Original costume design by Tanya
Moiseiwitsch for William Hutt as
Argan in *The Imaginary Invalid*,
1974

Original costume design by Robin
Fraser Paye for Stephen
Russell as Claudio in *Much Ado
About Nothing*, 1980

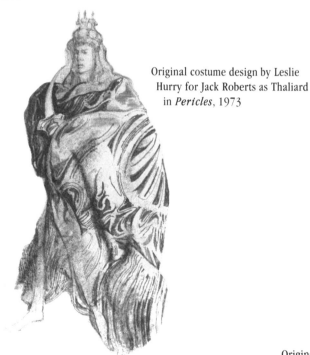

Original costume design by Leslie
Hurry for Jack Roberts as Thaliard
in *Pericles*, 1973

Original costume
design by Brian Jackson
for Robin Gammell as Oberon in
A Midsummer Night's Dream, 1960

From the collection of the Stratford Festival Archives

·S·T·R·A·T·F·O·R·D·

Stratford

The First Thirty Years

JOHN PETTIGREW AND
JAMIE PORTMAN

Foreword by *Robertson Davies*

VOLUME II:
1968–1982

Macmillan of Canada
A Division of Canada Publishing Corporation
Toronto, Ontario, Canada

Canadian Cataloguing in Publication Data

Pettigrew, John.
  Stratford: the first thirty years

Includes index.
In slipcase.
Contents: v. 1. 1953-1967—v. 2. 1968-1982.
ISBN 0-7715-9809-2 (set).—ISBN 0-7715-9882-3
(v. 1).—ISBN 0-7715-9883-1 (v. 2).

1. Stratford Festival (Ont.)—History.
2. Theater—Canada—History. I. Portman,
Jamie, date. II. Title.

PN2306.S72S7 1985   792'.09713'23   C84-099732-9

V.2

49,740

Material from Sir Tyrone Guthrie's *A Life in the Theatre*
(New York: McGraw-Hill, 1959) reprinted by permission.
Material by Walter Kerr from the *New York Herald Tribune*
© I.H.T. Corporation. Reprinted by Permission.
New York Times reviews by Brooks Atkinson, Clive Barnes,
Richard Eder, and Walter Kerr
copyright © 1953/54/55/56/57/59/68/76/78/80
by The New York Times Company.
Reprinted by permission.

Edited by *Patricia Kennedy*
Copy-edited by *Eleanor Sinclair*
Designed by *NewtonFrank*

Macmillan of Canada
A Division of Canada Publishing Corporation

Printed in Canada

·S·T·R·A·T·F·O·R·D·

Contents

1968-69

The Board of Governors had considered several possible new leaders, but when the time for a decision arrived, it was happy to approve Langham's recommendation that Jean Gascon and John Hirsch take over the artistic direction, with William Wylie heading the business end. The board and Langham agreed that the new leadership should really be a triumvirate, but since Hirsch did not wish to be tied down to the Festival for the whole year, and since the board came to feel that one of the new artistic directors should be senior to the other, Gascon became executive artistic director and Hirsch associate artistic director. It was planned that Gascon should report to the board on artistic matters and Wylie on business matters, but in practice over the years Wylie did an increasing amount of all reporting—partly because of his strong personality and his competence, partly because Gascon was never much interested in matters administrative and was more than content to leave things to Wylie, whom he knew to be devoted to the artistic side and knowledgeable about it. Oscar Shumsky had resigned as director of music; Victor di Bello, music administrator since 1962, was also entrusted with the Music Festival, and by the end of 1968 had been formally named director of music.

There were no major policy changes, Gascon and Hirsch making it clear that they would build on the traditions of the past. Most of the company remained under the new leaders, both of whom stressed their belief in ensemble playing as central to Stratford's

1

success. Some young actors were given their first leading roles in 1968: Jane Casson, James Blendick, Neil Dainard, and Eric Donkin. No stars were imported, but two young and virtually unknown members joined the company in leading roles: the French-speaking Canadian, Louise Marleau, and the American, Christopher Walken.

One custom was abandoned: the playing of the National Anthem before all performances. Stratford's tradition had been to play arrangements of "God Save the Queen" to suit the spirit of the play being performed, and there had consequently been versions cacophonous, hilarious, sombre, and gay. The arrangements had become an attractive feature of the Festival for many visitors, and frequently drew applause, but they were abandoned because there was no way in which the Festival could reconcile the demands of those who wanted "O Canada", those who wanted "God Save the Queen", those who wanted no anthem, and those who objected to varying arrangements.

With the new leadership came a natural freshness and excitement, some of which bubbled over into attractive new ventures: frequent workshop performances and readings, open to the public, in the rehearsal hall after performances; and also some free, informal one-hour concerts beginning at midnight and called "Music at Midnight". From all points of view the season was a success. All attendance and box-office records were broken, and the heavy losses of the past two years were not repeated, largely because tight controls on production expenses reduced them by more than $250,000 from the 1967 figure.

The concerts were well received, with India's sitarist and composer, Ravi Shankar, winning special acclaim. The four offerings at the Avon were also successful. The Royal Winnipeg Ballet returned for eight performances in July, presenting new works from its repertory, and Patricia Kern's Angelina dazzled audiences in Douglas Campbell's production of Rossini's *Cinderella*, drawing a five-minute standing and screaming ovation on opening night.

Waiting for Godot, which was William Hutt's first Stratford assignment as director, was auspicious. There were only eight performances, but the Avon sold them out, and critical tribute was highly favourable. The Canadian mime Adrian Pecknold (Lucky), James Blendick (Pozzo), and Powys Thomas (Vladimir) won praise, but chief acting honours belonged to Eric Donkin for an Estragon which was a fine blending of the peevish, the cowardly, the vicious, the absurd, the pathetic, and the obscurely dignified.

Gascon's production of Chekhov's *Seagull* drew respectable houses for its twenty-three performances, but reviews were mixed. There seemed to be general agreement that the production was rather too sombre and slow, with gloom being so pervasive at times as to come perilously close to burlesque. Mervyn Blake's Sorin and Marilyn Lightstone's Masha received special attention among the

Scene from the 1968 Avon stage production of Waiting for Godot, *by Samuel Beckett, directed by William Hutt, designed by Brian Jackson. L.-R.: Powys Thomas as Vladimir, Eric Donkin as Estragon, Adrian Pecknold as Lucky, and James Blendick as Pozzo. Photograph by Douglas Spillane, courtesy of the Stratford Festival Archives.*

minor roles; as Chekhov's villains, Arkadina and Trigorin, Denise Pelletier and William Hutt gave admirable performances.

Excellent though the Avon season was, the main excitement focussed on the Festival Theatre, though things began badly with Campbell's production of *Romeo and Juliet*. Panned by most reviewers, it drew only moderate, 78-per-cent crowds during its run. Louise Marleau had taken a crash course in English, but her speaking was inadequate—monotonously high-pitched and so heavily accented as often to be incomprehensible. Christopher Walken's Romeo was also generally considered weak, with Walter Kerr describing him as "the politest Romeo I ever saw—polite to his elders, polite to his inferiors, polite to the moon. You don't meet his mother, of course; but you can perfectly well hear her, upon discovering that mess in the tomb, saying, 'I just don't understand it, he wasn't the kind of boy to give trouble.'"

There were good performances from Kenneth Pogue (Capulet), Bernard Behrens (Friar Laurence), Neil Dainard (Tybalt), and Joel Kenyon (Benvolio), but the only really remarkable feature of the production was Leo Ciceri's brilliant and unconventional Mercutio —a man middle-aged, embittered, alone even in company, hiding from life behind a barrier of words and a visor of gaiety which was only apparent, never felt.

John Hirsch's production of *A Midsummer Night's Dream* had had a four-week pre-season tour to Montreal, Ottawa, and Ann Arbor, Michigan, helped by a Canada Council subsidy of $50,000. The houses for the two-week Montreal run were disappointing at 58 per cent, but Ann Arbor sold out, thereby ensuring a small profit for the tour.

The production of *Dream* was grossly marred by the gratuitous silliness of having Theseus's court, in Walter Kerr's words, "composed of arthritic crones and doddering Silenuses to no purpose that is ever made clear". One reviewer's complaint is typical:

> The lights went up on a rouged, cigar-smoking, bare-chested, hair-netted, bow-legged, octogenarian lecher of a Theseus in the process of being laced, gruntingly, into a corset, amid doddering courtiers ready to expire at a moment's notice. This was not promising. Worse followed. . . . He proceeded to guy Shakespeare's lines at every possible opportunity and found smut where it couldn't possibly exist, equating for instance that word of which he is so fond, "solemnity", with "sexual intercourse". He ogled a Hippolyta dressed in black and wearing black leather boots, a Hippolyta who was to make a later entrance cracking a whip with which she and Theseus had clearly just been having a wonderful time (reasonable enough, I suppose, since Theseus's age and physique obviously precluded more normal forms of sexual activity).

Such silliness was all the more regrettable because almost everything else in the production was praiseworthy: Stanley Silverman's music, which ranged from Mendelssohn to rock; the fairy world (always verging on the sinister); some very funny lovers led by Jane Casson's pouter-pigeon of a Helena; and a winning group of mechanicals led by Bernard Behrens's anxiety-ridden and accident-prone Quince. Special tribute was due Martha Henry's Titania for being both extremely sexy and extremely ethereal—"There has never been, I am certain, so right and so exciting a Titania," commented Berners Jackson. Douglas Rain's Bottom was a further good performance.

Hirsch's other production, entering the repertory July 22, was a smash hit. Peter Raby's adaptation of *The Three Musketeers* was directed with reckless abandon, and had forty scenes, a hundred duels, a seeming cast of thousands, and a costume and property budget that seemed to demand millions. (Actually, the 250 costumes cost very little, being for the most part made from end-of-line samples, some dating back to before the First World War, which Heeley had found in New York. Four tea chests crammed with magnificent materials cost him only $500.) The production moved very fast, so fast, Eric Christmas remarked, that at one point he saw Bernard Behrens playing a scene with himself. It was wonderfully wild, a gorgeous romp, and very busy: a mixture of three-ring

Scene from the 1968 Festival stage production of The Three
Musketeers, *adapted by Peter Raby from the Dumas novel, directed by
John Hirsch, designed by Desmond Heeley, music by Raymond Pannell.
L.-R.: James Blendick as Porthos, Powys Thomas as Athos, and
Christopher Newton as Aramis. Photograph by Douglas Spillane,
courtesy of the Stratford Festival Archives.*

circuses and Dumas and everything else that might be called
"camp", of Batman and Superman and pop art and every swash-
buckling scene that Douglas Fairbanks or Errol Flynn ever played in,
of dastardly villains and vixenish women and maidens or pseudo-
maidens in distress, of breathtaking gallantry and acrobatics (only
two professional acrobats in fact appeared), of incredible love-
making, of eye-smiting costumes and ear-smiting noise.

Martha Henry's Milady bared her beautiful arm at regular intervals
to reveal the fleur-de-lis token of shame; Kenneth Pogue's Bucking-
ham expired by millimetres, summoning up his last reserves of
strength to totter with exquisite gallantry and pathos before the
portrait of his queenly lover.

Mia Anderson's Constance was put out of her misery by Milady's
poisoned wine, but not before she had oozed equally exquisite
pathos all over the stage; Leo Ciceri's Richelieu emerged from the
trap, resplendent in red cloak, to engage in foul machinations and to
hiss (and occasionally be hissed). Lurid seductions and rapes were
initiated by both sexes and carried to successful conclusions in

Scene from the 1968/1969 Festival stage production of Tartuffe, *by Molière, translated by Richard Wilbur, directed by Jean Gascon, designed by Robert Prévost, music by Gabriel Charpentier. Centre front: William Hutt as Tartuffe; Rear, L.-R.: Robin Marshall as Laurent, Douglas Rain as Orgon, Leo Ciceri as Cléante, and Kenneth Pogue as the Officer. Photograph by Douglas Spillane, courtesy of the Stratford Festival Archives.*

almost every scene. Eyes flashed, and so did swords, decapitating candles and bushes and people. Yet, through it all, Douglas Rain's D'Artagnan managed to keep his head and live to ensure that Milady would lose hers at the hand of the man whose brother she had so deeply wronged. Pleading "I'm too young to die," Milady left the stage with head held high to the end; her exit was followed by a most satisfying off-stage clunk. So was evil punished, and some of the virtuous survived to continue their disgraceful behaviour and to reap their unjust rewards.

But if *The Three Musketeers* was the crowd-pleaser, the great miracle was Jean Gascon's production of Molière's *Tartuffe* in the rhyming-couplet translation done by Richard Wilbur (who thought the presentation "faultless") and set around 1830. Early houses were small, but for the last three weeks of its abbreviated run, the production sold out, and long queues again formed for rush seats and returns. Cohen thought it "muted and denatured Molière", but his was a lonely voice amidst a chorus of praise as universal as has greeted any production at Stratford. Tribute was paid to Wilbur's translation and to Gascon's direction, marked, wrote Herbert Whittaker, "by classic serenity and power, by restraint and discipline, by faultless taste and harmony". There was praise for all the performers, but especially for Stratford's two leading actors—William Hutt as Tartuffe and Douglas Rain as Orgon.

One reviewer found Douglas Rain's Orgon a perfect match for William Hutt's Tartuffe. Of Rain he wrote: "It says much for his performance that he was not acted right off the stage, that he left no doubt Orgon is the play's central character." And what of Hutt? In Clive Barnes's words: "With the gait of a praying mantis and a graveyard growl, Mr. Hutt, obsequiously arrogant, cut a fine and spectral figure of hypocrisy." But it is Walter Kerr's awed eloquence in the *New York Times* on June 23 under the headline "Stratford Tartuffe Greater Than Superb" that demands quoting at length:

Mr. Gascon's mounting of Molière's play for the Stratford Shakespeare Festival is not just a superb "Tartuffe", though it is that. A man would have to be mad to expect a better production in his lifetime, or even to have hoped for so good a one. It is, furthermore, not simply an extraordinarily funny "Tartuffe", slapping us awake and into laughter where we've always dozed before. It is a *seriously* funny "Tartuffe", deriving its comedy from fierce concentration on what it is reasonable to expect of dimensional human beings. And it is something more again than a particularly effective production of a particularly interesting play. It is the stage at peace with itself, quietly proud of itself, sensually aware of itself, uncluttered, uncompromised, serenely at home with its simplest methods and most profound materials. It is the stage satisfied to be the stage and making the magnificent most of it. . . .

Perhaps a word about Elmire, the wife Tartuffe so lusts after, is in order. Martha Henry plays her as a woman who cannot be surprised. She is herself reserved, immaculately self-contained, gently delicate. But she is informed. She has a body. She knows precisely its various possible uses, understands without pretense or dismay Tartuffe's crafty designs upon it. She is a good woman but never an innocent one. *He* may be evasive, circuitous; she is too supple and intelligent to engage in affectation. She would smile knowingly at his overtures and never humiliate him, if he were any other man, any less devious man. As it is, she stands her ground, cool, worldly, and in her worldliness as generous as a woman may be.

Miss Henry, who is most remarkable, gives us this woman whole; because she does, because she creates a three-dimensional creature who must be circled to be approached, she gives us a great deal of Tartuffe, too. He is indirect and treacherous in the patterns he must make if he is to surround her. We see in the counterdance of intelligences, the contending shapes of the play. And because Miss Henry is all of these things, she can, unpredictably but inevitably, make suddenly explosive comedy out of a perfectly ordinary straight line, a mere exit-and-entrance line. She has told her husband of Tartuffe's lust and her husband has defied her to prove it. "Send him to me" is the line, and it is merely meant to get a servant off and Tartuffe on. "*Send* him to me!" blazes Miss Henry, appalled that any aspersion could be cast on her ability to provoke lust, confident as a lion tamer unafraid of the cage, seeming to roll up her non-existent sleeves and look prettily forward to a contest from which she must emerge triumphant as Minerva. . . .

The company is virtually flawless. Mr. Hutt, a hypocrite put together out of a bust of Beethoven and the remains of Mr. Hyde, sits erect and trembling as a grasshopper while he waits out a woman's virtue; Douglas Rain, as the gullible Orgon, fastens his attention so fiercely on his mentor that he seems a reflecting pool, dancing insanely to another's rhythm; Barbara Bryne plays the eternally obtuse grandmother of the family like an eagle in severe mourning; Mia Anderson's quivering daughter, a wrinkle-nosed rabbit with almost enough courage to nip at one corner of a cabbage leaf provided no one tells her not to, is delightful; and Leo Ciceri's reading of the common-sense speeches that measure out and then frame the play could not be more persuasive.

Richard Wilbur's excellent translation has been used and finally done justice. The players neither sing-song nor suppress the end-stop rhymes, so unfamiliar to our ears; they absorb them instead, keeping them just within consciousness and leading us to look for them, subliminally, as bright little tenpenny nails in an advancing structure.

"Before the festival," wrote American critic Julius Novick, "nobody knew how good Canadian acting was; now, it puts us to shame." Happily, something of this production survives in the Caedmon recording.

The 1969 season again set attendance and box-office records, but artistically it was a letdown and also a less happy experience for the company and the theatre staff. The season was extended by two weeks to twenty weeks and the policy of opening productions "cold" was finally abandoned. An extra week of student performances was scheduled for the final week of May, and the first week of June was given over to previews of *Hamlet*, *The Alchemist*, and

Measure for Measure. For some actors, the season began on January 5 with rehearsals for a CBC television production of *The Three Musketeers*, which was shown on March 19. For others, work began on January 20 with rehearsals for the tour of Hirsch's *Hamlet* and Gascon's *Alchemist*. This tour opened at Chicago's Studebaker Theater for three weeks on March 3 before moving on to Ann Arbor for two weeks, and to Montreal's Théâtre Maisonneuve for the final week, April 8 to 13. Then, at the end of the Stratford run, both plays went to Ottawa to launch the Stratford National Theatre's inaugural season at the recently opened National Arts Centre. In November the Arts Centre hosted Stratford's first studio presentation of four one-act plays by Jean-Claude van Itallie. Ottawa, too, saw a special children's production of John Hirsch's *Sauerkringle*, and late in the year, a three-week tour of schools in the Ottawa region. Despite mixed reviews, the box office was good on the spring tour, and near-capacity audiences attended the Ottawa performances of *Hamlet, The Alchemist*, and *Sauerkringle*.

One important development early in the year was the final departure of Tom Patterson from the Festival. He was developing plans in association with Duke Ellington for a Stratford-based theatrical producing and consulting company.

The Festival abandoned its operas, since Gascon had recognized that they were both costly to the Festival and showed little prospect of growth or of developing significance. Although Julian Bream conducted a master class in guitar, the music workshops were also abandoned. Di Bello did, however, arrange some concerts in the Avon by the "Stratford Festival Orchestra", and the music season enjoyed some successes. Open-air concerts on the main island in Lake Victoria were well received, and the Sunday concert series was the most successful it had been to date, selling out five of the eight concerts. Nevertheless, on balance, the music season wasn't a success, and while Bream, the National Youth Orchestra, and Elisabeth Schwarzkopf drew plaudits, the critics roasted a high proportion of the other concerts. The orchestral events scheduled for the Avon were mainly critical and box-office failures, and at the end of the season di Bello resigned.

Another major resignation in 1969 was that of John Hirsch. He had found it difficult to adjust to playing second fiddle to Jean Gascon after years of running the Manitoba Theatre Centre, and he had been sharply critical—sometimes offensively so, in the judgment of some senior members of the organization—both of the Festival and of its leadership. After many years of unremitting hard work, he was also, as he told the board, tired out and he needed an extended sabbatical. On top of everything else, his two 1969 Stratford productions were judged artistic failures by the leading critics.

With 93-per-cent houses at the Festival Theatre, *Hamlet* was the box-office hit of the season, but it was ill received by experienced reviewers. There was praise for Angela Wood's Gertrude and Neil Dainard's Laertes, and for the gravediggers and the players—but that was about all. The Ghost, suggested one reviewer, was "about as thrilling as a detergent commercial", while "Leo Ciceri's Claudius —with reason—seemed afflicted with boredom." Kenneth Welsh's Hamlet, the critic commented further, "threw the verse away, belting out the soliloquies as if anxious to get them over with and never for a moment seeming actually to think about anything: his Hamlet was immensely energetic, but also unprincely, unpoetic, uncomplicated, and uninteresting."

It was at the Avon, however, that Hirsch verged on disaster with a new musical comedy, *The Satyricon*. Despite 86-per-cent houses, it was a financial catastrophe; the $109,000 production budget was overrun to $193,000, while box-office receipts were only $95,700. Peter Raby, who had returned to England, had been expected to provide a script based on Petronius's curious work; instead, mid-April saw the new literary manager, Tom Hendry, faced with the difficult task of writing a show in a few weeks. The result was promoted as being the kind of thing which would upset the morality squad. Most reviewers actually liked the brassy performance, but they also found the book thin, and the production not only vulgar but tasteless, especially in its attempts to be contemporary and Very Relevant. This was most obvious in some sermonizing lyrics by John Hirsch on the evils of our world and its parallels with that of Petronius. The *Detroit Free Press* suggested that the production was "completely tolerable, I would think, only to drama lovers like the man in the orange chiffon scarf and white harem pants in the row in front of me". Cohen, still wincing from a recent National Arts Centre première of a play called *Party Day*, was also unimpressed: "It is a wretched piece, which effectively supersedes such other numbellicitous nonsense as *Party Day* in the extreme of its inadequacy."

The Satyricon gave way in August to Jean Gascon's highly praised production of Peter Luke's *Hadrian VII*, presented under Festival auspices but with a special company headed by Hume Cronyn in the title role. Robert Fletcher's designs were sumptuous, and Cronyn was generally thought very fine. At the end of its Stratford run, the production set off for a thirty-eight-week tour of the United States. It had its problems on the road: in parts of the Midwest, audiences boycotted a play about "the Pope", and in several cities the company ran into the new problem of audiences being afraid to venture out at night. In February of 1970, thought was given to abandoning the tour in Philadelphia, but attendance picked up, and the schedule continued as planned. The tour enjoyed critical acclaim and even ended up with a modest profit.

Gascon also had two productions at the Festival Theatre. One was a revival of *Tartuffe*, with several cast changes, including Donald Davis as Orgon and Angela Wood as Elmire. (For the first time Douglas Rain was missing a Stratford season, and his wife, Martha Henry, was also absent with him in England. The production held up very well indeed; the odd critic even thought it improved, and Cohen seemed to have changed his mind and gave it a rave review.)

Gascon's new Festival Theatre production was Ben Jonson's *The Alchemist*. For years, people had insisted that Gascon and Jonson were the perfect pair, but this production of *The Alchemist* suggested that Gascon was in fact not on Jonson's wavelength, and neither pace nor style was quite right. The production moved too slowly, and, while Eric Donkin's Dapper and William Hutt's Sir Epicure Mammon showed what should be done, too many of the other performances were insufficiently extravagant. Nevertheless, considering that the playwright was not popular in our time and scarcely known to most Canadians, an average attendance of 87 per cent was a remarkable achievement.

The least popular of the Festival Theatre productions, with 81-per-cent houses, was *Measure for Measure*, directed by David Giles, familiar to Canadians for his work on the television serial *The Forsyte Saga*. Reviews were very mixed, but Bernard Behrens's Pompey and William Hutt's benign Duke won many tributes.

During 1969, the Festival passed the 500,000 mark in attendance for school performances. The students had come from 4,500 different schools, and 60,000 of them had come from the United States. The 227 school performances had cost the Festival more than $2 million, of which only $1.2 million had been recovered, $300,000 of that in supporting grants from the Ontario Department of Education. It was estimated that another half-million students had attended regular performances. As the board president remarked in his annual report, the Festival was making a major contribution to the educational process. Some idea of the need for such contributions was provided in a 1969 survey showing that only four per cent of Canadians had ever attended a live performance of music, ballet, and drama.

1970

In 1967, Vic Polley had turned down the position of general manager, largely because he felt that Stratford was overreaching itself—that frequent tours and productions elsewhere would strain the Festival's resources too much. Early in 1970, many Stratfordites were agreeing with him. Gascon was haggard from overwork, and the board acknowledged that he must have senior artistic help. The theatre staff was also under heavy pressure.

The spring tour, longer than ever before, took *The Merchant of Venice* and *The School for Scandal* to the University of Illinois for a week in mid-February, to Chicago's Studebaker Theatre for a month, to Montreal's Théâtre Maisonneuve for two weeks, and finally to Ottawa's National Arts Centre from March 30 to April 25. Ottawa came close to selling out, and box office increased substantially in Montreal, but Chicago cost the local sponsors money, despite 90-per-cent houses in the final week. March saw a second three-week school tour in Ottawa, this time of Peter Hay's *As You Like It*. Like the play offered on the first school tour late in 1969, this proved controversial and too heady for some tastes, and a projected third tour had to be cancelled. There were also studio productions at the National Arts Centre of three one-acters by Slawomir Mrozek and of James Reaney's *The Easter Egg*. Meanwhile, the Arts Centre's thrust-stage auditorium was offering repertory productions of Brendan Behan's *The Hostage* and Boris Vian's *The Empire Builders*. It was a busy, even hectic, time.

Scene from the 1970 Festival stage production of The School for
Scandal, *by Richard Sheridan, directed by Michael Langham, designed
by Leslie Hurry and assistant designer, Jack King, music by Stanley
Silverman, lighting by Gil Wechsler. L.-R.: Jane Casson as Mrs.
Candour, Blair Brown as Maria, and Eric Donkin as Sir Benjamin
Backbite. Photograph by Douglas Spillane, courtesy of the Stratford
Festival Archives.*

The Festival welcomed back many familiar faces in 1970. The
four designers whose names over the years are linked most closely
with Stratford were there: Tanya Moiseiwitsch and the "Banner
Brigade" of Leslie Hurry, Brian Jackson, and Desmond Heeley.
Michael Langham returned to direct *School for Scandal*, and among
the leading players back again were Marcel Marceau, Irene Worth,
Douglas Campbell, Eric House, Kate Reid, Robin Gammell, and
Donald Davis. The unusually high proportion of new faces included

directors Kurt Reis, Colin George, and Peter Gill from Britain, and Chattie Salaman of the Comédie de Saint-Etienne. Visitors engaged for major roles included the Guthrie Theatre's leading lady, Helen Carey, and, from Britain, Maureen O'Brien, Gordon Jackson, and Stephen Murray.

The playing season at Stratford was cut back two weeks, mainly because of the tour activity, and only one preview of each of the three opening plays at the Festival Theatre preceded the June 8 first night. Jean Gascon's production of *The Merchant of Venice* opened the season, with most reviewers praising Donald Davis's dignified Shylock, Gabriel Charpentier's music, and Heeley's designs, but finding Maureen O'Brien an uninteresting Portia, and the production as a whole solid but also dull, slow, and uninspired. The wildly extravagant caricature of Eric Donkin's Aragon was probably the most memorable aspect. His "blinking idiot" looked and walked rather like a drunken whooping crane in a mini-skirt, and spoke like a soprano hypnotized by a metronome, while his arrogance and confidence in his own infallibility were nicely stressed by his arrival with a retinue of churchmen prepared for the immediate wedding that his brilliant intellect promised. Audiences were convulsed by this naughty but hilarious performance. The production surprised many by becoming one of Stratford's biggest box-office successes, playing to near-capacity houses throughout the run.

Langham's bold and brassy production of Sheridan's masterpiece *The School for Scandal* was dazzling and a great favourite with critics and public, playing throughout its run to standing ovations and excellent audiences. Stanley Silverman's music—of which the production made unusually extensive use—and Leslie Hurry's designs were highly praised. Langham's genius was everywhere: in his fresh approach to the play; in the freezes for asides and expository information; in the acrobatics of the speedy scene changes, performed "with an agile precision", remarked Berners Jackson, that seemed "to defy the laws of gravity and the geography of collision"; in crisp speech and vigorous action; in its success in making a proscenium play look as if it had been created for a thrust stage. There was an abundance of imaginative business.

The cast was everywhere admirable, but Robin Gammell's Joseph Surface was miraculous. The reviewer for the *Journal of Canadian Studies* commented that this Joseph was

> very obviously Charles's brother and no relation at all to Fielding's Blifil with whom Joseph is so often compared. He was not the hypocrite but the man who enjoys playing a role for all it's worth, and who invited *us* to share his enjoyment in, in Lamb's phrase, "the downright *acted* villainy of the part".... Sentiments were telegraphed several miles ahead by a stance and voice change; Mr. Gammell's Joseph was a baritone for himself, a fruity tenor for

sentiments, and a falsetto for those extremely frequent moments when his plans go awry. And so far from being shrewd and calculating, this Joseph was rather the most accident-prone of men. For him to think was to be whomped: it became altogether clear that his real talent was for getting himself into the most terrible scrapes, and his real genius for then compounding his mistakes. Mr. Gammell's Joseph thought himself terribly clever, but he never was really in control of anything, not even his body and voice, both of which kept playing terrible tricks on him.

Peter Gill's production of *Hedda Gabler* was a failure, despite the odd glowing review. Almost everyone agreed that the production should have been in the Avon, for the Festival stage simply did not seem able to accommodate this claustrophobic play, and Gill appeared to increase the natural problems by making extensive use of the balcony, by having Judge Brack enter by the centre aisle, and by having Hedda shoot at him in this location. Moreover, the cruelty of the stage was displayed: Irene Worth could not, on that stage in 1970, look twenty-nine, and in Ibsen things like that matter greatly. The supporting roles were well played, with Gordon Jackson outstanding as Tesman, but Miss Worth often seemed to be in a different play from the rest of the cast. Many first-night reviewers found the production too sombre, but as the season progressed, Miss Worth appeared to play the role for every laugh that could possibly be wrung from it, and as the discords became strident, the production degenerated into a shambles.

Jean Gascon's production of *Cymbeline* was the North American professional première of the play. It entered the repertory on July 21 for a limited run of nineteen performances. One would never have guessed that the play had been rushed in rehearsal, with the company and technical staff working unusual hours to get it ready. Although some reviewers thought the play crude and not even worth producing, this was a fine production of a most curious work, a compendium of the sublime, the ridiculous, and almost every theatre cliché and convention. Gascon refused to succumb to the temptation to guy the play or to avoid the laughter prompted by its frequent absurdities; he proceeded straightforwardly, putting his trust in Shakespeare, even though a play like *Cymbeline* must have given him some doubts about the wisdom of such a course. He was greatly helped by a Stonehenge setting, by Tanya Moiseiwitsch's designs, and by Gabriel Charpentier's score with its mixture of weird electronic music and more conventional attributes.

The performers threw themselves into their assignment with an appropriate reckless abandon. They included Kenneth Welsh as Posthumus, Powys Thomas as Cymbeline, Pat Galloway as his nameless queen, Robin Gammell as a hilarious Cloten, and Leo Ciceri as Iachimo.

Scene from the 1970 Festival stage production of Cymbeline, *directed by Jean Gascon, designed by Tanya Moiseiwitsch, music by Gabriel Charpentier, lighting by Gil Wechsler. Barry MacGregor as Jupiter. Photograph by Douglas Spillane, courtesy of the Stratford Festival Archives.*

The production had many memorable if bizarre aspects: the guying of "Hark, Hark, the Lark" in a manner that must have left Schubert writhing in his grave, since it ended with an incredibly unmusical rendition of the word "Arise!" from a Cloten who obviously confused larks with vultures; the Guthrie-like pageantry of the stylized battle scenes; a bat that entered the theatre and the spirit of the occasion at one performance and took a special fancy to Cloten and his mother; the arrival of thunder, lightning, smoke, and an eagle the size of a steam locomotive, who turned out to be Barry MacGregor playing Jupiter; the delightfully ridiculous procession of recognition scenes, which followed what must surely be the most necessary and splendiferous intervention of a *deus ex machina* in all drama. MacGregor, incidentally, had played in *Cymbeline* at

Stratford-upon-Avon, and he insisted on a part in the Canadian production. He possibly came to regret his insistence, as his make-up for his brief intervention as Jupiter took ninety minutes to apply; then, strapped into a harness which gave him absolutely no freedom to move, he was pushed for his entrance down a small track to the edge of the balcony, from which he thought nightly he was sure to be precipitated.

The music program, with Andree Gingras now in charge as music administrator, was severely cut back in 1970. Plans had been presented to the board in January for a co-operative opera-and-ballet program with the National Arts Centre and the Manitoba Centennial Corporation. Mario Bernardi had hoped that Mozart's *Abduction from the Seraglio* might appear at the Avon with the National Arts Centre Orchestra in the pit, and he also recommended a visit from the Royal Winnipeg Ballet. Since it was estimated that the four-week season would lose $186,000, however, the board had little choice but to turn down the proposals. Sixteen concerts were held in the Festival Theatre on Saturday mornings and Sunday evenings. Audiences were disappointing, with those on Saturday averaging about four hundred and the Sunday concerts playing to about half capacity.

For the first time, the Avon was reserved exclusively for drama. The schedule started well there with Patrick Crean, the Festival's fencing master, doing four performances of *The Sun Never Sets*, his own one-man show about the last glories of the British Empire as seen through the eyes of Rudyard Kipling. Crean was followed by a popular week of Marcel Marceau, and he in turn gave way to three fairly experimental modern plays. There had been delays in setting the Avon season because of the opera proposals, and Gascon was late in choosing his three plays and did so in a state of something approaching desperation. His decisions proved unhappy. None of the three productions reached the 40-per-cent level in attendance, despite frantic and costly efforts by the publicity staff, and many regular visitors thought the Festival's reputation tarnished by the Avon offerings.

The first of the three was unquestionably the most hated production in Stratford's seventeen-year history, despite its brief run of eleven performances and gallant attempts by the two-man cast of Roger Blay and Arnold Soboloff. The play was *The Architect and the Emperor of Assyria* by Spain's Fernando Arrabal. The printed program contained comments so pretentious as to read like a burlesque of pretentious program notes:

When one is "inside" one of his plays, one is pulled down into the deepest recesses of human experience—down among the archetypes. There reigns the Great Mother Figure, performing her castration rites, and one is drawn upwards towards magical phenomena and mystical aspirations.

Few people seemed to get "inside" the play or to be drawn anywhere except to the exits. At all performances, members of the audience left in droves, some of them addressing rude remarks at the stage as they went.

Arnold Wesker's new play, *The Friends*, fared better, but not much so. It was not one of Wesker's major works, and skilled playing could not mask the fact that much of the text seemed to need rewriting and that the second half was anti-climactic. Slawomir Mrozek's absurdist *Vatzlav* was a much more satisfying play and might have won better houses had not dissatisfaction with the earlier entries convinced audiences that this particular Avon season should be given a miss by the time it opened on August 11.

The season's most unhappy event, in August, was the sudden death of Leo Ciceri, in a car accident. He had been a fine and unselfish actor, who knew as much as anyone at Stratford about the importance of company teamwork, who cheerfully undertook more than his share of unrewarding roles, and who gave generously of his time in helping others to share his love of his craft and his skill in it. He had been an absolutely reliable supporting actor, and he was to be missed in succeeding years. The Festival established a scholarship fund in his name to provide an annual grant to a student attending Montreal's National Theatre School.

Another sad event was the departure from the Stratford scene in October of Vic Polley after sixteen years of devoted service to the business end of the Festival. No man in the organization was more loved or respected, and as a Stratford native with a strong sense of civic duty, a war veteran, and a former alderman, he was regarded by Stratford citizens as their main guarantee that Stratford still mattered in Festival thinking. Apart from work directly connected with his official position, he had done much over the years to help sell the Festival to the unconverted. He had, for instance, worked away at a number of citizens opposed to the Festival, inviting them to the theatre and giving them tickets. He converted a fair number of them, many through their children, who had been given free tickets and then insisted on taking their parents to the theatre to show it off to them. However, Polley's relationship with William Wylie had been difficult from the beginning. The two were very different, Wylie bearing some resemblance to the standard image of the efficiency expert. Though some people found him abrasive and tactless, even rude, Wylie was respected for his abilities and for his dedication to the Festival, but Polley was the man the Festival staff loved. They had become accustomed to working through Polley, and tended to go to him rather than to Wylie. Finally, Wylie insisted that Polley must go, and Polley resigned.

There was a huge explosion in Stratford. The community felt that first Patterson had been pushed out, and now Polley, and that the community itself was being threatened by the Festival and insufficiently appreciated. Both Ian Lindsay, Chairman of the Board, and Wylie made tactless statements—which they later regretted—in the heat of the moment, further inflaming a situation that was extremely badly handled and in which Wylie had, in fact, exceeded his authority. As Floyd Chalmers put it in a letter written at the time, the "summary nature of the execution" had nothing to commend it.

The editorial and correspondence columns of the *Beacon-Herald* reverberated with cries of outrage, but throughout the whole sorry mess, Polley refused comment and behaved with an exemplary dignity that some of the other participants would have done well to follow.

The November 30 annual meeting of the members of the Festival Foundation proved stormy. Tom Patterson gave a long, prepared speech highly critical of the Festival for what he saw as its loss of the original vision. He was upset with the fate of the Music Festival. He said that the people of Stratford had "been treated with contempt— treated as peasants!" He urged the Festival's general manager and president to resign. There was a reminder by board member Russell Payton, former president of the Canadian Opera Company, that the Festival, faced with the certainty of another Music Festival loss exceeding $200,000, had had no choice but to do what it had done, and that opera could be presented only if heavily subsidized. Payton's comments soothed ruffled feelings to a degree, but wounds remained.

Nine days after the season ended at Stratford, many members of the company began a four-week run at the National Arts Centre of *Cymbeline* and a revival of *Tartuffe* (William Hutt had returned from work at Chichester to repeat his title triumph, and Donald Davis and Angela Wood were back as Orgon and Elmire). However, relations with the National Arts Cente had become strained. The Centre had been unhappy with Stratford's studio and school productions and was disturbed that it had not been consulted about Hirsch's departure. It also felt the Festival had broken an agreement in its decision to abandon opera. Furthermore, with grants frozen, the Centre was having financial problems, and it felt that it could provide more varied entertainment itself for the amount of money being spent on Stratford's Ottawa productions. The Centre noted it could import Shaw Festival offerings at less than half Stratford's costs. The concepts of the Stratford National Theatre of Canada and Ottawa as a winter home were, for all practical purposes, no more.

Stratford's year had been frantic, and on the whole neither very successful nor happy. Certain problems were becoming very clear. Could the Festival and its artistic director stand the strain of tours and the Ottawa relationship? What should the role of music be at the Festival? How much priority should Shakespeare receive in programming? There had been considerable criticism of 1970's thin Shakespeare ration. The company also missed several of its leading performers: William Hutt, Martha Henry, Tony van Bridge, and Douglas Rain. Within the company itself there was a definite sense of fragmentation. In 1970 there was an unfortunate gulf between the Avon and the Festival theatres; not one director, actor, or designer had worked in both. For seven productions there were seven designers. Only Gascon directed more than one production. Four of the six leading roles in *Hedda Gabler* were played by visiting actors, who appeared only in that one production. There was an embarrassingly large number of new and temporary faces in the company, and it was clear that some merely competent players had been imported for roles that could have been played at least as well by Stratford regulars. Gascon, lacking the international contacts or prestige that other Stratford artistic directors had had, seemed to some observers to be floundering about with stop-gap imports instead of trying to build a regular company. Policy decisions respecting the Avon Theatre were obviously needed, but were not being made. Once again the Festival seemed to be drifting without adequate control or advance planning.

But one picture was much brighter—the financial picture, and this despite an increase of well over $500,000 in production expenses and a record operating loss before gifts and operating grants of more than $850,000. With the annual appeal again bringing in more than $200,000, and the materialization of operating grants of $660,000 (including $510,000 from the Canada Council), the Festival had a modest income for the year instead of the losses of the past several years. The 88-per-cent box office at the Festival Theatre was encouraging. However, the organization had built up a serious accumulated deficit of more than $600,000, a situation resulting partly from the freezing of all government grants three years before, but mainly from the financial problems of Langham's last two years. Other artistic organizations were also in financial difficulty, and a joint approach by some of them to the Province of Ontario produced results. The Province agreed to retire 54 per cent of the accumulated deficits of each organization, and in July 1970 Stratford received a payment of $315,336. The Canada Council agreed to retire the balance over five years. Conditions were naturally laid down: the groups would no longer be permitted to accumulate large deficits, and any future deficits would have to be retired before further grants would be given. As Wylie commented, "This one move has done more to improve the financial condition of these organizations than anything since the formation of both councils by wiping the record clean and taking measures to ensure it stays clean."

To conform with new regulations of the Canada Council and the

Ontario Arts Council, which recognized rent but not depreciation of fixed assets, the Festival Foundation was in 1970 divided into the Stratford Shakespearean Festival Holding Foundation and the Stratford Shakespearean Festival Foundation of Canada, the latter being the operating company and the former owning the real estate.

At the beginning of the year, the Festival had provided statistics on its revenues and expenditures, showing that 19 per cent of its revenue came from government grants, 9 per cent from gifts, and 72 per cent from box office, while of expenditures 9 per cent went to administration, 14 per cent to publicity, 3 per cent to each of finance, repairs, and renovations, and 71 per cent to production.

An interesting contrast was revealed in Europe, where some theatres at that time were 85 per cent state-subsidized. It was also clear that government grants to Stratford did not come close to equalling the tax revenue generated by the Festival. Such anomalies were to become even more evident over the next decade.

·C·H·A·P·T·E·R · X V I I·

1971-72

New box-office and attendance records were set in the 1971 season, which was extended to twenty-two weeks. The first two and last six of these weeks were devoted to school performances, and 1971 set records for those as well, with 83,000 students attending. To save the tedious and time-consuming work of re-rehearsing touring productions to adapt them to the thrust stage, the spring tour of Hutt's production of *Much Ado About Nothing* and Gascon's production of John Webster's *The Duchess of Malfi* played only at Minneapolis (February 24 to March 13) and the National Arts Centre (March 22 to April 17). Minneapolis audiences were disappointing; although *Much Ado* drew 90-per-cent houses, *The Duchess of Malfi* attracted only 60 per cent. Ottawa attendance was good, and in both centres the productions were hailed as artistic successes. Plans for a fall tour were abandoned, with Gascon insisting that the Festival administration needed time to catch its breath, plan ahead, and get some rest from the kind of pressure of the year before. The Festival was also discovering that tours would almost always have to go out without visiting stars, since they were reluctant to commit themselves to ten-month seasons.

In May, while the company was in rehearsal, news arrived of the death of Sir Tyrone Guthrie. A memorial service was held in the theatre at the same time as one at the Guthrie Theatre, which sent a message to Stratford: "Our two theatres stand as the most abiding

Scene from the 1971 Festival stage production of The Duchess of
Malfi, *by John Webster, directed by Jean Gascon, designed by Desmond
Heeley, music by Gabriel Charpentier, lighting by Gil Wechsler. Pat
Galloway as the Duchess of Malfi. Photograph by Douglas Spillane,
courtesy of the Stratford Festival Archives.*

memorial to his life and to his beliefs.'' And so indeed it is. Nathan
Cohen also died in the spring of 1971; his regular seat was endowed
in his memory and a memorial plaque placed on it by the Festival.

William Hutt's production of *Much Ado*, set in what Hutt called a

"Beardsley-Hilton" atmosphere with lavish art-nouveau designs by Alan Barlow, was uneven and undistinguished except for Hero (Pamela Brook) and Claudio (Leon Pownall). Most reviewers were hostile, but, as always, the play proved a great crowd-pleaser. The next night, Gascon's production of *The Duchess of Malfi* was most impressive. Early houses for a work with which most Canadians were unfamiliar were only 50 per cent, but enthusiastic reviews and word-of-mouth led to sell-outs during the final weeks of its abbreviated run. It was a triumph for Gascon, whose direction was marked by absolute confidence in Webster, the company, and the stage, and by a consequent economy in every respect: in the acting, in a minimum of props, and in a bare stage, unmodified in any way. Only at one point were all the stops pulled out—in the Loretto or excommunication scene, where force was given to the play's stress on the Church as symbolic of the cruel destinies that shape our ends and on the agonizing ironies of the human condition. With clouds of incense, pealing organs, opulently costumed priests, and a heavily gowned Bishop, whose very entrance with a swinging ponderousness of movement was awe-inspiring, this was probably the most lavish use of the spectacular in Stratford's history.

Three actors stood out. Barry MacGregor turned the seemingly thankless part of Antonio into a most rewarding one, showing himself to be a fit husband for the Duchess. Powys Thomas was strong in the play's most challenging role of Bosola. But the evening belonged above all to Pat Galloway, usually thought of as a comic actress, in her first Stratford lead. Her Duchess was true magic, rising to that rare level precisely because, cast in a role that ought to be merely pathetic, the Duchess refused to co-operate. Merely to pity her, as Miss Galloway showed, would be to insult a character so magnificent it cannot pity itself.

Peter Gill's version of *Macbeth* was somewhat bewildering. It may have been that he was anxious to exemplify the truth of David William's observation during the season that some directors just have to prove they are still twenty-six. It may have been that Gill's primary aim was to show that worse travesties of the play than Peter Coe's were possible; opinion was divided as to which version won. Gill appeared to see *Macbeth* as a political play in which the Folk destroy all leaders. It opened with the Folk releasing their witches as a means of destroying Duncan. It ended with the Folk, mouths smeared with blood, appearing to have supped to the full on the remains of Macbeth. The play's central character became, in fact, this Chorus of Folk, generally carrying on as the Poor who are always with us, but at times appearing to turn into the equivalent of Vietnamese peasants or the riot police of Mayor Daley's Chicago. Mr. and Mrs. Macbeth (Ian Hogg and Pat Galloway) seemed to have instructions to subordinate their roles to the Chorus and to ensure that audiences were forced to understand that *Macbeth* is a play without poetry, grandeur, imagination, or power. Scotland was such a curious place that one came to wonder why Macbeth should ever want its throne. The conglomeration of Aztec, Chicagoan, and Vietnamese seemed perverse. As in Coe's version, Scottish table manners were appalling: the unfortunate company members at Macbeth's banquet had to eat—off the floor—dishes of rice, which for one performance were made even more unpalatable by a back-stage wag who mixed green peppermints into the mess. There were other curiosities: a teetotaller of a Porter; three Macduff children who were bathed, coddled, lullabied, and inspected for dirt in their ears; and a young Siward stabbed in the back despite the text's protestation that he had "his hurts before"—"on the front". Roasted by the reviewers and loathed by most of the cast, the production played all season to packed houses.

Ben Jonson's *Volpone*, which entered the repertory late in July, was directed—for the most part brilliantly—by David William. It was generally agreed, however, that it was a mistake to move a work so rooted in its own particular time into the nineteenth century. William was also injudicious in retaining almost uncut a sub-plot generally considered insufferably tedious. However, there was praise for William's skill in blending Jonson's difficult mixture of the hilarious and the suave, and for the impeccable performance of Mervyn Blake (Corbaccio), Douglas Rain (Mosca), and William Hutt (Volpone).

The production featured one of Stratford's more memorable props: a bed which seemed inspired by the boudoir tastes of *Playboy* magazine publisher Hugh Hefner. The production opened with Volpone, resplendent in fox furs, on the bed in front of an inner stage stuffed with "sacred treasure". While a large choir and a bevy of organs accompanied his adorations, Volpone stood in glory on the bed, which gradually parted in the middle to reveal his gold in the trap under it.

After the debacle at the Avon the year before, Gascon took no chances in 1971. He offered a season of classic French farce. In July, that old chestnut, *An Italian Straw Hat*, held sway, with Robin Gammell portraying a Ferdinand for whom, wrote Berners Jackson, "perpetual frenzy has become a way of life". Jackson also liked Tony van Bridge's Nonancourt, terming it a "gross confection of cupidity and hypocritical sentiment". However, the production seemed to lack vivifying direction from Stephen Porter and was only moderately successful. It gave way in August to what many Stratford regulars considered to be the most hilarious production in the Festival's history: Gascon's scintillating production of Feydeau's *Le Dindon*, under the title of *There's One in Every Marriage*. The all-star cast was studded with Stratford favourites: Martha Henry (Luci-enne), Peter Donat (Pontagnac), Richard Curnock (Vatelin), Jack Creley (Roubillon), Tony van Bridge (Pinchard), Mary Savidge

(Madame Pinchard), and Joseph Shaw (Gerome).

The Feydeau marked one of those occasions when audiences complained about pains from excessive laughter. Perhaps the highlight was the scene in which Lucienne, thinking her husband has been cheating on her, offers herself to Roubillon, who has long lusted after her. In the *Journal of Canadian Studies*, Berners Jackson wrote:

> When Lucienne arrives, Roubillon has just spent a long night with his mistress of the moment and finds himself unable to accept this sudden bounty. Throughout this scene at Stratford, Mr. Creley played like a man in pain, the exquisite irony of his situation bearable only because his attempts to cope with the importunate Lucienne were interrupted by short periods of sleep. He managed the words but not the music of passion; his gestures were those of an heroic spirit who finds, in a moment of crisis, that the flesh is out to lunch.

Delighted Stratford buffs hoped Feydeau would become to the Avon in the early 1970s what Gilbert and Sullivan had been in the early 1960s. The production went to New York's Royale Theatre the following January, with everyone confident of success. Every New York reviewer loved it, with the exception of Clive Barnes, and such was the power of the *New York Times* that the production closed in two weeks. The experience hurt Gascon deeply, and he abandoned plans for a 1972 Feydeau production.

The music program used the same format as in years before: Sunday concerts and Saturday recitals of chamber music. ''Music at Midnight'' in the Art Gallery on eight evenings in July and August proved popular again, and there were three master classes. Under the directorship of Gerald Pratley, the International Film Festival was revived, using high-quality projectors from the Czech Pavilion at Expo. Though audiences were small for the ten-day season in September, the response was sufficient to ensure that the Film Festival would be continued.

The old Casino, or Festival Concert Hall, or Festival Exhibition Hall, came back into the picture again. It was now called the Third Stage and was planned as an experimental theatre for new work, with portable staging and tiers for chairs for an audience of about 250. The Third Stage was the home of a two-week run of *The Red Convertible* by the Colombian playwright Enrique Buenaventura. Most critics questioned the worth of the play, but most also thought Mari Gorman brilliant in the central role and also praised the direction of Michael Bawtree, now returned to the Festival after stints at Simon Fraser University and the National Arts Centre. Also at the Third Stage in July and August were appearances by the National Theatre of Puppet Arts, the Montreal Marionettes, and the Canadian Mime Theatre.

During the winter a sophisticated new lighting and sound system was installed in the Festival Theatre. The original simple system, in the capable hands of master electrician Len Smith, who had lit every one of the Festival Theatre's productions for the first eighteen years, had worked well. Nevertheless, equipment was wearing out and was becoming difficult to replace; by the standards of the 1970s, the system was primitive and expensive in terms of man-hours. Lighting effects were severely limited, and the expansion of the repertoire to works other than those of Shakespeare and his contemporaries demanded something richer. There was, moreover, the problem of spill-over of light from the stage; illumination of front-row spectators could be distracting. Robert Scales, who held a doctorate in theatre arts, was appointed technical director to supervise the installation of the system in association with Gil Wechsler, a lighting designer involved in many Stratford productions. The final cost exceeded $433,000, and installation work also exposed a need for nearly $100,000 worth of roof repairs. The Festival had hoped to pay the whole cost from the proceeds of a lottery in which it co-operated with eight other Ontario artistic organizations, but final proceeds were only $12,800, and another lottery in 1972 brought the Festival less than $2,800.

Fortunately, the Richard Ivey Foundation of London, Ontario, and the Kresge Foundation of Birmingham, Michigan, stepped in with grants of $20,000 and $100,000 to help with a difficult and unexpected financial problem.

The 1972 season began badly with the tour to Minneapolis and Ottawa. The two-and-a-half-week run at the Guthrie Theatre beginning February 23 saw a sharp drop in attendance from the year before, and although the Guthrie authorities remained pleasant, it became clear to the Stratfordites that, with the Guthrie Company now well established, Minneapolis would not in future be keen to act as a pre-season touring centre. Gascon's production of Musset's *Lorenzaccio* was not well received in Minneapolis, or in Ottawa during the one-month run there that began on March 20. Hutt's production of *As You Like It* proved popular, but with a drop of more than $40,000 in Canada Council support and disappointing box office, the tour had cost the Festival heavily and was to be the last of its kind.

The season at Stratford was unusually controversial, and protracted arguments were the order of the day in after-theatre discussions in the Chalmers Lounge and other cultural centres. About two productions, however, there was almost no controversy: Michael Bawtree's production of Goldsmith's *She Stoops To Conquer*, introduced late in July into the Festival Theatre for nineteen performances, and Albert Millaire's Théâtre du Nouveau Monde production in English of *La Guerre, Yes Sir!*, Roch Carrier's portrait of

Scene from the 1972/1973 Festival stage production of She Stoops To Conquer, *by Oliver Goldsmith, directed by Michael Bawtree, designed by Desmond Heeley, music by Raymond Pannell, lighting by Gil Wechsler. L.-R.: Mary Savidge as Mrs. Hardcastle (1972), Tony van Bridge as Mr. Hardcastle, and Alan Scarfe as Tony Lumpkin. Photograph by Robert C. Ragsdale, courtesy of the Stratford Festival Archives.*

wartime life in a Gaspé village. Virtually everyone agreed that both were brilliant; the former was also the season's box-office hit, playing to above 97-per-cent capacity, while the latter was a box-office disaster at 38 per cent.

Though Bawtree was directing his first production for the Festival stage, his active role in the organization over several years made him thoroughly at home with it, and he served Goldsmith well, not least by being unobtrusive.

Decoration for the Goldsmith play was stripped to the minimum, and there were no gimmicks. The production moved quickly and was energetic and vital. Nicholas Pennell, new to Stratford but familiar to Canadians as Michael Mont in the BBC's *The Forsyte Saga*, managed nicely to obscure the element of the ninny and the cad in his portrayal of the play's young hero. Pat Galloway was suitably pert and charming as Kate Hardcastle, and both were ably supported by Barry MacGregor's Hastings and the Constance of the visiting Anglo-American actress Carole Shelley. As the Hardcastles, Tony van Bridge and Mary Savidge made it clear that Goldsmith had them in mind when he created the roles, and a Festival newcomer, Alan Scarfe, was a most distinguished Tony Lumpkin. *La Guerre,*

Scene from the 1972 Avon stage production of La Guerre, Yes Sir!, *by Roch Carrier, translated by Suzanne Grossman, with Le Théâtre du Nouveau Monde company, directed by Albert Millaire, designed by Mark Negin, lighting by Gil Wechsler, music by Gabriel Charpentier. Jacques Thisdale as Henri. Photograph by Robert C. Ragsdale, courtesy of the Stratford Festival Archives.*

Yes Sir! also had an all-star cast, and the players of Le Théâtre du Nouveau Monde brought their usual style and sense of ensemble to a fascinating play. Critics raved—and people stayed away. Commented Berners Jackson:

In each year, numerous voices create the impression that the public is hungry for Canadian plays, and that, if Stratford is to fulfil its responsibilities—let alone its destiny—it must give stage room to some of these. Yet, when a good Canadian play is given an exciting production by a great Canadian company, the public response is disappointing, discouraging and depressing. Perhaps the voices can explain it; I can't.

There were odd people who professed to enjoy *Lorenzaccio* and even odder ones who judged it the season's best production. Most viewers, however, seemed to think the play unutterably dreadful, almost interminable, and creakingly inept, especially in being practically all talk and no action. Why, people wondered, was so much effort being expended on the work? Why, having produced it earlier, did Gascon decide to stage it again? The reviewer for the *Journal of Canadian Studies* shared the puzzlement of many over the casting of Pat Galloway in the hero's role:

> I felt sorry for everyone involved—especially me, and even more, perhaps, for Miss Pat Galloway who, for reasons I don't understand, had to play that epitome of the drippily uninteresting, the hero of the play. That Sarah Bernhardt performed in the role offers no justification for casting a woman as Lorenzo, any more than her Hamlet justified further female Hamlets. The programme note tried gallantly and obscurely to explain that to have a woman playing Lorenzo allows for "a highly complex human being rather than simply a categorized sexual one"—the point escapes me and it neglects the fact that Miss Galloway is emphatically categorized sexually as a person who will still strike one as exquisitely feminine if she were encased in a barrel of cement. Miss Galloway can no more play a man than, say W. C. Fields could have played Mae West.

The production tied the *Henry VI* of 1966 for the worst attendance record of any Festival Theatre production. It had 53-per-cent houses.

William Hutt's production of *As You Like It* played to excellent houses throughout its run. It was uneven, the Jaques for instance being so low-key that he almost failed to register at all. There were some memorable performances in minor roles, and Elizabeth Shepherd's bouncy and ebullient Audrey nearly stole the show with an engaging innocence and a display of bosom that led one reviewer to describe her as the two best things in the show. Edward Atienza, draped in a costume which made him look rather like a cheap mattress in the last stages of decay, was a marvellous Touchstone, his comic genius overcoming the formidable challenges of many lines that today are completely dead. Nicholas Pennell's Orlando performed the difficult feat of not being acted off the stage by Carole Shelley's Rosalind, to whom the evening clearly belonged. Casting Miss Shelley in her first Shakespearean role proved inspired. Her natural charm and gaiety were irresistible; her magnificently lithe body allowed her to move like an angel; her love for Orlando was genuine and wonderful. Above all, however, her fine comic timing resulted in one of the funniest Rosalinds ever.

King Lear, directed by David William, was a box-office hit, with houses almost equalling those for the Goldsmith play, but quarrels over this production's merits were perhaps the most intense of all. It was certainly uneven. Most people seemed agreed, for instance, that the American actor playing Edmund was disappointing, whereas Kenneth Welsh as Edgar gave perhaps his finest Stratford performance. The production began very strongly with William Hutt's Lear exuding power and foolishness, and getting fine support from Edward Atienza's Fool and the three daughters (Pat Galloway as Goneril, Carole Shelley as Regan, and Elizabeth Shepherd as Cordelia). Matters started disintegrating, however, in the heath scenes, where Stratford seemed mainly concerned with demonstrating its new sound system. Hutt became largely incomprehensible and his later Lear seemed pathetic rather than tragic, excessively humble and inadequately wise.

Controversy over Jean Gascon's production of *The Threepenny Opera* at the Avon centred on whether it was acrid and acrimonious enough, since Anton Rodgers's Macheath was deemed altogether too gentle by some playgoers, and whether it mattered very much that Lila Kedrova's Mrs. Peachum was often incomprehensible. On the latter point, Berners Jackson had no doubts:

> Miss Kedrova attacked the part with a gusto that threatened to dismember it. Her Mrs. Peachum was not so much a character as a phenomenon. She has one of those faces where emotions register themselves as prototypes. Mrs. Peachum's smirk, for instance, struck one as the model from which all lesser smirks had been derived. Her gestures, turning her back on Peachum to guzzle surreptitiously from a bottle, ironing a beggar's clothes, etc., were vigorous, uninhibited, exaggerated to the point of parody. Crammed into an indescribable garment, her shapeless body still carrying a hint of former glories, she seemed indestructible, propelled by a vitality that nothing could erode. Miss Kedrova played much of this in a broadly comic way, and I must admit there were times when I wasn't sure what she was up to, and that to this moment I'm not clear as to what her conception of Mrs. Peachum may have been. Yet, she went about it all with such zest and high spirits, and so compelling is her presence on the stage, that I enjoyed every minute of it. . . . Here was a Mrs. Peachum! When comes such another?

Jackson also had no doubts—nor did anyone else—that Denise Fergusson was "the definitive Jenny. In a to-hell-with-it coiffure, grotesque scarlet rouge, and a psychic state as vicious and resentful as the satire in her songs, Miss Fergusson hipped her way through the melodrama, a night prowler with the face of a harpy and the body of a panther."

The show, the first musical at the Avon for some years, was very popular.

The music program offered an attractive innovation that year: a special *Music for a Summer Day* on August 25. It began at 9:30 a.m. with a coffee klatsch in the Festival Theatre. At 10:30 the Beaux Arts Trio performed, at noon Jean-Pierre Rampal gave a concert, and at 2:30 the New York Philharmonic Orchestra took over the Festival Theatre. At 5 p.m., the Dorion Woodwind Quintet performed at Rothman's Art Gallery, and at midnight the Canadian Brass concluded events with a concert on the island in Lake Victoria. The $20 ticket included breakfast, a picnic lunch, and an outdoor supper, in addition to the musical feast. Attendance at the International Film Festival increased remarkably. On August 27, Tony van Bridge, looking more Chestertonian than G.K.C. himself, gave a one-man show based on Chesterton's writings. For this twentieth season, the Festival mounted an impressive exhibit at City Hall, dealing with the history of the theatre and of the city itself.

Michael Bawtree arranged a challenging all-Canadian program at the Third Stage. A two-week run of a new play, *Mark*, written by Betty Jane Wylie and directed by William Hutt, was not well received, but the other productions were successes. There was a one-week revival of Gabriel Charpentier's opera, *Orpheus*, originally commissioned for the opening of the National Arts Centre in 1969; a version of *Pinocchio* adapted and directed by John Wood, which pleased children of all ages and played to 111-per-cent capacity for three weeks; and Murray Schafer's opera, *Patria*, which ran at 110 per cent for three performances. The Third Stage season was very expensive, since the board had proceeded in the spring on verbal assurances from the Ontario Arts Council and the Canada Council that necessary money would be forthcoming for the proposed program. In fact, the Ontario council gave nothing, and the Canada Council gave $35,000 of the $50,000 that had been expected of it. Later seasons also proved expensive, and four years later Robin Phillips announced a temporary closing of the Third Stage; whether the costs incurred were justified was the burning question. Probably the Third Stage's major importance lay in its contribution to Canadian opera. It was really the only outlet in Canada for contemporary Canadian opera, as was stressed in Lord Harewood's report on the state of opera in Canada.

In 1972, the Ontario Ministry of Industry and Tourism conducted the most detailed survey of Festival visitors so far undertaken (excluding school and Film Festival audiences). Among the findings: the average visitor had attended Stratford five times; 26 per cent were making their first visit; the proportion of U.S. visitors was steadily increasing, with 43.7 per cent of visitors coming from the U.S. in 1972 and accounting for 54.8 per cent in ticket sales; and the largest single age group was people in their twenties.

·C·H·A·P·T·E·R · XVIII·

1973-74

Early in January 1973 the company gave two public dress-rehearsal performances of its two touring plays: a revival of *King Lear*, and a new Gascon production of *The Taming of the Shrew*. The performances were in the Avon and used the portable steel touring set (known among company members as the Iron Curtain), which roughly approximated the Festival stage in appearance. Then it was off to Montreal for an eleven-day run that was very well received and heartened the company for what was to be its longest tour to date — subsidized by $200,000 from the Department of External Affairs. On January 24 in Copenhagen, the company gave a command performance of *The Shrew*, which pleased the Danish Queen so much that she returned three days later with the Queen Mother. There followed two days in Utrecht and one in The Hague, four days in Warsaw and two in Cracow, and two one-week runs in Moscow's Art Theatre and in Leningrad. On March 7, the company returned to Toronto and a warm welcome from Stratfordites. Members of the company made many new friends, and the tour had been most happy and successful in every way; nowhere was there an empty seat in the house, and receptions were rapturous, the highlight being the nine-minute ovation for *Lear* on opening night in Leningrad. There was only one sour note: some company members had picked up parasites from Leningrad's water, and a few remained affected all summer. It was somewhat ironic that the company

Scene from the 1972 Festival stage and 1973 touring production of
King Lear, *directed by David William, designed by Annena Stubbs,*
music by Louis Applebaum, lighting by Gil Wechsler. William Hutt as
King Lear. *Photograph by Robert C. Ragsdale, a.r.p.s., courtesy of the*
Stratford Festival Archives.

enjoyed so remarkable a European success with a *Lear* that did not
really show it at its best, and with a *Shrew* that many considered the
only really weak production ever mounted by Gascon for the
Festival.

Back at Stratford there had been two sad deaths. The popular box-
office manager, Ken Bell, died in January after fourteen years of
service to the Festival, and Bill Wylie died very suddenly on April
22. Bruce Swerdfager became acting general manager and assumed
the post permanently in September. The Festival had been fortunate

in having his services at a difficult time. As an actor in the first company, later as company and theatre manager and then comptroller, and as the man who had supervised the Avon restorations, he was well equipped for his new responsibilities. The others rallied around him, and he proved a most successful and popular leader.

The season opened on June 4 without its leading lady, since Pat Galloway had broken bones in her leg and ankle in an accident. Anni Lee Taylor stepped into the breach as Kate in *The Shrew*, and Pat Bentley-Fisher was an admirable replacement as the Kate in the revival of *She Stoops To Conquer*. (Later in the season, Miss Taylor herself was hospitalized, and Nicholas Pennell injured his ankle and had to perform with a marked limp.) Goldsmith's play, with Amelia Hall taking over as Mrs. Hardcastle, seemed as fresh as ever, and played to excellent houses. However, *The Shrew*, although a box-office success, was an artistic disappointment, memorable mainly for some clever props and bits of business. Gascon abandoned the play's frame, introduced some *commedia dell'arte* elements, and presented the work as a precise piece of clockwork—crisp, fast, noisy, and very professional, but mechanical, inhuman, and increasingly strained.

The season's major disaster was David William's production of *Othello*. William had directed the leading Israeli actor, Nachum Buchman, in a triumphant *Othello* for the Habimah Theatre, and although Buchman had no English, William thought he could learn the language adequately and repeat his earlier success. William proved wrong, and Buchman's performance was often incomprehensible and almost always embarrassing. Martha Henry's moving and gutsy Desdemona and some fine moments from Amelia Hall could do nothing to redeem a doomed production. Given the virtually unanimous distress over this offering, the 72-per-cent attendance was remarkable.

Over his many years at Stratford, Jean Gascon directed surprisingly little Shakespeare, and except for *Cymbeline* had never seemed really at home with him. Now, in 1973, he showed again that he was attuned to the romances with a stunningly beautiful production of the rarely performed *Pericles*. This is a strange play, much of it extremely awkward, nearly half of it probably the work of some hack. The few directors who had ever tackled it tended to seek refuge in extensive cuts, spectacular effects, or gimmickry. Gascon instead proceeded as he had with *Cymbeline*, straightforwardly, and gave the audience the finest of all his Shakespeare productions. It had a stripped and clean simplicity, and while the text was occasionally modified, the changes were always faithful to the spirit of the play.

As Gower, the medieval poet who presents the play in long Choruses, Edward Atienza was masterly. Clearly regarding himself

Scene from the 1973/1974 Festival stage production of Pericles, *directed by Jean Gascon, designed by Leslie Hurry, music by Gabriel Charpentier, lighting by Gil Wechsler. L.-R.: Tony van Bridge as Simonides (1973), Martha Henry as Thaisa, Nicholas Pennell as Pericles, and Edward Atienza as Gower. Photograph by Robert C. Ragsdale, a.r.p.s., courtesy of the Stratford Festival Archives.*

as the writer, director, lighting designer, and chief star, Gower meandered through the court of King Simonides to make actors freeze, burst into speech, or fall in love; he delighted in playing little jokes on the audience; full of self-adulation, he invited viewers to savour the perfection of his Latin. In short he "charmed" (in both senses of the word) his audiences into accepting the old folk tale for the joy it can bring. Tony van Bridge contributed another definitive performance as Old King Cole (alias Simonides), with whose first entrance the play took off from its inevitable rocky beginnings. Like Atienza, van Bridge oozed charm, and had a fine time pulling Pericles' leg by accusing him of being a vile seducer.

Angela Wood gave a highly stylized portrayal of the dastardly Dionyza, and Martha Henry was beautiful and moving as Pericles' wife, Thaisa. Amelia Hall was not at all lovely as the epitome of a

Byzantine madam. Ably abetted by three exhausted whores clearly capable of infecting men with every known disease, she bestrode the stage—flat-footed, horrible-voiced, garishly wigged—making the question "Are you a woman?" put to her by another character a more than reasonable one. Pamela Brook's lovely Marina was all the things that impossible and delightful young lady should be, and Pennell used his lithe body and rich voice to excellent advantage as Pericles. The reunion between father and daughter was played with a simple and touching honesty.

Gascon had toyed with the notion of a season of Victorian melodrama at the Avon, but finally decided on two Russian plays: Turgenev's *A Month in the Country* and Gogol's *The Marriage Brokers*, both directed by William Hutt. They did disappointing business, neither making 50-per-cent capacity. Public and critics alike tended to find Turgenev's play old-fashioned and not to their taste, but a minority admired the sympathetic direction, Brian Jackson's impressive sets, and performances by a fine cast headed by Dawn Greenhalgh's Natalia. An equally talented cast, with Leonard Frey as Podkolyossin and Roberta Maxwell as Agafaya, did justice to Gogol's play and was often uproariously funny, but it could not hide the essential thinness of the work.

Another International Film Festival played to good houses, but the role of music in the Festival was further diminished in 1973 when the Sunday concerts were discontinued. Two days were set aside for *Music for a Summer Day*, and there were eight Saturday-morning concerts. Otherwise, music was restricted to a continuation of the midnight performances during July and August and master classes in guitar and flute. The Third Stage had a most successful season despite a new opera, *Exiles*, which struck most people as having an insufferably silly book and being otherwise pretentious. Henry Beissel's children's play, *Inook and the Sun*, which utilized Felix Mirbt's marionettes, played to full houses, however, and so did Michael Ondaatje's *The Collected Works of Billy the Kid*, a Festival commission. The story of the legendary outlaw, with Neil Munro as Billy, music by Alan Laing, and direction by John Wood, was dramatized by Ondaatje from his own book—a work that won the 1970 Governor General's Award for Poetry. This poetic theatrical western was greeted with considerable acclaim, and was to be widely performed in later productions in various parts of Canada.

Gascon's tenure was nearing its end. A year before, he had told the board he would be leaving the Festival at the end of 1974; the resulting search processes led to the appointment of Britain's Robin Phillips. Meanwhile Gascon's final year was shaping up as one of the busiest in the Festival's history.

To begin with, there was a CBC videotaping of *She Stoops To*

Conquer. This was the first time a Festival production had been taped on stage before a live audience. The next concern was an Australian tour; over the years the Festival had received several invitations to perform down under, and finally was able to accept one extended by the Adelaide Festival of the Arts and the Elizabethan Theatre Trust. On January 10, the seventeen-member cast commenced rehearsals of Molière's *The Imaginary Invalid*. On February 7, the group left Perth County, Ontario, and two days later was in Perth, Western Australia.

It was high summer in Australia, and the players had three days of rehearsal on a new stage set designed back in Canada but built in Australia (all props and costumes had been brought over from Stratford). There were ten performances in Perth, twelve in Melbourne (where temperatures of more than 100 degrees kept attendance down slightly), seventeen in Adelaide, and fifteen in Sydney. Reviews were enthusiastic, and Australian hospitality was remarkable; hosts included Tom Brown, who had served the Festival under Guthrie and Langham nearly twenty years earlier. Company members found themselves thoroughly spoiled, and, as William Hutt remarked, their love affair with Australia was "flagrant". The cast managed to do a lot of swimming; one of the ladies, rescued from the clasp of a jellyfish by a young Australian, promptly proceeded to get engaged to him. The company returned to Stratford on April 8, exhausted and exhilarated by what Hutt called "one of Stratford's happiest and most memorable ventures" abroad. Two weeks later, on Shakespeare's birthday, it was announced that Gascon had won the $50,000 Royal Bank Award for his contributions to Canadian theatre, and rehearsals were broken off for an impromptu celebration.

The season opened with Gascon's production of *The Imaginary Invalid*. Reviews tended to be negative. Some reviewers seemed to have been expecting another *Tartuffe* and ignored the fact that Molière's last play is far less complex and more farcical than its illustrious predecessor. Foreign critics were generally impressed: Clive Barnes loved it, and the *Manchester Guardian*'s Gareth Lloyd Evans had high praise for "a heart-rising, belly-tickling exhibition of an exquisitely light-fingered production. . .and comic acting of a quality I have not seen in England this many a long day". By general agreement, Tanya Moiseiwitsch's design work was a delight. As Toinette, Pat Galloway proved yet again that she was born to play soubrettes, especially when assigned such untruthfully funereal lines as "The poor deceased has passed on." As the Invalid, William Hutt rather resembled a Bugs Bunny with ear disease, a Bugs Bunny who had lost not only his marbles but even more of his lower jaw. His relish in his diseases and the infinite variety of enemas that were his to enjoy was the ultimate in greasiness, and his capacity for self-

Scene from the 1974 Festival stage production of The Imaginary
Invalid, *by Molière, translated by Donald M. Frame, directed by Jean
Gascon, designed by Tanya Moiseiwitsch, music by Gabriel Charpentier,
lighting by Gil Wechsler. William Hutt as Argan, Pamela Brook as
Angelique. Photograph by Robert C. Ragsdale, a.r.p.s., courtesy of the
Stratford Festival Archives.*

pity was monumental. Hutt had a fine time, but he didn't neglect
Argan's more human moments. This character must finally attract
some sympathy: buried deep within him there is a heart that is
prone—if only metaphorically—to liberal bleeding, and thus he
can be twisted by others at will. This capacity for sentimentality at
its most maudlin emerged in Hutt's characterization, because he
gave his Argan a kind of wide-eyed baffled innocence that made him
extremely vulnerable. This Argan lived in a world that seemed to

exist mainly to preserve him in a state of perpetual astonishment.

The second night saw Gascon's *Pericles* back, as fresh as ever, and once again establishing itself as the season's best production. However, Michael Bawtree's production of *Love's Labour's Lost* was less successful. It did receive better reviews than *The Imaginary Invalid*, and there was praise for Alan Laing's music, Pennell's Berowne, and Hutt's revival of his Don Armado of ten years before. But the court scenes did not really work, largely because the leading ladies, Dawn Greenhalgh and Pat Galloway, looked uncomfortable as the Princess and Rosaline. The *Journal of Canadian Studies* commented: "This must be the first *Love's Labour's Lost* on record in which Katharine has shown the other ladies how to do it—Marti Maraden, a Stratford newcomer, is a young actress of enormous promise whom the Festival must, as Jeeves would say, grapple to itself with hoops of steel."

King John, directed by Englishman Peter Dews, joined the other plays on July 23, and won high praise from the critics. The production was straightforward and well-spoken, and notable for the highly pictorial quality and stillness of much of the staging. Edward Atienza was brilliant in the title role, his John seeming always to be trying hard to play a role for which he was lamentably unfitted; but the generous underplaying of the Bastard's role by Douglas Rain was perhaps carried too far, to a point where the character became unexciting.

Gascon's final season was of high over-all quality, and his last production as artistic director was a delight, as a kind of old-home-week atmosphere prevailed at the Avon in a romp through Offenbach's frothy *La Vie Parisienne*. Douglas Campbell returned to do silly things as the Baron de Gondremarck, and to be encumbered by the Baroness of Marilyn Gardner (Mme Gascon in private life). Gascon's brother Gabriel came from Paris to play Gardefeu. Old friends associated with the production included Robert Prevost, Jack Creley, and Barry MacGregor. Mary Lou Fallis and Anne Linden alternated in the role of Gabrielle. Everyone in the cast seemed to be having a lot of fun, and so did audiences. Unfortunately, the 63-percent houses indicated the error of turning the Avon over to a single production for a full ten weeks.

The major offering at the Third Stage was John Wood's excellent production of *Walsh*, a good and honest play by Vancouver's Sharon Pollock, which deals with the conflict Major Walsh of the North West Mounted Police faces because of his affection and sympathy for Sitting Bull, the man who had triumphed over Custer at Little Big Horn, who Walsh has been ordered to send back to the United States. Once again, however, audiences averaging only 59-per-cent capacity challenged the Festival's policy of trying to present Canadian plays.

Houses were better for a children's play, *Ready Steady Go*, by Calgarian Sandra Jones, and Michael Bawtree's two operatic productions sold out. Maureen Forrester was dazzling in Gian-Carlo Menotti's *The Medium*, and Garnet Brooks sang Everyman and Phyllis Mailing Paramour in composer Charles Wilson's *The Summoning of Everyman*, with libretto by Eugene Benson.

Raffi Armenian, conductor of the Kitchener-Waterloo Symphony Orchestra, who had taken over as Festival music director after the resignation of Andree Gingras, arranged five Sunday concerts and the customary master classes and Saturday-morning concerts, and also formed a new group, the Stratford Festival Ensemble. Attendance was again disappointing.

The tenth International Film Festival featured Dilys Powell as critic-in-residence. School performances were abnormally low—a freak situation caused partly by a teachers' strike in Michigan and partly by daring programming, which included none of the well-known plays that were regularly included in the North American school curriculum.

In an interview with Julius Novick in 1968, Gascon had remarked:

> There is a danger here of stagnation. It's probably the most important and organized company on the North American continent. But the danger of it is that it could become an institution. People get self-satisfied. . . .
>
> The people. . .are hoping to see the pageantry—the trumpets and the banners and the whole bit. It's very hard to break that pattern, but it must be done.

There had been some criticism that Stratford had indeed succumbed to the very danger Gascon had described. It was said by some that Stratford was becoming decadent and taking on the character of a mausoleum or a museum. Some said there was too much opulence, an excessive emphasis on spectacle and lavish costume at the expense of the inner life of the drama.

Following Gascon's retirement, the claims of decadence were to be put forward routinely, as if accepted matters of fact. "We have only," wrote John Fraser in the *Globe and Mail* on July 17, 1976, "to cast our minds back a very few years to remember the tedium and mediocrity that were the trademarks of a Stratford Festival pompously encumbered with a false sense of its own grandeur." Robin Phillips was to be credited by Clive Barnes for bringing about a renaissance, and by others with breathing new life into a corpse. Yet it is difficult to regard these sentiments as anything more than mythology. The Gascon years were often uneven; they had yielded their share of failures and the occasional disaster. The programming, however, had often been daring—far more so, in fact, than that of some succeeding years. To schedule *Love's Labour's Lost*, *King John*, and *Pericles* in one's final season is not playing it safe, nor is producing the kind of works offered at the Third Stage, nor is trying to fill the Avon with Arrabal, Wesker, and Mrozek.

Curiously, the facts seem to be the opposite of the myth: Gascon in many ways was—if not always wisely—the most adventurous and experimental of all Stratford's artistic directors. Perhaps the myth was partly attributable to the general truth that a high proportion of the productions during his regime were of relatively simple plays calling for relatively simple effects: a thin work like *Lorenzaccio*, when apparelled as richly as a major Shakespeare work, inevitably takes on the characteristics of a costume piece, and can lead to complaints about hollowness. Be this as it may, the image of the "decadent" Stratford of the early 1970s must surely be questioned.

This is not to say that Gascon had been the perfect leader. He was often indecisive, and prone to procrastination followed by hasty decision. He had not grappled successfully with the problems of musical programming and of the Avon Theatre. Many of the actors from Britain and the United States had not been selected wisely, and with only a handful of exceptions, he had not succeeded in attracting real stars to Stratford. Nor had he kept together the solid core of players whose sense of ensemble had characterized much of the greatness of Langham's final years; instead, there had been a heavy turnover of actors from one season to the next.

On the other hand, Gascon had a warm and Gallic personality and was a fascinating man; people found him easy and interesting to work with and felt he had helped to foster a very real sense of the Festival as a co-operative venture. Everyone trusted him, and he enjoyed great loyalty from his associates. Gascon used to insist that the main thing holding a theatre together was love, and under his leadership the Festival had generally been a happy place to work. He had shown courage in tackling rare plays himself, and had enjoyed some major successes with them. He had contributed some of Stratford's most distinguished productions: *The Dance of Death*, *Tartuffe*, *Hadrian VII*, *Cymbeline*, *The Duchess of Malfi*, *There's One in Every Marriage*, and *Pericles*. He had proved a most successful director of opera. Furthermore, he did more for Molière in English-speaking Canada, and perhaps in North America, than any other individual.

The New Beginning

Nationalist juices were flowing in Canada during the 1970s, particularly in the world of the theatre, so it was predictable that the decision to hire England's Robin Phillips as the Stratford Festival's new artistic director would spawn criticism. What was not expected was the degree of hostility that erupted among the more militant ranks of the Canadian theatre when Phillips's appointment was announced.

The board was astounded, because it felt that it had pursued the search for Gascon's successor in a careful and responsible manner. Gascon had given the board eighteen months' notice, which was sufficient for him to complete the 1974 season and which gave the board ample time to fulfil its crucial responsibility. Under the chairmanship of Berners Jackson, the search committee had worked hard and listened to many authoritative advisers. The major source on British possibilities was Ronald Bryden, dramaturge for the Royal Shakespeare Company and for a period the man who had ascended to Kenneth Tynan's plum post as theatre critic of the *Observer*. Bryden had the additional qualifications of having spent many years at school and university in Canada and of having visited the Festival several times to participate in the Stratford Seminars. Among those he recommended most highly were Michael Blakemore (who proved unavailable) and Robin Phillips, the thirty-two-year-old artistic director of the Greenwich Theatre, and a former associate director of both Exeter's Northcott Theatre and the famed Bristol Old Vic. Phillips's career had been extraordinarily successful. His reputation as a whiz kid had begun while he was still a student at the Bristol Old Vic School, where his obsession with knowing everything there was to know about the theatre made him equally adept at dressing a wig or building a set.

During the 1960s he established himself as an actor. He was a member of Laurence Olivier's Chichester Festival Company in 1962, and later began landing key television and film roles. He appeared in several episodes of the BBC's enormously popular adaptation of *The Forsyte Saga*, played the title role in a star-studded film version of *David Copperfield*, and won the coveted lead in the 1968 screen version of Evelyn Waugh's *Decline and Fall*.

Despite these successes, a directing career was becoming increasingly attractive to Phillips. Although he continued to perform until 1972, he was convinced that he possessed neither the vocal power nor the physical presence to become a major actor. By 1966, a directing career had become his primary goal. By 1969, when he staged a critically acclaimed production of Chekhov's *The Seagull* in suburban London, he was well on the way to achieving that aim. Other directing triumphs followed: the London première of Edward Albee's *Tiny Alice* with David Warner and Irene Worth; a controversial West End production of *Abélard and Héloïse*, which later toured the United States; a controversial treatment of *Caesar and Cleopatra* with John Gielgud at Chichester; and an unorthodox treatment of Shakespeare's *The Two Gentlemen of Verona*, which appalled the Royal Shakespeare Company hierarchy while delighting critics and public.

During this period, Phillips came to the conclusion that he badly wanted a theatre of his own. He was touted as a candidate for the artistic-directorship of the Chichester Festival, but that job went to Keith Michell. Instead, Phillips took over the tiny Greenwich Theatre in London's dockland. It was such a shoestring operation that Phillips even found himself cleaning the washrooms. Yet, his prestige was such that he was able to attract such major names as Mia Farrow and Joan Plowright to perform for him at meagre salaries.

But Phillips remained unsatisfied, confiding at one point to a friend: "I really want my own theatre, and I may have to emigrate to get it." He began thinking about Canada and about Canadians he had known at the Bristol Old Vic School. They had been enthusiastic about the future of theatre in their own country. Could there possibly be a place there for him? He even wrote Gascon at Stratford, checking out the possibilities for work, and received a negative reply; by coincidence this exchange took place at the same time that Phillips's name was assuming increasing prominence on the

Stratford board's list of potential artistic directors. In the summer of 1973 he was on the short list of six candidates and was invited over to Canada to view the facilities and meet the board.

Phillips was overwhelmed when he first entered the Festival Theatre and saw the stage. Having successfully directed at Chichester, he was familiar with the pitfalls of the thrust stage, but he saw immediately that Stratford's design offered a new and exciting challenge. He was less excited by the type of work being done on that stage, and impressed board members with a quick but perceptive analysis of one particular production's shortcomings and what could be done to set them right.

The board found Phillips an attractive and exciting candidate. Phillips was more ambivalent. The Festival Theatre fascinated him; the institution itself made him wary. One of the reasons for his disenchantment with British theatre was that he felt that it had lost its spark, that its classical productions tended to be dusty museum pieces. He had coined a phrase—"the semaphore thing"—to describe the tendency of many British stage performers to declaim and telegraph their emotions. In a *Maclean's* magazine interview with David Cobb in 1977, he recalled his first contact with Stratford:

I came, liked the place—and found the acting to be much the same tired old semaphore business that there is in England. What was the point? That's what I wanted to get away from. So when the Board asked me how I'd like this sleepy little town, I replied that it wasn't for me. But there was one woman on the Board, Barbara Ivey, from London, Ontario, who started talking very passionately about what the Festival needed. It *had* to go forward, she said, it couldn't stand still, it couldn't be smug. She wasn't a great talker, but I've dealt with boards before and I've never known anyone talk with such passion about a place. Barbara made me realize there was a job to be done, that should be done.

Barbara Ivey recalled later:

To me, Robin was a shot in the arm. The Festival was reaching the point where it needed a shot in the arm, yet when Robin first came over, he looked so incredibly young and shy. At the same time, there was no question but that there was a vitality and vision there. It's awkward conducting interviews with prospective candidates for a job. There we were on one side of the table, and there he was on the other, and we knew we wanted him. Therefore, it came as a bombshell when he initially said that he didn't think he was the type of person we wanted, that he didn't think the Board was committed enough to change.

The board's search committee had by this time faced up to some hard decisions. It had narrowed the field down to two candidates—Phillips and William Hutt. The ultimate choice facing it was far from easy, especially since Hutt was widely known, respected, and deeply loved in Canada. Moreover, the board suspected that the appointment of an Englishman would enrage many Canadians. Hutt would have been the safe and popular choice and a good artistic director, but the board decided on Phillips, one reason for the preference being his considerably greater directorial experience, another a conviction that Stratford needed fresh ideas and something of a shaking-up of a kind that it expected Phillips would give.

Barbara Ivey's passionate plea was the deciding factor in Phillips's decision that he did, after all, want the job. John Killer, who was Phillips's first board president, said that he and his colleagues were particularly impressed by the young Englishman's practicality. They saw him as a welcome contrast to Gascon, a man capable of remarkable productions, who, however, lacked the planning abilities or the scope and vision so evident in Phillips. Nevertheless, the decision to go for Phillips was a bold one.

The announcement of the appointment, at the end of the 1973 season, caused a storm of protest—with Stratford, Phillips, England, and especially the board being vilified. Some of the criticism was considered and responsible; most was intemperate; some, like Tom Hendry's heavy-handed piece of sarcasm in *Saturday Night* magazine in February 1974, was simply vulgar.

The nationalist opposition manifested itself in some distinctly unpleasant ways. Back in England, Phillips began receiving hate mail so offensive that he couldn't bear to discuss it years later. During a CBC radio interview, he was slapped across the face with a rubber glove by Don Rubin, a free-lance commentator and the American-born editor of the vociferously nationalistic *Canadian Theatre Review*; Rubin explained that he was acting on behalf of John Juliani, an avant-garde director, in challenging Phillips to a duel.

The nationalist faction made such a commotion that it might have seemed the entire Canadian theatre community was united in opposition to Phillips. Such was not the case. Many theatre people believed that artistic expression should really know no frontiers. Many more were appalled by the juvenile behaviour of the militants. William Hutt, the man who lost out to Phillips for the job and who was to become one of his most loyal lieutenants, was aghast at the way some colleagues were behaving. "Robin's reception," Hutt told *Maclean's* in 1977, "was graceless, witless, ludicrous and cement-minded."

However, there was a degree of criticism that was thoughtful and responsible, even though it appeared to many to be framed within too narrow a context. It reflected an anger based not so much on the fact that the board's search committee had approached Phillips, but on the fact that it had pointedly neglected to approach the most eligible of all Canadian candidates—John Hirsch.

Why had Hirsch been passed over? After his artistic partnership with Gascon had fallen apart in 1969 at Stratford, Hirsch had continued to develop his international credentials, enjoying a productive New York period which included stagings of such varied works as *Galileo*, *Saint Joan*, *The Time of Your Life*, and the Broadway première of Joseph Heller's *We Bombed in New Haven*.

Ironically, Hirsch, a man of pronounced internationalist sensibility, was a particular darling of Canada's nationalists. Nevertheless, more thoughtful members of the theatre community did feel Hirsch had been unjustly treated, if not insulted, when the Stratford search committee failed even to approach him. This led to a questioning of the very processes and philosophy underlying the events that led to Phillips's hiring.

In the spring of 1974, Hirsch was among seven Canadian directors who presented a protest manifesto to the board. The others were Bill Glassco, Martin Kinch, George Luscombe, Leon Major, Henry Tarvainen, and Keith Turnbull. Robertson Davies had aided them in the drafting of the document, to ensure a responsible and diplomatic tone. The manifesto was delivered to board representatives at a Sunday-afternoon meeting in April in the Ontario Arts Council office in Toronto. It raised some provocative questions about the Festival mandate:

To the Stratford Board:

We have asked for this meeting because of our concern for the future of the theatre in Canada, and our conviction that the Stratford Festival must play a dominant role in that future. In the broadest terms, we ask what your long-range plan is for the Festival, and what steps you hope to take to integrate it with Canadian theatre.

When Stratford was founded, it began a new era in Canadian theatre, and we have benefited from its enterprise and courage. Now, it appears that the theatre we represent is taking one direction, and Stratford another. During the past twenty-five years theatre in Canada has advanced to a direction that Stratford does not reflect. Canadian theatre is now working consistently to present world theatre in Canadian terms, to reveal a truly Canadian sensibility, and to advance, under the best circumstances at its command, Canadian plays, and the work of theatre artists in every field. The time has come when we have a right to expect leadership from your theatre, which is the national theatre of our country whether it accepts that title and the accompanying burdens or whether it does not. Your theatre receives the largest public subsidy of any theatre in Canada, and we think the time has come for some public statement as to its function, and its plans for fulfilling that function.

We fear that Stratford's seeming lack of a coherent long-term policy will bring about a divergence of aims and ideals which can only work against the development of a truly Canadian theatre and thus, in larger terms, against the development of a Canadian culture. We do not want to see two theatres in Canada—ours, and yours—one firmly national and the other imitatively international.

We are not so naive as to think that Canadian culture can develop without playing its part in the Western World of our time, nor are we so nationalistic as to wish to exclude from Canadian theatre anything that can nourish and enlarge it. But we are convinced that a Canadian sensibility is now a fact in the theatre as in the other arts, and we are anxious to serve it and strengthen it in a realistic way.

May we therefore offer for discussion the following points which seem to us to outline what Canada might expect from its national theatre, and assert that the theatres we represent have tried to embody some of them, acknowledging that none of our theatres have been able to encompass them all:

(1) That a national theatre should interpret the classics of world theatre, and explore the literature of world theatre in the light of a Canadian sensibility, which would imply that it would also,

(2) Use the best theatrical talent of the country to give something more than perfunctory attention to plays of Canadian origin that need the resources of the best equipped and most highly subsidized theatre in the country.

(3) That it should nurture growing theatre talent by providing it with the opportunity of working with the most mature and experienced theatre talent in Canada.

(4) That it should exploit the human resources of Canadian theatre by giving mature and experienced Canadian directors, designers, and actors an opportunity to extend their talents within this country, and should bring back artists who have gained experience abroad.

(5) That it should enrich our theatrical life by bringing the finest world theatre artists to Stratford from time to time as guests and exemplars, but not as permanent appointees.

(6) That it should represent the best that is Canadian in the theatre for audiences here and throughout the world.

A national theatre is a national resource of incalculable influence and significance. We feel that Stratford should take its responsibilities as a *de facto* national theatre more seriously than it has done in the past; specifically we suggest that your board be less heavily weighted with members whose realm of expertise is finance, and should include patrons and practitioners of the arts and a greater representation from the world of scholarship. We suggest that the board, rather than its artistic direction, be ultimately answerable to Canada for what is done in its national theatre.

We urge you to reconsider your position with which our own is inextricably linked. It is because of this link that we appeal to you now in a spirit in which co-operation and criticism are necessarily mingled, but in which the will toward co-operation is certainly dominant.

The meeting between board members and theatre directors proved unsatisfactory to both sides. The board saw the directors' manifesto as yet another instalment of the attack being levelled against Phillips because he was English. Keith Turnbull, who was present at the meeting, said later that the directors felt frustrated, in view of the care they had taken in framing a document that was not in any way a personal attack but rather attempted to raise practical and philosophical questions about the Festival's future. Turnbull expressed the sense of frustration in a memorandum sent to directors who had not attended the meeting:

> The barriers of understanding on all but the most obvious and naive levels were enormous, and more often than not absurd. Not one of the Board members seemed capable of getting beyond the fact that they felt their aims and functions were completely reflected in what they are doing at present and in the recent past and that the prospects for the future were in doing it all a bit better.
>
> The recurrent theme was how valuable this "dialogue" was in spite of the fact that they found everything we were saying totally incomprehensible at best and we found everything they were saying all too clear. It was even suggested that a permanent platform for discussion be established on a regular basis irrespective of the fact that nothing was accomplished on the first attempt.
>
> However the "isn't this wonderful we're getting together and listening to the profession" guise was quickly dropped when they discovered that, as had been clearly stated at the beginning of the meeting, we still intended to give our initial statement to the press. We were all somewhat dumbfounded by the violence of their reaction to this suggestion as I think we all felt the statement to be as considered, sympathetic, and middle of the road as one could be. . . .

The controversy caused Phillips great anguish, and for years afterwards he would talk of the "insults" he had had to endure during his early years in Canada. The manifesto, despite its moderate language, upset him further, particularly because he felt he was already preparing a new Festival scenario which would allay much of the criticism. His sense of being isolated increased further as a result of a dispute with the Festival press office over the most appropriate time for releasing his own plans.

So shaken was Phillips by the controversy that he contemplated returning to England. His board president, John Killer, was instrumental in prevailing on him to stay. Says another board member of the day, "I have no doubt that Robin would have gone back to England had it not been for Killer's support and commitment. What also sustained Robin was his view that this was a remarkable theatre capable of doing the best stage work in the world."

On behalf of the board, Killer eventually responded to the directors' manifesto:

The Stratford representatives were very pleased that the submission of the Directors was in so many ways in accord with the thinking of our Artistic Director designate, Mr. Robin Phillips. We believe that Mr. Phillips' plans. . .answer most of the submissions of the Directors and, in fact, open a challenging new future for the dramatic arts in Canada. Those plans demonstrate the very reasons Robin Phillips was selected artistic director of the Stratford Festival.

It was clear from Killer's statement that the dissident directors had, however, struck a sensitive nerve with their suggestion that the Festival Board "be less heavily weighted with members whose realm of expertise is finance". Killer clearly was disturbed by the implications of this proposal:

Speaking for myself, I could not accept this suggestion because I believe the members of the Stratford Board at present represent an effective balance between the arts, finance, fund-raising and the City of Stratford. Without going into a long discussion of the merits of each of these influences, I suggest that the balance presently represented has proven itself the most effective to the Festival's destiny.

For support, Killer cited a key recommendation from *The Awkward Stage*, an influential theatre study report commissioned by the Province of Ontario: the report said appointments to Boards of Governors of theatre organizations should be

on the basis of the following major responsibilities: (a) fiscal management and operations, (b) fund-raising and applications for grants, (c) provision of experience and knowledge in such fields as law, accounting, construction. Members should be in sympathy with the objects of the organization rather than in command of its artistic activities.

Killer continued:

Mr. Phillips' recently announced plans herald an exciting new era for the Stratford Festival and we hope for theatre across the country. It will be an era which will see closer communication than ever before among those in the Canadian theatre community. The Stratford Board is fully committed to these plans and eager to give Mr. Phillips every co-operation in their implementation.

The controversy left its legacy. At the time, Phillips himself commented on the situation: "I'm not at all resentful about the turmoil of the nationalist issue. I think that some of the methods used are very silly, but the root cause is very deep and very important. I resent some of the scheming, particularly from people who are afraid to stand up and protest for themselves."

Robin Phillips was taking over Stratford in a volatile climate for which he himself was not responsible. There were voices of temperance and moderation on both sides. But where emotions ran high, particularly among those insisting that a Canadian should run Stratford rather than the best man available, there was a tendency to forget that directing classical theatre and directing contemporary theatre could involve very different disciplines, and that success in running a theatre dedicated to twentieth-century plays could mean little in a theatre where the focus was on Shakespeare.

In the years that lay ahead, Phillips was to overcome much of the apprehension stemming from his appointment. Nevertheless, issues underlying the 1973-74 controversy, especially those dealing with nationalism and board responsibility, continued to simmer and were to reach boiling point again in 1980 with a crisis that was to threaten the very future of the Stratford Festival.

Shortly before he left the Festival, Jean Gascon insisted on the need for fresh thought and direction. "I honestly hope that Robin will take a new tack, that he will find new ways of waking the place up, a new vision. Stratford must be challenged with new vision. In every department. The place always needs to be shaken up, every aspect of the organization."

Phillips needed little prompting. Arriving early in 1974 as artistic director designate, he devoted much of the following months to familiarizing himself with the Canadian theatre scene. He travelled across Canada, meeting colleagues and scouting out potential actors for Stratford. He looked closely at all aspects of the Festival structure itself, and at the time the dissident directors were preparing their manifesto, he was already putting the finishing touches on his own proposed strategy.

In a prepared statement, he declared:

> There is a legitimate challenge to theatre in this country today, but it is not really a new challenge. It comes along *with* every generation, in every society. It is the challenge to open the doors to the new and untried, to build on the experience of the past, to embrace the thoughts of the young and to recognize that to embrace does not necessarily mean to surrender. In short, the challenge is to act as a *conscious* and willing connector between the past and the future. A clear voice that speaks of today—that is, actually, the essence of our job in theatre. It is possible to step with, to step aside or step back, but it takes courage and sensitivity to step forward without ignoring the remarkable achievements of the past.

Phillips's tone was conciliatory towards the wider Canadian stage community, and it was evident that he was uncomfortable with the "national theatre" label which had been affixed to Stratford. He had clear ideas about what the Festival's place should be, but he was by no means indifferent to the role of other Canadian theatres:

In terms of the works of classic theatre, Stratford achieved this aim at the outset, setting a standard by which other theatre experiences could be judged and providing audiences with new sight-lines and new perspectives. The Stratford idea was revolutionary. And the theatre experience came as a revelation. The Stratford experience forced everyone involved in theatre around the world to rethink and revise ideas which had been nurtured on the proscenium arch. Today, the wheel has come full circle and the challenge lies in rethinking and revising ideas nurtured on the experience of the past twenty-one years.

This is a demand on theatres across the country, not solely on the Stratford Festival. If we all put our minds and our hearts to meeting it, then we can together get on with the job of creating a national theatre, not in any one location or serving any one city or province but stretching from one end of the country to the other and making a statement that is truly Canadian—transcending differences of geography and economics to find the underlying pulse of this country and give it a voice. This demands from all of us a breadth of vision far greater than has ever been achieved in any other country in the world. This is the kind of contribution that can and must be made. This is what the entire theatre community must work towards.

The idea of the only possible Canadian national theatre being made up of the sum of its parts was not a new one. Indeed, it had been floated a few years previously by the Canada Council in one of its annual reports. Phillips's views may have erred on the side of idealistic theorizing, and when he did attempt to apply them, they didn't always work. But from the beginning he was painfully conscious of Stratford's isolation from the Canadian theatre scene in general, and made various attempts—some successful, others less so—to remedy the situation.

Within a few weeks of his arrival he recommended the establishment of boards of associate directors for each of Stratford's three stages, with the purpose of ensuring channels of access with other major theatres in Canada. Each group would be headed by one person resident in Stratford. Others would be in residence in theatres across Canada. Among those named to the positions on June 13, 1974, were Jean Roberts of the National Arts Centre in Ottawa, Christopher Newton of the Vancouver Playhouse, John Neville of the Citadel Theatre in Edmonton, John Wood of the Neptune Theatre in Halifax, and the Toronto Tarragon Theatre's Bill Glassco, who had been one of the directors who had signed the manifesto expressing concern over Phillips's appointment. In a further effort to reduce Stratford's supposed isolation, he proposed extensive Canadian tours. These early initiatives had merit, reflecting Phillips's sensitivity to the concerns of the wider Canadian theatre community. But for a number of reasons, some logistical and some financial, they were not to last.

Phillips was an artist who relied on a well-honed instinct, whether he was running a theatre or directing a play. He was a newcomer, but instinct told him the Festival had reached a plateau in its development. He was concerned—as Gascon had been—with the need for new directions. He also worried that no new generation of actors was looming on the company horizon.

"It didn't seem terribly in touch," he recalled later. "It was like going down a country road, turning a corner, and finding a Ruritanian something. I didn't feel that Stratford was making contact—not at any rate on the basis of what I had been seeing across the country."

He looked at some Stratford productions and saw "a lot of crazed clowns, a lot of energy, but often little more. Actors can do any amount of springing about a stage, but in the final analysis they can't camouflage the fact that they're not doing real work underneath." Phillips was painfully aware of nationalist doubts over the seeming lack of a meaningful Canadian context for a classically based repertory theatre, and although nationalist extremism angered him, he did share some common philosophical ground with his critics. In addition, Phillips had his own pronounced ideas of how to do classical theatre—ideas that had plunged him into hot water with the establishment back in England.

> I couldn't see a relationship between the country and the Canadians I had met on my travels on the one hand and the classical theatre being offered at Stratford on the other. I couldn't see any human connection. It was as though we were saying period people were not real, that they were painted dolls running around.

He saw a special need to train Stratford's actors beyond their often impressive level of achievement. A Canadian classical company in the mid-1970s must, he felt, relate more to modern life and be capable of exploring a play's connection to a "now" sensibility.

Phillips saw the company as the heartbeat of the Festival, and he thought it was necessary to abandon the practice of maintaining a separate group of actors for each theatre. He was influenced partly by economics: without a fully integrated company whose members were efficiently cross-cast in a variety of productions, there would be an inevitable increase in costs. But Phillips was also harking back to Tyrone Guthrie and his belief that an examination of the text—by designers and actors as well as directors—was the basis of good classical theatre. In a message to Festival patrons in the 1975 souvenir program, Phillips wrote:

> The idea of one Company that is equally at home on any of our stages and that works from a basic premise in its approach to all Festival productions is inherent in this over-all aim. This is why we are trying to develop a single Festival Acting Company rather than have a separate group of actors for each theatre.

Scene from the 1975 Avon stage and touring production of Two
Gentlemen of Verona, *directed by Robin Phillips and David Toguri,
designed by Molly Harris Campbell, lighting by Gil Wechsler, music by
Martin Best. L.-R.: Nicholas Pennell as Proteus, Stephen Russell as
Valentine. Photograph by Robert C. Ragsdale, a.r.p.s., courtesy of the
Stratford Festival Archives.*

Nevertheless, within the context of this long-range commitment,
Phillips did launch a key training initiative in the form of his new
Young Company. The word "Young" created some confusion,
implying that it was some sort of student endeavour, and Phillips
took pains to explain that it referred "not so much to chronological
age as to attitude or viewpoint". Hence, it contained not only

promising younger actors but such seasoned artists as Nicholas
Pennell, Jackie Burroughs, and Bernard Hopkins. Furthermore,
Phillips acted deliberately in assigning the Young Company *The
Two Gentleman of Verona* and *The Comedy of Errors*.

> These were the two earliest Shakespearean comedies I could find and
> they are reasonably straightforward. They were plays where I felt it
> would be possible to show that excess energy was not the same thing
> as vitality, plays which I thought could be related to the present. I
> wanted a feeling of beginning, of starting something, of a young
> Shakespeare being done by a young Company with the realization of
> a hard path to travel. Some members of the Company had no experi-
> ence, some a little and some a great deal—but all were starting a new
> journey.

The Young Company would tour Canada during the late winter
and spring, and then perform at the Avon during the summer. At the
time, Phillips hoped its members would "remain together for
several seasons, eventually joining the Festival Stage company or the
Third Stage, or working outside Stratford for a period of time and
then returning to us". He saw it as "potentially the most totally
practical theatre school on the continent". By 1978, however, the
Young Company had to all practical purposes ceased to exist, and
Phillips could claim a fully integrated acting company sharing all
three stages. Nevertheless, the venture proved to be one of the most
significant of Phillips's early years.

The Young Company was also a key element in Phillips's grand
strategy to restore the fortunes of the Avon, which he saw as a poor
relation that deserved to be treated with more respect as the Festival
Theatre's talented offspring. In 1971, William Wylie had remarked,
"Nobody is in charge of the Avon and everybody is in charge of it.
Nobody lives there. We have to make that theatre somebody's home,
for whatever purpose, if it's ever going to have a policy of validity."
Phillips was determined to make the Avon "somebody's home" and
to take full charge of it. He appointed himself director of the Avon
stage and made Hutt director of the Festival Theatre. (Michael
Bawtree's appointment as director of the Third Stage proved short-
lived when he left Stratford in the autumn, so Phillips took on that
responsibility as well.) Phillips moved boldly with the Avon: his
ultimate aim was the extension of its season—once only six weeks
long—to full parity with that of the Festival stage. Through the
Young Company, he would be legitimatizing the Avon as a Shakespeare house—while also scheduling works of other playwrights
there. In the process, he would be guaranteeing good audiences for
the Avon and also reducing problems experienced during tours in
the past, when thrust-stage productions found themselves having to
perform on a proscenium stage.

There were other major changes in the offing. Phillips made it clear to the board that he wanted major physical alterations in all three Stratford theatres. The Third Stage was given a new modified thrust stage, and seating capacity was increased by fifty. The Avon received a $165,000 face-lift. It was redecorated in black and gilt, with many dark mirrors, while the stage was extensively modified, extended to cover the orchestra pit, and framed with modular panels. There was a further important innovation at the Avon—a permanent basic or "box" set, of simple architecture, capable of economically housing both classical and modern works in a repertory situation. In the years that followed, it made the Avon financially viable as a repertory house and, in Phillips's words, "saved the Festival a fortune".

The most radical changes were reserved for the Festival Theatre, and some traditionalists were quick to howl sacrilege. Both Langham and Gascon had wanted the balcony on the Festival stage to be mobile, but had been unable to win the board's agreement because of the cost. Phillips shared the concerns of his predecessors, stressing the need

for a more anonymous space to retain the individuality of the theatre, yet provide greater flexibility for those working in it. While it does enhance the more robust works of Shakespeare, the balcony has an inherent aggressiveness inimical to the staging of other works. Any portrayal of innocence becomes an all but insurmountable problem. The harsh and angular appearance of the background introduces an alien element, establishing an internal dichotomy that cannot help but inhibit the production. The concept of the audience within the action must not be lost but, equally important, the action itself must not be at odds with the physical structure of the stage.

The solution to this problem is a mobile balcony, which can slide back and forth to leave a bare wooden semi-circle as the playing area, when a bare semi-circle will best suit the moods of the play. It is essential that the balcony become manoeuvrable, but it is equally essential that it never be completely removable. . . .

The revisions open up exciting new possibilities for the Festival Theatre, particularly in the realm of music. Opera, musical comedy, operetta and oratorio can all be staged effectively and the absence of the balcony will also facilitate orchestral work on a much larger scale and vastly improve acoustics for music.

Phillips won the board over, and, at a cost of $175,000, the balcony was made mobile during the winter of 1974-75. The change was widely publicized, but other modifications to the stage attracted little attention—significant though they were. In fact, the changes were greater than any others, apart from those of 1962. The step down from the edge of the area covered by the balcony was

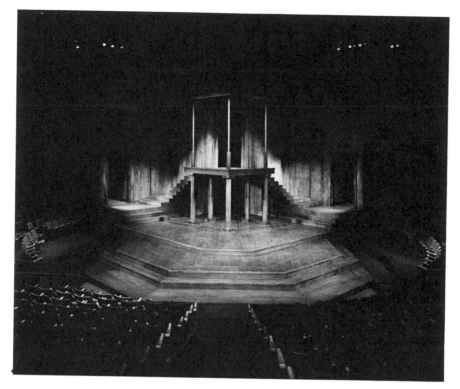

The Festival stage, 1975-6, with Measure for Measure *balcony roof and pillars and an extra step in front. Photograph by Robert C. Ragsdale, a.r.p.s., courtesy of the Stratford Festival Archives.*

moved forward to a point about the centre of the main acting area, and that area was widened by covering the steps to the sides of the stage. The main back entrances were pushed forward to reduce the time needed to get people on and off stage (this change led, however, to acoustics problems and the entrances were pushed back again for the 1977 season). A canopy supported by three slim pillars was erected above the balcony; it too disappeared in 1977. The whole of the main acting area was made level with the area under the balcony, thus eliminating the step at centre stage.

Another major change under Phillips was the appointment of a head of design. Daphne Dare's association with Phillips dated back to the Bristol Old Vic, and she was now one of the United Kingdom's most respected designers. (One of her early assignments was creating monsters for the first two years of the cult television series *Dr. Who*.) When she agreed to fill Stratford's new design post, she undertook to help develop promising young Canadian talent; and the impressive legacy of this commitment was evident to the end of the Phillips regime.

Early in February 1975, the Young Company presented its two

touring productions to enthusiastic audiences at the Avon. It launched its tour in Winnipeg February 10, and then moved on to Saskatoon, Regina, Edmonton, Calgary, Vancouver, and Victoria. *Comedy of Errors* then played three weeks at the National Arts Centre in Ottawa, and both plays were put on for two weeks in April in Montreal. Reviews were generally favourable, but ticket sales (particularly in the West, where there were complaints of high prices) were disappointing, and the financial losses were heavy. In any event, Robin Phillips's first major test would be his actual Stratford season.

1975

Robin Phillips acted quickly and successfully in establishing a remarkable relationship with his actors. Asked later to comment on Phillips's impact on the company, William Hutt didn't even hesitate: "There are three immediate points to be made about Robin. One was his blinding intelligence. The second was the excitement he generated of an atmosphere within which one could create. The third was that he gave us a sense of future, of vision, of progress."

Martha Henry had heard of Phillips's reputation even before he arrived. "An actress friend from England had said to me, 'I'm working with this wonderful director, and you simply must work with him because he's absolutely brilliant.' Then, lo and behold, there he was at Stratford." Henry's first glimpse of Phillips was in the Festival Theatre's Green Room. "My first impression was—how beautiful, shy, and gentle he was. He showed great care for us, and came to every table to shake our hands."

Both Hutt and Miss Henry were typical of company members who felt that Phillips had opened up new artistic horizons for them personally. Martha Henry recalled:

Coincidentally with Robin's arrival, I had the feeling I had gone as far as I could. There hadn't been any real teaching in recent years at the Festival—and I believe we all need to be taught and to continue learning. I was having to deliver large things in terms of perform-

59

ances, yet I wasn't sure how I was getting there. The underpinnings were fading away, and what I seemed to be left with was the shape rather than the substance. I learned a great deal from Robin. He was very minute in seeking to create an awareness in us of what we were doing.

Not only did Hutt continue to give memorable performances during the Phillips years, but he was also one of his most loyal lieutenants. Shortly after Phillips was appointed, he had written Hutt a warm and friendly letter, saying he knew of Hutt's high reputation and expressing the hope that the two of them could work together. Hutt was both touched and impressed by the tone of the letter. "I responded to Robin, saying that his was an extremely generous response and that I would be happy to work for him when he got out here."

Shortly after Phillips took charge of the Festival, he made a suggestion to Hutt. "I think we should walk through this building just to be seen together—to see that we care." And the two of them did walk through the building together, stopping and chatting with people. Hutt saw it as an extraordinarily generous gesture on Phillips's part.

Phillips endeared himself to Hutt in other ways as well. During an early office conversation, Phillips started looking at Hutt with great intensity. Then he became rather embarrassed. "I'm looking at your nose," he confessed. Hutt found himself totally disarmed by this comment.

> I know what my nose looks like. It's fairly prominent, and the older I get and the shorter my chin gets, the more prominent it becomes. But I really admired Robin for saying this. There was no equivocation— he was looking at my nose. That says a great deal about Robin and a great deal about his impact on the Festival. It was an approach he used on other actors in rehearsal. In effect, he would say, "I'm looking at that thing which makes you unique, really human. That's an element we want to know and to explore and to release—especially to release if you have protective feelings about it."

It was Hutt who was assigned direction of Bernard Shaw's *Saint Joan*, the play which officially opened the 1975 season. It was the Festival's first Shavian offering and Phillips did not schedule it until he had received the blessing of the Shaw Festival at Niagara-on-the-Lake. Some Stratford-watchers were to suggest later that Phillips could not have chosen a more appropriate season opener if he wished to give an example of the type of bad museum theatre he wished the Festival to abandon.

Writing in *Saturday Night* in September 1975, Martin Knelman caustically suggested that the play proved suitable to the occasion, and commented with devastating accuracy on the psychology of a Stratford season opening:

Opening night at Stratford is still a stuffy, square event. The lords and ladies of Upper Canada arrive in their chauffeured limousines and, as the trumpets blare, make their way across the lawn and through the theatre lobby in dinner jackets and long dresses. The evening represents an uneasy get-together of culture and big business, and the procession looks like the grandest, blandest wedding of the year. Many of the people in this audience don't go to plays the rest of the year, and they're not ready for anything innovative or terribly imaginative. For them, the theatre still represents what the Marx Brothers were demolishing in *A Night at the Opera*—a pompous institution which draws people of a certain social position who wish to be congratulated for being civilized as well as rich. It's a gala, dress-up, formal occasion; and the style of the play should ideally be in keeping with this tone of decorum. There must be a certain amount of pageantry and spectacle, and the actors are expected to march about in puffily elegant costumes, looking like stuffed vegetables and reciting the kind of elevating speeches that people might remember memorizing for the final exam in high school.

Saint Joan was to evolve into one of the best productions of the season. But on opening night, with its slow pace, it pleased few in the audience. Some leading critics were appalled. Urjo Kareda reported in the *Toronto Star*:

Oh, the dismay. Robin Phillips's new regime at Stratford has begun with a flashback—not to say a throwback—to the bad old days. William Hutt's production of *Saint Joan*—stuffy, overdressed and pompous—is virtually a summary of what needed to be changed at this institution. . . . There is the predictable casting of certain major roles; there are the meaningless crowd scenes, full of stiff, concerted laughter; there is a stage draped in silk flags; there is the lavishly garbed procession from stage left to stage right, serving as no more than a cue for a "Wasn't that pretty?" round of applause.

Kareda was upset by designer Maxine Graham's "fussy, frilly outfits" and irked by Pat Galloway's Joan.

Her attempts at simplicity are arch and superficial, and she somehow lacks the force personality to make the character seem believable for a moment. She lacks an ecstatic purity, a tower of inspiration. You doubt whether this Joan could inspire Boy Scouts across an intersection, let alone armies or nations.

Dave Billington of Southam News Service was higher on the Galloway performance, suggesting she had "triumphed over the chaos and mediocrity which surrounded her", just as Joan did in the fifteenth century.

The *Globe and Mail*'s Herbert Whittaker was more generous to the production, suggesting that the play was knowledgeably and respectfully handled, and arguing that the leading lady had met the role's biggest challenge: "The Galloway Joan is...spiritually inspired beyond doubt, and that is after all the hardest and most important achievement in playing Shaw's heroine, for unless you can accept her inspiration, the whole evening can dwindle into theatrics."

Whittaker also took a close look at the Festival Theatre stage, having had some reservations about Phillips's changes. He found himself reassured:

> The open stage itself had first to be examined with some suspicion for big changes had been bruited about. But if the famous portico stage Tanya Moiseiwitsch had designed for Tyrone Guthrie is now capable of retreat, there were no signs of instability last night. Its top step had increased in area, its upper platform lost a parapet but gained a canopy which maintained the dignity to which we have been long accustomed as centrepiece of this great theatre.

The Festival Theatre's second night featured a sunny and straightforward *Twelfth Night*, directed by David Jones of Britain's Royal Shakespeare Company and designed by Susan Benson. It featured some excellent performances from Frank Maraden (Aguecheek), Marti Maraden (Olivia), Kathleen Widdoes (Viola), Leslie Yeo (Sir Toby), and Tom Kneebone (Feste). With 93-per-cent houses, this proved the Festival Theatre's most popular offering. However, what gave this production its particular glory was the fact that it marked the Festival debut of Brian Bedford, an artist who was to remain a mainstay of the Stratford Company over the next decade as one of its most popular lead actors, and also as an enterprising director.

Bedford played Malvolio—and imbued the character with supreme self-satisfaction, snobbishness, and smugness incarnate. The production was set in Jacobean times, and Bedford's Malvolio was attired in Puritan dress.

Urjo Kareda was delighted with this "preening, pontificating booby on intimate speaking terms with the Deity. The actor's collection of condescending smirks and self-assuring smiles is miraculous and the detail of his performance of the letter scene, manipulating the audience with deadpan amazement, is a consummate achievement in comic invention."

The British-born Bedford had forged an early reputation in his native country, playing Hamlet for the Liverpool Repertory Company, and later making an impact in London's West End in Peter Brook's production of Arthur Miller's *A View from the Bridge* and in Peter Shaffer's first stage success, *Five Finger Exercise*. Bedford later travelled with the Schaffer play to the United States, where he eventually made his home and established his reputation as a fine classical actor further in appearances with the American Shakespeare Festival and the APA Phoenix Repertory Company.

Phillips saw a shortage of leading males as one of the Festival's weak spots, and he respected Bedford's quality and experience. He also felt at this stage of his Stratford stewardship that he should not feel too isolated, and he saw in Bedford, a person of similar background, a colleague who would share the same theatre language and sensibility.

Comedy is the hardest kind of theatre to act, and Phillips knew Bedford to be marvellous at comedy—a gift which showed up frequently in future years. But Phillips also revealed Bedford as a master of brooding drama by assigning him the role of Angelo in *Measure for Measure*, the third play to open at the Festival Theatre that week.

Martin Knelman concluded that the production's most stunning performance was "Brian Bedford's weak and creepy Angelo, who with close-cropped hair connects alarmingly with our impressions of Nazi demons and the prison guards in the movie *Les Ordres*. Bedford's impact is all the more amazing if you've seen him as Malvolio the previous night."

This was not a *Measure for Measure* that aimed for frivolity as an alternative to dealing with the play's more troublesome aspects. Knelman was not the only critic to find contemporary parallels. The production reverberated, in Associated Press writer William Glover's words, with "a post-Watergate relevancy". The Boston *Globe*'s Kevin Kelly noted that William Hutt's Duke, "for all the ribbons on his uniform, for all his regal bearing, could be any hierarchical authority in any century," just as Bedford's Angelo, "his self-servingly corrupt Deputy, could be any latter-day Nixon flunky."

Measure for Measure was Phillips's first Festival production, and it dazzled audiences and critics, playing to 90-per-cent attendance. It also ushered in a new approach to the classics. It was a most compelling production, hard and spare, uncompromising in its exploration of the text, crisply spoken, fresh in its responses to many aspects of the play. As he was so often to do with Shakespeare's "problem" plays, Phillips moved *Measure for Measure* closer to our own times, in order to help audiences relate to its concerns. Designed with dark, brooding brilliance by Daphne Dare, it was set in Vienna just before the First World War, when the Austro-Hungarian Empire was about to collapse forever. Dare presented a cruel world of bars and bolts and—in nunnery as in prison—of iron bars and metallic echoes. It was a world in which there was little communication, one in which Angelo's desk, massive and scrubbed by a brigade of servants for several minutes before the action began, became a kind of voluntary prison, imposing barriers between himself and others. There was little fun in this Vienna wasteland. Isabella, who was grippingly portrayed by Martha Henry, emerged as a poignant victim—a woman who finds that the security of her religious order is useless, that it cannot save her from the cruelties and horrors of a world she neither knows nor wishes to enter. Abhorson (Daniel Buccos) was as icy an executioner as could be imagined, and the normally amusing Barnardine (Michael Liscinsky) was brutish and irremediable evil incarnate. There was no justice in this world, no love, no happy ending. Isabella was left alone at the end, in one of the most compelling images in the Festival's history, removing her coif and glasses, apparently planning to immerse herself in the world's evil, contemplating a forced marriage to the Duke, and exuding profound spiritual agony.

With *Measure for Measure* Phillips also declared his hostility to the old-fashioned declamatory way of doing classical theatre. "Of course, there are places in plays where people do lecture," he has said. "But it doesn't make sense if everybody's making speeches and proclaiming all the time. It becomes deeply boring." With such productions as *Measure for Measure* and the 1977 *Richard III* and the 1978 *The Winter's Tale*, he sought to make audiences listen to (and perceive) classical theatre in a different way. "I don't believe Richard III spent all his time screaming and shouting. He also spent time whispering and muttering. Because Shakespeare's language is great doesn't mean it has to be declaimed. Even gods can be invoked with a world-weary sigh and a shrug instead of a scream."

This was one of the messages delivered to cast members during those early rehearsals of *Measure for Measure*. "I believe earth-shattering emotions are tiny: one of our most devastating weapons is the Bomb, yet it results from the tiniest splitting of the atom. *Measure* has huge emotions, but it's ridiculous to feel you have to rant and roar and spew emotion all over the stage."

The *Toronto Star*'s Urjo Kareda was quick to seize on the significance of this approach in his enthusiastic review the following day:

> People caught their breath to hear murmured conversations. Flickers of emotion were caught from faces which seemed suddenly intimately close. Nuances were captured and held for lengths with later details. The accumulation of tension hovered over the action with electrifying intensity. Robin Phillips, directing his own first Festival Theatre production, has created an awesomely detailed, brilliantly acted response to one of Shakespeare's most complex and fascinating plays.

Both Bedford and Martha Henry delivered particularly striking performances, but there were other outstanding characterizations as well. Richard Monette's whining, sneering, insufferably vulgar Lucio loomed large as he wove his way in and out of events, ready at any moment to take centre stage. Bowler-hatted, frock-coated, and

Scene from the 1975/1976 Festival stage production of Measure for
Measure, *directed by Robin Phillips, designed by Daphne Dare, music by
Louis Applebaum, lighting by Gil Wechsler. L.-R.: William Hutt as the
Duke, Michael Fletcher as Escalus, Leslie Yeo as the Provost, Brian
Bedford as Angelo (1975), Martha Henry as Isabella, Kathleen
Widdoes as Mariana (1975), John Innes as Friar Peter, and Richard
Monette as Lucio. Photograph by Robert C. Ragsdale, a.r.p.s., courtesy
of the Stratford Festival Archives.*

armed with a cane, all of them somewhat battered, he was seedy and
nasty—the kind of person who tips his hat with one hand while
smearing mud with the other. Then, there was William Hutt as the
Duke, a role he had played in a previous Festival era. Now, under
Phillips, he found the characterization to be one of the most
disturbing assignments in his career.

From the beginning, Phillips sought to inject into his actors the
idea that their function was to do more than just turn out plays, that
they were all there at Stratford to explore these plays in an atmosphere that enriched and enlivened them. Company members
became quickly aware of one key aspect of his approach: his
readiness to accept what they did in rehearsal on the most basic of
terms and then seek to develop these actions within the context of
the play. Hutt was particularly sensitive to this approach during the
rehearsals for *Measure for Measure*:

> The role of the Duke disturbed me because the entire rehearsal
> process made me examine in a very still, smooth, pool-like atmo-
> sphere the dark corners of my own life. Robin as a director instinc-
> tively senses the subcutaneous vibration. He sees things that an actor

isn't even aware he's doing, and can recognize something that the actor is trying to say but is afraid to say. An almost insignificant gesture can achieve enormous significance in his mind.

Meanwhile, members of the Young Company had been having similar experiences. Phillips saw the whole venture as one of sharing a new beginning, for himself as much as for his players:

> In ways I was more inexperienced than other company members, whether they were on the Festival stage or in this Young Company. I had never done anything like this before. I had never started a Young Company. I had never run a theatre like Stratford before. I had never worked in this country before. I had never directed much Shakespeare before. I wanted us all prepared to stand together and say, "This is a beginning and we have much to learn."

Because of the pre-season tour, the Young Company productions of *The Two Gentlemen of Verona* and *The Comedy of Errors* were the earliest into rehearsal. During the beginning weeks, Phillips spent a good deal of time on games and improvisation. He was concerned that some players lacked sufficient stamina to run the extra mile demanded by classical theatre. Nicholas Pennell, a senior member of the Young Company, was struck by Phillips's abilities as a teacher. This quality was decisive in commanding an incredible love and respect among the actors.

Phillips was excited by the acting talent within this group, but he was frustrated by the actors' obvious lack of contact with the classics. Working on a particular scene with one actress, he gave vent to his concern:

"You sort of act like old movies," he said.

"But that's all most of us ever see."

"But that's not how you grasp a role," he shot back. "It's not being Veronica Lake or Doris Day. Better to relate it to real experience—like going to Loblaw's or the post office."

Phillips found himself "astounded" by the experience. "There was this huge lack, this great waste. I was seeing all these gifted young actors, yet so many of them had this idea of copying whatever they encountered in other performances."

He told Young Company members that their involvement in theatre required more than a desire to emulate. He went further: in his effort to drive home his concept of "company" and of "sharing" he instituted a strategy known as "the hot seat". Company members sat in a circle; then, recalls one participant,

> each member of the company told you what he thought of you. It was a dreadful thing. It was very scary. It was dangerous. It could only be done by someone who knew he had control of the situation. [It was this kind of action that led some of Phillips's critics to complain that

he manipulated his actors.] People resisted Robin in this exercise, and of course it was manipulative, but only because he wanted our work to be good. Most of us realized he had this important purpose—which was to build a solid ensemble over the years. To create ensemble, you have to break down barriers and create trust. That's why Robin resorted to techniques like this—to enable us to know each other at all levels.

The two Young Company productions, which were co-directed by Phillips and Vancouver-born choreographer David Toguri, were bright, inventive, and unorthodox. They overflowed with acrobatics, immense energy, and more than a little irreverence. Phillips's policy of encouraging young designers was vindicated by the contributions of Jeffrey Sisco (*The Comedy of Errors*) and Molly Harris Campbell (*The Two Gentlemen of Verona*).

Sisco's Conestoga wagon dominated the stage for *Comedy of Errors*, functioning as a kind of tiring room; as a cornucopia disgorging scores of actors and acrobats; as a priory; and as a convenient wall on which to hang beer-mugs, pieces of laundry, and other assorted items. The play was set in a curious kind of American Midwest around the 1880s. There were cowboys, an abbess wearing workboots, a sequence burlesquing movie westerns, and a great deal of catchy music composed by Alan Laing with lyrics reputedly written by Phillips himself. The centrepiece of this excursion into vaudevillian Shakespeare was the double pairing of Barry MacGregor and Richard Whelan as the boys from Syracuse and of Nicholas Pennell and Bernard Hopkins as their Ephesus twins. They all rang their various changes with unremitting vigour. The *Globe and Mail*'s Herbert Whittaker heralded the production as "a romp for all who can stretch their minds in making *The Comedy of Errors* laughable".

Whittaker was also pleased with *The Two Gentlemen of Verona*:

It is a play full of verbal conceits, of romantic inconstancy strung on slight plotting, which shuffles four lovers, the whole best recalled for one lyric, "Who Is Silvia?" It may still be so recalled, for Jackie Burroughs brings her delicate and haggard beauty to grace the role of Silvia, beloved of both Proteus and Valentine, the aforementioned Gentlemen.

Phillips has matched new conceits to old. His characters are jet-set playboys and playgirls, posturing their loves slightly and gracefully. Does Phillips wish to extract a virtue from this play? I suspect so and that his irreverence is paying off for him. It shows off the kind of playing, the kind of company he is after. Spontaneity, ambivalence and theatrical chic are the banners of his outward walls, and in choosing both *Two Gentlemen of Verona* and *The Comedy of Errors*, he can train his young company to his methods without being distracted by the screams of the stuffy and set of ways.

Scene from the 1975 Avon stage and touring production of The Comedy of Errors, *directed by Robin Phillips and David Toguri, designed by Jeffrey Sisco, lighting by Gil Wechsler, music by Alan Laing, arranged and directed by Berthold Carriere. Jackie Burroughs as Adriana, Bernard Hopkins as Dromio of Syracuse. Photograph by Robert C. Ragsdale, a.r.p.s., courtesy of the Stratford Festival Archives.*

And there *were* screams from some quarters. The *Toronto Sun*'s McKenzie Porter argued that modern-dress productions of Shakespeare—particularly the modern dress used in *The Two Gentlemen of Verona*—were an insult to taste. Phillips was no doubt prepared for these complaints, since much of this production of *The Two Gentlemen of Verona* was a carry-over from his Royal Shakespeare Company treatment, which had so outraged the traditionalists. In any event, the general verdict was favourable for a production set in a never-never period that was fifty per cent 1920s Italian Riviera and fifty per cent Vic Tanny health resort, and that featured such accessories as cocktail bars, beach balls and beach boys, transistors, swimming pools, and society magazines. Silvia (Jackie Burroughs) was a flapper who made her initial entrance doing a cartwheel. Speed (Bernard Hopkins) showed up with a bicycle. Richard Curnock's Eglamour resembled Colonel Sanders, and at one point was called upon to stagger across the stage burdened under the weight of a large parrot cage, several mink stoles, a butterfly net, numerous suitcases, camping stools, and safari gear.

Reviewers generally agreed that the nonsense not only was fun in itself but supported a production that was, in its essentials, pure and clean.

In late July, Phillips unveiled his second Festival Theatre production of the season—an extravagant treatment of Bertolt Brecht's *Trumpets and Drums*, which brought members of the Avon troupe and main-stage company together. Brecht had taken George Farquhar's comedy *The Recruiting Officer* and had changed its setting to the American Revolution in order to declaim against the miseries of war.

There were those who thought the production Phillips's first big disaster at Stratford and who deplored its flashy effects and composer Alan Laing's cheeky music. At one point the Captain Plume of Gordon Pinsent (brought in late to replace Brian Bedford, who was suffering from a back ailment) engaged in a comical billiard match with a mustachioed Jackie Burroughs, whose Victoria Balance was currently posing as the gallant Ensign Wilful. At another point, a chorus sang "You've seen the Severn, but have you seen the Mississippi" on a black-lit stage flashing with white gloves.

Urjo Kareda reported in the *Toronto Star* that

> The production has great things in it without being a brilliant production, just as the play had great Brecht touches without being great Brecht....This *Trumpets and Drums* lacks any sense of narrative flow. Even more damagingly, it doesn't yet possess the precise inter-connection of Brecht's ironic effects. But it does contain some bits and pieces which rouse and shine.

Some of those shining moments were provided by Jackie Burroughs's elegantly funny Victoria, Tom Kneebone's obsessive Sergeant Kite, and William Hutt's hilariously decadent Captain Brazen. *Trumpets and Drums* was, by consensus, minor Phillips. But behind the scenes it assumed far greater significance, because it changed the way in which Stratford actors were cued to go on stage. Until *Trumpets and Drums* arrived, a system of backstage light cues was used to inform actors when it was time to appear on stage. Phillips was astonished to discover when he came that performances were not being piped into the dressing rooms. He saw an analogy with a symphony orchestra:

> It was as though the woodwind had not been listening to the strings. Obviously every section of an orchestra must be ready for its particular entry. It must understand how it fits and complements the musical passages that came before it. The same rules apply to ensemble acting. Well, when I first went to Stratford, the actors never had to do any of that. There was no way of listening to a show in the dressing room. Instead, you just sat there and waited.

Phillips decided there would be no backstage light cues for *Trumpets and Drums*. This meant the actors had to take their own cues: they had to wait in the wings as it were and listen. It was hard for them to listen, because some of them were so far back that it was difficult to hear.

"I don't care what you have to do in order to hear," Phillips told the company. "If necessary, you can crawl right up the tunnel and be almost kneeling on the stage so that you can hear. You must be wherever you need to be in order to pick up your cue from the script."

The show evolved—in Phillips's words—"with everyone lying around anywhere they could in order to hear. Consequently, there was a vitality from that show. There was a real harmony." Having made his point, Phillips ensured that, in future seasons, sound would be piped into the dressing rooms from the live performance on stage.

Instinct had guided Phillips's choice of plays for his first season. He had deliberately programmed a wide range in an attempt to get a personal feel for the audience. The same week that *Trumpets and Drums* opened on the Festival stage, the first major production of an American play in Stratford's history opened at the Avon. It was the *The Crucible*, Arthur Miller's lacerating drama about the seventeenth-century Salem witch hunts. Director John Wood fashioned a gripping production, which generated an almost unbearable psychological tension. At Stratford, *The Crucible* emerged as a drama framed in darkness, with the Avon stage a yawning void in which the citizens of Salem worked out their appalling destinies. The visual impact was heightened by the grim simplicity of Susan Benson's design concept and Gil Wechsler's stark lighting effects.

Critical reaction was mixed over the performance of American Stephen Macht as the doomed farmer John Proctor, whose rebellion against the witch-hunting hysteria of his neighbours has fateful consequences; Urjo Kareda praised Macht for the "integrity and emotional tenderness" of his characterization, but was bothered by muddiness of diction. Highest praise was reserved for Martha Henry's portrayal of Mary Proctor: Kareda called it "magnificent" and at the end "almost unbearably moving, simply by the strength of the emotions she must hold back". A further brilliant performance was supplied by Douglas Rain, who instilled into the character of the merciless deputy governor Danforth a quality of dreadful conviction. With 98-per-cent attendance, *The Crucible* was the Avon's biggest hit that season.

The Third Stage provided a variety of fare. Opera was represented by three works: Richard Strauss's *Ariadne auf Naxos*, Canadian composer Harry Somers's *The Fool*, and Jean Vallerand's *Le Magicien*. Raffi Armenian was music director for all three works, with Jan Rubes staging the Strauss and the Somers and Pat Galloway directing the Vallerand. The attractively mounted productions featured fine performances from a talented company which included Mary Lou Fallis, Gary Relyea, D. Glyn Evans, and Brian Roberts. Unfortunately, the productions played at the height of summer, and the chief memory for many audiences was the unbearable 100-degree-plus heat inside the Third Stage—a heat that left both spectators and performers soaking. Attempts by the fire department to cool down the interior by spraying the roof of the building with water had little effect.

The latter part of August saw three further Third Stage openings. *Oscar Remembered* was twenty-two-year-old Maxim Mazumdar's extraordinary one-man show, which appraised the life and career of Oscar Wilde through the hothouse sensibility of Wilde's young friend, Lord Alfred Douglas. Mazumdar's portrayal of "Bosie" Douglas—directed by William Hutt—was heralded by Herbert Whittaker as a "rare achievement".

Bill Glassco, a member of the group that initially questioned the board's reasons for hiring Phillips, was brought in to direct *Kennedy's Children*, Robert Patrick's bittersweet play about a group of characters in a New York bar giving utterance to the pain, joy, and puzzlement of the confusing 1960s. The play was essentially a memory piece, but Glassco directed it with sensitivity and intelligence, and the cast—which included Richard Monette, Denise Fergusson, and Brenda Donohue—responded splendidly.

An additional August opening at the Third Stage resulted in the roughest press reception of the summer. Canadian playwright Michael Tait's *Fellowship* was a murky drama about sex, religion, loving, dying, and madness. Set in an old Toronto house inhabited by a group of Anglican breakaways awaiting the Second Coming, it featured the terrible death of a child as well as the on-stage crucifix-

Scene from the Third Stage (1975) and Avon stage (1976, 1979)
production of The Importance of Being Earnest, *by Oscar Wilde,*
directed by Robin Phillips, designed by Molly Harris Campbell, lighting
by Robert Scales. L.-R.: Pat Galloway as Gwendolen Fairfax (1975-6),
William Hutt as Lady Bracknell, and Nicholas Pennell as John
Worthing. Photograph by Robert C. Ragsdale, a.r.p.s., courtesy of the
Stratford Festival Archives.

ion of a maddened priest. Tait's uncompromising but lurching
script was ultimately unsatisfying, despite Bernard Hopkins's gallant direction and notable performances from Lynne Griffin as a
troubled teen-ager, Robert Benson as her father, and Neil Vipond as
the tormented priest. *Fellowship* was a critical and box-office
failure, and it provided fuel for those who questioned the inclusion
of Canadian works in the Stratford repertoire. However, as later
years proved, the *Fellowship* debacle did not diminish Phillips's
commitment to Canadian playwrights.

The season's final production arrived at The Third Stage in late
September. It was never intended as a major offering. The tourists
had disappeared, and Phillips viewed it as essentially a local treat
for the company and the people of Stratford. Instead, all eight
performances sold out, and the processes of legend-making had
begun. The play was *The Importance of Being Earnest* and it was
remounted for the Avon stage in 1976 and remounted again in
1979. It became one of Phillips's best-loved productions.

Its initial reputation—or notoriety—was due to the casting of
William Hutt as Lady Bracknell, the announcement of which pro-

voked predictable complaints about drag-show gimmickry from the purists. The indictment proved unfounded.

The production had its genesis near the end of 1974, when Phillips and Hutt were discussing plans for the 1975 season. Phillips wanted to finish with something special: "I think we should end the Third Stage season with something we do mainly for ourselves—a play done simply for its style." Phillips argued that there was a need to examine a play for its own value—for example, he said, a play like *The Importance of Being Earnest*. To which Hutt replied: "Why not? I've always wanted to play Lady Bracknell."

Hutt recalls that Phillips's reaction to this comment was instantaneous. "I looked at him. Those brown eyes became like saucers. I knew exactly what he was thinking, and I said, 'Now, just a minute, Robin. I was being half serious and half frivolous.' He said, 'No, I think it's a wonderful idea.'" They continued to discuss the idea, and finally Hutt agreed to play Lady Bracknell, but only on condition that Phillips direct.

Phillips quickly made it clear that the venture was a serious one. He was determined to do Wilde's classic comedy with the style, elegance, and sense of period that it demanded. He held his first rehearsal in his own old-fashioned house on Douglas Street. He had prepared a fragrant dish of pot-pourri, which he passed around to cast members assembled in his cluttered Victorian parlour. "Smell that," he told them. "That's the smell of the nineteenth century." Then he produced a bottle of Air Wick. "Smell that. That's the twentieth century. Learn to understand the difference." Phillips had his cast participate in a revealing pencil-and-paper game to help emphasize the fact that Oscar Wilde was somewhat more than a creator of glittering farce. He reeled off a succession of quotations by Oscar Wilde and Anton Chekhov and asked his listeners to identify their author. Most of the cast scored eighty per cent wrong. Phillips then pressed home a further point not normally appreciated: Wilde and Chekhov were of the same generation and died only a year apart. He urged the company to think more about historical context.

Phillips repeatedly urged his cast to treat the play with respect. This resulted in a confrontation with Kathleen Widdoes, who had been cast as Gwendolen and insisted on seeing the production as some kind of silly joke. Midway through rehearsals, Widdoes found herself replaced by Pat Galloway.

Nicholas Pennell, who played Jack Worthing, always argued that Lady Bracknell was essentially an asexual character, and that therefore the casting of a male was legitimate. By the time Hutt had done the role in three different seasons, he found himself in full agreement: "The thing that astonished me about the play—you might say it is the play's one fault—is the reference to Lady Bracknell's two children. In view of the way Oscar Wilde wrote this character, I really could never understand how Wilde could possibly let her go through a second conception."

The warmth of critical response was genuine, not only for Phillips but also for a fine cast which also included Marti Maraden (Cecily) and Richard Monette (Algernon). But the highest praise was reserved for Hutt. The *Globe and Mail*'s new theatre critic, John Fraser, was ecstatic:

> In case anyone was still sniggering about this fine actor taking on such a role, the program provided pictures of both Alec Guinness and Laurence Olivier making similar dramatic sidesteps. The pictures weren't necessary. Hutt, who bore a frightening resemblance to the pictures of the late Queen Mary, turned in a flawless performance. He rarely succumbed to any of the obvious temptations, and by conducting himself so seriously, he became the most genuinely funny thing the whole season had to offer. He correctly interpreted Lady Bracknell as sexless but fierce, and before he was through, one was convinced that the fox fur around his shoulders had never been killed but rather taken live and placed there after a stern look from Lady B.

The Festival Ensemble, under Raffi Armenian's direction, provided a series of Sunday concerts, and there were two concerts by outside artists, Cleo Laine and Bruce Cockburn.

Stratford again hosted an International Film Festival in September under the leadership of Gerald Pratley.

At the Stratford Shakespearean Festival Foundation's twenty-third annual general meeting, board president John Killer was able to report that Phillips's first season had proved to be an "overwhelming critical and box-office success". Attendance was up 36,000 over 1974, rising to a record 437,302 for a twenty-one-week season. A box-office gross of $2,638,000 represented a rise of nearly a quarter of a million dollars over 1974. Fund-raising increased by twenty per cent over the previous year to a total of $285,000. Citizens of Stratford alone gave $42,000, the equivalent of $1.70 per person. The season ended again with an accumulated operating deficit—a manageable $86,000.

Killer's year-end report politely rebuked the nationalists who had been attacking the Phillips appointment, asserting that *Measure for Measure* provided

> indisputable proof that great theatre and Canadian theatre can, and should, be synonymous. William Hutt, Martha Henry, Brian Bedford, Richard Monette, Kathleen Widdoes, and others in the cast were responding to one another, not as Canadians to Americans or British, but as artists engaged in a collective effort to make palpable the inner world of the play. . . . Taken alone, this one production is a persuasive

enough argument against placing considerations of nationalism above all else in an artistic enterprise.

The 1975 season saw a number of senior staff appointments. In addition to naming Daphne Dare new head of design, the organization appointed Gary Thomas, formerly the Festival's accountant, as administrative director, and Douglas Allan to the newly created post of head of publicity. There was one further appointment of great significance when Phillips wooed Urjo Kareda away from the *Toronto Star* to become the Festival's new literary manager. Kareda was to become one of the most important components of the new regime.

In the spring, when Phillips was about to unveil his first season, he had called his company together. "I want you to remember that the work you're doing is beautiful," he said. "If the press is negative, it's against me, not you. I believe in your work absolutely and I want you to believe in it absolutely."

Phillips had worked hard that first year to forge strong bonds with his company. They would continue to the end of his regime.

·C·H·A·P·T·E·R· XXI·

1976

In the winter of 1975, during a break in rehearsals for *The Two Gentlemen of Verona*, Phillips had taken actor Nicholas Pennell aside. "Can I speak to you?" he said. "You're going to play Hamlet next year." Pennell recalled that he was flabbergasted at the time: "The 1975 season hadn't even opened, yet here was Robin saying I was going to do Hamlet the following year. There was an implicit message here: he was telling me to start planning my life a bit in order to meet the challenge." Pennell found this incident a characteristic Phillips tactic: "Nothing Robin ever said or did was ever wasted, whether in rehearsal or in a social situation. He had this irritating perception of how people worked and of how their individual needs could best be served."

Phillips was a firm believer in advance planning. He also believed in innovation, which is why his 1976 season was to feature not one Hamlet but two, with Pennell and Richard Monette alternating in the role. This successful venture in double casting was but one example of the fresh breezes blowing through the Festival. This was the year that saw British actress Maggie Smith begin a long and productive association with Stratford. It was the year that saw the traditional music programming and the film festival sacrificed to the greater needs of the Festival's primary mandate, which was to put on plays. It was the year that saw an increased commitment to Canadian drama. It was the year in which Phillips solidified his power over all aspects of the Stratford operation, while also ominously revealing that crushing burdens of responsibility were imposing limits on even his remarkable stamina. Finally, it was the year that marked the start of a breach between Phillips and John Hirsch, the man who was ultimately to succeed him.

There were fears that 1976 could be a tough season financially for Stratford. Total spending was to increase from $3,919,676 in 1975 to $4,746,893 in 1976, with inflationary pressures being cited as the main reason for the jump. But outside factors were also causing concern. Tourism in major centres within Stratford's orbit was well below expectation. The Montreal Olympics threatened to become a major competitor for tourist dollars. Inflation was forcing many people to re-evaluate their spending habits and to reapportion funds accordingly. Yet, at the end of 1976, John Killer was able to face the annual general meeting and proudly report that for the first time in the Festival's history it had passed the half-million mark in attendance. The 518,421 tickets sold represented an 18.5-per-cent increase over the previous year. This translated into a box-office gross of more than $3.7 million, an increase of more than $1 million over 1975.

Killer offered some perceptive comments on the nature of the season that had given rise to these figures:

> It does not necessarily mean that half a million people agreed with everything they saw on stage. It does not mean that they all left the theatre comfortably reassured that the Shakespeare parade was marching in customary fashion. On the contrary, many people found that attending the Festival this year was a reasonably demanding exercise. Some long-held ideas were challenged, and these challenges demanded mental response. But I think the figures tell us that our audiences were not only willing but eager to provide such response, to have their ideas challenged by productions that were stimulating and thought-provoking.

Killer was correct in asserting that the season posed new challenges. Indeed, it left many audience-members and critics polarized in their reactions to what transpired on the Festival and Avon stages (the Third Stage was closed to the public that year and used for company workshops). Inevitably, Phillips assumed an even higher profile, and in the process became a greater source of controversy. However, his artistic vision continued to generate the kind of excitement that paid off at the box office in the face of considerable odds.

In a winter interview with *Performing Arts in Canada* magazine, Phillips said that he had no regrets about his move to Canada.

> I have only gained enormously by being here. I've found a much freer approach to the classics here, with no great past memories of how classics ought to be done. By "here" I mean Canada. Indeed at

Stratford, a strain of production values has grown that was perhaps slightly too Old Vic of the 1950s and it will take a while to step away from that. . . . I find here that the questions thrown at me from actors are refreshingly straightforward and direct.

Phillips also admitted the truth of a rumour already prevalent in theatre circles—that he would make comments to an actor about his personal life in order to put him in the right frame of mind for a role. However, he went on to stress two important points about such an approach. The first: "The techniques of rehearsal are a private matter between director and actors." And the second: "Anything is permissible if it will produce something more real and true from the actors involved." Phillips also responded to another charge that was frequently levelled against him during his Stratford years—that he favoured a strongly authoritarian approach in his relationship with the company. Phillips denied this, and replied:

I like actors constantly to be challenged and asked to be part of the production as a whole. I have to be authoritarian when actors get trapped into being other than themselves, when they fall back onto effects from somewhere, or somebody else. Often, for instance, when I criticize designers, they'll think it's because I'm trying to be forceful, trying to impose my ideas. That isn't so. I'm forcing them to think *personally* about the text, to respond personally to it, and not to come up with somebody else's—Tanya Moiseiwitsch's or Leslie Hurry's or whoever's—solutions. And however democratic you want the organization to be, finally one person still has to pull all the departments together, to make sure that everybody is doing the same play.

Phillips also explained his choice of *Hamlet* and *The Tempest* for the 1976 Young Company (these plays were far into rehearsal by January). He noted that the year before, he had

thrown the Young Company into the deep end with plays—*Two Gentlemen* and *The Comedy of Errors*—of which, if they failed, people could always say, "Oh well, they were never good plays anyway, one must allow a few excuses." With *Hamlet*, nobody can say, "Well, the play itself doesn't work." The company must now test its mettle against a—if not *the*—masterpiece.

Phillips bristled at the interviewer's suggestion that *The Tempest*, like *Hamlet*, was a "crowd-pleaser". "Since when," he shot back, "is *The Tempest* a crowd-pleaser?"

Hamlet and *The Tempest* were slated to bow in at the Avon in opening week, but prior to the official Festival run they had a brief tour that began on March 4 at Kingston and then continued with engagements at Montreal's Place des Arts and Ottawa's National Arts Centre. The plays were co-directed by Phillips and William Hutt,

Scene from the 1976 Festival stage and Avon stage production of
Hamlet, *directed by Robin Phillips and William Hutt, designed by*
John Pennoyer, lighting by Gil Wechsler, music by Berthold Carriere,
basic set designed by Daphne Dare. Richard Monette as Hamlet.
Photograph by Robert C. Ragsdale, a.r.p.s., courtesy of the Stratford
Festival Archives.

with lighting by Gil Wechsler and music by Berthold Carriere.
Hamlet designs were by John Pennoyer and those for *The Tempest*
by John Ferguson.

The casting of two Hamlets stemmed from Phillips's conviction
that, in Monette and Pennell, the Festival possessed two fine young
actors who deserved the opportunity to tackle perhaps the most
demanding role in the Shakespearean canon.

Monette confessed that the assignment frightened him, but he
also knew that he was being given the opportunity to purge himself
of demons that had been pursuing him for more than a decade.
Twelve years before, at the age of nineteen, he had played Hamlet
for Toronto's Crest Theatre, and the reviews had been devastating.
He particularly remembered one notice which began: "If your
name is Richard Monette, read no further." Unfortunately for
Monette, he ignored that advice, and the ensuing slam haunted him
for years. Early in rehearsals, Phillips asked his actors to tell him, in
one word, what the play was about. Monette did not reply "poli-
tics" or "revenge" but simply "ME". Twelve years and twenty-three
other Shakespearean roles after his earlier ordeal, he was tackling
Everest again.

Phillips eventually insisted that the two actors watch each other
in rehearsal, an experience that proved both fascinating and

unnerving for them. By this time each was set in his own distinctive interpretation. Nevertheless, Monette suffered a temporary identity crisis.

As he told Myron Galloway of the *Montreal Star*:

> The effect was rather strange and unexpected. For instance, there were certain lines that I'd gone over at great length, trying out first one and then another of two different ways they could be interpreted. I made what I thought was my choice, but my option was still sort of open in my mind. Then when I saw Nicholas and discovered he'd made an opposite choice to mine in some instances, I knew I was stuck with my choice. In other words, I didn't have a choice then. He'd taken the choice away from me.

Was this good or bad? "Good, I think, because it made me solidify my own interpretation. We're both going to be very different and Nicholas is so good that I'm frightened all over again."

As for Pennell, Hamlet was a role he had never expected to play. He remained convinced no other director would ever have given him the opportunity, and saw it as an example of the way Phillips trusted his actors. Pennell believed one of Phillips's greatest gifts was in helping actors to explore a text and in making them feel it was as much a voyage of exploration for him as for them. "With Robin in charge, with his energy, enthusiasm, and passion, you felt you could do anything. You were not afraid of failure, but welcomed it." At one point during rehearsal of the soliloquies, Phillips tied Pennell to a chair in order to prevent the actor from resorting to physical exploration in tackling Hamlet's complex thought processes and to force him to examine the text itself while sitting still, unable to smooth over its difficulties with extraneous business. Pennell had always felt it rather vulgar to show powerful emotions so nakedly on stage, and he credited Phillips with releasing this inhibition.

He told Galloway:

> Phillips allowed us both to play the role as we felt it should be played, and he waited and watched until we each came up with something that was uniquely our own. . .something that came closest to expressing our own very different personalities, and when that happened that's what he developed as our interpretation. The best way to explain it perhaps is to say that he acted like an orchestral conductor directing a piano concerto. A case of two performances of the same concerto with two different soloists.

He found it an extraordinary experience to watch Monette's Hamlet. "I was amazed to find how we had taken such different directions in our interpretation of some aspects of the character and how, in other aspects, those different interpretations would converge."

Scene from the 1976 Festival stage and Avon stage production of
Hamlet, *directed by Robin Phillips and William Hutt, designed by*
John Pennoyer, lighting by Gil Wechsler, music by Berthold Carriere,
basic set designed by Daphne Dare. Nicholas Pennell as Hamlet.
Photograph by Robert C. Ragsdale, a.r.p.s., courtesy of the Stratford
Festival Archives.

The Festival's double-header *Hamlet* was generally well received
when the production opened the Avon season in early June. "To see
Richard Monette's direct and wonderfully straightforward Hamlet is
to see, at long last, a Canadian Hamlet," declared the *Globe and
Mail*'s John Fraser. "Is a great Canadian Hamlet important? No, not
really for anyone else, but for Canadians it is crucial because in
achieving it we are set free from the kind of inferiority complex that
has plagued us for far too long." The British-born Pennell's poetic,
tear-stained Hamlet was in notable contrast to the edgy quality of
danger inherent in Monette's interpretation. It also had its fans,
among them U.S. critic Norman Dresser, who praised Pennell for
the emotional colour with which he invested his portrayal.

The *Toronto Star*'s new drama critic, Gina Mallet, deemed the production "sombre to drab" and felt it lacked a strongly imposed point of view. But she considered Monette and Pennell to be worthy contenders for the role:

> There can be few actors so dissimilar as the volatile Monette and Pennell the cool technician. They play Hamlet like two sides of the same person.
> Monette is witty and romantic. Sometimes, he even acts as if he were playing Mercutio, the dashing cavalier of *Romeo and Juliet*. He snaps with sarcastic relish; ill-concealed impatience fuels him. This Hamlet, one feels, would have no trouble fitting deed to action. He would have polished off Claudius and jumped into bed with Gertrude and be damned to everyone else. It makes for a lively evening, but ultimately a rather superficial one. Hamlet changes continuously, each soliloquy a revelation of altered vision, and the actor must let the man visibly ripen.
> Pennell is a naturally more introspective actor, and he speaks the blank verse better. Monette tends to punch out the lines in two-word bites. But there is a shyness in Pennell; he never seems convincing as a man rocked to the core of his being. This is a nice boy who's gone astray, taken drugs perhaps, and lost those English schoolboy manners that got him through so many scrapes before. However, as Hamlet becomes increasingly detached, Pennell gains in authority. He has a gentle speculative quality that makes a poignant catharsis of the final bloodbath.

The verdict of critics was more mixed for Michael Liscinsky who played Claudius and for Pat Galloway and Pat Bentley-Fisher who alternated as Gertrude (the only other rotating role in the production). Ophelia's mad scene also disturbed some critics for what seemed to be gratuitous cruelty: actress Marti Maraden appeared with her arms bound to a yoke. But there was much praise for Eric Donkin's Polonius.

The Phillips-Hutt production of *The Tempest* conjured up magic from the very first moment. The Avon stage was at the beginning a black box, which was empty save for one item: a triangular piece of white suspended canvas. The lights dimmed. There was the crash of thunder and the roar of winds. Lightning flashes revealed figures clinging frantically to ropes. There was the clamour of voices. Then, as calm returned, a red disk was seen glowing in the distance, a disk that ascended from left to right and changed colours from red to blue to silver grey. It was a stunning opening for a production that paid particular attention to visual imagery in an attempt to sustain the quality of Prospero's magical isle. The Boston *Globe*'s veteran critic, Kevin Kelly, wrote that Stratford's *Tempest* came very close "to being a work of considerable art". However, he felt the low-comedy scenes involving the Stephano of Richard Whelan and the

Trinculo of Barry MacGregor were somewhat overdone, and he was uncertain about Prospero:

> William Hutt, with thick gray mane, his form voluminously kaftaned and leaning on a staff, looks like a mix between Moses and the standard fountainhead of a lion. Hutt is sometimes so sonorously dignified that Prospero's humanness seems questionable. But he is, no question, a majestic figure, and handles the role well.

Kelly was delighted, however, with Miranda and Ferdinand: "Marti Maraden and Jack Wetherall are so joyously contagious their exuberance makes the audience burst into applause."

Kelly also liked the production's two most controversial performances—the Caliban of Richard Monette and the Ariel of Nicholas Pennell. Gina Mallet complained that Monette played "this contradictory and mythopoeic figure, who fulfils so aptly the colonist's bigotry about the natives, as a caricature of the hunchback of Notre Dame." Kelly, more approvingly, deemed Monette "scurvily fine". Monette himself, in an interview before the opening, described the role as the kind of risk he enjoyed taking. "No one but Robin would have the imagination to cast me as Caliban. I play him as retarded— i.e. politically, sexually, economically, linguistically, and physically. . . ."

Pennell found the idea of playing the spirit Ariel almost as startling as that of playing Hamlet. "Listen," he told Phillips, "I'm thirty-seven. I'm a basso-profundo. I'm hardly suited. . ." To which Phillips quickly replied: "Maybe that's why you should do it."

It was an unorthodox Ariel. The part, one of the shortest in Shakespeare, contains only about a hundred lines, but Pennell was on stage for almost the entire play. In a late-summer interview, Pennell admitted that the device had "irritated the pants off some people". During rehearsals, the cast had worked on psychological exercises in an attempt to identify with the play's unique "space". Believing that the magic of *The Tempest* must go beyond the sleight-of-hand, the performers actually tried to project thought waves to one another. Explained Pennell: "There's a circle around each person—an aura, if you like, but I hate the word. Within a certain distance, we become aware of someone there; then there's a danger point one must not go beyond. With eyes closed we tried to see if we could detect it. It worked out as those things do— sometimes it worked, sometimes it didn't." Questionable though the benefits of this exercise may have seemed, it did reflect the determination of those involved in the production to give *The Tempest* the ethereal quality it so often lacked. Kevin Kelly concluded that the use of Ariel was perhaps the most striking example of how well the production had succeeded:

Ariel, very nearly "invisible", white from the top of his head to his feet (his costume is white Nineteenth Century bathing attire—tank top and knickers), is followed by ten silent spirits (in their leader's costume but black). Ariel looks like a robot from "Space: 1999". He moves in slow motion, lifting knees high, coming to rest like a wound-up, now exhausted toy, his heels softly touching the ground four times before his invisible weight settles down. For most of the play the spirits do nothing but trail him, starting, moving, kneeling, swaying at arbitrary moments in the text, a group of ballet dancers oddly paralytic. They seem anxious, extraneous, a stylized after-thought. For a long while I found them distracting. Then, as the play continued, they were more effectively used. Strangely, the more I accepted their staring presence, the more mysterious they seemed, the more genuinely airy inhabitants of Prospero's island. One of Phillips's best touches is the amplification of Ariel's lines—an other-worldly echo to his speech. The mood, in general, is marvellous: wailing winds, smoke-swirling light, distant music.

Opening week at the Avon was completed by a remounting of *The Importance of Being Earnest*, with Barry MacGregor replacing Richard Monette as Algernon. The critics raved, and the production became one of the season's big money-makers. As for the Avon itself, its new status was now firmly ensured as a result of a second season of imaginative programming.

The impact of the Avon's fare was all the more impressive in view of the high-powered talent lined up for the Festival Theatre's opening week. Not only was Maggie Smith playing two major roles —Mrs. Millamant in William Congreve's *The Way of the World* and Cleopatra in Shakespeare's *Antony and Cleopatra*—but Hume Cronyn and his wife, Jessica Tandy, were also joining the company. The Canadian-born Cronyn would be on view opening week as Shylock in *The Merchant of Venice*, and Miss Tandy would play Lady Wishfort in *The Way of the World*. The presence of such luminaries prompted the usual objections from nationalist factions that Stratford was once again falling victim to the dubious tempta-tions of the star system. Such complaints unjustly neglected the very real commitment that a leading international artist like Maggie Smith was prepared to make to the Festival and its company.

Despite Phillips's international reputation as a director, he was still shy of celebrities. The name of Maggie Smith as a potential company member had been broached to him by Urjo Kareda, among others, but Phillips was still astonished by his own boldness in approaching her when she was playing Toronto in a touring produc-tion of *Private Lives*. "I decided to call her and tell her that if she'd like to escape for a weekend we'd come and collect her." Miss Smith's playwright husband, Beverley Cross, called back and said they would love to get out of Toronto. Phillips took them for a weekend at a cottage near the Lake Huron resort town of Grand

Bend. It was an enjoyable time. Phillips had assumed that he and Miss Smith had never met. It turned out they had worked together years before; he had played Orsino and she Viola on a recording, and Phillips had also been an assistant director for a production of Anouilh's *The Rehearsal* in which she had a lead role.

Beverley Cross always took care of Maggie Smith's professional interests, protecting a sensitive artist as much as possible from the more troublesome demands of stardom. It was Cross who would communicate offers of roles to her or requests for interviews. Such was his role with respect to Stratford. ("She and I have never had much communication other than work," Phillips was to declare later.) Following the Grand Bend weekend, Cross said to Phillips, "If you ever have anything for Maggie to do, I'm sure she would be interested in doing it." Phillips threw out a couple of ideas, Cross relayed them, and the answer was yes. "It was as simple as that," Phillips recalled incredulously. "By asking her if she'd like to escape for the weekend, we won her for the company."

She was one international star prepared to make an ongoing commitment to the Festival.

The approach from Stratford came at a fortuitous time for Maggie Smith. She was dissatisfied with her career and felt she was no longer fulfilling her potential. The charged political atmosphere of the British classical theatre scene frightened her—she hadn't been with the National Theatre since 1971—and she didn't really enjoy the commercial film industry. She had also become alarmed at what was happening to her in the course of an eighteen-month North American tour as Amanda in *Private Lives*.

In a Stratford interview she said:

A long run in a single part can be wearing, and it can be dangerous. We arrived in Chicago with *Private Lives* and suddenly the audiences seemed different. The play suddenly wasn't funny. It was a very, very peculiar feeling for me, and I started looking at my own portrayal. What had happened was that, as the run continued, I had gotten so accustomed to laughs that I started playing for them. My performance got broader and broader, and more out of touch with Coward.

When Maggie Smith arrived in Stratford on March 1 with her husband and two children (by a previous marriage to actor Robert Stephens), she settled quickly into the life of the community. She was a star who shunned the trappings of stardom. Press interviews unnerved her, and she loathed watching herself on the cinema screen. The Academy Award she won for her performance in *The Prime of Miss Jean Brodie* had ended up back in her English home as a doorstop. In Stratford she was determined to pursue as natural a life as possible. She settled with her family into an attractive old house and registered the children at local schools, where they quickly made friends.

Stratford, where she was to spend four summers, proved to be a lifeline. She no longer had to deal with lengthy runs of a single play. Instead, there was the continuing challenge of "rep" and the joy of once more being part of a company. Of the 65 company members listed alphabetically on the back of the Festival's 1976 brochure, she was Number 58.

What happened to her during her long *Private Lives* tour could not happen in a classical repertory situation. "I'm playing both major and supporting roles," she reminded an interviewer. "That's one of the attractions. Everybody is just as scared as everyone else. We all level out. Playing several roles keeps you on your toes, and that's something I need right now."

What struck other members of the company was her determination to be one of them and not to flaunt her international reputation. "Of all the stars, she was the most committed to the company," recalls Nicholas Pennell. "Her presence intensified our over-all work level. All of us benefited from her presence. In return, I think Stratford provided her with her most productive period as an actress." Urjo Kareda found her to be "fiendish" about her commitment. "Her loyalty to the entire organization was never recognized. She had this incredible firmness of purpose. She took part in the classes. She attended rehearsals even when she wasn't called."

Phillips found her remarkably untemperamental: "The only temperament she ever showed was due to her inability to suffer fools gladly. Otherwise, she couldn't have been easier. She was a marvellous, marvellous woman who was totally professional. I've never worked with anybody like her." Phillips considered her honesty to be a significant factor in her acting. "She's incapable of reflecting anything that isn't truth. Whenever there were things awry, as in the *Private Lives* tour, it was only a question of removing the excesses. She is so guarded in her private life but on stage she's not guarded at all."

Her first reaction had been "absolute panic" when Phillips offered her the roles of Millamant in *The Way of the World*, Cleopatra in *Antony and Cleopatra*, Masha in *The Three Sisters* (a late season offering), and Mistress Overdone in his revival of *Measure for Measure*. Cleopatra frightened her the most: "I thought the part was beyond me. I didn't think it was within my range. Yet, on the other hand, I've always thought that an artist should seek to stretch oneself. Robin persuaded me, and now I'm grateful to him for asking me."

The Way of the World officially opened the Festival Theatre season June 7, and the consensus was that Maggie Smith outshone the over-all production. Phillips had not initially planned to direct this play. However, his first choice, British director William Gaskill, had wanted to do Congreve's classic comedy in blue jeans, and Phillips felt this would be unfair to Stratford audiences. He then approached Mike Nichols, who was interested but unable to commit himself to a three-month rehearsal period. Phillips, who had hoped to be able to concentrate on *Antony and Cleopatra*, a play he knew to be fraught with difficulties, was forced to take on *The Way of the World* as well.

The Ottawa *Citizen*'s Audrey Ashley echoed many critics when she heralded the Millamant of Maggie Smith and the Lady Wishfort of Jessica Tandy as "the brightest spots in what was an unaccountably long, and often dull evening". Doug Bale of the *London Free Press* found the evening a dreary, tedious bore with "no sense of period, no sense of social climate, no sense of humor and no sense of drama".

There were glimpses of the production that might have been, a production that explored with depth and compassion a society in which the spinning of a witty epithet was considered more substantial and less dangerous than establishing a relationship, and in which good taste was considered a greater mark of civilized life than good sense. Yet much seemed static, with occasional visual awkwardness raising questions about the appropriateness of the Festival stage for a play of this nature.

There were some positive endorsements of the over-all production. John Fraser in the *Globe and Mail* found it a sterling and happy occasion, praising Phillips's straightforward direction and Daphne Dare's evocative designs. In the *New York Times*, Walter Kerr judged it "the most successful" of the three Festival stage productions opening that week.

However, the *Toronto Star*'s Gina Mallet remained disturbed by the style:

> The audience can be made to feel they are choking on champagne, sneezing over the bubbles, even as they keep drinking. Or they may feel they have strayed into opera; first a male quartet, then a mixed duet, now a chorus and then an aria. Robin Phillips's production is weightier than either of these alternatives. He has erred on the side of humanity. It's all very well to emphasize that real human beings are inside these brittle figurines, but it is fatal to try and make them tell the plot in logical fashion. We simply do not want to know what they are doing, but to enjoy them as they are. Instead, Phillips makes every line tell the story, and the result is that Congreve's delicate strokes of wit are all too often blown out of proportion into pseudo-epigrams.

The verdict was generally cool towards Jeremy Brett's portrayal of the mischievous Mirabell: Gina Mallet found him sombre and Walter Kerr accused him of "nibbling so rapidly at his mots that he seems an underfed squirrel". The critics were more positive towards Alan Scarfe for his portrayal of the conniving Fainall, Tony van Bridge for his entertaining work as the gauche Sir Wilfull Witwoud, and Jackie Burroughs for her eccentric approach to the role of Lady Wishfort's maid. But they polarized again with respect to Jessica Tandy's Lady Wishfort. The Ottawa *Citizen* found Miss Tandy "a model of wit and clarity". Walter Kerr was enchanted.

> Miss Tandy, scowling at a servant for serving her cherry brandy in a container the size of an "acorn", plays an aging, heavily enamelled dowager who controls the purse strings of the plot. She raps her dependents to order with a stout tongue and a sometimes candid, sometimes self-deluding appraisal of her own chances for coaxing a bit of romance back into her life.

Gina Mallet, however, was not enchanted. "It's enough to make one cry," she declared. "Tandy is an actress of simple purity who could, I am sure, create a character simply by reading the telephone book. But fine as her moments are when Wishfort is revealed as a pathetic, painted jade, she can no more essay the character's broad vulgarity than Buster Keaton could talk."

The only true unanimity was for Maggie Smith. Praising her as "the most successful and most curious creature" in the production, Walter Kerr used the occasion to reflect on her uniqueness as an actress:

> Miss Smith has more or less taken over the snake-charmer's concession in that continuing sideshow we call the theatre, and has, in the last 10 years or so, laid waste more living rooms, chaise longues, leading men, ottomans, vanity tables and handy bric-a-brac than any other enchantress in the business.
>
> She coils around things, and they disappear in small puffs of smoke, leaving only her violent red hair and her small contrite mouth behind as a memento of the holocaust. Usually, it's a comic holocaust; Miss Smith makes annihilation funny.
>
> What didn't figure in the least was the way she'd choose to play *The Way of the World*. She's Millamant, of course, haughtiest of the haughty, witty even before breakfast, so swift and lethal of tongue that one of the fops-about-town who appears early in Congreve's elaborate conceit announces that he wouldn't go near her "were she as Cleopatra". (Since we can also see her as Cleopatra in Shakespeare's *Antony and Cleopatra* the very next night or so, we are in a position to appreciate the gentleman's apprehension.)
>
> But let the chaps talk. When Miss Smith comes on as Millamant, she does indeed prattle on until someone must point out that she doesn't give fair play. She prattles about the papers she uses as hair-curlers, about suitors, about landscapes and lying and the unreliability of love.

And yet if there's one thing she is not, it is too mighty, too overwhelming, too bright. She's almost hinted, right from the beginning, that she talks to keep her composure, that language is her last line of defence, that she's secretly more vulnerable than anyone on stage. She is magnificent.

Critics were in far more agreement over Bill Glassco's production of *The Merchant of Venice*. They liked Hume Cronyn's Shylock and disliked virtually everything else. The *Globe and Mail*'s John Fraser called Cronyn's performance masterly and bristling with self-righteous indignation. "It is a daring and honest interpretation and comes across very strongly. But when you leave this *Merchant of Venice*, you end up not caring very much for anyone who appears in the production. Everyone is rather hateful."

Gina Mallet had initial hopes that Cronyn was

> going to chuck convention and give us a Shylock as engagingly villainous as *Richard III*....But that hope evaporated. And Shylock sank without a trace into the bog that passes for Bill Glassco's conception of the play. Did I say conception? Rather it seems we are witnessing a country house party where all the guests have been loosed in charades, and the biggest ham wins the day....Jackie Burroughs makes of Portia a hearty hockey captain. She is so aggressive that you keep hoping she will slip on a banana peel. Nick Mancuso's Bassanio is a refugee from the movie *The Godfather*; he grunts his lines as if he was chewing bullets.

The Merchant of Venice was the season's big failure. It also renewed the debate about the use of guest directors—in particular, *Canadian* guest directors—at Stratford. Glassco was a revered figure in the Canadian theatre community, he had been a leader of the alternative movement in the early 1970s, and he had also signed the nationalist manifesto protesting Robin Phillips's appointment to Stratford. Having successfully directed *Kennedy's Children* at the Third Stage in 1975, he had been invited back to do *The Merchant of Venice* on the treacherous Festival stage. It was an intimidating leap for a director who had made his reputation mounting works in a tiny warehouse theatre. However, when Glassco was announced as director of *The Merchant of Venice*, many in the theatre community heralded this as a long-overdue vote of confidence by Stratford in Canadian directing talent. When Glassco failed, many of those same voices saw the whole episode as evidence that guest directors—especially Canadians—were being set up to fail in order to make Phillips look good. This mythology gathered momentum as the years passed, although it was not supported by the facts.

The truth of the matter was that choice of guest directors had posed insoluble problems for the Festival from its very beginnings. To begin with there was the treacherousness of a stage which had taken even Langham years to master and which was to frustrate Phillips on occasion. Further difficulties were posed by the logistics of rehearsals. Because Stratford was a repertory theatre, with company members rehearsing several plays at the same time, rehearsal periods of three months or more were not uncommon. This created difficulties in finding outside directors willing to commit themselves to such an extended time period. The directors themselves had to share time with other directors and other productions, with the result that a daily rehearsal period for a particular play was often an impossibility. Guest directors were, in Urjo Kareda's words, "floored by the scheduling difficulties".

However, there was a more serious problem, having to do with the psychology of a permanent company. It was a problem that had plagued alien directors since the Festival's earliest days when Cecil Clarke encountered hostility from his actors simply because he wasn't Tyrone Guthrie. "Once you establish a good relationship with a company, it's difficult for them to accept another director," Phillips once commented. "And if you also happen to be running the theatre it can cause you great difficulty." Phillips was to have the same trouble as his predecessors in finding good directors with whom company members, particularly leading actors, were willing to work. Just as musicians in a symphony orchestra could cause problems for a visiting conductor with whom they lacked rapport, so could members of a permanent theatre company distrust a guest director. Some senior company members such as William Hutt were willing to work with virtually any guest director and seek to adapt themselves to that director's style. Others would balk at taking lead roles in any production that Phillips wasn't directing. Two members of the cast for the critically acclaimed 1975 production of *The Crucible* complained to Phillips about Canadian director John Wood, saying they would never work for him again. Phillips, a keen admirer of Wood's work, respected their wishes, but also was determined to have Wood back, and finally succeeded in signing him again for the 1978 season.

Phillips had also imposed a rule on himself with respect to treatment of guest directors. The rule was to remain aloof from their productions unless he was asked for input. Not only was Glassco coping with the Festival Theatre stage, he was also coping with what he considered to be the intransigence of Jackie Burroughs and Nick Mancuso and the growing unhappiness of Hume Cronyn. In fact, Cronyn appeared in Phillips's office frequently, asking him to intervene. Phillips was concerned, but he was to stress later that he continued to keep his distance because Glassco had not invited him to attend a rehearsal. Phillips's position was a controversial one, which was not shared by all artistic directors. However, it was moulded by his own traumatic experience with the Royal Shakespeare Company when that theatre's hierarchy, led by Peter Hall, attempted to sabotage his production of *The Two Gentlemen of Verona*. Phillips was determined that in any theatre he ran, the territory of his guest directors would be respected.

Phillips's own production of *Antony and Cleopatra*, which opened June 9 at the Festival Theatre, again divided the critics. Phillips had aimed for an intimate, even domestic, approach, arguing that he was tired of seeing kings and queens walking around in crowns. "I don't see *Antony and Cleopatra* like that. It is a basic story of a middle-aged love affair. . . .It is an extraordinarily lonely play."

This approach didn't appeal to *Detroit News* critic Jay Carr, who told his readers the following day that the production lacked an inner life. He wondered whether Phillips was spreading himself too thin by directing too many of the season's productions, and contended that *Antony and Cleopatra* marked a lapse back into the kind of "bland ceremony" Phillips was supposed to combat:

> Maggie Smith is an arrestingly statuesque Cleopatra, and her death scene, played atop a three-tiered platform with a long cape trailing behind in a wonderful art nouveau swirl, is at least visually striking. Here she has size and dignity. But elsewhere, the series of sculptured poses with which she negotiates the role seem to drain it of impact.

Gina Mallet found the production a chilly substitute for what should be a blaze of Mediterranean passion, and suggested that to cast Miss Smith as Cleopatra was akin to setting down a Wren church amid the Pyramids. She found the relationship between Maggie Smith's Cleopatra and Keith Baxter's Antony "archetypically English" in nature, involving two people terrified of physical demonstration.

There was also critical scorn for Daphne Dare's costumes. "The soldiers look like pretty boys with their chic mid-calf white boots and pleated skirts," wrote Jay Carr. But there was praise from most critics for Alan Scarfe's icy Octavius, Max Helpmann's sly Lepidus, and Bernard Hopkins's humorous cameo as the man who delivers the asp to Cleopatra.

However, the production also won some strong affirmative votes. In the *Vancouver Sun*, Max Wyman unequivocally labelled the production a masterpiece. "This is theatre to make you weep—an honest human telling of this most human of all love stories, and one we can with clear conscience allow to stand high with all our finest memories."

Wyman approved of the portrayal of Antony by Keith Baxter, a British actor brought in after John Colicos turned down the role in favour of a $250,000 movie offer. "Far from the unbridled sensualist and doting vacillator that some have made of this role, Baxter's Antony is a man of troubled conscience, a man who senses that duty calls him elsewhere yet is reluctant to be true to his human instincts."

And what of Maggie Smith? Said Wyman:

> This may be no Cleopatra you have ever known, but what makes it so penetrating is the fact that she is at once so normal and so special. She is the embodiment of every impulsive romantic, building a life on her emotions, because that is the only way she knows, but dreadfully insecure about it all, anxious and worried and desperate to do it well and properly—though never, of course, prepared to admit any of that to the person it is all concocted for. It is a masterly and perceptive piece of playing.

Writing in *Saturday Night*, Martin Knelman observed that this Cleopatra was "not a femme fatale; she's a woman made helpless, in spite of her power and wealth, by being desperately in love." In the *New York Times*, Clive Barnes was ecstatic:

> Miss Smith's Cleopatra was the best I have ever seen—I would rank it, for example, as equal to and because of its youthfulness, more persuasive than Edith Evans's, and better than such Cleopatras as Peggy Ashcroft, Margaret Leighton and Janet Suzman. It has such immediacy and spirit, there is a kind of wistful grandeur, yet above all a womanliness that most Cleopatras disregard.

There was one particularly notable aspect to the production: it gave Phillips his first opportunity to display the new flexibility of the Festival Theatre stage. It took six workmen only twenty minutes to move the balcony off the stage by utilizing a new hydraulic system. The balcony's removal provided Phillips with a wide central entrance for armies marching five abreast. It also allowed him to mount a pier-like platform for the death scenes of Antony and Cleopatra. Critical disagreement notwithstanding, the production played to 94.8-per-cent attendance over twenty-eight performances.

By the end of opening week, Phillips was exhausted. He had never intended to direct so many productions himself, but as he told Sidney Edwards of the London *Evening Standard*, "we were let down for various reasons by several directors and so I decided to take them on." He had suffered a further blow in early January when Urjo Kareda, his new literary manager, was seriously injured in an automobile accident and lost to the Festival until September. Board president John Killer was to acknowledge later that Phillips had been subjected to almost "inhuman" demands that year—a factor that may explain the crisis precipitated by an interview a tired and distraught Phillips gave to Max Wyman of the *Vancouver Sun*.

Phillips was upset by the media response to much of opening week. He was also distressed by what he deemed a lack of support from the wider theatre community. For that reason, he told Wyman, he had decided to leave Stratford when his current contract expired at the end of the 1977 season.

"You know the ludicrous storm I came in under," he said. "It has quietened down on the public front, but it hasn't behind the scenes. You'd be amazed at the number of Canadian actors approached for this season who said they weren't interested." He said he was grateful for the praise of foreign critics (the *Evening Standard*'s Edwards had written a front-page story demanding that *Antony and Cleopatra* be invited overseas for the Royal Jubilee celebrations), but he was more concerned with the Canadian response. "It's marvellous to get that kind of encouragement from England, but this is where we sell most of our tickets, and if the Toronto and London, Ontario, media dismiss us as a load of rubbish, who's going to come to us?"

Two days later, he expanded on these views in an interview with Southam News Service:

> I have single-handedly fought the battle that has been levelled against me for a very long time. Few voices have been heard raised in my support. I can't continue heaving the heavy stone up the mountain by myself. I haven't forgotten the attack that went on when I arrived. There were no voices raised that were supportive, and even now I don't feel I have a community of interest backing what we're trying to do at Stratford.

The decision to leave in 1977 was taken in the heat of the moment, in the view of those closest to Phillips. "He still hadn't learned to roll with the punches," one former colleague recalled later. "He would read a negative notice and conclude that the author hated him. Yet all he needed to do was to talk to these people, to disarm them with his candour, to make them feel they were sharing his dream. He was hurt by the failure of people to understand what he was trying to achieve."

There was also the problem of workload, of a sense of isolation. He once said to his publicist, Douglas Allan:

> There's a big difference between England and here. In England, I can reach the point where I'm ninety-nine per cent there and something's not jelling and I can call Olivier or Gielgud to sit through a rehearsal and tell me what's wrong. I would know they'll be absolutely honest and that I can completely trust them. Who can I call here?

Many in the theatre community interpreted Phillips's determination to leave in 1977 as a resignation threat aimed at winning more concessions from the board. It was not to be the last time such a charge was levelled at Phillips, and it was one which both he and board members considered to be highly unfair. "At no time did I witness any pyrotechnics or ultimatums from Robin," commented one veteran governor.

By June 15, the Festival board was expressing public sympathy and support for Phillips. Said board chairman John Killer:

> I know that Robin has been overworked. We've been very much aware of it and concerned by it, but there's little we can do about it. I hope when Robin has had a chance to rest a bit and recharge that we'll be able to change his mind. What he's making abundantly clear is that he has to feel there's a clear understanding of what he's trying to do here. I hope there will be sufficient reaction to his statements, not only by the public. The board here and the artistic community at large can make Robin feel that what is happening here is significant.

In later comments to the Toronto media, Phillips emphasized that he would fulfil the commitment of his existing contract, and that whatever happened, he intended to remain in Canada. He also reiterated what his goals had been for Stratford, which were to make the Festival the focus of Canadian theatre work, employing more Canadian directors and designers as well as the best Canadian acting talent.

Some of the pithiest comments on the furore came from *Toronto Sun* columnist George Anthony:

> He [Phillips] is obviously overworked—and underpaid, I'm sure— but what has defeated him finally (if only temporarily) is the Great Canadian Put-Down. We greeted him the way we greet most foreign artists, by challenging him to verbal and physical duels; and once he got things rolling (and did he ever, with the two biggest box-office advance sales in Stratford's history) we showed him the sort of provincial hostility that explains why British statesmen still refer to us as the *colonies*. What Phillips failed to grasp is quite elementary; it's simply that Canada is not afraid of Failure—it's afraid of Success. Until he truly absorbs this lesson he will always be discouraged, because discouraging new concepts, new ideas or, God forbid, new *risks*, is what Canadians as a people do best. His resignation, however, does not become really effective until September 1977, after Stratford's much-anticipated 25th anniversary season, and I have a sneaking suspicion he'll lose more battles but win the war in the end. I have never encountered a director who inspired such reverent respect and downright devotion from performers on all levels, be they apprentice, actor or marquee-lure star; and Stratford has never before had an artistic chief capable of attracting so many stars to its

stages. I don't think Stratford is ready to give that up. I don't think we are either—but we may have to head for the nearest shrink, collectively, to overcome our Great Canadian Hang-Up before Phillips can get back to business. That business, incidentally, is not dry-cleaning, or wine-tasting, or plumbing. That business is show business—and Robin Phillips has already proved that he knows his business very well indeed.

Board members and Phillips met frequently over the next three months to discuss problems, and on September 15 Killer announced that Phillips had agreed to remain as artistic director with a new five-year contract. Killer's statement indicated that Phillips had regained confidence and that he enjoyed support for his vision. The contract, said Killer, was "an expression of our firm determination to give him every assistance in...carrying out his plans for the future, plans which we think are not only exciting but capable of raising the Festival to new heights of artistic achievement."

However, there were those who also saw in these developments an expansion of Phillips's power to an unprecedented degree. September also saw the resignation of Bruce Swerdfager as general manager. Significantly, he was not replaced.

The prevailing mythology was that Phillips hadn't wanted a general manager because he wanted total control for himself. Both Phillips and board members were to argue later that this was far too simplistic an interpretation. Swerdfager's predecessor, William Wylie, had been a conspicuously powerful general manager—so much so that few artistic directors would have found the situation acceptable. Jean Gascon, who disliked many areas of administration, was prepared to defer frequently to Wylie. Phillips was not content to delegate details automatically. Not only was he fanatical about ensuring that a budget was stretched to its limit, but he also expected the right of final approval on all aspects of Festival operation, from the uniforms worn by ushers to the quality of paper stock used in Stratford publications.

Following a heart attack, Swerdfager had to ration his time and was unable to work the hours he had before. There was also friction with Phillips. Phillips had prepared an organizational chart that provided for all authority to flow through him; the exception was Swerdfager, who, at the insistence of some board members, continued to have access to the board. By 1976 it had become apparent that authority could not be shared between Phillips and Swerdfager. The chemistry at the Festival had changed since the days of Jean Gascon and strongman Bill Wylie. Swerdfager eventually resigned, and Phillips found himself in full control.

This did not, however, mean that Phillips had opposed the appointment of a general manager. To be sure, the powers of Stratford's artistic director had been redefined and—in the process

—increased, but they were no different in degree from the powers long enjoyed by artistic directors in many of Canada's regional theatres, where boards had decided it was best to have one person in sole authority. But these other theatres did have an administrator or general manager in a key number-two position to take some of the workload off the artistic director. Stratford, after 1976, did not. Gary Thomas, who had taken over Swerdfager's own comptroller's position when Swerdfager moved up to general manager, became treasurer and assumed some new administrative duties. However, by decision of the board rather than by demand of Phillips, there was no general manager. Before he had even accepted the job, Phillips had warned the board he was not an experienced administrator. He did not believe that his need for ultimate control was inconsistent with the need for a top-flight general manager. "Why can't you find someone to help me?" he pleaded with one board member during one of the many periods when his workload became too crushing. Comments this same board member: "Don't assume Robin wanted the general manager's position abolished. The fact of the matter is that it was a majority of the board which was responsible for not putting in a new general manager with redefined responsibilities and for taking some of the load off Robin." This action, with the additional burden it placed on Phillips, subsequently proved a big factor in the traumatic events that almost destroyed the Festival in 1980.

Meanwhile, the remainder of the 1976 season was attracting considerable acclaim. A revival of *Measure for Measure* opened June 30 with Douglas Rain chillingly replacing Brian Bedford in the role of Angelo, and Maggie Smith flashing with brief, garish brilliance as Mistress Overdone.

July brought a major première of a new Canadian play. It was *Eve*, Larry Fineberg's adaptation of *The Book of Eve*, the Constance Beresford-Howe novel about a woman who quits her comfortable Montreal home to live alone on an old-age pension in a seedy flat. Bruce Swerdfager had sent the book to Jessica Tandy, suggesting it as a possible vehicle for her talents. Tandy, a distinguished international actress, was enthusiastic, and both Phillips and Kareda shared her enthusiasm. Fineberg, a gifted young Toronto playwright, found the experience frequently taxing—mainly because of the leading lady's demand for rewrites—but the end product, directed by Vivian Matalon, was a critical and box-office triumph, playing to

Scene from the 1976 Avon stage production of Eve, *by Larry Fineberg, based on the novel* The Book of Eve *by Constance Beresford-Howe, directed by Vivian Matalon, designed by John Ferguson, lighting by Gil Wechsler. Jessica Tandy as Eve. Photograph by Robert C. Ragsdale, a.r.p.s., courtesy of the Stratford Festival Archives.*

99.4-per-cent capacity in its thirteen-performance run at the Avon. The success of *Eve* vindicated Kareda and Phillips in their contention that Canadian drama did have a place in Festival programming. The *Globe and Mail*'s John Fraser said that Fineberg had written a tour de force for a great actress, Jessica Tandy. "It is absolutely contrary to anything we have ever seen her in before, or expected to see her in, and it is done so compellingly that she practically whips us into believing her against all our better judgments." Fineberg proved unintimidated by the episodic nature of the plot and came through with a fluid, dramatically aware text, bolstered by strong drawing of characters and a sensitive ear for easy, naturalistic dialogue. Augmented by the tasteful, economic direction of Matalon and shabby authenticity of John Ferguson's sets, the production proved to be a memorable occasion.

The summer also brought the final Festival Theatre offering of 1976—Phillips's regal production of *A Midsummer Night's Dream*, with Hume Cronyn as Bottom, Jessica Tandy doubling in the roles of Hippolyta and Titania, and Jeremy Brett doubling as Theseus and Oberon. Visually, it was an eye-filling event, with designer Susan Benson decorating the early court sequences in rich blacks and golds, which provided a sumptuous contrast to the gossamer delicacy of the later forest scenes. Alan Laing's music was a cunning and fascinating melding of Elizabethan and contemporary idioms, and Michael Whitfield's lighting was subtle and evocative.

It was a production of translucent beauty. But both in 1976 and in its 1977 revival, it left many critics more admiring than enthusiastic. John Fraser noted that Phillips had the handicap of working in the shadow of Peter Brook's audacious and radical treatment of the *Dream* for the Royal Shakespeare Company:

> Phillips has not pulled off a greater version, far from it in fact, but he has pulled off a different and highly credible tableau, one that is both controversial and saleable, which is a nice combination if you can manage it. In place of spareness and lyricism, Phillips and his dazzling designer, Susan Benson, have offered us something unique, for they have hung an Elizabethan court masque upon a hazy summer's dream and given us a vision of Gloriana herself—Elizabeth I. . . . And so those noble and quaint Athenians from a midsummer's revel are made to do double service by playing out the play as evoking the glory and ethos of that long and noble Tudor reign.

Fraser felt that some of the comedy scenes were too bumptious, and that Phillips had banished the play's lyricism and mystery. But he approved of the contributions of Cronyn and Miss Tandy, Tom Kneebone's Puck, and Nick Mancuso's Lysander. He also said there was no way one could diminish the significance of a production of the *Dream* which used the glory that was Elizabeth as its conceptual springboard. "What Phillips has done, and it is a crucially

Scene from the 1976 Festival stage production of A Midsummer
Night's Dream, *directed by Robin Phillips, designed by Susan Benson,
music by Alan Laing, lighting by Michael J. Whitfield. L.-R.: Jessica
Tandy as Hippolyta, Richard Partington as Demetrius, Denise
Ferguson as Helena, Nick Mancuso as Lysander, Mia Anderson as
Hermia, William Needles as Egeus, and Jeremy Brett as Theseus.
Photograph by Robert C. Ragsdale, a.r.p.s., courtesy of the Stratford
Festival Archives.*

important achievement, is so to blitz our minds with this unexpected new look at a famous play that we can suspend comparisons
and judge it for its own sake.''

There were no critical reservations about the season's final production of Chekhov's *The Three Sisters*, which opened at the Avon
in early September. It marked John Hirsch's return to Stratford as a
guest director and his reunion with a playwright whom he revered.
Phillips had delivered him a remarkable cast: Maggie Smith, Martha
Henry, and Marti Maraden as Masha, Olga, and Irina; Keith Baxter as
Vershinin; William Hutt as Chebutykin; Pat Galloway as Natasha;
and Eric Donkin as Ferapont. Daphne Dare was the designer, and her
contribution was credited with reinforcing the text to a memorable
degree.

The critics hauled out the superlatives. A typical reaction was that of Gina Mallet, a writer not always favourably inclined to Hirsch's work:

> To see Chekhov's *Three Sisters* is to watch someone you love dying, a draining experience that leaves only mindless platitudes and insubstantial expressions of love and grief. Thus it was last night at Stratford's Avon Theatre when John Hirsch's intricate production of *The Three Sisters* opened. This is the final show of the Stratford season this year, and ineffably, it overshadowed all that has gone before.

Miss Mallet had particular praise for the direction:

> To this dense web, Hirsch has brought his own spinning wheel. He has made his company an ensemble. The actors remain individual without ever breaking the integrity of the whole. They never go off stage, it seems; they simply move to other parts of the house or garden or into the town where, no doubt, they are continuing their oblique conversations and whispered confrontations.

To the critics, this was the kind of guest director Stratford needed. Hirsch, one of the most distinguished figures in Canadian theatre, seemed destined to play an important role during the Phillips regime, for it was clear that his past Stratford association and his remarkable gifts as a director made him an ideal choice for future guest assignments.

However, Hirsch was not invited to direct again by Phillips, and members of the Hirsch camp were quick to suggest that he had blotted his copybook by having the temerity to be successful in a theatre where guest directors were supposed to fail. After all, they asserted, hadn't Phillips been upset when an enraptured Maggie Smith publicly wondered where Hirsch had been all her life?

If Phillips was consumed by jealousy, he didn't show it. Indeed, on more than one occasion he was to pay public tribute to the high quality of Hirsch's production of *The Three Sisters*. Furthermore, when a crisis was mounting four years later over the appointment of a new artistic director, Phillips was the one who urged the board to give Hirsch serious consideration as his successor.

Nevertheless, Phillips did decide he didn't want John Hirsch back as long as he was running Stratford. Problems between the two artists began with Hirsch's initial arrival back in Stratford, when he complained that Phillips had failed to extend him a proper welcome. Rehearsals for *The Three Sisters* weren't yet due to begin, and Phillips heard about Hirsch's unexpected appearance in the Festival building second-hand. "He had not been to see me. He had not said he was coming," Phillips recalled afterwards. "Had I known, I would have made sure he had a welcome befitting him."

Scene from the 1976 Avon stage production of Three Sisters, *by Anton Chekhov, directed by John Hirsch, designed by Daphne Dare, lighting by Gil Wechsler. L.-R.: Maggie Smith as Masha, Marti Maraden as Irina, Amelia Hall as Anfisa, and Martha Henry as Olga. Photograph by Robert C. Ragsdale, a.r.p.s., courtesy of the Stratford Festival Archives.*

Once rehearsals were in progress, word drifted back to Phillips that Hirsch was criticizing his operation of the Festival. He later clashed with Phillips over certain members of his cast and tried to have them removed, but Phillips would not budge.

However, the big breach occurred a week before *The Three Sisters* opened, when the *Globe and Mail* published an interview Hirsch had given John Fraser. In the text of the interview, Fraser observed that Phillips was making more money than any director in Canada's history because he was—in addition to his Stratford salary—being paid a handsome sum for each of the seven productions he had directed that season. The statement was untrue. Phillips read the interview early on the morning of August 27, picked up the telephone, and called Fraser at home. "He was furious," recalls Fraser. "I have never heard such language. Phillips asked me the source of my information. I replied, 'Who do you think?'"

That was enough for Phillips. "I cannot believe that you would print such a story without checking your facts," he raged at Fraser, and then he called Hirsch, who denied having given any such information. However, Fraser was later to name Hirsch as the specific source of the charge. He claimed that during the interview,

Hirsch had said of Phillips's workload, "Why do you think he directs so many shows?" A year later, Fraser joined Phillips for dinner at the Church Restaurant in Stratford, and again confirmed that it was, in fact, Hirsch who had supplied the misinformation.

Phillips continued to feel that his reputation had been seriously compromised, and that it had caused damaging fall-out at a time when he was trying to win the trust of the theatre community. "For a long time, people looked at me with grave suspicion, assuming that I was in fact receiving all this extra money, and I finally had to get the board to write letters to the newspapers."

Phillips was by this time acutely aware of the guest-director problem. He was desperate to secure people of Hirsch's calibre. "Nevertheless," he recalled later, "I made the decision that I would never again have anything to do with him as long as I was artistic director."

The month of September also saw an important educational venture unfold, when third-year students from Montreal's National Theatre School spent almost a month in Stratford rehearsing scenes from two plays under Robin Phillips's direction with Maggie Smith and Martha Henry assisting. The rehearsals were organized in the same way as regular company sessions, and the same demands were made on students as were made on professional actors. Design students worked under Daphne Dare, preparing costumes and properties. The reaction of one student, Robert Ruttan, was typical:

> It was without question the single most valuable learning experience of our training. We were not only able to observe top-level professionals both in performance and rehearsal, but we also received the benefit of their comments on our work. We were especially fortunate in having an opportunity to be directed by Robin Phillips. He understands the needs and concerns of students who are still unsure of what they wish to accomplish artistically and are only beginning to develop their techniques of expression. He managed to draw more out of us than we realized we had to offer. While this left us drained at the end of every day it somehow also had an invigorating effect— making us eager to give that much more.

The 1976 season marked the end of musical programming, save for pops. Raffi Armenian resigned as director of music, complaining that the present regime was unsympathetic to the classical aspect of Festival programming. The six chamber concerts presented at the Festival Theatre in 1976 incurred a net loss of $36,000, once more proving that serious music was a losing proposition at the Stratford Festival. Some of Phillips's allies on the board felt he had little sympathy for musical programming, but they also acknowledged the validity of his argument that producing plays was Stratford's essential concern. The Festival's official statement cited several factors as contributing to the end of its current music program:

> First, at a time when mounting costs and cutbacks in grants are forcing the Festival to search for a way to avoid cutbacks in the program of drama planned for the Avon Theatre next year, it is not sound economics to continue with a peripheral program that is a constant drain on the Festival's financial resources.
>
> The Festival is essentially a drama program and we owe our first allegiance to the development and expansion of drama on our stages. If music were more closely integrated with over-all Festival policy, it might have been possible to observe allegiance to both. But as now constituted, the music season is a separate entity, totally unrelated to the development of the Festival as a whole. Ultimately, there must be a single artistic policy encompassing both drama and music, as they relate to the Stratford Festival.
>
> This policy has not evolved to date and it is, therefore, necessary at this time to re-examine the possibilities for music at Stratford, and to attempt to bring the two elements together. We cannot reach this objective and at the same time maintain our present music policy.
>
> However admirable it is artistically, the ensemble is composed of members of the Kitchener-Waterloo Symphony Orchestra and as such enjoys a natural liaison with that organization rather than the Stratford Festival. Even the master classes were held in Kitchener this year, removing the music program even further than in the past from the Festival itself. Our involvement becomes meaningless when master classes conducted under Stratford Festival auspices must take place in Kitchener.

The board argued that in financially difficult times it could no longer subsidize chamber music to the tune of $36,000 or more a year. Berthold Carriere succeeded Armenian as director of music.

The year also saw the demise of the film festival. Cancellation of the 1976 festival—which would have been the twelfth—was announced in August. Reasons given by the board and the administration were financial. The film event was a low-priority item at Stratford; in addition, there were fears that necessary government aid would not be forthcoming. Film Festival director Gerald Pratley tried to be philosophical. "What's the use of fighting to be where we are obviously not wanted?" he asked. "Theatre festivals seldom want to be bothered with film festivals—this we know. Film is always the stepchild. We owed our existence at Stratford to Bill Wylie, the former general manager. When he died two years ago, we knew that Stratford was waiting for an opportunity to drop the film program."

The 1976 theatre season proved a spectacular financial success. Net profit for the season totalled $214,517, a figure large enough to take care of a previous accumulated deficit of $86,056 and leave a healthy surplus of $128,461.

·C·H·A·P·T·E·R· XXII·

1977

The 1976 season had been launched with a marathon succession of seven openings in four days; however, because of the two *Hamlet*s, only six productions were involved. In 1977, the opening-week pressures intensified, with Phillips crowding seven separate productions into four days. It was an experience press personnel would not easily forget. Neither would company members, some of whom found themselves on stage in three different plays within a twenty-four-hour period.

Opening day, June 6, set the tone, with *Romeo and Juliet* premiering in the afternoon at the Avon and *A Midsummer Night's Dream* in the evening at the Festival Theatre. June 7 saw a matinee of Ibsen's *Ghosts* at the Avon and *All's Well That Ends Well* on the Festival stage. June 8 brought another afternoon opening at the Avon with Strindberg's *Miss Julie* and an evening unveiling of *Richard III* at the Festival Theatre. Friday, June 9, saw only one opening—Ferenc Molnar's *The Guardsman* at the Avon.

The opening-week pressures proved intense. But there were convincing reasons for this marathon. Some fifty critics from Canada and abroad were attracted to Stratford that week, and the cumulative impact of so many productions within such a brief period of time left them in awe. As one critic said at the end of the week, "I'm exhausted, but I also feel I have shared in something wonderful." Despite dark mutterings about the back-breaking schedule, Phillips was prepared to defend it to the hilt. One of his main motivations, he argued in an interview, was concern over ticket sales:

> In that opening week, we're getting virtually everything into our repertory program, and this is good for the box office. In past years, when we used to have a number of major openings later in the summer, there were problems. The box office tended to be weak after the first opening week in June, and wouldn't pick up until July when a greater choice of plays was presented.

This is not to say that the week was a total success artistically; but it did create a climate of excitement unique in the Festival's history. One writer concluded that the week left him in a stage of "catatonic euphoria". The openings were also cunningly orchestrated, reaching a spectacular climax with two of the season's most memorable productions.

Stratford's twenty-fifth season had a significant emblem: a red Tudor rose on a white maple leaf superimposed on a silver-anniversary shield. The Festival remained dedicated to its legendary Tudor playwright, but it was also reaffirming its commitment to Canada. There were eighty-three members in the company. Only three— Maggie Smith, Brian Bedford, and Margaret Tyzack—were imported stars. Of the remaining eighty, fifty-two were native-born Canadians, and a further twenty-six had lived or worked in Canada for a significant part of their adult lives as landed immigrants or citizens. Furthermore, younger members of the company were being given the opportunity to join the top ranks of Festival performers—among them, Stephen Russell, who moved up to a major role in *A Midsummer Night's Dream*, and Jack Wetherall, who played Orlando to Maggie Smith's Rosalind in *As You Like It*.

Despite this visible commitment to Canada, nationalist factions were to cause the 1977 season serious problems. Indeed, the troubles had begun the previous autumn when the Festival lost one of the key members of its 1977 company—Kate Reid. Phillips had been anxious to bring this remarkable Canadian actress back to Stratford for the anniversary season, and her agreement influenced the planning of his program. When, ultimately, Miss Reid had second thoughts about committing herself to such a lengthy season, Phillips was left without a mature actress capable of playing three particularly taxing roles—the Countess of Rousillon in *All's Well*, Mrs. Alving in *Ghosts*, and Queen Margaret in *Richard III*.

Needing a fast replacement, Phillips turned to England and hired Margaret Tyzack, an actress best known for her work in BBC Television's *Forsyte Saga* series. Canadian Actors' Equity barred her on the grounds that a Canadian should have been hired, and then reversed its decision after Phillips reminded the union that he had been burdened at the eleventh hour with the need to find someone good enough to take on roles originally chosen for a Canadian star. By December, Equity militants had forced their executive to reopen the Tyzack case. The executive grudgingly decided that Miss Tyzack could still join the Stratford Company—she had, after all, signed a contract in good faith—but it again warned Canadian directors that they must look to Canada first in casting future roles. Phillips was disturbed that no one seemed to be prepared to acknowledge the fact that more Canadians would be working at Stratford in 1977 than ever before. Some members of the press were angered over Equity intransigence. Commented Gina Mallet, herself a comparatively recent arrival in Canada: "Canadian actors should get the lion's share of work in their own country, but a bout of isolationism could retard the development of Canadian theatre itself. On a short-term basis, actors and directors from countries with richer theatrical resources provide Canadians with a training that is generally not available here."

Ironically, it was an imported director, David William, who was to open the Festival on a low note with a disappointing production of *Romeo and Juliet*. Its biggest problem was that it lacked the glow and passion of youth. Richard Monette and Marti Maraden were two of the most attractive young performers at Stratford that year, yet they perversely brought to the characters of Shakespeare's star-crossed lovers exactly the type of maturity that Romeo and his Juliet didn't need.

British critic Robert Cushman suggested to readers of the London *Observer* that William's visit to Canada "seemed hardly necessary, especially since his starting point seemed to be the Old Vic of the Fifties at its fussiest and most pedestrian". Writing in *New York* magazine, Alan Rich suggested that William should have been more ready to wield the editing scissors. "An uncut *Romeo*, with all its snide boisterousness left intact and its speeches droning on like so many doctoral dissertations, dulls the impact of the few poetic moments that have made the play famous." Canadian critics were also generally negative. The *Globe and Mail*'s John Fraser was impressed by John Ferguson's stately thrust set and earth-coloured costumes, but concluded that the production was "remarkable only for the lack of real thought and inspiration behind it". He accused William of being so concerned with brandishing constant stage business that he ignored the need for "interior magic". Fraser also found some of the characterizations bizarre. "In Leslie Yeo we are confronted with an Archie Bunker of a Capulet. John Goodlin's Escalus is more of a game referee than a feared and respected prince, and, in the most quixotic casting of the lot, that fine actor Nicholas Pennell is for some reason allowed to transform the mercurial Mercutio into an aging and disturbingly-decadent hanger-on." Fraser chastised the Festival for not having the courage to take a risk with *Romeo and Juliet*: "some of the younger and aspiring talents at Stratford might have had a better go at it than this lot. Indeed, it was a heaven-sent and obvious opportunity, capriciously missed."

The highlight of the opening, for many dozing patrons, was the sudden emergence of an Avon Theatre bat, which made several dramatic swoops at the balcony. "I'm not at all sure it wasn't scripted in," commented Fraser sardonically.

The revival of *A Midsummer Night's Dream* was one of the season's big hits, playing to 95-per-cent houses. Maggie Smith was now taking the dual role which had been assigned Jessica Tandy the year before, and Alan Scarfe was Bottom. Several critics were ecstatic, among them Jack Tinker of the London *Daily Mail*. He felt the production ranked with Peter Brook's celebrated version in terms of excitement, originality, and impact. He singled out Maggie Smith for special praise:

> She plays the dual role of Hippolyta and Titania as twin manifestations of the first Elizabeth. The opening image is of Miss Smith's splendid, isolated Gloriana alone on stage staring desolately across space and time. Gradually, the play swirls to life around her in the shape of a formal Elizabethan masque. It is ravishingly dressed in black, white, gold and silver—beautiful beyond a fault. . . .it is no cosmetic creation. It sends echoes through the text which linger in the senses. The magic of this enchanted production is. . .a rare kind. I shall forever be haunted by Miss Smith's gilded Gloriana.

But again, as was the case with the 1976 original, other critics were more cautious. The choice of play for 1977 was apt, what with Stratford celebrating its twenty-fifth year on one side of the Atlantic and Queen Elizabeth II observing her Silver Jubilee on the other. What better reason for presenting *A Midsummer Night's Dream* as a masque from the court of Elizabeth I? Nevertheless, the end result still troubled some reviewers, among them Gina Mallet of the *Toronto Star*:

> This is the first *Dream* I have seen which is dominated by the rustics' own show. Usually it's Bottom, adorned in the ass's head, who steals the show. Sometimes it's a bitter-sweet beauty and the beast encounter between Bottom and Titania. Here, however, the worthies suck up all the attention. Alan Scarfe is a gently whimsical and naive Bottom who dreams of love with the Queen and is at once funny and touching; the Snug of Bernard Hopkins, the Quince of Rod Beattie and Starveling of Frank Maraden all project an earthy simplicity that is irresistible.
>
> Upstairs, as it were, everyone is highly neurotic. Barry MacGregor and Maggie Smith double in the roles of Theseus-Oberon and Hippolyta-Titania, but beyond the announcement of that fact there is little to differentiate the characters. MacGregor plays both as a chairman of

the board, apt for the dull Theseus but far too bland for the emotional Oberon. Maggie Smith looks like a carbon copy of Elizabeth I and acts that way, too—fine steel tempered by wit but rarely softened by tenderness. The disappointment is that she makes Titania such a mope. There is not even an erotic twinge when she falls in love with Bottom; she appears merely to find comfort in stroking his furry head.

Miss Mallet was happier with Jack Wetherall, finding he had the makings "of a charming, fuddle-headed Demetrius", and with Martha Henry, who "if derailed from the laugh track could be a heart-wrenching Helena". Lewis Gordon's Puck she found to be a "pantomime dame":

"The oddest thing about this production is that as an idea it seems so foolproof and complete. Just how and where the life went out of it cannot be assessed immediately."

However, the following afternoon saw the opening of one of the season's palpable hits—Ibsen's *Ghosts*. It was the production that introduced Margaret Tyzack to Stratford audiences and that helped silence nationalist complaints about her presence in the Festival Company. Gina Mallet suggested that of all that summer's Stratford performances, Margaret Tyzack's portrayal of Mrs. Alving was the one all young actors should be certain to see.

Praise was virtually universal for a production that also featured Nicholas Pennell as Osvald and William Hutt as Pastor Manders. The reaction of Jay Carr of the *Detroit News* was typical:

Ibsen was a fierce moralist, and the Stratford production, staged by Arif Hasnain, projects this with urgency and freshness, with the conflict being framed by the invaluable Margaret Tyzack as a radiant Mrs. Alving, in burgundy gown and brave smiles, and the smugly monstrous Pastor Manders, who has a well-developed sense of everybody else's responsibility, but never allows his religion to stand in the way of his convenience.

Not that all the characters aren't solidly drawn. These include Marti Maraden's hard little climber, Eric Donkin's disarmingly folksy blackmailer, and Nicholas Pennell's Osvald Alving, the doomed son who sits drooling, idiot-like at the end, his brain rotting with the syphilis his promiscuous father brought into his blood.

Ghosts played to 87-per-cent capacity during its thirty-five performances, and some critics thought it the best production of the Festival. However, the production also sparked a behind-the-scenes drama which in turn renewed debate about guest directors. John Wood had originally been assigned *Ghosts*, but had been forced to withdraw because of prior commitments. The job was then given to Arif Hasnain, recently appointed artistic director of the Manitoba Theatre Centre and an artist who had worked at the Third Stage

Scene from the 1977 Festival stage production of Ghosts, *by Henrik Ibsen, directed by Arif Hasnain, designed by John Pennoyer, lighting by Gil Wechsler. Nicholas Pennell as Osvald, Margaret Tyzack as Mrs. Alving. Photograph by Zoë Dominic, courtesy of the Stratford Festival Archives.*

during the Gascon years. Rehearsals began at the end of March, and there was conflict between cast and director almost immediately. Margaret Tyzack was particularly troubled by Hasnain's introspective method and his insistence that his actors "discover" the right approach for themselves. She felt she and her colleagues deserved greater guidance from their director.

Phillips, fearing a repetition of the *Merchant of Venice* situation of the year before, was anxious to soothe both performers and director. He conceded privately that Hasnain's directing style was the opposite to his own, but he also felt that the cast should try to make the necessary adjustment. But Margaret Tyzack became more and more vocal about her unhappiness, complaining not only to Phillips and other company members but also—unbelievably—to the press. In interviews with some critics she warned that she was prepared to speak out publicly in response to any review that credited Hasnain with the success of the production—assuming, of course, that it was a success.

When *Ghosts* finally opened, some reviews did play down the director's contribution while acclaiming the performances. The experience shattered Hasnain. The situation also distressed Phillips. Unlike Glassco a year before, Hasnain had invited Phillips to look at his production in rehearsal. Phillips did so, discussed problems openly with Hasnain, and in his words "we reached agreement on what should be tried." Phillips sympathized with the frustration of some members of the cast of *Ghosts*. But he also hated to see visiting directors "on the firing line". Acutely sensitive to rumours that he and the cast had taken over full direction of *Ghosts*, he took the unprecedented action of speaking to some critics the evening before the opening to emphasize to them that *Ghosts* was still very much Hasnain's own production and that they were in for an outstanding theatrical experience.

The afternoon opening of *Ghosts* on June 7 was paired with an evening opening at the Festival Theatre of *All's Well That Ends Well*. Expectations were high for the latter production. For one thing, there was the nostalgic aspect: in this twenty-fifth season, the play was again being designed by Tanya Moiseiwitsch, who had designed the only previous production back in that historic first year in the tent. Secondly, the Royal Shakespeare Company's David Jones was back to direct. Admirers of Jones's 1975 *Twelfth Night* were confident that he wouldn't let them down.

However, the resulting production was more respectable than inspiring. A strong cast, which included Margaret Tyzack, Martha Henry, Nicholas Pennell, William Hutt, and Richard Monette, was unable to prevent this curious play from being its usual glum, unlikeable self. The production had its champions, notably John Fraser, who acclaimed the "joyous high spirits" of Martha Henry's Helena and praised David Jones for offering "uncluttered and unmolested Shakespeare". *New York* magazine's Alan Rich was also impressed:

> Helena, its heroine, is one of Shakespeare's wisest women, comparable to Beatrice and Rosalind in her wily insight into male foibles, superior to them both in her drive toward her goal, baffling only in that her goal—the weak and licentious Bertram—is so infinitely not worth the pursuing. David Jones...directed a beautiful performance, full of lights and shadows; Martha Henry and Margaret Tyzack

...dominated, but Richard Monette as the Falstaffian swindler Parolles also did a commendable job.

On the other hand, most playgoers would probably have sided with Rich's veteran colleague, Elliot Norton of the Boston *Herald-American*, who admitted that he was tempted to shout "Get on with it" during the performance. "The pace is so slow that at times the most patient play-goer is apt to find himself—or herself—wondering if this comedy, which ends well, will ever end."

Canadian director Eric Steiner's production of *Miss Julie* was the Avon's June 8 première. It attracted the lowest audiences of the season, chalking up only 65-per-cent capacity over its twenty-three performances. Earnestly staged by Steiner and misguidedly performed by Domini Blythe as Julie and Douglas Rain as the manservant, Jean, it emerged as a dry and lifeless piece of theatrical taxidermy. What was so inexplicable was an almost total lack of sexuality in a production that should have been seething with sexual repression and hysteria. The production's one virtue was the strikingly angled set, a triumph in ultra-realism, designed by Daphne Dare, the person who also had designed Phillips's celebrated 1971 production in Britain.

However, memories of the *Miss Julie* disaster were erased a few hours later with the blockbuster première of *Richard III*, featuring Brian Bedford in the title role, with direction by Robin Phillips, costumes by Daphne Dare, and music by Louis Applebaum. This was destined to be one of the most truly historic productions ever to surface at Stratford, and some playgoers with long memories confessed that it was superior to the legendary Guthrie-Guinness version of 1953.

The opening tableau was striking. With the balcony stored behind the scenes, the Festival Theatre stage became a dark, oppressively empty expanse, which gradually was taken over by shifting shadows of a doom-haunted court. Max Wyman of the *Vancouver Sun* was typical among critics who were mesmerized by the astonishing impact of Richard's first appearance.

Bedford's Richard is a small, crouching, spindle-shanked man. His concave chest and wide shoulders, curved and tapering to his skinny waist and hips, give him the threat of a hooded cobra. His rimmed eyes are blinking, restless, anxious, unexpectedly choleric. His mouth is vicious and tight, curved down, unforgiving. Nothing about him is soft. He limps, and yet there is about him an unstoppable energy. He has a withered hand in a black leather glove, yet he's a swordsman better than most. He paces like a crippled animal, hunched, restless, bitter, pouncing without warning. "Off with his head" becomes a mere aside.

This was not the charming monster inherent in so many portrayals of Richard III. But it was equally enthralling. The production carefully orchestrated its effects, eschewing spectacle until a remarkable coronation scene, which offered a special kind of horror in the sight of this warped and stunted creature groping his way up to an oversized throne and then squatting there like a repellent mockery of divinely anointed kingship.

There were the three awesome encounters with the three queens. Margaret Tyzack's mad Queen Margaret hurled forth her imprecations in a scene rendered all the more gripping by two remarkable devices: the fact that Bedford's Richard ignored her with chilling indifference, and that at the same time the use of sound amplification for her speeches caused them to echo back in grim portent of things to come. Maggie Smith's bereaved Queen Elizabeth emerged as a genuinely tragic figure, fighting to salvage the last remnants of her shattered family. As for Martha Henry's Anne, she helped supply some of the most sexually charged moments of the production as she was perversely wooed by Bedford's Richard over the corpse of the father-in-law he has just killed.

Several critics focussed on one of the most characteristic aspects of a Phillips production—his passion for detail. Commented Maureen Peterson of the *Ottawa Journal*:

> There is not a single scene that does not bear the stamp of the director's attention. Characters on the fringes of the story seem to have been rehearsed as principals. Stephen Russell and Joel Kenyon, as Richard's thugs, to name just two of the literally dozens in the cast, dispatch George, Duke of Clarence, in his cell as if this were the pivot of the story. . . . Every spoke of the wheel is sturdy and equal to the next.

Alan Rich had expressed doubts about Phillips's *A Midsummer Night's Dream*. He had no reservations about *Richard III*, finding it

> entirely brilliant, wonderfully uncoiled around the breadth of the Festival Theatre's thrust stage, its centre splendidly filled by the quietness of Bedford's delivery, and with a battle scene—armored men and draped horses ringing the acting area with jets of fog arising mid-stage—that has to be the finest staging of combat I've yet witnessed.

Robert Cushman, a critic who had followed Phillips's career since its beginning in Britain, declared that Phillips had

> flowered majestically at Stratford. . .his production of *Richard III* ranks with the finest Shakespeare I have ever seen. Richly spectacular (gorgeous Plantagenet costumes, caparisoned horses, flights of arrows in a battle fought not faked), it is never overblown. The text is taken literally, both as a ritual—with Miss Tyzack a fearsomely crazed choric Margaret still roaming about in battledress as she mentally

Scene from the 1977 Festival stage production of Richard III, *directed by Robin Phillips, designed by Daphne Dare, music by Louis Applebaum, lighting by Gil Wechsler. Martha Henry as Lady Anne, Brian Bedford as Richard III. Photograph by Zoë Dominic, courtesy of the Stratford Festival Archives.*

relives the Wars of the Roses—and as psychology. Mr. Bedford's opening soliloquy is full not of actorish glee, but, as the lines suggest, of corroding resentment. He enters through the audience and, with his hump to us, surveys the set: one man against the world. It is this solitariness—which rises to a dapper tense eroticism in the seductions of Anne and Elizabeth—that wins attention and even, though the production is exact and unsparing in its depiction of tyranny, respect. It seems fitting that he should impale himself on Richard's sword having whispered "My kingdom for a horse" in agonised wonder: all that for this.

Richard III was the kind of production worth preserving in some form, and this might have happened had not nationalism once again reared its head. CBC Radio proposed to commemorate the Festival's twenty-fifth season with a stereo version of the Stratford production. Because it viewed the production as an historic one, it naturally wished to use all members of the actual cast. However, the plan was sabotaged by the Association of Canadian Television and Radio Artists, which exercised its power over CBC programming by refusing to grant work permits to Maggie Smith, Margaret Tyzack, and Brian Bedford. ACTRA refused to accept the argument that this was not a new production for radio, but rather a momentous stage production worthy of preservation. It also ignored the fact that the three foreign stars were already in Canada, courtesy of its sister association, Equity. Instead, it proceeded to fan the flames of resentment even more strongly when its president, Donald Parrish, suggested that if the CBC were that anxious to do a Stratford production of *Richard III*, it could easily replace Bedford, Tyzack, and Smith with understudies. On grounds of principle, the Festival could not submit to ACTRA's blackmail. The radio version was shelved; ACTRA by its intransigence had denied several dozen bona fide Canadian performers the extra income that would have been due them had the CBC proceeded. Not for the first time, and certainly not for the last, did Stratford Company members find themselves at odds with their nationalist brethren. One of the most outspoken was company member Pamela Hyatt, who fired off an open letter to Parrish, denouncing him for his statements.

"I cannot believe the gibberish that appears to be moving out of your mouth and into print. You state that Brian Bedford, Maggie Smith, and Margaret Tyzack—the British stars of this production—can easily be replaced by their Canadian understudies for CBC's taping. Dear God, Donald, what utter tripe!" In the letter, she also chastised her stage union, Actors' Equity, for being too preoccupied with nationalism, saying the last Equity meeting on this issue "was so revolting I almost upchucked. The screaming egomania and tasteless attitudes evidenced by many of Canada's well-known actors shocked me." In a subsequent interview, Hyatt termed ACTRA's action chauvinistic and ignorant, charging it was dominated by "a very vocal, well-organized minority in Toronto—many of whom cannot be properly called working professional actors". Meanwhile the stage production was to top the Festival Theater attendance, grossing $756,000 and playing to 93.7-per-cent capacity.

Phillips capped his opening week with *The Guardsman*, Ferenc

Molnar's beguiling comedy about a jealous actor who tests his wife's fidelity by posing as an amorous army officer. The Avon run was a near sell-out, with attendance reaching 98.6 per cent of potential over twenty-nine performances. The production was also significant because it established Maggie Smith and Brian Bedford as a superb comedy team, which in turn proved to be a potent box-office commodity in the years ahead.

Admittedly, there were threats of an early shipwreck for this pairing the previous winter when Phillips had directed them in a dry-run production of *The Guardsman* for the cavernous Ahmanson Theater at the Los Angeles Music Center. Bedford and Miss Smith were uncomfortable with the size of the house and feared disaster for the type of intimate production envisaged by Phillips. After the run had opened and Phillips had left Los Angeles, they began to broaden the comedy. Those who saw the production at this point were to report that Maggie Smith was slipping back into the mannered excesses that had blemished her career prior to her association with Stratford. Halfway through the run, Phillips slipped back unannounced and was enraged at what he saw on stage. Versions of what happened backstage were soon to become part of the Phillips mythology: Phillips himself was later annoyed by reports that a furiously slammed door caused $1,000 damage. What is certain is that Maggie Smith and Brian Bedford were so shaken by the extent of Phillips's anger that they wondered whether they would make it to Stratford that summer. Reflecting back on the incident, Phillips admitted that he was cross. But he had also discerned the explanation for what had happened:

> With people as marvellous as Megs and Brian, there is always a reason if they're that naughty in a show—it was the desperation of trying to fill that house with a very fragile piece. It was an absolutely monstrous house, and if I was angry it was because I was deeply upset at what I was seeing. It was Maggie at her worst. But one had to see why she was doing it. She was trying to get that subtlety a thousand miles off to the seats. When we got back to the Avon, we started again and of course they were magnificent.

Some critics had reservations about Phillips's direction of this final opening-week offering. Gina Mallet, for example, felt the production tended to amble rather than to bubble. In contrast, Alan Rich felt he had ended a hectic week by attending "a little jewel, a perfect leavening for night after night of resolutely uncut classics". However, there was considerable agreement concerning the comic chemistry created by the pairing of the two stars. Commented Gina Mallet: "When on stage together, Bedford and Smith merge life into art and the art of acting into the roles themselves. They contest each other for every laugh, trying every now and then to catch the other off balance, in the very way their other selves, the Actor and Actress, struggle for supremacy in their little comedy.''

It had been an exhausting, artistically uneven, but ultimately exhilarating week. Such was the post-mortem verdict of critics. Gina Mallet did deplore the lack of strong male actors in a company dominated by world-class actresses, and concluded that the season had yielded no ensemble acting to rival that of Hirsch's *Three Sisters*:

> However, it says something about the general level of the acting and productions this year that the disappointments only slightly diminish the achievements. The happy impression is that Phillips now has the measure of the Festival and is trying to use it in the broadest possible way to meet his own ambitions, the aspirations of theatre in Canada and the needs of audiences which come from all over North America.

The raves continued to pour in. ''There is more good theatre just now in a backwoods Ontario town than in any of the world's theatre capitals,'' wrote Martin Knelman in *Saturday Night* magazine. ''A company to match the best in the English-speaking world,'' declared Ronald Bryden in *Maclean's*. ''We have seen productions and performances to make our own National Theatre tremble,'' asserted Britain's Jack Tinker. The time was clearly ripe for Phillips to push his next big plan, one that had been taking shape in his mind since the days when he was running Greenwich. Phillips and board president John Heney unveiled the scenario at a press conference in late July. The Festival board had unanimously approved a proposal which, in Heney's words, would ''radically alter the future of the Stratford Festival and ultimately have an influence on all Canadian theatre''.

At the heart of Phillips's grand plan was a new facility to be called Stage One. This was a building that would be constructed behind the Avon Theatre on property already owned by the Festival and that would house a drama school, an experimental theatre, training facilities for directors and designers, and ultimately a TV and film studio to record festival productions for the world market.

Also announced were three-year contracts for fifty members of the Festival Company and a new playwrights' project under which six Canadian writers would be hired to do new works or adapt classics for the Festival's various stages.

Phillips's remarks at the press conference were enthusiastically applauded by company members, and glossy brochures outlining the Stage One project were handed out. What was lacking was any detailed information on how much it would cost or how it would be financed.

Phillips was the latest in a succession of artistic directors to be troubled over the Festival's difficulty in fulfilling the second key directive of the Festival's charter. The first—"to advance the development of the arts of the theatre in Canada"—had, in his view, been achieved. The second directive—"to provide facilities for education and instruction in the arts of the theatre"—was quite another matter, and he told the press conference that this had become "an urgent, imperative issue".

He argued:

> [it] has been apparent to those who not only understand this theatre's function and stature, but also concern themselves about its future that there are several major gaps in our structure. We are deficient in the key areas that have always represented the very heart of the Stratford Festival: training and communication. The future rests in understanding one's priorities....This single building, Stage One, will allow us to look with boldness and imagination into our own future.

The educational side of the scheme represented yet another attempt by a Festival artistic director to solve a nagging problem. Stratford was already providing on-the-job training for younger actors, but this was, in Phillips's words, "training provided on the run, in and around rehearsals and productions". Stage One offered the boldest solution yet, although it was also evident such a plan could pose a direct challenge to Montreal's National Theatre School.

However, the revolutionary aspect of the Stage One idea was found in its futuristic vision of a Stratford Festival capable of harnessing the new technology. Even in the days when Phillips was running his little theatre in Greenwich, he talked about the need for film and television facilities. In Stratford, these ideas took firmer shape. "Are we running the right kind of theatres any more?" he kept asking. "How can we continue to fulfil our artistic commitment and also safeguard our future? Twenty years from now, will people still be able to drive down the 401 to our plays?"

When Phillips had agreed to a new five-year contract the season before, he had asked for the board's support in establishing a film and television centre and for a facility that would also provide more suitable quarters for Third Stage presentations. He had floated the idea publicly at a businessmen's banquet in Toronto. Now he had received the green light, and at his Stratford press conference he asked his listeners to share his vision with him:

> A quarter century ago, Stratford, with an act of daring and imagination, created the theatre of the future. But the world changes swiftly, and that future must constantly be re-defined: Stage One will be prepared to meet the new future of technology.

At just the time when the feasibility of touring is becoming prohibitively costly, technology is providing more and more advanced means of reaching new audiences: films, TV, video cassettes. We want to link our resources of talent with the potential of the communications media. Stage One will make this possible. (On June 22, 1977, the Stratford Festival welcomed its seven-millionth visitor after 24 years, but an audience of seven million is merely a modest-sized one for an hour of prime-time television.) We repeatedly get offers, both from the CBC and the Public Broadcasting System in the United States, to record our productions; we feel very strongly, however, that we want to experiment with the methods of media recording, and we want to do those experiments on our own ground, at Stage One.

It was a bold and exciting concept—one that was to seem more and more valid as the years passed—but it never came to fruition. The price tag for Stage One in its entirety could have been as high as $15 million. Within two years, the Festival would be hitting rough financial waters. The project went on indefinite hold, sparking rumours that Phillips was furious with the board for letting him down. "That's incorrect," recalls one former board member. "Robin was a visionary, but he was also a realist. He understood the plan wasn't feasible at this time."

However, there was also no doubt that Stage One frightened some Stratford-based board members in the breadth of its vision and that they were not anxious for it to go ahead. They feared erosion of the Festival's home base, which had been the cornerstone for twenty-five years. They were suspicious of the growing number of board members from larger cities outside the Stratford area. "There was terrible polarization," recalls one governor of the day, "and this geopolitical thing could create genuine difficulty. Whether they were prepared to admit it or not Stratford members were not 100 per cent comfortable with the way the Festival grew and developed under Robin. They felt it was getting away from them." Stratford governors were also to be apprehensive about another pet project of Phillips's: establishing some kind of performing presence in Toronto.

Two plays opened on the Festival Theatre stage in mid-August. Marigold Charlesworth's production of *Much Ado About Nothing* was a major failure. Robin Phillips's production of *As You Like It* was to become one of the major triumphs of his regime.

Much Ado proved a particularly unhappy experience for many of those involved. Again, Phillips was anxious that a Canadian direct this play, and Marigold Charlesworth was one of several people approached. Phillips was impressed by her track record, which included six years directing plays on the challenging stage at Ottawa's National Arts Centre. Furthermore, he was conscious of a disturbing degree of male chauvinism in Canadian theatre when it came to top jobs, and he was acutely aware that a woman had yet to direct at the Festival Theatre. The signing of Charlesworth signalled his determination to alter this situation.

Phillips was to contend afterwards that Marigold Charlesworth had mastered the troublesome Festival stage with remarkable ease. Nevertheless, there was considerable friction at rehearsals over the director's approach to both play and company. There was particular tension between Miss Charlesworth and Martha Henry, who felt the production was wrong-headed in its dramatic interpretation. In addition, performers felt they were being treated like a jobbed-in cast. "This approach mangled any possibility of exploring a play on a true company basis," said one performer.

The reviews were devastating, with only Martha Henry emerging relatively unscathed. The Toronto *Globe and Mail*'s new critic, Bryan Johnson, said that Miss Henry's Beatrice "wove a thread of sheer excellence which tied together a rather frayed *Much Ado About Nothing*". Johnson felt that Alan Scarfe's Benedick was no match for her—that he was "as much Beatrice's equal as Marty Feldman is that of Maggie Smith".

Gina Mallet detected the "stink of formaldehyde" in the production and complained of "an unhappy melange of accents and mannerisms". She also suggested that the production was an insult to Stratford's reputation:

> When lutes and viols summon our attention; when a graceful dance makes a full stop to the evening; when entrances become mini-pageants or steps from a ballet; when lines are treated with a trudging literalness that forces the life from a play; when character is trodden down by plot, and language overcome by shenanigans—then we are in the presence of embalmed Shakespeare, a theatrical form which debases the playwright much the same as pidgin English debases the language.

Miss Mallet was not enamoured with *As You Like It* either, suggesting that the experience was akin to a Mozart opera being jazzed up by Leonard Bernstein. Other critics were far more favourable. *As You Like It* played to 93-per-cent houses over its fourteen performances in the late summer and fall of 1977, and when revived the following year for twenty-two performances, it played to 98.4 per cent of capacity and chalked up a staggering $472,055 at the box office.

The production was notable for its visual beauty. British designer Robin Fraser Paye's late-eighteenth-century setting was inspired by the water colours of Thomas Rowlandson. The centre balcony had been replaced with a gnarled but magnificent tree in silvery blossom. The cast was stunning: Maggie Smith as the banished Rosalind, delectable in her first trouser role for Stratford; Jack Wetherall moving to new prominence within the company as Orlando; Domini Blythe as Rosalind's faithful cousin Celia; Brian Bedford in an extraordinary performance as a rueful but charitable Jaques; Bernard Hopkins as a rotundly sardonic Touchstone. The production was a beguiling amalgam of the visual and the musical (with Berthold Carriere's fine score helping fix the mood), emerging finally as an exquisite watercolour fixed in the timelessness of the imagination.

Noel Coward's *Hay Fever* was the Avon's autumn attraction. Directed by Phillips, designed by Daphne Dare, and featuring Maggie Smith and William Hutt as Judith and David Bliss, it predictably played to capacity houses over its fourteen performances. However, some critics felt that the production lacked unity, and that several performers lacked control. Cited as a major offender was Maggie Smith, who was back to her old, bad comic excesses. Hutt was credited with the most controlled performance and the one closest to Coward's sensibility.

The season had proved a spectacular success. With a full, twenty-two-week schedule at both the Festival and the Avon theatres, the final box-office tally stood at 88 per cent of capacity, with five of the ten productions topping 90 per cent. Total attendance of 504,963 marked a slight decline from the 1976 figure of 518,421, but box-office grosses reached $4,237,106, as opposed to $3,714,798 the previous year. Fund-raising activities produced $410,000. Meanwhile, Phillips and his colleagues had been keeping a tight lid on expenses. In spite of inflation, production costs rose modestly from $2,915,963 in 1976 to $3,128,997 in 1977; operating and maintenance rose from $724,594 to $745,016; and administration expenses actually dropped from $494,916 to $399,580. By the end of the fiscal year on October 31, the Festival could report a net income for the season of $471,249 and an accumulated surplus of $599,710. It was an astonishing achievement, but it was also one that was not to be repeated.

Mid-term Report

"I can whip myself up to keep others charged and buoyant," Robin Phillips once declared, "but each time I'm left a little emptier." The accuracy of that self-appraisal was to be borne out by the end of 1978, but when the year began, Phillips's Stratford reign was at its peak, and it seemed that nothing—absolutely nothing—could go wrong.

Phillips's most visible achievement in the eyes of the public was what had been happening on Stratford's two stages. In both volume and variety, his output as a director had been staggering. It had also been popular with ticket-buyers. By the end of his third season, Phillips had directed fourteen productions. His predecessor, Jean Gascon, had taken seven seasons to direct sixteen. As for Michael Langham, he had directed eighteen plays in the course of thirteen shorter seasons. It had not been Phillips's intention to load so many productions onto his own shoulders, and certainly the numbers would have been fewer had he been more successful in securing guest directors. But even with more help in directing, his output would still have been formidable. Phillips was in many ways a workaholic. He also believed it would be sloughing off his responsibilities as Festival head if he didn't direct a reasonable number of productions. Moreover, he was acutely aware of cost, which is one reason he was so enraged by John Hirsch's suggestion that his main purpose in directing so many shows was in order to inflate his own income.

Scene from the 1977/1978 Festival stage production of As You Like It, *directed by Robin Phillips, designed by Robin Fraser Paye, music by Berthold Carriere, lighting by Gil Wechsler. L.-R.: Domini Blythe as Celia, Bernard Hopkins as Touchstone, Bob Baker as Le Beau, Maggie Smith as Rosalind. Photograph by Robert C. Ragsdale, a.r.p.s., courtesy of the Stratford Festival Archives.*

"Robin was not only a brilliant artistic director," recalls one board member, "he was a bargain. By doing more and more shows himself, he saved us money."

Indeed, Phillips's sense of fiscal responsibility endeared him to those board members who still cringed at the memory of the horrendous over-runs in budget which had occurred at Stratford in some earlier years. Although total budgets did increase substantially during the Phillips years, they were consistent with expanded activity and supported by realistic income projections.

Board members were to look back with awe on Phillips's financial performance. "He had a genius for figures and for stretching a dollar to the last cent," recalled one. "Unlike some artistic directors he never believed he had the right to demand the moon and that marketing would sell anything. Robin had this curious, old-fashioned notion about the importance of responsible budgeting and keeping down costs." One project close to Phillips's heart was staging the Benjamin Britten opera *Death in Venice*. He ordered a cost projection, and when he discovered the venture would cost $1 million, he gave up the rights. "He said the Festival couldn't afford it, and the decision was typical of his incredible financial responsibility."

Part of the prevailing Phillips mythology was that he was constantly at war with the board and that he blackmailed and manipulated its members into giving him what he wanted. It was a rumour that deeply disturbed him. "There is no way I can dump on that board," he has said. "It's a total myth that I was constantly at war or that I made unreasonable demands. Indeed, if I were to list people who were important to me, the names of my first two presidents, John Killer and John Heney, would certainly be there." There were tensions, however, and they were to increase during the final phase of the Phillips regime, when the very future of the Festival seemed in jeopardy. Furthermore, there was always apprehension among some board members, particularly those based in Stratford, over Phillips's expansionist plans, and over his reluctance to waste time socializing. "Let's face it," observed one long-time governor. "Some of the Stratford people wished the Festival was still an eight-week event. The more it grew, the more the locals feared a loss of power."

However, for most of Phillips's reign, experienced board members discounted the significance of the friction, arguing that it was part of the give-and-take relationship that existed between any artistic director and his board. Phillips could be a master politician when it came to selling the board on a scheme, but he also respected the board as final authority. One board member recalled: "The board was never asked to make a commitment without being fully aware of what that commitment was, but Robin would never stay in the room for the vote. He was absolutely meticulous. He never took the line of, 'If you don't do this, I'm out.' His attempts to resign were always triggered by exhaustion."

Phillips's relationship with the board marked one area in which he made an impact. Even more significant, however, was his relationship with his staff, from the lowliest usher to the most senior member of his acting company. "The people in the building were devoted to him," recalls Nicholas Pennell. Barry MacGregor, who was company manager, said Phillips always had time for ordinary staff members. "He knew everybody on staff and what everybody did. He astonished people with so many facets of knowledge. He could do things most artistic directors couldn't do. He could actually sew costumes or dress a wig."

What struck those who worked for Phillips was the incredible energy he generated. Urjo Kareda found that Phillips had "an uncanny power" to make people give of their best:

> It was a very intense, high-spirited sensation. It was like being part of a close-knit family, a feeling intensified by our being together in this tiny city. Robin's hold wouldn't have been so powerful if we all hadn't been excited by our work under him, but he had this incredible shrewdness about how to run all parts of a theatre. He had the ability to choose talented people in all kinds of departments and to

inspire them to do their best. The festival under Robin was a highly custom-made machine.

Kareda had never encountered a director who worked better with actors, and by 1978 the loyalty of the vast majority of company members was unqualified. They accepted the fact that he could be tough and terribly demanding. Max Helpmann, the Australian actor who gave some of his finest performances during the Phillips regime, was once asked to describe his mercurial young artistic director. Replied Helpmann: "He's a genius—a fascist but a genius." Some perpetual Phillips detractors outside the organization would make comments about an artistic director who had a finger in every pie—even to the point of personally putting the trim on his actresses' dresses. But company members like Marti Maraden saw this as an example of caring:

> I owe Robin practically the biggest debt I owe anyone. In 1974, when I was playing a small role in *Love's Labour's Lost*, he recognized what he thought was some promise. He brought me up gently, giving me important smaller roles one season and graduating me to larger ones the next. He always stood by me and he always believed in me.

Miss Maraden was not an actress who viewed Phillips through rose-coloured spectacles. She felt she was luckier than some of her young colleagues who, in her opinion, had been pushed too rapidly into more taxing assignments only to find themselves unable to cope emotionally or professionally. And in 1977 she raised eyebrows when she told *Maclean's* magazine: "He knows just how to keep actors guessing. There's a lot of the bastard in Robin. He's *very* wicked." Queried about the comment six years later, Miss Maraden remained unrepentant. "That's exactly what I meant to say. However, I've always accepted the fact that you can't have democracy in a theatre. It simply doesn't work. Secondly, people don't understand that you can get cross with a person, call him wicked, and still be terribly fond of him."

She felt that Phillips had a particular knack for making fledgling members of the company feel important:

> In a crowd scene, he had the gift of making each person in the crowd feel he was a living, breathing human being. He spent extraordinary amounts of time working out tiny bits of character business for each person. He was always worrying that people in a crowd tended to lose their identity.

William Hutt was struck by Phillips's strategy of illuminating a play by examining one particular moment of it:

> What he was seeking was the sort of precision which required that we examine every moment for its reality. Some of the detailed things

which Robin was doing—details in terms of his direction, for example—were intended to illuminate not just minutes of time but seconds, and if an audience was perceptive it could see what Robin, the play, and the company—these three elements put together—were all about. During rehearsals he tried and tried to induce, perhaps even seduce, his actors into a realization of the connection between two particular lines.

Company members repeatedly argued that if Phillips was authoritarian, he was authoritarian in the right way. Some actors were frightened by him. Barry MacGregor was one of the many who were not:

> He didn't intimidate me. He never frightened me. I knew he could make me do what he wanted, because he had this immediate ability to size up an actor and how he could best relate to a character. Yet at the same time he maintained a calm atmosphere of the most incredible freedom. He preferred to start with a blank sheet. He wanted an actor to make choices.

(However, it could be a different story when Phillips was overworked or ill. Nicholas Pennell had a graphic insight into what this could mean when he was rehearsing *Private Lives* for Phillips later in the season. "Robin was ill and it was alarming. It was shocking to be in a rehearsal period at such a time, because when the beam, so to speak, was not working, you were terribly aware of its being cut off.")

The winter and spring of 1978 were deemed by many to be a peak time for the Stratford Festival. Urjo Kareda had advice for a recently arrived colleague: "We all have to realize that Robin is the star of this place. Accept that, and we'll get a lot done." Yet teamwork was very much a part of the Phillips regime. "He was never hard-line," recalled Douglas Allan. "It was nonsense that he surrounded himself with yes-people. In truth, he despised them. He wanted honest reactions. Yet, there's no doubt that his own enthusiasm and descriptive abilities had such a contagious effect that you wanted to support him."

Phillips could be a master psychologist. "He could have an extreme effect on women," was the recollection of one staffer. "He engendered loyalty and love. He created this effect of vulnerability that made one want to protect and mother him." Douglas Allan recalled Phillips's willingness to take the rap when something didn't work. "He never tried to hide behind his ego. He never tried to blame someone else when a mistake was made. If wrong, he always took the total blame." Furthermore, Phillips was accessible to people with problems at all hours of the day—and night. Worried actors would call Phillips at home in the middle of the night and he would tell them to come right over. Recalled Nicholas Pennell: "I can't think of one member of the company who didn't go to Robin's house at least once at three in the morning when he needed help and had to talk out a problem.''

However, the image of Camelot was not total. Zoe Caldwell suggested to *Maclean's* magazine in 1977 that visiting the company was like visiting a Communist country. '' 'How are you?' I say, and everyone replies, 'I'm-very-happy-and-Robin's-a-genius.' '' Some younger company members who had received initial encouragement from Phillips were later to feel that he would play favourites and then get bored with them; other performers saw this as a sour-grapes response from people obsessed with the need to be continuously "stroked, patted on the back and praised".

Some senior company members who were intensely loyal to Phillips felt his own loyalties were sometimes misplaced. "He was an attractive human being," recalled one actor. "He was always touched when people professed loyalty and devotion to him, and he reciprocated in kind. But sometimes his loyalty was misplaced. There were those who were regarded as special members of an inner cabinet, yet it was inevitable that a person like Robin would attract some people less than greatly talented." Douglas Allan felt that in some ways Phillips was too accessible, with the result that people took advantage of him. "The board expected too much of him. So did members of his staff and company. He needed people to have faith in him, but he ended up coping with demands and responsibilities over and above the call of duty."

But there were times when Phillips's extreme secretiveness left colleagues muttering in frustration, times when he kept important plans as well as looming problems to himself. "He was secretive by nature," recalled one senior staffer, "and it could cause problems for various departments. People could be begging for important information, but he simply wouldn't provide it until he was ready. It was part of his personality."

There were those who felt the euphoria that Phillips generated tended to conceal serious organizational problems: "It was like being on an extraordinary high which ultimately had to crash," recalled one close colleague. "In the process, people were used badly." However, Douglas Allan saw the situation in a different perspective. "Robin's big error was to fail to ensure that the board gave him a general manager he could work with and trust."

Such was the character of the Stratford Festival under Robin Phillips midway through his reign. If there were rumblings, they were subdued. The energy and enthusiasm remained high. "Working for Robin," Urjo Kareda once remarked, "is an act of faith." But it was faith that seemingly worked miracle after miracle. Or, as Nicholas Pennell phrased it: "With Robin's energy, enthusiasm, and passion, you felt you could do anything."

1978

In an unprecedented early move, Robin Phillips had announced his 1978 season before the 1977 one even opened. The plans proved somewhat premature. By the time 1978 actually arrived, three of the plays—Shakespeare's *Troilus and Cressida*, Goldoni's *La Locandiera*, and Euripides' *The Bacchae*—had vanished from the scheduling, and others had been added. Nevertheless, Phillips's revised season was still awesomely ambitious. It would include six Shakespeare plays: a revival of 1977's *As You Like It*, the first Festival production of the gory *Titus Andronicus, The Merry Wives of Windsor, Macbeth, The Winter's Tale,* and *Julius Caesar*. Other major productions would include John Whiting's *The Devils*, Leonard Bernstein's *Candide*, a new version of Chekhov's *Uncle Vanya* by Canadian playwright John Murrell, a risky one-man show by Barry Collins called *Judgement*, a dramatization of the love letters of Héloïse and Abélard, Noel Coward's *Private Lives*, and two new works: *Haworth: A Portrait of the Brontës* by Maggie Smith's playwright husband, Beverley Cross, and *Devotion*, a commissioned Canadian play by Larry Fineberg. All this was scheduled for the Festival and Avon theatres, but in addition the Third Stage was to reopen with three more new Canadian works: Tom Cone's *Stargazing*, Larry Fineberg's new treatment of the Medea story, and Sheldon Rosen's *Ned and Jack*—plus, as a final fillip, four playlets by Samuel Beckett.

It added up to eighteen productions in a season extending from June 5 to October 14—a dramatic change from the two plays offered in a tent for six weeks a quarter of a century before. "Thor's hammer strikes again!" muttered one disgruntled member of a Toronto alternative theatre community, which had decidedly mixed feelings about the increasing amount of activity occurring at Stratford under Phillips.

Productions were in rehearsal by the New Year, and Phillips was back working an eighteen-hour day. Nevertheless, he found time to launch a public debate with the Canadian government over its arts-funding policies. The event that triggered Phillips's ire was the decision of Secretary of State John Roberts, the federal minister responsible for cultural policy, to award Ottawa's National Arts Centre a special $1.1 million grant to enable it to create a new resident theatre company that not only would perform at the NAC, but would also take to the road with productions in both English and French. The operation was to be headed by Phillips's Stratford predecessor, Jean Gascon, and its funding had come out of a special government allocation earmarked for projects that would strengthen national unity. The effect of this special allocation would be a total federal subsidy for the Arts Centre of more than $10 million for the forthcoming fiscal year.

Phillips considered it unconscionable for Ottawa to show such favouritism with direct grants to the Arts Centre at the same time that it was maintaining restraints on the Canada Council, the independent agency responsible for funding other theatres. In an interview with Canadian Press, Phillips made headlines across the country by describing the federal government's conduct as shameful, unforgivable, and presumptuous lunacy. He made it clear that he was speaking on behalf of Canada's theatre community in general, and not indulging in special pleading for Stratford. "Ottawa," he asserted, "is getting far too much money at the expense of all the other theatres; it really is a shameful distribution of finances, and I think it's extremely unfair."

He argued that someone had to speak on behalf of smaller theatres because many of the latter feared they would receive no funding whatsoever if they complained publicly. He took particular exception to press reports that labelled the Arts Centre operation a new national theatre company, and recalled that Gascon had once tried to apply that title to Stratford. He said he had dropped the name when he took over the Festival because

it's not the national theatre and never will be. The national theatre of Canada is the theatre of the nation, coast to coast. This country is far too big to say we are going to have a national theatre in Ottawa. It may be where all the politicians are, and I think it is shameful and a real disgrace that this should be happening when the Canadian Opera Company and the National Ballet don't have a home.

Phillips's blast didn't please John Roberts. It also provoked a rebuttal from Donald MacSween, the National Arts Centre's Director General. MacSween accused Phillips of inaccuracy in his statement, and denied that the government was supporting the Arts Centre at the expense of other theatres. MacSween argued that Roberts had managed to secure money for specific purposes of national unity—money that would otherwise not have been available for the Canada Council or for other theatres. Phillips, although emphasizing that he had no quarrel with the National Arts Centre and applauding the idea of a permanent acting company there, nevertheless stuck to his guns in a letter published in several Canadian newspapers:

> I am angry that the Secretary of State has seen fit to fund one theatre so extravagantly while ignoring the legitimate needs of so many others. In fact, I am angry that the Secretary of State has seen fit to do any funding at all. The Canada Council is the agency best equipped to handle funding of the arts. It was established for this purpose and it has been doing the job effectively for many years. I object to the manner in which the Secretary of State has stepped in and in effect taken over the Council's function. In so doing, he has threatened the growth and perhaps even the survival of many worthwhile, struggling performing arts organizations. The allocation to the National Arts Centre is not being made over and above normal allocations to the Council. There is only so much government money available for the arts. The fact that the Council has had its funds cut back is, therefore, not at all surprising. It is a logical move to fill one hand by taking from the other. This is the gist of my argument and my objection. As I said, my quarrel is not with the National Arts Centre. It is with the way the Centre, and the rest of us, are being used.

For the first time in its history, the Festival had been drawn into a major public argument about government cultural policy. The incident reflected Phillips's conviction that Stratford should be playing a more significant role in the wider Canadian stage community and that when other theatres were in trouble, the Festival had a duty to use its enormous power and prestige to redress a wrong. It was not the last time he would find himself playing an activist role in shaping government cultural initiatives. His growing concerns in this area constituted a rebuttal to those who doubted the depth of his commitment to Canada's artistic life.

Again, opening week was marathon time at Stratford, with eight plays premiering over four days. But there was a further change in the form of a "Gala Shakespeare Revel" which actually launched the 1978 season on June 5 at the Festival Theatre. (Unlike the earlier attempt at a gala in the mid 1960s, this one preceded any play premières.) It was Phillips's attempt to find a solution to the problem of an opening-night audience that was more interested in the social aspect than in the play being presented. To be sure, there had been nothing during Phillips's regime to match the notorious occasion during the Gascon era when an impeccably tailored but totally inebriated first-nighter actually threw up in the aisle of the Festival Theatre. Nevertheless, Phillips felt his company deserved a more alert and attentive audience for an opening play than it normally received. As one Festival staffer confessed: ''The Gala is just to get the socialites out of the way so we can get down to serious theatre.''

The event was a two-hour grab-bag, featuring members of the Festival Company doing bits and pieces of Shakespeare (Phillips joined Martha Henry for a scene from *The Merchant of Venice*), plus appearances by Canadian Opera Company and National Ballet members. The Gala proved entertaining, and an appropriate mood of celebration prevailed. A similar event would launch the 1979 season as well, but it was to be the last. There were grumblings from first-night dignitaries and many board members, who felt that a first night demanded the actual presentation of a play. Phillips deferred, while continuing to contend that his solution was a sensible one and that the board had been silly not to retain it. ''The problem was that it left the VIPs in a cleft stick. They felt guilty about indulging in the social side that night and not staying on to see any plays. It was obviously more than they could bear.''

The serious business of play-making began the following afternoon at the Avon Theatre with Phillips's production of John Whiting's *The Devils*. Based on Aldous Huxley's *The Devils of Loudon*, it was inspired by a real-life case of demonic possession afflicting a group of nuns in seventeenth-century France. Despite a powerful production approach, complete with savage design concepts from John Pennoyer and highly dramatic music by Berthold Carriere, the production was not an audience success, attracting only 53-percent attendance for its twenty-six performances. Phillips saw it as an excellent vehicle for Martha Henry, who delivered a lacerating performance as the sexually tormented Sister Jeanne. Nevertheless, critics tended to be lukewarm. Richard Eder of the *New York Times* felt that Phillips had stressed all the faults of what was already a ''swollen rhetorical work'', and was particularly incensed with the production's attitude to the character of the womanizing priest, Grandier:

He dresses up Nicholas Pennell as Grandier in a white soutane that looks like a hussar's great-coat. With his robe, his blond hair and beard, and his melancholy, he is made into a Christ-like figure, and this is plain nonsense. The lighting, picking out each figure like cheap religious art, the dramatically asymmetrical poses, the quavering voices all help turn a poor play into a dreadful opera.

The opening of *The Merry Wives of Windsor* the evening of June 6 at the Festival Theatre introduced an important new figure to Stratford audiences. Born in Montreal and trained in England, Peter Moss had remained overseas to work as associate director of the Crew and Phoenix theatres. He came of a generation of actors and directors who used to swear that they would never work at a large Establishment theatre like Stratford. But Moss wanted to return with his family to Canada, and, well aware of Phillips's reputation, he sought an interview in 1976. A half-hour meeting between the two turned into a four-hour conversation. "We got on fantastically well," Moss recalls. "It sounded as though he was doing exactly the things I wanted to do." Subsequently, Executive Producer John Hayes called him and offered him a position as an assistant director. Moss was back in Canada and working at Stratford by February 1977. "Robin tossed me into the deep end with *Richard III*. It was trial by fire, but I passed." Later in the year, Moss was appointed as a director with special responsibility for the Third Stage, but, as it turned out, he was to make his major impact at the Festival Theatre.

The Merry Wives of Windsor was not the most desirable vehicle with which to debut. Moss thought it a fiendishly silly play, and suspected that if it hadn't been written by Shakespeare it would never be done. However, his production proved to be an often engaging treatment of an impossible comedy. Moss and designer Phillip Silver chose to set the play, not in the Elizabethan period, but in early Restoration times, when the Puritan influence remained strong and when the appearance of frayed remnants of the bygone Cavalier period, in the persons of a down-at-heels Falstaff and his cronies, helped underline the social upheavals that had been occurring. In approaching *Merry Wives* as an essentially middle-class play—perhaps the only genuine middle-class play Shakespeare ever wrote—Moss attempted to create something more than a one-joke entertainment about the tricks played on an aging knight. Most critics displayed a charitable kindliness towards *The Merry Wives*, although they were hard-pressed to conceal their dislike for the material. And some critics were jubilant, among them the *New York Times*'s Richard Eder, who applauded Moss for "a lovely, unforced and continually revealing production".

Eder had praise for the entire cast: Alan Scarfe's "funny and rounded portrait" of the jealous Ford; Domini Blythe and Jennifer Phipps, who played the two wives "with a sense of comedy rather than farce"; the Slender of Tom Wood, who played this extinguished suitor as "a kind of Woody Allen without desire". However, Eder devoted most attention to the Falstaff of William

Hutt, because this was the performance which gave the production its true sensibility:

> All these characters are funny but they have a reasonable human purpose as well. There is an underlying dream quality to *Merry Wives* and magical glints of it appear throughout the production, culminating with a bamboozled Falstaff stumbling about Windsor Wood wearing a deer's head. It is simply a comic sight: William Hutt's bearded face with antlers on top. Then he puts up both hands and does indeed look like a stag, one that covers its mouth in regret for having been human and having said foolish things.
>
> Mr. Hutt is a funny Falstaff and an affecting one too, but with the lightest of autumnal touches...he is tired, poor and at the end of his devices....Mr. Hutt plays Falstaff old, with self-knowledge, rather than self-pity. It is a self-knowledge that holds him to his jokes and outrageous hopes, not like a man deluded, but like one who gives full measure to his role in a life that he knows to be a delusion.

Merry Wives predictably was a big seller, playing to 96-per-cent attendance over its four-month run.

Uncle Vanya, which opened the afternoon of June 7 at the Avon, proved to be one of the season's outstanding events. It also launched a significant new chapter in the Festival's relationship with the Canadian writing community, and showed the influence that Urjo Kareda was now playing in artistic planning. "Urjo was crucial to this entire period," Phillips was to say later. "After the actors and Daphne [Dare], if any one person played a major role in the success of these years, it was him." Phillips had a genuine commitment to new scripts. He believed new work was a particularly desirable challenge for a company that would otherwise be involved almost completely in material from the classical period. However, Phillips and Kareda also believed that Canadian playwrights could help the Festival fulfil its classical mandate as well by providing new versions of foreign-language classics. Many existing translations were of inferior quality, and a good case could be made for filtering Chekhov or Goldoni through a particular Canadian sensibility. John Murrell, an accomplished and sensitive dramatist, struck Kareda as being ideal for such an assignment. The critics agreed when they saw Murrell's version of *Uncle Vanya*.

"Well, it's true," rhapsodized Gina Mallet in the *Toronto Star*. "A good Canadian adaptation of a classic is a boon. John Murrell's new adaptation of *Uncle Vanya* opened yesterday at the Avon Theatre, and almost immediately the spirit of the Stratford Festival rose. It is both lucid and idiomatic and plays easily and naturally." Martin Knelman in *Saturday Night* felt that Murrell had caught exactly "the subtle comedy and melancholy ripeness of this great Chekhovian work".

Scene from the 1978 Avon stage production of Uncle Vanya, *by Anton Chekhov, in a new English translation by John Murrell, directed by Robin Phillips and Urjo Kareda, designed by Daphne Dare, music by Berthold Carriere, lighting by Michael J. Whitfield. L.-R.: Helen Carscallen as Marina, Marti Maraden as Sonya, Martha Henry as Elena, Max Helpmann as Professor Serebriakov. Photograph by Robert C. Ragsdale, a.r.p.s., courtesy of the Stratford Festival Archives.*

Kareda shared co-director's billing with Phillips, who respected his colleague's remarkable insight into Chekhov. "In one sentence," Phillips once remarked, "Urjo could totally change our conception of what we should be doing." The production featured some of the Festival's most high-powered talent: William Hutt as Vanya, Brian Bedford as Astrov, Martha Henry as Elena, Marti Maraden as Sonya, and Max Helpmann as an old scrounge of a professor. Gina Mallet felt that some of the casting was capricious and some of the timing quirky, with the result that farce tended to win out over comedy. In contrast, American critic Martin Gottfried hated everything he saw that opening week—except *Vanya*. The latter, he wrote,

captures the beauty of Chekhov's dramatic orchestration. It grasps the sublime grace of his compassion, his ability to deal with boredom without being boring; to make the extraordinary out of the ordinary. Brian Bedford's bewildered Astrov, Martha Henry's flirtatious Elena, and Marti Maraden's frustrated Sonya are but three subtly drawn characters in a perfect ensemble.

Vanya ran for thirty performances, and attracted a respectable 85.6-per-cent capacity.

The Festival Theatre's evening performance of *Macbeth* opened with a clever device. The house lights remained up as the three witches and assorted Scottish soldiers assembled on the stage of the Festival Theatre. Then, as the witches looked ominously upwards, the house lights went down, presumably to signify the descent of darkness on the soul of man. It was a promising start. Unfortunately, many critics felt that darkness had descended on the soul of the production as well. Nothing Robin Phillips did at Stratford provoked as much controversy as his production of *Macbeth*, which struck many as the most somnambulistic attempt at Shakespeare to plop onto a Stratford Festival stage in years. Starkly designed by Daphne Dare and starkly staged with a degree of stylization which, in the view of many first-nighters, weighted the entire occasion with lead, it seemed to reaffirm the superstition that *Macbeth* is a play that jinxes even the best directors.

It did have its admirers, one of them Max Wyman of the *Vancouver Sun*. His comments approvingly conveyed the mood of this production:

> The supernatural magic and mystery that lie at the heart of the play and its plot—the witches, the appearance of Banquo's ghost, the hallucinatory dagger, the moving of Birnam Wood to Dunsinane—are given short shrift. They are, it seems, nothing but figments of the heated imagination of a man who is somehow fatally wrong in the head.

In place of "misty supernaturalism" Wyman found "contemporary theatrical trickery of a high (and somewhat distracting) order". Wyman applauded the "steely coolness" of a production reminiscent of Ingmar Bergman's *The Seventh Seal*—a production that went for the "psychological jugular" and was "far more intent on the conflicts that exist within Macbeth and his lady than in all the external trappings". However, Wyman also noted an even more significant characteristic. This, he declared, was "a Macbeth stripped to the spirit, a dissection of blackness. Austerity is the keynote. This is a Macbeth with the sharp, *stark simplicity of classic Japanese theatre*."

Wyman later discovered from conversations with Phillips and his actors that a great deal of attention had in fact been paid to Japanese theatre over the previous three months. Occupying a prominent place in Phillips's office was a massive picture-and-theory book on Japanese theatre. The aim was not to copy such theatre literally but to benefit from its concern for simplicity and austerity, to see it as a means to an end. Phillips's aim was clarity, discipline, and proper focussing of energy. "The more you dig into the plays, the more you think, Jesus, every syllable ties up with the other. It's the most extraordinary pattern of intellect, very difficult to get one's head around." Phillips's concern that his actors be ruled by concentration, discipline, and order was such that he sent two individuals on patrols around the corridors beneath the Festival Theatre stage during performances to make sure that everyone was concentrating on the product—no quiet card games were allowed in this situation. "The way we are trying to work, we must have everyone's total energies focussed on the stage," he told Wyman, stressing that he had been bursting with pride at the opening-night performance of *Macbeth*. "This is a very brave company. Their response has been extraordinary. They have great faith. . . .Some scenes don't work— I'm aware of that, and I don't know how to answer their questions about them because I can't find the answers for myself yet. But we give as much excitement as we can, with as much as we've got."

Unfortunately, most critics didn't share this enthusiasm. There was considerable praise for the Lady Macbeth of Maggie Smith. There was also general agreement about one stunning theatrical moment: the murder of Banquo occurred in sudden darkness on an uninhabited stage—yet in what seemed only a few seconds of time, the lights came up to reveal a noisy banquet in progress. But one striking scene was not enough to salvage the production.

Gina Mallet wrote:

Very stirring and enormously theatrical as this scene is, it is almost unique in the show. For three hours, Shakespeare's fastest-paced, hottest-blooded tragedy, packed with the most violent and bloody poetry, proceeds at a snail's pace. [Douglas Rain's Macbeth] never shares anything with us. He simply marches on stage and delivers his speeches as if talking to himself, chucking away some of the most splendid words Shakespeare ever wrote. I don't believe his face changed expression once. He not only put off communication with us, but worse, with his wife, who is played by the luckless Maggie Smith. [She] does her best in her reformed Stratford style—hands still, voice sincere—and comes over just as the old saw says, as the perfect wife. But this is a macho play and Lady Macbeth cannot hold it together any more than she can wash the blood from her hands.

Some critics such as Martin Knelman considered the production Phillips's biggest Stratford failure. Phillips himself cheerfully acknowledged that his production had enraged many critics, but also maintained to the end of his regime that it had been undervalued. He could also point to sales figures that once again demonstrated the imperviousness of *Macbeth* to criticism. The play had more performances (thirty-nine) than any other Festival Theatre offering that season, yet it managed to chalk up a remarkable 97.3-per-cent attendance, which translated into box-office revenues of more than $800,000.

As with *Uncle Vanya*, Phillips shared co-directing billing—this time with Eric Steiner, the gifted young Toronto director. The innovation was to continue to the end of Phillips's Stratford tenure. The type of co-direction differed from play to play on the basis of what parties were involved. When Kareda joined forces with Phillips to stage a Chekhov play, the situation was, in Kareda's words, "a shared feedback system" in which Kareda had "input on casting and conceptualizing". In the case of Peter Moss, Phillips was able to rely on the ability of a trusted and experienced colleague to take over the majority of rehearsals when necessary and thereby help ease his work burden. With other colleagues, such as Steiner, Phillips was again seeking solutions for the problems of new directors working at Stratford. He had remained troubled by Bill Glassco's experiences when directing *The Merchant of Venice*. He was aware that for a quarter of a century many visiting directors had faced a chronic problem of winning acceptance from the company, and that outside of Stratford the opportunities were rare for them to tackle classical works. Above all, there was the challenge of the Festival Theatre with its thrust stage and 220-degree audience arc.

"It was and is a fiendishly difficult theatre," Phillips was to recall. "To make it work requires skill, knowledge, love, and a great deal of collaboration among all involved in a production." His invitation to younger directors was essentially one of "come and learn". Suggestions that his directing colleagues were no more than glorified coffee-fetchers angered him. Instead of listing them in the general credits on the printed program as "assistant directors", he elevated them to co-directing status:

> They had to have shared billing with me. To be sure, with most productions I did most of the talking and made many of the final decisions, but that doesn't diminish in any way the importance of the people who worked with me. With *Macbeth*, Eric Steiner's involvement was marvellous. It was invaluable. It was only right to share billing as director. It helped ensure them the respect to which they were entitled. Hopefully, as well, it enabled them to get a feel of what the company was like without being shafted. It also allowed actors to get to know some of these people, to acquire a feeling for who and what they were.

Musicals became part of the Festival package in 1978, with Leonard Bernstein's *Candide* premiering at the Avon Theatre on June 8. The Stratford production was based on a reshaped version prepared by Harold Prince, and it ended up playing to 86.5-per-cent capacity. Reviews, however, were generally lukewarm. The production had been staged by Lotfi Mansouri, general director of the Canadian Opera Company, and there had been problems in rehearsal. Many connected with the production felt that the most valuable input had been supplied by choreographer Brian Macdonald, who mounted some glittering musical numbers and who also ended up supervising the transfer of the show to the Festival Theatre for four performances.

Richard Eder of the *New York Times* found Edward Evanko "a sprightly and attractive Candide", and admitted that Caralyn Tomlin managed an "agile coloratura" as Cunegonde. However, Eder found the production only "marginally competent" and charged that some scenes looked "like the production of a high school whose budget has been voted down". American critics, schooled to the Broadway tradition of impeccably mounted musicals, tended to be harsher to *Candide* than did their Canadian counterparts. Martin Gottfried was devastating:

> To Leonard Bernstein's *Candide* goes the distinction of being the season's biggest embarrassment. Stratford's talent for professional patina evidently doesn't extend to Broadway musicals. Your garden-variety dinner theatre would have ejected this shabby orchestra and gauche performance. Nowhere is Stratford's plush campiness more apparent than in this production. . . .

Gottfried was not enamoured either with *The Winter's Tale*, which opened at the Festival Theatre the evening of June 8, but here he was very much in the minority. This production, co-directed by Robin Phillips and Peter Moss, was hailed by *London Free Press* critic Doug Bale as "the sleeper of the year". Myron Galloway of the *Montreal Star* deemed it a "ravishingly beautiful production", which succeeded by making the most of the play's fairy-tale elements. Featuring Brian Bedford as the jealous King Leontes, newcomer Margot Dionne as his wronged Queen, Martha Henry as her loyal friend, William Needles as the courtier Camillo, and Graeme Campbell as the braggart Autolycus, it provided some of the strongest ensemble acting of the season.

Some critics were bothered by the late-nineteenth-century setting. Others felt that the production took the title too literally and that the end result was excessively wintry. (Richard Eder in the *New York Times* applied the adjective "Arctic".) But it found a big fan in Bernard Levin, the waspish critic for the London *Sunday Times*, who came to Stratford that year "prepared to make allowances" and then found himself forced to back down on his "patronising presumptions" after experiencing "some of the most beautiful and interesting Shakespeare I have seen for many years". He was struck by the naturalness of *The Winter's Tale*:

The conversational tone, as though the play had been rehearsed for years without losing its freshness, was impressive, and even more so was the use made of anachronism; in Act IV, for instance, it seemed quite natural for the courtiers, snatching a break in a corridor while the denouement they are describing is being finally sorted out upstairs, to light up the cigarettes that they had clearly been dying for while on duty.

The *Guardian*'s Michael Billington thought the production as good as any he had seen of a difficult play:

Its first advantage is that it sets the Sicilian section of the play in a Tsarist court of poker-backed formality, evening dress and potted plants. Immediately, this establishes an atmosphere of repressive (and repressed) autocracy. It also provides a tremendous frisson when Brian Bedford's dry and contained Leontes launches into venomous sexual jealousy in which words like "sluiced" and "slippery" leap out of the text....Bedford, with his wire-drawn smile, plastered-down hair and nutmeg-grater voice, also confirms what his Richard III showed last year—that he is the best classical actor not seen on the English stage.

Levin was struck by Martha Henry (an actress new to him), describing her as "an elemental force in her furious loyalty" to the Queen. He also admired the final scene. "And when the statue stepped down from its pedestal, before a huge bank of candles, lit one by one from tapers as we watched in rapture, the full force of the play's unmistakable redemptive message was felt." Phillips's determination to take chances with young new performers also reaped dividends: as Hermione, Margot Dionne established herself as a stunning new presence. Gina Mallet found her "a classic, chiselled beauty who manages to pull off the rare feat of making goodness attractive". Daphne Dare was responsible for the evocative pillared set concepts and the sumptuous costume designs. Louis Applebaum supplied the music, and in so doing contributed to one of the production's high points, Graeme Campbell's robust rendition of "When Daffodils Begin to Peer". *The Winter's Tale* was not a box-office blockbuster. Its 81.5-per-cent attendance was well below the whopping attendance figures racked up by *Merry Wives, As You Like It,* and *Macbeth*. But for most of those who saw it, *The Winter's Tale* was to glow in the memory as one of the most brilliantly realized offerings of the Phillips era.

British journalist Barry Collins's play *Judgement* lasted for only an hour and forty-five minutes, without intermission. By Stratford standards, it was brief, but that didn't make the experience any less harrowing, either for theatre-goers or for actor Richard Monette, who was its sole performer. The subject was cannibalism. The play was inspired by an incident that took place in the closing weeks of the Second World War when a group of captured Russian officers

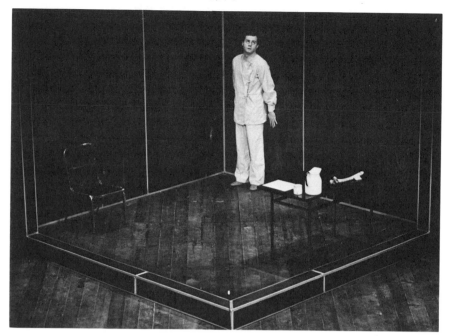

Scene from the 1978 Avon stage production of Judgement, *by Barry
Collins, directed by Robin Phillips, designed by Michael Maher, lighting
by Michael J. Whitfield. Richard Monette as Officer Vukhov.
Photograph by Robert C. Ragsdale, a.r.p.s., courtesy of the Stratford
Festival Archives.*

were locked in a cell and abandoned by the Germans. By the time
the Red Army arrived on the scene, only two of the officers were still
alive; they had survived by eating the flesh of their colleagues.

The play was a monologue, an account by the sane survivor of the
horrors of his ordeal and the appalling outcome. Phillips mounted a
cold and uncompromising production, trapped in a grimly institu-
tional set designed by Michael Maher. Monette, dressed in white
pyjamas, told his story articulately and with a minimum of emotion.
Some critics felt that the mood was almost too sterile; others felt
that emotional distancing was necessary because the real power of
the play rested in the words and their underlying philosophy, and
that there were more horrifying implications in the cool, rational
pleading of such a case than there would be in a display of
anguished theatrics. Monette's performance was an endurance test
as much as anything else. When Peter O'Toole had played the role
in Britain, he had read from a script. Monette memorized the entire
role—it took him more than three months to learn it—and in
performance was restricted to five basic gestures. Talking about
Judgement many years afterwards, Phillips paid tribute to
Monette's involvement and wondered at his own temerity in scheduling the play: "My goodness, what a huge risk it was when you look

back. I must have been crazy to attempt it." The play ran for sixteen performances through the summer, but by Stratford standards it was a major box-office disappointment, attracting less than 50-per-cent capacity.

However, *As You Like It*, which returned triumphantly on June 9, was the Festival Theatre's biggest hit of the season, playing to 98.4-per-cent capacity and earning $480,000 over its twenty-two performances. Max Wyman summed up the quality of the play in three succinct words. "It's a caress," he said. Most critics felt the same. Bernard Levin felt that in Maggie Smith's Rosalind he had seen "one of the definitive performances of a lifetime". Michael Billington was also enthusiastic. As he wrote in the *Guardian*:

> This was acting of an unaffected beauty that lit the comedy with a strange sadness. No question that Miss Smith's Rosalind was fathoms deep in love; witness her entranced walk around Orlando when she first sees him, her constantly buckling knees, her dreamy abandon. But it was also a performance of great wit (seeing Orlando for the first time when she's in male attire, Miss Smith instinctively covers her crotch) and a sad awareness that such a rapturous emotion must be transient. Miss Smith looked a picture (to be precise, a Gainsborough lady). More importantly. . .she pierces the heart.

During rehearsals for *As You Like it*, Phillips had discouraged Miss Smith from resorting to her more effective comic mannerisms in order to depict Rosalind's giddiness of love. "Be serious," he told her. "Don't try to make the audience laugh. Try to make them cry." She accepted this advice and, in the words of one admiring colleague, "she gave Robin exactly what he wanted and ended up being even funnier."

The other big accolade went to Brian Bedford for his remarkable Jaques. As Bryan Johnson declared in the Toronto *Globe and Mail*:

> Bedford could just pack up the Festival and take it home with him if ownership were established on stage. Twice already this week he has staked claim to being the best actor in Stratford, and his Jaques last night was still more dazzlingly captivating than the one he wowed us with last year. Some might argue, in fact, that he's made the melancholy traveller so charming by now that he no longer performs Jaques' function: to tartly undercut the sweet, pastoral Forest of Arden scenes. Even if that were so, it would take a grumpy purist to object.

The most puzzling production of 1978 was *Héloïse and Abélard*, which opened at the Avon Theatre on June 17. It proved to be little more than a platform reading by Ted Follows and Dawn Greenhalgh of poet Ronald Duncan's reworking of the celebrated twelfth-century love letters exchanged between Peter Abélard and his beloved Héloïse. The set was clearly borrowed from *The Devils*, which was sharing the Avon repertory, and the experience was grimly static and untheatrical. In view of the fact that the Festival was asking the same ticket price for this non-event as it was for such other, fully mounted Avon productions as *Uncle Vanya* and *Candide, Héloïse and Abélard* emerged as something of an audience rip-off. Nevertheless, it played ten performances during the season (with Roberta Maxwell and Jim McQueen also appearing on certain days) and drew a respectable 73.9 per cent at the box office.

Dominion Day weekend brought a significant event: the reopening of the Third Stage to the public with a new mandate emphasizing Canadian works. The aim was to provide a theatre where young directors could work with young writers, whose scripts were being developed by Urjo Kareda. *Ned and Jack*, a new work by Vancouver playwright Sheldon Rosen, opened on June 30, and Larry Fineberg's new version of *Medea* on July 1. Later in the summer, the Third Stage would house *Stargazing*, by another Vancouver writer, Tom Cone, and an evening of four short works by Samuel Beckett.

It was inevitable that Kareda was to become a key figure in the Phillips regime. His original basis for giving up a drama critic's post and joining the Stratford operation was, in his words, to help Phillips "plan things".

"I'm someone for Robin to bounce ideas against, someone for him to work with and talk to," he said in an interview during this period. "We discuss season plans, casting problems, production concepts, individual performers and their potential." Typical Kareda duties included reading and recommending the texts to be used for the Festival's Shakespearean productions, preparing lists of middle-range actors and actresses for Phillips's consideration, travelling to theatres in other parts of Canada "to keep in touch with what is going on", and simply sending out "idea balloons" to Phillips. Kareda was often to share the frustration of colleagues over Phillips's frequent secretiveness and—when he was under pressure or felt he was being attacked unfairly—his defensiveness. But Kareda was also forthright in his admiration, even though his views offended those members of the alternate theatre movement who had also viewed Kareda as their champion and who saw his move to big Establishment Stratford as a sell-out.

As Kareda told the *Globe and Mail*:

When you see the degree and loyalty of affection Phillips inspires in so many people who work here, you also realize that there's a lot of animosity and jealousy lurking about elsewhere. Anyone who draws such a strong positive response usually gets a fair deal of hatred as well. It goes with the territory. This has to be coupled with the fact that Phillips was an outsider coming in and there is as much of a ritualistic hierarchy of theatre here as anywhere else.

But I'll tell you one thing. One keeps hearing that he's supposed to be a tyrant and I can assure you I have absolutely no interest in working for tyrants of any sort. I've never seen this alleged despotic temperament. Of course he has tough decisions to make. . . .For the most part, though, he tends not to come rushing forth with answers but with sophisticated questions. He has incredibly accurate instincts and he understands Shakespeare better than any number of scholars or pseudo-scholars. Robin is one of the most deep-thinking, intuitive and generous men I have ever met, and he has my absolute respect. I would kill for him.

Kareda was invaluable to Phillips in many areas of the Festival's operation. But from Kareda's perspective, the most important feature of his job was the commitment he made to Canadian writers. New scripts were commissioned. All unsolicited scripts were read carefully. The commitment was fully supported by Phillips, who always believed that producing new Canadian scripts should be part of the Festival's mandate. Kareda forged particularly strong links with Western Canadian playwrights—John Murrell in Calgary and a group of outstanding talents associated with Vancouver's New Play Centre. (A further reason for looking westward was the continuing hostility and lack of co-operation of many members of the Toronto drama community.) Kareda made the acquaintance of several West Coast writers when he conducted a workshop in Vancouver. He also discovered some promising scripts, one of them *Ned and Jack*. He reported back to Phillips that the latter play was a wonderful vehicle for Stratford actors because of its quality of language and imagination.

Ned and Jack proved a positive beginning to the new Third Stage season. Rosen's play was inspired by the real-life friendship that existed between two remarkable men, John Barrymore and Edward Sheldon. The latter had been a respected American playwright in the early years of this century, but before he was thirty he was struck down by an appalling form of arthritis which was eventually to leave him totally blind and immobolized for the remaining half of his life. Yet, despite these terrible disabilities, Sheldon maintained a remarkable contact with the world he loved through friends and admirers. The play conceives for the audience one turbulent night in the relationship between Barrymore and Sheldon—the opening night of *Hamlet* in 1922, an event Sheldon is too weak to attend. In the small hours of the morning, a flamboyant Barrymore makes his entrance up the fire escape and through the French windows. Still in his Hamlet costume and armed with three bottles of champagne, he has come to celebrate. What follows is a session that moves from celebration to recrimination to despair and ultimately back to celebration.

In a script overflowing with dramatic tension and rich, evocative language, Rosen examined a crisis affecting not one but two remarkable characters. Canadian actor and director Sean Mulcahy, assigned

Scene from the 1978 Third Stage and 1979 Avon stage production of
Ned and Jack, *by Sheldon Rosen, directed by Peter Moss, designed by*
Shawn Kerwin, lighting by Harry Frehner. L.-R.: Alan Scarfe as John
Barrymore, Jack Wetherall as Edward Sheldon. Photograph by James
A. Hockings, courtesy of the Stratford Festival Archives.

to review the 1978 season for *Performing Arts in Canada* magazine, found *Ned and Jack* one of the three outstanding events of the
summer (the others were *The Winter's Tale* and *Uncle Vanya*).
Mulcahy was so fascinated by Rosen's play that he started looking up
every bit of information he could find about Edward Sheldon.
"When a play can do that for you, then it's got to be very good," he
pronounced. The most favourable critical response was reserved for
the text and for Alan Scarfe's bravura performance as Barrymore.
Jack Wetherall's Sheldon tended to be colourless, and Peter Moss's
direction was deemed sluggish. *Ned and Jack* played only ten

performances in the tiny Third Stage, to 78.1 per cent of capacity. It was to return in 1979 in a full-fledged production at the Avon. *Medea*, which opened the following afternoon, was not to be favoured with a similar endorsement, despite the fact that it surpassed *Ned and Jack* in attendance. Larry Fineberg's one-hour reworking of the Medea legend seemed pointless; the version was so scrawny and undernourished that it stripped the original not only of its psychological complexity but also of its narrative clarity. Patricia Idlette, an actress who had done good work for the company, delivered a trumpeting performance in keeping with director John Palmer's declamatory, sledgehammer approach.

Tom Cone's *Stargazing*, which opened later in the summer on August 25, also lasted only an hour, but the experience was far more enriching. The play, which had only six performances, tended to be undervalued. On the surface it was a comedy-drama about two brothers and their wives whiling away a summer's eve in Vancouver watching meteor showers from their sundeck. But what was really transpiring was a domestic *danse macabre*, which evolved into a probing examination of personal relationships and, more specifically, personal isolation.

Cone, a playwright with a musician's sensibility, didn't so much write this play as score it, with the four members of his star-crossed quartet working with bits and pieces of speech as fragmentary, yet as compelling, as the meteor showers. Thanks to the direction of the Vancouver New Play Centre's Pamela Hawthorn and the responsive work of four talented young company members—Bob Baker, Barbara Budd, Barbara Stewart, and Robert Ruttan—the production achieved the necessary blending of the emotional and the cerebral, and the right amalgam of melody, harmony, counterpoint, rhythm, and counter-rhythm.

Kareda saw the Third Stage as a potentially important forum for new writers. "It didn't have the curse of expectation that people had for the Festival and Avon theatres." Phillips shared this view, and also fought hard against what he termed "the deplorable tendency to equate the Third Stage with the third-rate". However, Phillips also believed that although the Festival should have a solid commitment to new Canadian plays, its very nature frustrated the fulfilment of that commitment. "The pressure on new Canadian works at Stratford is more than can humanly be expected of them— simply because they are surrounded by classics, by Shakespeare, Congreve, Wilde, and Chekhov." This concern was one big reason why Phillips was so anxious to find a Toronto home for the Festival. He didn't want anything elaborate, merely a modest playhouse which could serve as a home for new plays, safely distanced from the pressures of Stratford. Because of the resistance of some board members, the plan never materialized.

Meanwhile, as the Festival prepared to unveil its new-Canadian-play program, a major crisis had been developing behind the scenes. Phillips's drive and stamina had seemed doubly incredible because of a previous medical history that included a heart attack, a kidney removal, and an ulcer condition. At the start of the 1978 season, he had seemed in top form. By the middle of the month, as he was rehearsing Maggie Smith and Brian Bedford in *Private Lives*, he knew he was seriously ill. On June 20, Phillips announced that he had to undergo major surgery and that this would necessitate cancellation or postponement till future seasons of two productions he was scheduled to direct—the premières of Larry Fineberg's *Devotion* and of Beverley Cross's *Haworth*. A visibly ill Phillips continued with rehearsals for *Private Lives* but was finally forced to relinquish the final days of preparation to his co-director, Keith Batten. Before *Private Lives* even opened, he had flown to England to see the doctors who had treated him on previous occasions. They advised an immediate operation.

Phillips's illness received considerable publicity, and this cast a pall on a season which up to now had been so successful that it promised to break all previous box-office records. When *Private Lives* opened July 9 at the Avon, many in the capacity audience wondered if Phillips would be back next year. The apprehension was no doubt accentuated by the fact that this production of Coward's vintage comedy was deemed by many to be of near-classic quality. There was unhappiness over the performance of Andrea Martin—a skilled comedienne who had made a considerable reputation as part of the satirical Second City team—in the role of Sybil Chase. But there were few reservations about Maggie Smith and Brian Bedford as twentieth-century theatre's most celebrated warring couple or about Nicholas Pennell's accomplished work as Victor Prynne, the hapless creature whom Maggie Smith's Amanda was to marry and then abandon in favour of ex-husband Elyot (Brian Bedford).

Sean Mulcahy found the production a high-water mark of the season: "I had seen the play so many times, acted in it so many times, directed it so many times, that I wouldn't have thought I would be able to stay awake—but I reckoned without Robin Phillips." Mulcahy described the performances of Miss Smith and Bedford as "magnificent" and applauded Pennell for his comic expertise and for delivering "one of the best performances of Victor I've seen". *Private Lives* chalked up 100 per cent of capacity over its twenty-six performances. But, for a time, playgoers were wondering whether it would be the last Phillips production ever to play Stratford.

Phillips's surgery had proceeded satisfactorily in England. Nevertheless, while recovering at his parents' home, he dispatched a letter to Board of Governors president John Heney. It was his notice of resignation, effective in November. The news hit Stratford like a thunderbolt. Phillips himself declined to give reasons for his decision. The Festival board decided simply to mark time until Phillips's return, although it did acknowledge that his contract permitted him to invoke a four-month notice-of-resignation clause. Heney set up a special committee to meet Phillips once he returned from Britain and expressed the hope that some arrangement could be worked out so that Phillips would agree to stay. The one journalist who managed to make contact with Phillips at this time was Gina Mallet. In their conversation, he stressed that his recent surgery was not a factor in his decision.

Meanwhile, speculation mounted over Phillips's real reason for leaving. Inevitably, the most prevalent one was that he was indulging in a mere ploy to wrest more artistic concessions out of the board and that he was upset over the increasing probability of a delay in his Stage One plans. The theory was discounted by Festival officials.

What was certain was that the board was in an unenviable situation. Phillips's impending departure would leave little time to set up a new regime for 1979. To add to the uncertainty, Phillips himself had started outlining 1979 plans only a month before he had submitted his resignation. The *Stratford Beacon-Herald* sounded alarm bells in a July 18 editorial:

> Robin Phillips has done a great job for Stratford and the people of this community are indebted to him for his work here. We hope that he will soon be well and that he can be persuaded to carry on his work in Stratford for at least another year. In the meantime, the Festival is in a difficult position. If Phillips does not come back, it will be extremely difficult to find a man of his imagination, energy and dedication to replace him. Especially on such short notice.

The real explanation for Phillips's latest attempt to quit was the most obvious—although it was not one designed to satisfy those who preferred to believe that he was once more resorting to blackmail tactics to get his own way. The reason for this midsummer crisis was simply that once again Phillips had overextended and overexerted himself. He was tired. His state of mind came as no surprise to those who had talked with him over the past year about the toll which running a massive organizaton like Stratford exacted. By this time, Phillips had already gone on record as saying that Stratford should examine the feasibility of having an artistic director who was an administrator, and who didn't have to direct plays; privately he had confessed he would be far happier in some sort of ''resident director'' capacity which would free him of the onerous responsibility for the over-all Festival operation.

In late August, Phillips finally felt able to discuss the reasons for his resignation letter publicly. In an extraordinary interview with Bryan Johnson of the *Globe and Mail*, he said he was "simply going through a difficult period, a time of self-doubt". He had talked to other directors, among them the Royal Shakespeare Company's Trevor Nunn. "They say it's something everyone has to face. But it's really hell when you're going through it." He stressed that his doubts were "entirely artistic". Physically, he now felt "fine". But he hinted that his own personal evaluation of his work was far harsher than that of most critics. Asked if he thought the Festival was in artistic trouble, he replied:

> Stratford isn't. I am. It's a kind of crisis situation. I suppose the more you do, the more doubt you have. The really deep-rooted problems are the ones you inflict on yourself. Finally, you know better than anyone when you've failed. You know whether you're communicating with your cast. They may think you're communicating better than any director on God's earth, but you may not be. And you're the only one who knows for sure.

He talked candidly about his own uncertainties over whether to part company with the Festival or not. "It's true I didn't really want to leave. The resignation started off by saying, 'Listen, I've got to stop for a while, and I don't know when I can come back, so the only fair thing for me to do is resign.'"

By the time Phillips had come out with this probing piece of self-examination, he and the board had reached a compromise about his future. He would take a year's paid sabbatical in 1979, but would oversee planning and casting of the season before taking his leave. The aim was to have world-class directors staging the plays; without that assurance, Phillips said, he would not have accepted such an arrangement.

The sabbatical proved somewhat illusory. Phillips was back directing some plays at Stratford in 1979, and he was once again to feel caught on the Festival treadmill. Once again the board had been given a respite from the event it most feared—the departure of Robin Phillips. But the events that occurred during the summer of 1978 were the beginning of the end for the Robin Phillips regime. Phillips knew it; even though he wouldn't be leaving immediately after all, there was no way he would continue to be artistic director after 1980. His challenge over the coming two years would be to force the board to face up to the inevitability of his departure. The fact that the board was unwilling to do so was to have near-catastrophic consequences in 1980.

Meanwhile, the 1978 season continued its record-breaking progress. The two new productions opened during August at the Festival Theatre. *Julius Caesar*, which premiered on August 15, was assigned to one of Phillips's favourite Canadian directors, John Wood, with Susan Benson designing. On August 26, the Festival would finally take the plunge and unveil its first production in twenty-six seasons of Shakespeare's bloodiest play, *Titus Andronicus*. Brian Bedford was making his directing debut, and Desmond Heeley was returning for the first time in several seasons to design the production.

The two productions provided a resounding if somewhat controversial climax to the season. *Julius Caesar* would play to 89.6-percent houses over its fourteen regular performances and to 97.5-percent for its twelve school performances. Nevertheless, several critics hated it, among them Noel Gallagher of the *London Free Press*, who complained of the "phlegmatic apathy" of the playing. Still, Wood's unorthodox production did find some champions. Lyle Slack of the *Hamilton Spectator* found a "mystical" quality in the occasion and applauded Wood for his "imagination, improvisation, and daring".

Darkness lay like a shroud over the production. It was present when the conspirators plotted to murder their leader, Caesar. It hovered ominously in the background as the Mark Antony of Stephen Russell delivered his funeral oration. Even after the conspirators were vanquished and dead at the end, the darkness remained, ever more heavy and stifling, continuing to close in despite the apparent heralding of renewed peace and stability. Michael J. Whitfield was the lighting designer responsible for much of the production's brooding atmosphere, and his effort was complemented by composer Alan Laing's haunting sound effects— hysterical cries in the night, the distant slam of a dungeon door. The only true illumination came during the assassination of Caesar, and so great was the contrast that the white light in which the slaying was bathed seemed blinding and almost obscene; with the various conspirators plunging their daggers into the staggering body of Eric Donkin's Caesar, the event seemed as ritualized as an act of purification and as appalling as an act of desecration. It was a production of striking intimacy—highlighted by the daring device of having Antony deliver the funeral oration alone on stage without benefit of Roman rabble. It was a production that eschewed mobs; great events of history were subordinated within the dramatic context to character and psychology.

It was not a traditional approach to *Julius Caesar*, nor was it likely to be a widely popular one. Much of the acting was of exceptionally high standard. Slack was struck by contrasts in characterization:

> Brutus (Nicholas Pennell) is a petulant and self-important leader; Caesar (Eric Donkin) is an irritable old man; Antony (Stephen Russell) is loyal but without human depth; Casca, who strikes Caesar

first, is a stupidly bitter young man (though Frank Maraden makes him briefly likeable with a stupendously entertaining description of Caesar being offered the crown thrice).

Slack reserved his highest praise for the Cassius of Alan Scarfe:

> It is Cassius who is the most interesting, the most creditable, the wisest of the assassins; Cassius who alone understands the importance of murdering Caesar and the repercussions it will cause; Cassius who submits in the end to the puritanical judgment of Brutus with a sense of the fatal; Cassius whose humanity finally makes us wonder about him more than anyone else in the play. Scarfe details his acting with long, pregnant hesitations, hard, knowing stares and a confident gait. He phrases words with flawless understanding and shades emotions with refinement along a black and grey continuum. He makes Cassius forgivable.

There was little critical polarization about Brian Bedford's fine directing debut with *Titus Andronicus*. William Hutt, who gave a powerhouse performance in the title role of Shakespeare's tragically maddened Roman, was to say afterwards that Bedford should be congratulated not only for his gifts as a director but also for his accomplishment as an editor. A difficult and often unwieldy text had been trimmed into a tight, taut, immensely theatrical experience.

The play's stomach-churning brutalities remained: at least twelve violent deaths, the rape and mutilation of Titus's daughter, Lavinia (her tongue is torn out and her hands are cut off), and the final grisly scene which sees the villainous Tamara unknowingly eat a pie that Titus has prepared from the chopped-up remains of her children. How did Bedford manage to make all this palatable? Gina Mallet's *Toronto Star* review gave the answer:

> He has taken this Sam Peckinpah movie vehicle and rendered it, first, as a revenge story, taut as a rubber band, each cruelty built to its own climax, and then as a mirror for the fall of Rome, underlining the single moral to be drawn from the bloodbath—that when private loyalties are allowed to usurp public ones, there can be neither justice, peace, mercy, not to mention civilization.
>
> Bedford sets a brisk pace right away. I don't believe there's been a more exciting opening act at Stratford this year than that of a divided Rome welcoming Titus home from war. The atmosphere is thunderous with menace; Desmond Heeley's costumes boast a barbaric magnificence that banishes any petty emotion. William Hutt's entrance as Titus, bathed in the golden glow of the tombs of his fallen sons, is like the sun blazing before it is eclipsed by the moon.

Mallet also credited the company with "an uncommon virility" in performance:

Hutt reveals an unexpected tragic power as Titus, a great soul branded with insoluble bitterness. Alan Scarfe, too, has never been better than he is as Aaron the Moor, flaunting the oily charm of Iago. Paul Batten is noble and touching as Bassanius; Domini Blythe makes pain palpable as the helpless Lavinia. Max Helpmann is a touchstone of common-sense and human compassion as Titus's brother.

Titus played only nine performances and attracted only 65.7 per cent of capacity. But it became one of the most talked-about productions in the Festival's history and was to resurface in 1980.

Despite the turmoil and uncertainty caused by Phillips's illness and threatened resignation, the twenty-three-week season proved the most successful in Stratford's history in terms of attendance. A record 557,991 customers attended a total of 396 performances. Box-office revenues reached a new high of $4,636,502. Yet, an ominous financial note was struck at the annual general meeting on November 25, when retiring president John Heney reported a net loss from operations of just under $200,000.

> We are fortunate indeed to have a surplus carry-forward to offset this, but it is a grave reminder of the plight that we and other artistic organizations are in. We are caught in the middle of inflationary cost increases and frozen or reduced grants from government. We must find new sources of revenue and redouble our efforts in fund-raising.

Because of mounting financial anxiety, the minimum membership fee in the Festival Foundation was raised from $20 to $25.

It was amidst gathering financial clouds that the Festival began preparing for 1979 and Robin Phillips's penultimate season as artistic director.

·C·H·A·P·T·E·R · XXV·

1979

Robin Phillips's 1979 sabbatical proved at best to be only partial. He remounted yet another production of *The Importance of Being Earnest*, and directed the Festival's late-autumn blockbuster, *King Lear*, with Peter Ustinov. However, Phillips also took on a third directing chore when he found himself faced with the loss of Michael Langham, who had initially agreed to do the Festival Theatre's opening production, *Love's Labour's Lost*. Phillips had been banking heavily on Langham's return. For one thing, Langham was a distinguished former artistic director who, in Phillips's opinion, had been absent even in a "visiting" capacity for far too long. Secondly, Phillips was well aware of the legendary status of Langham's 1961 Festival production of *Love's Labour's Lost*, and he felt that Langham's mastery of this intricate and challenging comedy made him the best possible person to do it again.

However, when Langham's New York commitments made it impossible for him to come to Stratford after all, Phillips and Urjo Kareda took over co-direction of *Love's Labour's Lost* themselves. To be sure, Phillips was reducing his workload considerably in directing only three productions out of that season's fourteen. Nevertheless, his rehearsal schedules were such that he could not remain away from Stratford for any major extended period. After a six-week winter holiday he was back at work, and he was to admit later that, marvellous as his vacation was, he never really stopped thinking about the Festival and its problems. "It took the first three weeks to relax and the last three to gear myself up for starting again," he told Janice Lindsay in an interview for the *Canadian* magazine. "I was sitting on the beach with the complete works of Shakespeare. It's terrible to lie there and think of something that sorts out what's been worrying you in the text and not be able to look it up, so the Shakespeare goes with me everywhere. It's very boring for everyone else."

At the close of the interview, Phillips commented about the continuing pressures of the Stratford job:

> In Stratford I feel desperately cut off from the rest of the world. I miss things like the Victoria and Albert Museum in London. You didn't have to go often but you knew you could and when you did it was extraordinarily fulfilling. But it's not location. It's the nature of the job, really, and you can only do it for so long before you have to force yourself to stop, to live, refuel, feed on something rather than pouring things out all the time. I can whip myself up to keep others charged and buoyant, but each time I'm left a little emptier. So I've set a kind of deadline for myself to stop directing, just for a bit, and have a complete change of environment. I hope it won't mean leaving Stratford forever, but that will depend.

The 1979 season was not without its bold and adventurous aspects. Festival Theatre programming included *Love's Labour's Lost*, *King Henry IV, Parts I and II*, and—later in the season— *Othello*. The Avon season was notably catholic and innovative: a production of *Richard II* featuring three pairs of actors alternating as Richard and his nemesis, Bolingbroke; *Happy New Year*, a musical version of Philip Barry's *Holiday* with unpublished songs by Cole Porter; a new version of *Ned and Jack*; and that ever-dependable ticket-seller, *The Importance of Being Earnest*. Coming up later at the Avon was the North American première of Edward Bond's *The Woman* and the eagerly awaited *King Lear*.

Third Stage activity also looked promising: *The Taming of the Shrew*, the première of Canadian playwright Steve Petch's *Victoria*, and a new version of Federico García Lorca's *Yerma*. The season would impose a considerable load on Peter Moss, who was directing the two *Henry IV* plays, *Ned and Jack*, and—with Kareda —*The Woman*, while also overseeing Third Stage operations. However, the most striking aspect of 1979's directing roster was the preponderance of woman directors who had been lined up to help stage the season. They included avant-garde British director Pamela Brighton, who was now a resident of Canada, Kathryn Shaw and Pamela Hawthorn from the West Coast, Zoe Caldwell, and Frances Hyland. The line-up was in marked contrast to the continuing male-dominated nature of other major theatres.

Concurrently with planning the 1979 season, Phillips was bringing Stratford into a more active involvement in the wider Canadian theatre scene. The Festival was now a member of the Professional Association of Canadian Theatres, and Phillips startled delegates to the winter PACT conference in Victoria by showing up in person and taking a prominent part in discussions. Some hard-core representatives from the Toronto theatre community remained hostile, but other PACT members welcomed his input. "As soon as Robin started speaking," one said later, "we knew he was going to be an enormous asset to the association." Phillips's unhappiness over the federal government's special funding of the National Arts Centre had made him increasingly aware of the importance of government cultural policy in the country's artistic life. He became a member of a small PACT task force which was helping the Opposition Conservative caucus hammer out a policy on arts funding in anticipation of the next federal election and agreed to prepare the final PACT position paper on the subject.

The need for a better deal for the arts seemed all too evident by the end of a 1979 Stratford season that left the Festival with a deficit. Many Stratford regulars considered the season something of a "downer". They were conscious of a lack of stars—only a late-arriving Ustinov filled this category. They missed the opening-night excitement which permeated the 1977 and 1978 seasons. Yet, in many ways, 1979 was undervalued, on the basis of both its programming and its artistic achievement.

Thunderbolts and rain greeted the June 4 opening night, which, for the second and final time, was a special Gala performance. The theme was 1979's The Year of the Child. Guest performers included folk-singer Odetta, members of Les Grands Ballets Canadiens in scenes from choreographer Brian Macdonald's version of *Romeo and Juliet*, and the Ontario Youth Choir. (The latter so impressed Phillips that he decided Stratford should have its own youth choir the following year.)

The next afternoon it was down to business with the Avon unveiling of a rewritten version of Sheldon Rosen's *Ned and Jack*. Alan Scarfe repeated his bravura performance as Barrymore, but there was a new Edward Sheldon in the person of West Coast actor Jim McQueen. Gina Mallet had had reservations about the play a year before, but felt that the small-scale Third Stage might have inhibited its emotional scope. Now she found her reservations even more pronounced on seeing it again on the larger Avon stage. As she told her *Toronto Star* readers,

It is rare if not unknown to watch a play and gradually come to the conclusion that it would be far better as a one-man show. Yet that's the case with *Ned and Jack* . . . . [It] is only half a play in its present state, but cut to ninety minutes, with the character of Ned eliminated entirely, the result could be an actor's tour de force. In fact, it could be Alan Scarfe's tour de force if he were allowed to run away with the legend of the hard-drinking, wenching, despairing and surely magnificent John Barrymore, one of the most influential actors in this century. But as the play is, Barrymore gets all the best lines and all the laughs but he can never escape the chains of Ned.

Miss Mallet felt that, although Jim McQueen's performance was a distinct improvement over that delivered by Wetherall in 1978, the character was simply not credible. She also complained of the "funereal pace" of Peter Moss's direction.

Other critics were more positive. Audrey Ashley of the Ottawa *Citizen* felt that Scarfe's was one of the week's two outstanding performances (the other being William Hutt's Lady Bracknell). And Dave Billington of the *Edmonton Sun* was high on both play and production. He did, however, deem the opening a "qualified" triumph:

> I say qualified because the Toronto critics still hate the play....But most of the rest of the critics, including myself, loved the play.... Alan Scarfe's Barrymore is the best thing I've seen him do....Puffed with vanity, boozy and arrogant, he is also bitterly self-critical and dismissive of the importance of a stage performer. Yet beneath this there is a warmth and a love for the stricken playwright, a love which will not allow sentiment and self-pity to destroy Sheldon. Jim McQueen's Sheldon is the perfect match for Scarfe, as subtle as Scarfe is flashy and as quietly dignified as Scarfe is noisily self-destructive. The play's climactic scene is loaded with power....

Ned and Jack took in $61,882 at the box office, a figure representing 61.8 per cent of capacity, during its nine-performance run. This was by no means the worst box-office showing of the season, and Phillips was to remain an eloquent champion of the play, arguing that it proved that new Canadian drama could have a legitimate place in main-stage Festival programming.

Love's Labour's Lost, which opened the Festival Theatre season the evening of June 5, chalked up quite a different sales record, one that astonished Phillips and Kareda, who had feared a box-office problem. The production had been scheduled for forty-five performances through to November 2; with Langham directing, the risk of such a lengthy run for a difficult play seemed worth taking. Yet, without benefit of Langham and without benefit of imported stars, *Love's Labour's Lost* ended up doing 85-per-cent business and achieved record new sales figures by taking in an unprecedented $946,358 at the box office. For those Stratford-watchers who were bemoaning the lack of big international stars this season, the success of *Love's Labour's Lost*, with its dependable roster of veteran company members, constituted a formidable rebuttal. Further-

Scene from the 1979 Festival stage production of Love's Labour's Lost, *directed by Robin Phillips and Urjo Kareda, designed by Daphne Dare, music by Berthold Carriere, lighting by Michael J. Whitfield. L.-R.: Barbara Maczka as Katharine, Domini Blythe as Rosaline, Martha Henry as the Princess of France, Barbara Stewart as Maria; far right: William Webster as Boyet. Photograph by Robert C. Ragsdale, f.r.p.s., courtesy of the Stratford Festival Archives.*

more, the production itself earned general approval from the critics. Writing in *Saturday Night*, Martin Knelman found it "a handsome, mellow production of one of Shakespeare's most difficult and rarely seen comedies". Noting that the play's linguistic jests tend to intimidate a modern audience, Knelman said the production sought a "fresh view" by placing the story in the Bloomsbury period:

> Daphne Dare seizes the opportunity with costumes and a set full of autumnal elegance. The regular Company is shown to good advantage with strong performances especially by Alan Scarfe as the King, Richard Monette as his wily chief side-kick Berowne, and the magnificent Martha Henry as the Princess of France (even if she looks a little over-ripe for the part). I could have done without some of the campier effects in the low-life comic interludes, but even staying in a wheelchair, Max Helpmann as the hilariously pompous, beard-stroking schoolmaster walks off with the show.

Some critics saw Helpmann's performance as a spoof of Canada's eminent man of letters, Robertson Davies, who was reviewing the season for CBC Radio—but Knelman reported that Professor Davies, "who happened to be sitting next to me, was not among them."

Julius Novick, critic of New York City's *Village Voice*, was similarly impressed. (Novick had a special interest in Stratford that year since Robin Phillips was one of five directors appointed to the new administration of the Vivian Beaumont Theater in Lincoln Center—others included Woody Allen and Sarah Caldwell—as part of the latest attempt to make that beleaguered operation work. The Lincoln Center scheme was never to come to fruition.) Novick felt that the 1979 season was not one of Stratford's greatest. But he found his trip worth while because of *Love's Labour's Lost*. "Under the golden willow tree Daphne Dare has designed, Mr. Phillips and Urjo Kareda have staged a golden production," he wrote. Novick acknowledged that the production had

> sight-gags aplenty, but there is little of the desperate, frantic, irrelevant buffoonery to which this play drives most directors. I enjoyed particularly Frank Maraden as that pathetically grandiloquent grandee, Don Adriano de Armado, and Richard McMillan as the breezy peasant boy, Costard, but this *Love's Labour's* is an ensemble success, which is to say, a directorial success.

Love's Labour's Lost was not the only directing triumph that week. Peter Moss's productions of the two parts of Shakespeare's *King Henry IV* constituted one of the major artistic achievements of the season and firmly established the thirty-three-year-old director as an exciting asset to the Stratford organization. Not only did Moss approach the text with imagination and intelligence, he also again asserted his authority over the hazardous Festival Theatre stage. The productions opened on two successive evenings, and abounded in lively incident, clarity of narrative, and scalpel-sharp delineation of character. Yet, the ultimate vision was surprisingly dark and brooding. The production tingled with boldly contrasting images. On the one hand, there was the regal aspect, dominated by a majestic climax, with Richard Monette, as the newly crowned Henry V, clothed in regal blue and towering over his subjects. But Moss and his designers, Daphne Dare and John Pennoyer, were interested in a graphic depiction of the low life as well as the high life of Henry IV's England. The garments of many of the characters, like the lives they had been leading, were soiled and decayed. The scenes in the Eastcheap Tavern reeked of debased poverty, with Martha Henry, in a garishly brilliant cameo as a scraggly, pox-ridden Doll Tearsheet, even being required to vomit into a pail. What emerged from Moss's productions was not simply a vivid staging of a great Shakespearean chronicle play, but also a tragi-comedy with an uncompromising vision of human fallibility.

In his rave review of a "superb" Part I, the Toronto *Globe and Mail*'s Bryan Johnson reported on an evening of "pleasant" shocks. "Stephen Russell, who was mistaken for a cigar-store Indian at times last year, has made an amazing transformation as Hotspur. He stalks the stage like a great, glowering beast of prey, venting his rage in volcanic eruptions." Johnson was also pleased with the play's other "great" character: the corpulent Sir John Falstaff, who on this occasion was played by one of the company's least corpulent actors, Lewis Gordon. Johnson felt that Gordon's small but nimble presence was a handicap, but that the actor nevertheless succeeded. "Falstaff," he wrote, "is not so much the butt of jokes as a catalyst for them, and his cowardly behavior makes a strange kind of sense. Gordon has captured at least half these qualities and suggested the rest, no small victory for a thin man."

Critical praise continued following the première of the play's second part. Gina Mallet lauded Douglas Rain's Henry as

> the finest, most spine-tingling performance to be seen so far this year. ...Before our eyes, he picks up the smallish part of King Henry and inflates it into a starring role....He makes of the dying Henry an engrossing complexity, an ambitious, selfish, bitter man nagged by an uneasy conscience and haunted by the possibility that others are plotting to do to him what he did to Richard II.

Miss Mallet was struck by the power of the over-all acting. "Moss deserves a great deal of credit for inspiring or perhaps providing the environment for a raft of excellent performances, some from actors who have not had a chance to be much noticed or who have not seemed to have fulfilled their potential before." She had reservations about Gordon's Falstaff, arguing that the gallantry of his portrayal could not overcome a serious piece of miscasting. But, as compensation, she found an endearing performance of Justice Shallow by Cedric Smith, who played this dotty jurist "in the manner of an alert and slightly balmy bird considering the wonders of civilization as represented by Falstaff".

The stature of Moss's treatment of the *Henry IV* plays made their box-office failure all the more disappointing. The chronicle epics had always been hard to sell at Stratford, and 1979 proved no exception. Part I had been scheduled for forty-three performances with a potential gross of more than $1 million. It ended up selling only $535,795 worth of tickets and barely making 50 per cent of capacity. Part II fared even worse; with thirty-eight performances and a potential gross of $940,234, it attracted only 47.5-per-cent attendance and grossed $446,341. On some nights attendance in the 2,200-seat Festival Theatre dropped to as low as 10 per cent. For an organization that budgeted its seasons on a miniumum 75-per-cent box office, the showing of the two Henry plays had serious implications.

The Avon was also having its own box-office problems, and again a chronicle play was being cited as the culprit. *Richard II* eventually played forty-nine performances and ended up doing 60.8-per-cent business. (By contrast, the third go-around of *The Importance of Being Earnest* played to 88.5-per-cent houses over forty-two performances and grossed $80,000 more.) However, customer resistance to yet another chronicle play was probably strengthened as a result of the nature of the production. There was, of course, logic in allowing playgoers the opportunity to see *Richard II* and *Henry IV* in their historical sequence, but there seemed no logic at all in making the two productions seem as though they originated on different planets.

The style of *Richard II* was not calculated to win over playgoers who preferred hearty theatricality in their history plays. John Barber of the London *Daily Telegraph* gave an accurate report of the opening performance on June 6, featuring Nicholas Pennell as Richard and Rod Beattie as Bolingbroke:

> Something remarkable has happened at Stratford. A woman director, in charge of an almost all-male cast, has found a way of staging Shakespeare differently from anything seen before. Zoe Caldwell, the actress, offers an interpretation of *Richard II* so severe, and so clinically austere, as to chill the blood. She has locked the play into the deep-freeze of ritual.
>
> The tragedy is that of an egoist, pitifully inadequate as a ruler, who relies on his God-given status as king to fight off the threat to his throne from a practical and ruthless man of affairs, Bolingbroke. It can be a thrilling dramatic experience.
>
> Miss Caldwell wants something else. She uses a bare stage with a white Japanese screen at the back, and five white steps. The costumes are so clean that they give the actors a story-book artificiality. Often they stand motionless in symmetrical patterns. They speak with a measured pace, a majestic insistency which sets the verse to the tick-tock of a metronome. In some ways this alienation effect fits a highly stylized play. It drives one to listen hard to the words. But the words seem to belong to the cold print of a text. They are rarely allowed to be the outpourings of passionate men.

Barber admitted that this "icebox Shakespeare" was of interest—as an experience. "But it denies the theatre the right to contribute a humanity which the mere reader may not be able to imagine for himself."

Zoe Caldwell had inherited the stark design concept which was so instrumental in determining the production's ritual quality. It had been worked out by Phillips and designer Daphne Dare prior to her being engaged as director—and clearly signified another chapter in Phillips's continuing and often maddening flirtation with the trappings of Japanese theatre. However, Caldwell was prepared to embrace the concept (apart from successfully winning a battle to get her actors back into traditional tights, a costuming practice disliked by Phillips and Miss Dare). Reviewing *Richard II* for the *Globe and Mail*, Herbert Whittaker said it was clear this director wished "to force our attention back to the words themselves, and to do this without the customary aids—the violent reactions, the swift realignment of figures and other devices coined by Stratford in the past to ease us through the history book."

Some critics were polite enough to call the venture a brave failure. Others were more violent. Terry Doran of the *Buffalo News* called *Richard II* an "unqualified disaster" and was unimpressed by the motives underlying the production concept. For him, the experience simply added up to bad theatre:

> The set consists of two levels connected by a flight of five stairs, white as motif, with a back-drop resembling an ultra-modern office divider stood on end and having in its centre a kind of garage door that goes up and down to allow entrances. Besides being meaningless and dull, it is functionally unfortunate. It imposes a rigid formality on the playing space that is reflected, with a vengeance, in the performances. The production progresses in a series of...frozen, petrified ceremonies. Adolescent spear carriers are plunked about in muscle-builder poses to suggest court life under Richard II. The staging is so wooden that it causes Bolingbroke to call out something like "who comes there," only to discover that he who comes approaches from the blind side.

Dutiful critics attended the production three times in order to see all the leads, and perhaps the most unfortunate aspect of this *Richard II* was that controversy concerning its style tended to overshadow the fact that several company members were delivering performances of genuine quality.

First came the Pennell-Beattie teaming. There had been problems between Pennell and his director during rehearsals, and the resulting performance was curiously sphinx-like, if not wax-like, to the extent that Richard's true regality seemed suppressed and the tragic impulse stillborn. Yet, the performance again displayed Pennell's remarkable skill with Shakespeare's poetry. In contrast, Beattie's Bolingbroke was, in the words of Trish Wilson of the *Kitchener-Waterloo Record*, "a stiff and occasionally shrill nobody".

The second pairing worked better. Emotional instability was the hallmark of Frank Maraden's Richard. Herbert Whittaker felt Maraden brought "useful hints of paranoia, neuroticism and treachery to his portrait, sliding down into self-pity". Adding to the fascination of Maraden's portrayal was an unsettling aura of kingliness: even when at his most base and self-pitying, there was an awareness of being an anointed king whose destruction would be an offence against order. Paired against Maraden's Richard was the robust Bolingbroke of Jim McQueen. Whittaker felt this portrait of a usurper strong enough to snatch a kingdom was the Bolingbroke portrayal which "most satisfactorily leads us to the powerful study of a guilty king which Douglas Rain provides in the two parts of *Henry IV*."

Gina Mallet concluded that the most balanced pairing came from Stephen Russell and Craig Dudley. "They both bring a sense of human personality struggling beneath the lines.... They too share a breadth of humanity, an emotional resonance." Russell evoked a "genuine current of emotion" in the deposition scene, and Dudley's Bolingbroke was "a dashing super-politician". But the *Toronto Star* critic was still bothered by a production which she saw as "more a format than a showcase for actors". Not only was she unhappy with the visual stylization, she also questioned the rotating casting:

> There's a notion around the Festival that leading roles in theatre may be changed as easily as leading roles are in ballet and opera. But surely there's a world of difference between an actor and a dancer or singer. Dancers and singers may be turned into physical instruments largely unmodified by personality. Yet an actor's art is inseparable from who or what he is, and the way he shares his personality with the audience. The fascination of a great Richard would come from the uniqueness of every aspect of his performance, the way a specific intelligence filters every line through a single set of attitudes and perceptions that can be duplicated by no one else. This production gives the impression of being committee-controlled.

Artistically, the week's one resounding disaster was *Happy New Year*. Phillips had long wanted a Philip Barry comedy as part of a Festival season, but he also felt that this was an American playwright of such uniqueness that he required a particularly perceptive and sensitive director. Barry's 1928 play *Holiday*, which was best remembered as a wonderful movie vehicle for Katharine Hepburn and Cary Grant, was on Phillips's list, but he didn't feel he was the right person to direct it. An apparent solution was found in veteran Broadway director and writer Burt Shevelove, who had prepared a musical version of the play, using unpublished Cole Porter tunes. *Happy New Year*, which opened June 9 at the Avon, was the appalling result. This limp and listless musical proved that Cole Porter, a composer of impeccable taste, had been right in his original decision to put some of his songs away in a bottom drawer and that Shevelove had been wrong in trying to resuscitate them. The production featured handsome costumes by Robin Fraser Paye and ingenious sets by Michael Eagan, but most critics found the adaptation and most of the performances an embarrassment. Eric Donkin won some praise for a dependable performance as the millionaire father, and there was considerable approval for Victoria Snow—described by Dave Billington as "a leggy youngster from

near Hamilton, Ontario, who has the voice, poise, looks and dancing ability to make a fine career for herself in musical comedy".
Despite the critical slams, *Happy New Year*'s fifty-three performances did 71.7 percent in sales.

Audrey Ashley, veteran critic of the Ottawa *Citizen*, was one of
those who found opening week disturbingly dull. She also had
harsh words for the company, finding many actors "too young and
inexperienced to have been given the roles of mature noblemen.
It's one thing to give these actors training; it's quite another to put
them in roles beyond their capabilities in important public appearances." On the grounds that "hope springs eternal", Mrs. Ashley
found herself looking forward to the later openings of the season.
"Perhaps they'll salvage Shakespeare's and Stratford's honour."

Dominion Day brought a solid, workmanlike production of *The
Taming of the Shrew* to the Third Stage. Guest director Pamela
Hawthorn showed that she had as confident a way with Shakespeare
as with new Canadian drama, and she refused to be intimidated by
the Third Stage's difficult "in-the-round" facility. The production
was notable for entrusting the role of Petruchio to Graeme Campbell, one of the most dependable but often underrated actors in the
company. The *Globe and Mail*'s new drama critic, Ray Conlogue,
found Campbell "magnificently and odiferously macho", but
added that until he arrived on the scene the Kate of Margot Dionne
was hard to take:

> She enters like a shark dumped into a swimming pool occupied by
> her father, the buffoonish Baptista, pouty Bianca and three of
> Bianca's suitors. She spits grape seeds, grapples with her skirt as if it
> were a straitjacket, and does not use the relief the text might have
> afforded her from her raw-throated and one-dimensional bellow.
> When her energy is focussed on Petruchio, the play takes off. The
> vulgar battles between the two, celebrated in one century and
> bowdlerized in the next, delighted yesterday's audience. Campbell
> ...plays Petruchio from the "home" position of a wrestler: legs bent
> and arms outspread, ready to grapple either pugnaciously or
> amorously. When dealing with her father he has the cloying, side-
> winding, open-palmed leering manner of the true rogue; with Kate
> he adds a brutal temper equal to her own.

With a strong supporting cast which included the comically gifted
Tom Wood as Grumio, Maurice Good as Baptista, and Lewis Gordon
as Gremio, *The Taming of the Shrew* played to standing-room-only
audiences for its twenty-seven performances.

On August 7, Edward Bond's *The Woman* opened at the Avon for
a fifteen-performance run which would eke out only 61.7-per-cent
attendance, and August 8 saw *Othello* arrive at the Festival Theatre
and settle comfortably in for a twenty-two-performance engagement which played to 81.2 per cent.

Scene from the 1979 Festival stage production of Othello, *directed by Frances Hyland, designed by Robin Fraser Paye, music by Norman Symonds, lighting by Michael J. Whitfield. L.-R.: Domini Blythe as Desdemona, William Needles as Brabantio, Alan Scarfe as Othello. Photograph by Robert C. Ragsdale, f.r.p.s., courtesy of the Stratford Festival Archives.*

Bringing Edward Bond's left-wing reworking of Euripedes' *The Trojan Women* to Stratford was a project dear to the hearts of Phillips and Kareda. They saw in the character of Queen Hecuba a marvellous role for Martha Henry. Some critics hailed Stratford's production, directed by Peter Moss and Urjo Kareda, as a major triumph. Others felt it was even sillier and more pretentious than the original 1978 treatment at Britain's National Theatre. Myron Galloway of the *Montreal Star* heralded *The Woman* as "a densely written work of epic proportions, combining a Shakespearean format with that of classic Greek tragedy". Galloway wrote that Martha Henry's Hecuba was "one of her greatest triumphs, combining a

classic grandeur with dimensional humanity of contemporary proportions which makes the character entirely accessible and completely sympathetic.''

Gina Mallet's view was quite different. She saw *The Woman* as
yet another of Bond's socialist revisions of history and ''an attempt
to prove that yet another ideal of Western civilization, the city-state
of Athens, was nothing more than a capitalist hell-hole....Bond
appears to be anxious to assert his superiority over everyone else.
And that's a little laughable. *The Woman* is so old-fashioned in its
rhetoric.'' She found *The Woman* deadly dull and lacking ''the
necessary wit, philosophy and character to make it come to life''.
She also found the production no equal to the one she had seen at
Britain's National. ''At the Avon, the play is compressed into talking
heads....the characters are so wooden they might have fallen off
the prows of Greek ships.'' The production had an impressive cast—
Martha Henry, William Hutt, Craig Dudley, and, in her Stratford
debut, popular Toronto actress Clare Coulter—but lack of public
familiarity with the play plus a number of scathing press notices
made it a box-office disappointment.

Frances Hyland's well-received treatment of *Othello* once again
refuted the myth that guest directors always fared badly at Stratford.
Having acted frequently on the Festival stage herself, Miss Hyland
knew it well. By the time she came to Stratford she had also
established herself as an able and intelligent director. Reactions
were mixed towards Alan Scarfe's portrayal of Othello. Doug Bale of
the *London Free Press* felt that instead of a character, Scarfe
emerged as a ''loud, tedious vacancy'', and Gina Mallet, while
applauding Scarfe's craftsmanship and intelligence, found that he
lacked the Moor's ''tantalizing majesty''. However, there was almost
universal agreement that Nicholas Pennell's Iago was one of the
acting triumphs of the season. ''This is the first time Pennell plays a
baddie,'' enthused Gina Mallet, ''and he flowers as never before.''
Playing with just enough of a Cockney accent to indicate that class
envy was one factor in Iago's malice, Pennell was consistently
engrossing and persuasive. Nicholas Pennell, reported Bale, ''is all
things Scarfe is not: clear, subtle, complex, forceful, fascinating.''
Bale also praised Domini Blythe's ''plausible'' Desdemona and in
particular Stephen Russell's Cassio, ''a strong, competent, reasonable soldier, whose only faults are a poor head for drink and an
ungenerous attitude to the poor townswoman who has the misfor-
tune to love him.'' Most critics found Robin Fraser Paye's designs
excessively prettified, but they praised the bluesy score, commissioned from composer Norman Symonds. And the production did
have mood. Commented Bale: ''Director Frances Hyland has done
very well at creating an atmosphere of danger, of nervous fear and of
the possibility of imminent random catastrophe.''

Steve Petch's commissioned play, *Victoria*, opened on August 8 at the Third Stage to unenthusiastic notices. It involved the talents of some excellent artists—Vancouver director Kathryn Shaw, talented young designer Sue LePage, and company members Karen Austin, Richard McMillan, Jennifer Phipps, and Tom Wood—but they couldn't make Petch's earnest but quirky script work. The failure of the play provided fodder for those who believed Stratford was wasting its time with Canadian drama. Perhaps the most explosive reaction came from McKenzie Porter of the *Toronto Sun*. He sat through this drama about "a Canadian family which, for some unexplained reason, have acquired a shack on the scrubby beaches of Baja, California" and deemed *Victoria* worthy of review only because of his conclusion that it was the worst play ever staged by the Festival. He fumed:

> Canadian authors often complain that their nationality denies them fame. Author Petch may lay claim to renown, or notoriety, simply because he is a Canadian, backed financially by artistic chauvinists with public money to throw around. Producers anywhere else in the English-speaking world would have rejected this script with a harsh laugh or diplomatic cough. Because I wish to protect their reputations I shall not mention the names of the distinguished Canadian actors who must struggle, without interval, through this pretentious, offensive, Canada Council-ish tarradiddle.

Yerma, the final Third Stage offering of the season, had been reborn as *Barren/Yerma* by the time it opened on August 25. It encountered critical hostility, too, but Phillips and Moss were to argue that it was one of the most worth-while ventures in Stratford's history. A translation had been commissioned from Canadian writer Kenneth Dyba, but director Pam Brighton wanted to treat Lorca's celebrated play about sexual infertility in a closed rural Spanish community as a springboard for something radically different. She wanted the locale changed to Southern Ontario and would suggest situations and viewpoints for a "collective improvisation" by the cast. Instead of biological infertility, the play would deal with a heroine who was intellectually sterile.

This was too much for the *Globe and Mail*'s Ray Conlogue, who exploded into print with a lecture on the dangers of this kind of venture. He conceded that this "hapless effort" had "guts and nerve, qualities notably absent at Stratford otherwise", but he felt the event was generally incoherent, and he expressed embarrassment at the spectacle of some cast members visibly drying up:

> To ask actors, especially actors who did not volunteer for the task, to improvise a two-and-a-half-hour drama—not a comedy, but a drama, for God's sake—is a delusion. For the most part they enter upon the

task with superb courage, much akin to the charge of the Light Brigade. But the result is mere banter about impersonal subjects—the third world, how grandma made love, and even children. Unsurprisingly, the banter is often amusing—the kind of improv that can be done by a group of intelligent actors. But the characters almost never engage each other *dramatically*....

In a subsequent article, Conlogue allowed Third Stage head Peter Moss the opportunity to respond. Moss admitted he had taken a risk in backing Miss Brighton's concept but argued that this type of "research and development" was part of what the Third Stage was all about. "Critics can't close a show," he told Conlogue with relief. The show played to more than 85-per-cent attendance and—declared Moss—the intermission talk proved that the show was working. "We challenged them," he exulted.

At 11 a.m. on Tuesday, August 14, the cast of *King Lear* assembled for its first rehearsal. Phillips joined his players in a large square of chairs, and asked the person on his right to identify himself, suggest what *King Lear* was all about, and then relate its action. The exercise continued around the circle until it reached the actor on Phillips's immediate left—Peter Ustinov. The familiar voice rang out: "The play is about senility." Phillips followed: "My name is Robin Phillips and I don't know what the play is about."

But, of course, it quickly transpired that Phillips had already done a lot of thinking about the play—to the extent of boldly setting it in the nineteenth century. He had arrived that morning with stacks of reference material. He told his players to read Thomas Hardy, which had the "right feeling" for a mid-Victorian *Lear*. He passed around books opened at specific illustrations. A procession of images unfolded, ranging from idyllic and idealized nineteenth-century poses to bitter cartoons satirizing the horrors of the Crimean War. Phillips talked about the need to get beneath the romantic veneer of the era, threw out images of the claustrophobia and repression of the society of the day, and referred to the "domestic idiocy" of Lear's court in the play's opening scene. Ustinov told an anecdote about an aging, dying, mentally askew General Franco refusing to let go, and drew a parallel with Lear. Phillips decisively rejected *Lear* as a play only appropriate for an ancient setting: "Stonehenge," he declared, "doesn't make any sense at all." That was the start of a genuine adventure in discovery.

The 1979 Stratford production of *King Lear* was a bold and unusual production of one of Shakespeare's most perplexing and challenging works. Maurice Good, the Irish-born actor who was understudying Ustinov, kept a journal of the day-to-day processes of creating the production. The resulting book, *Every Inch a Lear*, published by Sono Nis Press in 1982, provided an absorbing insight into the theatre's creative processes. It was a rich and unexpected legacy of the Phillips-Ustinov *King Lear*.

The production, of course, left more immediate legacies—in particular the impact of a Lear who dared to be funny. It had been Peter Ustinov's lifelong ambition to play the role, and indeed at one point he had negotiated with his American producer, Alexander H. Cohen, for a Broadway production, which never materialized. Maggie Smith had heard about Ustinov's interest in *Lear* when they worked together in the film *Death on the Nile*. She recommended Phillips to Ustinov as a potential director. Ustinov contacted Phillips and the two subsequently met in New York in November 1978. The result: Ustinov would star in a Stratford production of *Lear* which would be presented in association with Alexander H. Cohen, who would have the option of taking it to Broadway. The Broadway proposal never came to fruition, but plans for a London run at the Theatre Royal, Haymarket, were to start taking shape. The Theatre Royal's owners, Duncan Weldon and Louis Michaels, were anxious to have Ustinov on stage in *King Lear*, and after seeing the 1979 Stratford production, their enthusiasm for the project increased. Preliminary discussions were held about the possibility of taking a 1980 Stratford revival of the production to London. It was at this time that Phillips made Ustinov the fateful promise he would only be expected to return to Stratford for a second season if the London engagement became a certainty.

The 1979 *Lear* fascinated virtually everyone who saw it. The production had remarkable narrative clarity, with ensemble qualities which were always satisfactory and often outstanding in their ritualistic power. Phillips was acting in character in transferring the play from primitive times to a sombre nineteenth century—his favourite setting when he wished to rethink a troublesome Shakespearean play and give it more focus. With Ustinov supplying an unorthodox but gripping portrayal in the title role, and William Hutt delivering a memorable characterization as The Fool, the moral universe of *Lear* emerged as some sort of grotesque joke.

Several critics were bothered by the updated setting, among them Lawrence DeVine of the *Detroit Free Press*:

> Stratford's shrewd artistic director, Robin Phillips, who is as calculating as they come, has calculated strangely with his first Canadian *Lear*. Defying custom, he has updated the tragedy of the ancient king of Britain into a Continental 1860. The production is a prisoner of Robin Phillips. His updating—by an incredible 2,600 years—confines *Lear* to literalness. Ultimately, Stratford's and Ustinov's *King Lear* is a boulevard tragedy done popular-style, with a great deal of directorial and ensemble artistry, as if it were best O'Neill or second-best Molnar.

Clive Barnes took a different perspective in the *New York Post*.

He considered the mid-Victorian setting awkward as well, but he was fascinated by Ustinov:

> He still surprises me....He is one of the funniest Lears I have ever seen—and, moreover, he meant to be funny. Ustinov constantly provides a tragic edge of unlocated loss to his clowning....He really is fantastic. I did not like his Lear as a whole, but I loved some aspects of it, and I would never have missed it....Emotionally outrageous, intellectually persuasive, and providing an unanswerable answer to the conundrum of Lear.

Gina Mallet's *Toronto Star* notice caught the mood of the opening scenes

> in a sombrely respectable Victorian drawing room. It is apparent that the age's moral code has collapsed. Here's the sober old Earl of Gloucester drily explaining how he fathers a bastard. In dodders Lear wearing a rather rumpled uniform, and the sense of degenerating ability is confirmed....Arteriosclerosis is advancing, the mind wanders, Lear nods off. Suddenly awake, he's had enough. He's going to carve up his kingdom among these three daughters and make them do some work for a change. Then they can look after him while he roisters life away. But his favorite, Cordelia, won't play—the spoilsport.

Miss Mallet felt Ustinov came near to making comedy the touchstone of Lear's tragedy. But, despite his dominance of the production, she concluded that he remained too much the "fetching old man" and that he was reluctant to surrender to the madness of Shakespeare's poetry. Most reviewers found supporting performances uneven, with Ingrid Blekys's Cordelia the prime disappointment. Judgment was more positive for Richard Monette's Edmund, Douglas Rain's Gloucester, Marti Maraden's Regan, and Donna Goodhand's Goneril. But the most striking work came from a veteran company member and a newcomer. Commented Ray Conlogue in the *Globe and Mail*:

> What glue did attach the framework to Ustinov's Lear came from William Hutt's wondrous Fool and Jim McQueen's deeply felt Earl of Kent. The Fool, in a frock coat with a ludicrous scarf dangling below, hunched his hands behind his back to deliver useless epigrams with the sing-song voice of a batty rural vicar. Hutt did not overdo the wordplay, keeping his Fool as clear and malicious as a real one would dare to be. McQueen's Kent counterpointed this folly with a stance and vigor almost kingly in itself.

The nineteen performances of *Lear* were completely sold out before the production even opened at the Avon. Its success provided a late-season boost for an organization that had been watching over-all box-office returns with mounting consternation. However, Peter Ustinov's star turn in *Lear*, lucrative as it was, could not work the kind of miracle the 1979 season needed.

Phillips gave the word to reporters assembled in his simple, austere office the morning after the *Lear* opening. The Stratford Festival, he said, faced probable financial catastrophe unless there was a major increase in government funding. "We have literally reached the point of no return," he said. "Unless the arts councils have a major change of attitude next year, we could close. There is nothing more to pare and save. We can't expand to get more box-office. We are at breaking point."

Phillips's regime had been scoring such spectacular successes that it was difficult for many people to grasp the possibility of financial disaster for the Stratford Festival. After all, its earning power had been sensational—well above the fifty-per-cent-of-budget figure which was the standard target for other Canadian theatres. Phillips's point was that the Festival was dangerously reliant on box office, and that its government funding was woefully below a fair level. Given Stratford's abnormal dependence on box office and the massive size of its budget, a decline of even ten per cent below projected revenues could be devastating and leave the organization half a million dollars in the red. For 1979, the disappointing showing of the two *Henry IV* plays and *Richard II* was sufficient to plunge the season into a deficit situation—since virtually everything else was registering earnings substantially above budgeted figures—yet it was as vital a part of the Festival's mandate to mount the less saleable chronicle plays as it was to schedule the certain winners.

Board and staff members had long been impressed with the frugality of the Festival under Phillips. Now he let the public in on some of the cost-conscious measures that had been taken:

> How many people realize that the costumes in this year's *Love's Labour's Lost* are the costumes they saw in my very first production of *Measure for Measure* four years ago and in *Richard III* two years ago? Those costumes have gone through so many productions. Daphne Dare is very smart with the materials she uses. They're sturdy and tough, and if we're forced to make them work again and recycle them, that's what we do. I'm prepared to do any amount of this, because if you do it skilfully enough, the public won't recognize we're using the same costumes all the way through. That's how imaginative and economical we have to be.

But, he warned, there were limits. Goodwill was running short; too many people were working at Stratford for less than they deserved.

Phillips's warnings were greeted with scepticism in some quarters. The Stratford Festival still had the image of being a "fat cat" institution which was complaining with unnecessary stridency about its temporary financial problems. Actually, Phillips had shown great moderation in his public comments. The true state of affairs was more startling. The Festival's permanent staff was roughly the same size as it had been in 1970—yet it had expanded its season and increased the number of plays. In some departments, the number of employees had actually decreased from what it had been nine years previously. The publicity department, which had had five employees backed up by clerical staff in 1970, now had three, with the same number of clerical staff. There was no general manager. Robin Phillips didn't even have a full-time secretary; instead, he had a part-time secretary who also functioned as a stage manager. In 1974, the budget for mounting a major Shakespeare production was $20,000. In 1979, despite inflation, it was still $20,000. The Festival could even plead not guilty to charges that its finances would be more secure if it didn't squander money on "international stars". In truth, it could not come close to matching the type of salary available to such people in film or television, on Broadway, or even on a national stage tour. When they came to Stratford, it was mainly because of the Festival's growing international reputation and the artistic fulfilment it offered them. As for Canadian artists, many of them had been approached to join the company but had declined because they felt they could earn more money elsewhere. A 1978 study of ten Canadian performing-arts groups revealed that Stratford had the highest percentage of box-office revenue to total revenue, but that its government funding was lowest in terms of total revenue. Indeed, there had been a frightening deterioration in government grants—from more than twenty per cent of budget in 1970 to less than eleven per cent in 1979.

At the Festival Foundation's annual general meeting on December 8, board president Robert V. Hicks reported that the 1979 season had ended with an operating deficit of $647,119. Because of the surplus carried forward from the previous year, the losses were reduced to a net deficit of $245,395. Hicks cited several uncontrollable factors—the impact of inflation on travel costs and the dislocation caused by gasoline shortages in the United States, the home of so many Stratford patrons. But the major culprits were provincial and federal funding agencies. "Just as nature abhors a vacuum, the granting authorities seem to recoil from a successful operation that produces a profit," Hicks commented drily. He warned that the Festival could close after the 1980 season without a major transfusion of dollars.

The 1979 season was perceived in later years to be a disaster. "What went wrong this summer?" asked Gina Mallet in a *Toronto Star* column on December 10. She then gave the answer:

Poor scheduling, no stars and non-existent leadership. The season was a fiasco in terms of expectations. Robin Phillips has made Stratford into a great, non-stop series of openings. Great. But these openings had better be worth the trip. This year, they weren't. Stratford looked as if it was falling into the trap that the Royal Shakespeare Company had fallen into. It looked inward and concentrated on its company rather than on creating exciting theatre.

Miss Mallet brought up the controversial question of stars. "Unless there are stars/great actors, and not just from Canada, at the festival, Stratford isn't worthy of its name."

Yet, much of the season had been of genuine artistic quality. It had been bold and innovative. A production of one of Shakespeare's least marketable plays, *Love's Labour's Lost*, had registered the highest grosses for a single offering in Stratford's history—and had done so by drawing on the rich resources of the Festival Company rather than by relying on imported stars. The season, at twenty-six weeks, had been the longest ever. Attendance figures of 504,775 came close to matching 1977's 504,963. Box-office grosses set a new record of more than $4.7 million. It was a notable achievement, but not sufficient to keep pace with inflation or to compensate for a decline in real-dollar terms of government funding. The chronicle plays had always posed a marketing challenge; this year, customer resistance was sufficient to plunge the Festival into the red. Had the two parts of *Henry IV* and *Richard II* met revenue projections, there would have been no deficit.

Nevertheless, the portents for the future did not look good. Phillips was determined to deliver a blockbuster season in 1980 on as tight a budget as possible. But he had also reassessed his own future as a result of a sabbatical which, in the final analysis, had been anything but. An encounter with one board member during the 1979 season burned its way into his mind. The board member took Phillips to one side, and rebuked him: "You're not doing enough!" Phillips, thunderstruck, replied: "I'm already doing three major productions, and I'm supposed to be doing nothing." By this time he knew that his sabbatical was not going to work, and that he must quit as artistic director at the end of the 1980 season. This was the message he tried to convey to the board. Unfortunately, board members were not listening. The twin problems of artistic succession and looming deficits were to lead them into the morass of 1980 and the biggest artistic crisis in Canada's history.

1980

When Robin Phillips began planning his 1980 season, he decided that the Stratford Festival must go international with a vengeance. "That will be our emblem for the decade," he told a Toronto press conference on October 29, 1979. "Stratford in the 1980s will be exploring and exploiting its internationalism."

His remarks seemed certain to provoke the nationalists into full protesting outcry. But Phillips stated the case for this new mandate with persuasive logic:

Stratford's internationalism is developed from two powerful currents —the first, the development of Canadian talent to a standard of achievement which is recognized and honoured internationally; and the second, a need for and commitment to that very standard on the part of the international artistic community. In 1980, this will mean, at the Stratford Festival, a company led both by Canadian artists with major international reputations—William Hutt, Kate Reid, Hume Cronyn, Douglas Rain, Roberta Maxwell—and by international artists who have responded with total dedication to the quality of work which is available only at Stratford—Maggie Smith, Jessica Tandy, Brian Bedford, Peter Ustinov. They will perform a repertoire which will include, in addition to Shakespeare, works from Canadian, Russian, Italian, American, and English dramatic literature. They will join a Canadian acting company whose talents and standards of production have placed them among the top three companies of the English-speaking theatre world.

Plans were under way to send four plays—one of them Ustinov's *King Lear*—to London. Also in the works was a film version of *The Importance of Being Earnest*.

Phillips outlined a season of sixteen productions for 1980. It was actually the second 1980 list to be announced, the earlier one having been unveiled prior to the 1979 openings. Missing from Phillips's October announcement were such earlier entries as Shakespeare's *Coriolanus*, John Vanbrugh's *The Relapse*, Sheridan's *The Rivals*, and two new Canadian plays, John Murrell's *Parma* and Sheldon Rosen's *Choices*. By the beginning of 1980, the list had again been revised. A revival of the 1979 *Othello* had been dropped, along with another Murrell item, *Memoir*. Nevertheless, these final amendments to Stratford's twenty-eighth season revealed programming of exciting potential.

Yet another marathon week of openings was planned, beginning June 9 with John Gay's *The Beggar's Opera* at the Avon and Phillips's production of *Twelfth Night* in the Festival Theatre. June 10 would see three openings: two performances of *Henry V*, directed by Peter Moss, with Richard Monette and Jack Wetherall alternating in the title role, and the world première of Edna O'Brien's *Virginia*, with Maggie Smith as Virginia Woolf. On June 11 Brian Bedford's treatment of *Titus Andronicus* was back at the Festival Theatre and Tom Cone's new version of Goldoni's *The Servant of Two Masters* opened at the Avon. On June 12 Kate Reid and Douglas Rain would be in comic confrontation in *The Gin Game*, and on June 13 Maggie Smith and Brian Bedford would have their latest commercially potent reunion in *Much Ado About Nothing*.

Later openings would include John Guare's *Bosoms and Neglect*, with Kate Reid repeating her Broadway triumph in the main role; a dramatized version of John Aubrey's *Brief Lives* with Douglas Rain; *Foxfire*, a new play by Hume Cronyn and Susan Cooper, with Cronyn and Jessica Tandy starring; John Murrell's adaptation of Chekhov's *The Seagull*; Eugene O'Neill's *Long Day's Journey Into Night*; the three parts of Shakespeare's *Henry VI* in an evening-length condensation by director Pam Brighton; and, of course, *King Lear*.

The Festival's genially chaotic production of *The Beggar's Opera* proved an audience-pleaser, winning 93.6-per-cent attendance during its twenty-six-performance run. Directed by Phillips and the talented young Greg Peterson, and featuring lively musical arrangements and direction by Berthold Carriere, the production exuded a zany irreverence that disarmed critics. Michael Billington of the *Guardian* was pleasantly surprised:

Two things make the Stratford production unusual: a revue-like eclecticism and Phillips's ability to marshal vast numbers of people.

Scene from the 1980 Avon stage production of The Beggar's Opera, *by John Gay, directed by Robin Phillips and Gregory Peterson, set by Daphne Dare, costumes by Sue LePage, musical direction, choral arrangements, and orchestration by Berthold Carriere, lighting by Michael J. Whitfield, choreography by Jeff Hyslop, additional lyrics by Ned Sherrin and Caryl Brahms. Centre: Jim McQueen as Macheath. Photograph by Robert C. Ragsdale, f.r.p.s., courtesy of the Stratford Festival Archives.*

In England these days, five is quite a crowd on stage. But Phillips's *Beggar's Opera* populates the acting area with Hogarthian types: all scruffy wigs, dirty underwear and gin-spoiled countenances. This both suggests the teeming nature of Eighteenth-Century London and enables the director to magic MacHeath out of the crowd like some red-coated imp. More controversially, Phillips also makes several obeisances to Broadway routines and to modern swing, and even has MacHeath escaping from gaol to the strains of the Skye Boat Song, We'll Meet Again, and White Christmas. The result may be intellectually inconsistent. But it is also consistently enjoyable....

Ray Conlogue of the *Globe and Mail* found the event a "pleasantly gritty surprise". Phillips always disliked the idea of jobbing in a special cast to do a musical; he felt, rather, that it helped stretch members of an existing company to offer them this kind of special challenge. *The Beggar's Opera* offered ample justification for this approach. Commented Conlogue:

Jim McQueen's piratical masculinity was perfect for MacHeath, while Graeme Campbell took his knack for eccentric character roles a bit further with his gnawing, squint-eyed Peachum. Jennifer Phipps was a pleasant shockeroo as Mrs. Peachum, who doesn't mind MacHeath hanging but wouldn't mind a squeeze in the hay with him before he goes, either. Edda Gaborek as a goody-two-shoes Polly Peachum (she shows up in MacHeath's cell wearing a Red Cross uniform) was a giddy counterpoint to her romantic competition, the pregnant and murderous Lucy Lockit, played with baleful brows by Alicia Jeffery....David Dunbar stood out as Filch the pickpocket, silly and vulnerable but somehow always coming out on top.

Most critical reservations had to do with the presence of the new Stratford Youth Choir as chorus. Chosen through cross-country auditions, and financed by a special donations drive launched by Phillips, these thirty-two young singers, trained under the direction of Robert Cooper, appeared in *The Beggar's Opera* and four special concerts during the season. However, their presence in John Gay's raucous musical entertainment seemed inappropriately wholesome.

Twelfth Night promised to be notable on several counts. In the first place, Brian Bedford was recreating the Malvolio that had earned him such plaudits in David Jones's 1975 production. Secondly, Phillips was directing this popular Shakespeare comedy for the first time. Thirdly, the production marked the return of Kate Reid to the Festival Company after an absence of many years. Some critics found this *Twelfth Night* curiously subdued, even passionless. Set designer Daphne Dare and costume designer Ann Curtis had created an autumnal eighteenth-century world of ghostly, silvery leaves and quietly rustling silks. Yet even though the emotional terrain seemed almost too placid, the production did achieve unusual intimacy and warmth. "This *Twelfth Night*," declared Gina Mallet, "flows with sweet reason."

Bedford's Malvolio, who at one point materialized clutching a teddy bear, was more forlorn and vulnerable than in 1975. Once again he captivated audiences, prompting Mel Gussow of the *New York Times* to suggest Bedford should be granted "permanent tenure" in the role.

One of the production's outstanding performances was provided by youthful Richard McMillan as Sir Andrew Aguecheek. Gussow described him as "a scarecrow teetering on toothpick legs. A coward of 'dormouse valor', he seems to be in a constant state of flight and agitation, his feet automatically leading him in a direction opposite to all potential confrontation." William Hutt had portrayed Feste for the Festival previously, in David William's production. His characterization for Phillips was astonishing—a warmhearted aging retainer who had a passion for books and shuffled about in comfortable slippers and baggy jacket. Gussow saw him as

174

an old fool, a semi-retired clown. He is the opposite of a jackanapes—
a forlorn family retainer who exudes a maturity and wisdom. He is a
cadger as well as a codger, always seeking to double his remunera-
tion. The performance. . .is irresistible. In addition, Mr. Hutt, with a
voice of Walter Huston's warmth and vulnerability, sings "O Mistress
Mine" and other lyrics.

Australian actress Patricia Conolly divided critics with her Viola.
Gina Mallet saw it as "one of the most intelligent and sensitive
pieces of acting seen at the Festival in recent years". But Ray
Conlogue was bothered by "a nervous, ingratiating half smile
forever playing about her lips".

The production was bolstered further by Kate Reid as a Maria of
sharp intelligence and affecting good humour, Jim McQueen as a
robust Orsino, Pat Galloway as Olivia, and Lorne Kennedy as Sebas-
tian. Barry MacGregor's unorthodox but convincing Sir Toby Belch
provided sound vindication for Robin Phillips's often unorthodox
directing style. MacGregor had been having trouble with the role in
rehearsals, but Phillips came up with the abrupt if somewhat
terrifying solution. Recalled MacGregor:

> To give you an example of his astuteness towards each individual—
> which is probably sharper than Langham's—he came and sat in my
> dressing room at 1:15 in the afternoon on the first day we did *Twelfth
> Night* in public (a school preview) and said, "I think that Sir Toby
> should have a Scots accent." And I said: "Robin! It's forty-five
> minutes to curtain-up." And he said: "Well, try it. If you don't, I shall
> understand, because you may want to run it through mentally." And I
> thought: "Well, hell!" I sat there. It was like being struck in the
> mouth by a wet kipper. Anyway, I got up for Scene Three, which is
> the first scene that Sir Toby goes into, and I stood and the red light
> went on, and I thought: "Well, it's now or never." I went out, and it
> was like having the final pin placed, and there it was for me and him.
> And he said, "It worked." And it does—for me. I don't know, for
> some people it may not. But it was just like putting the final brush-
> mark to part of the canvas, and it also slowed me down, made me that
> fraction older.

Twelfth Night attracted 81.6-per-cent attendance, running
throughout the season, and grossed $804,807.

Peter Moss's theatrically effective productions of the two *Henry
IV* plays in 1979 had created high hopes for his treatment of *Henry
V*. Furthermore, there was the anticipation of seeing Richard
Monette, who had been such a fine Prince Hal the year before, show
how this same character adjusts to the mantle of kingship. Unfortunately, *Henry V* was one of the major disappointments of the
1980 season. Moss's production was static, and neither Monette nor
Jack Wetherall, who were alternating in the role, were convincing
monarchs. Striving for the summit, they ended up slithering for-
lornly on the slopes.

Wetherall's failure was somewhat more honourable and interesting. Although his Henry lacked the true stamp of kingship and leadership, he did convey some belief in divine grace, some clear sense of spirituality, some genuine awareness of being an anointed king. Wetherall couldn't deliver the charisma a Henry V ultimately needs; but he did convey the vulnerability of a young king facing his first terrible test.

Neither Henry was convincing as a leader worth following into battle, but the failure of Richard Monette's performance was the more maddening because of an earlier Hal which suggested he was tailor-made for the character. Commented the Vancouver *Province*'s Bob Allen, a Monette admirer: "In this production, he has mistaken affectation for acting, coupled with a tendency to deliver his lines in jerky little three-syllable chunks. His Henry is a pompous little chap who would scarcely inspire you to cross the street with him, much less follow him into a battle like Agincourt."

The ensemble work was stilted, and the company was not at its best, with several normally dependable performers behaving as if they had been embalmed. Some glimmers of life were provided by Amelia Hall as a true and touching Mistress Quickly and by Barry MacGregor cackling his way energetically through the role of the fanatically militaristic Fluellen. The best comic moments were probably provided by Rod Beattie as Pistol. Ray Conlogue felt this actor was finally realizing his potential: "This walrus-faced ruffian, arm upstretched and waggling an insolent glove like a fool's flag, rushes into battle to steal what he can: he is everything engaging in Henry's (and England's) brigand youth which must come to an end."

Henry V was not a success, drawing 59.8-per-cent attendance. Such was not the case with *Virginia*, which had virtually sold out its seventeen scheduled performances before it even opened. By frantic juggling of dates, Festival staff managed to find a place for three additional performances; even so, thousands of playgoers were turned away from one of the most acclaimed productions in the Festival's history. The play's style was stream-of-consciousness. Irish novelist Edna O'Brien's function was as much that of editor as that of author, since her text was drawn from Virginia Woolf's own writing. There were only three in the cast: Maggie Smith as Virginia; Nicholas Pennell, who played her father, Leslie Stephen, and later her husband, Leonard Woolf; and Patricia Conolly as her friend and lover, Victoria Sackville-West.

Edna O'Brien had been commissioned to write the play by the New York producer Arthur Cantor. Maggie Smith heard about it, reputedly through her London hairdresser, whom she shared with Miss O'Brien, and suggested it to Phillips as a possible vehicle for her at Stratford.

The end result was considered by most Stratford regulars to represent Maggie Smith at the peak of her Stratford achievement. Michael Billington had read an earlier draft of Edna O'Brien's script in 1979 and had found it unsatisfactory. But the *Guardian* critic was overwhelmed by what he saw in Stratford the following year. The week's real excitement, he told readers, was at the Avon with *Virginia*, "a play that give Maggie Smith the best role written for a woman since Jean Brodie was in her prime." Billington found O'Brien's script vastly improved:

She has. . .clearly put immense work into sculpting and refining it so it skilfully leads one through Virginia Woolf's life and, with the help of only two other characters, also conveys the world about her. It begins and ends with the words, "Something tremendous is going to happen." And in the interim it steers one through her mental break-downs, her appetite for the world of London literary life, her marriage to Leonard, her affair with Vita Sackville-West, and her suicide in 1941 in the belief that she was once again lapsing into insanity.

What both writer and actress managed to persuade us of, in two hours, is the extraordinary emotional volatility of Virginia Woolf. Maggie Smith, with her fine-drawn features, bears more than a passing resemblance to her subject, but this is acting, not impersonation. She conveys, with a sharp downward inflection, her distaste for the "animal vigor" of her half brother, George Duckworth, who noisily seduced her. She skips and quivers with life as Virginia and Leonard devour literary London—"Shakespeare would have liked us tonight," she cries full of brio. She steps back in initial apprehension at the sight of the printing press Leonard buys in Holborn Viaduct for under twenty pounds. And she suggests, through a delicate tightening of her body and narrowing of her gestures, a gradual withdrawal into solitude.

Miss Smith has no peer at conveying the qualities of passion and insecurity—qualities ideal for Virginia Woolf. But one must also praise Edna O'Brien's dramatic skill in composing the portrait. . .the rock-like compassion of Nicholas Pennell's Leonard and the spare clarity of Robin Phillips's production, which is one of his very best. Sound (clocks, planes, gently lapping water), back-projected images and light are used in a way that is pleasing without being obtrusive.

Ted Kalem in *Time* magazine was similarly exuberant:

This play is a tone poem, and it is surely Robin Phillips at the top form of his directorial career who has elicited from Maggie Smith this confluence of naked emotions. She is, from moment to moment, grieving, loving, bitter, wasp-witted, rapturous, valiant and a womb-ful of fear. Her most powerfully affecting sequence is the descent into madness, where terrifying apparitions of unreason flit like vampire bats through the buckling rafters of her brain.

Heightening the production's impact were the evocative costumes of Ann Curtis, the atmospheric lighting of Michael J. Whit-field, the quietly eloquent music of Berthold Carriere, and the remarkable set concept of Phillip Silver. The latter, according to Gina Mallet, "has designed a set that is memory itself, projections of the Woolfs' houses onto translucent screens set at angles to each other on a bare white stage, empty except for two cane armchairs." (And what material was used to give those screens their spectacular translucent beauty? Silver confided after the run that it was plain cheesecloth purchased from the local Woolco at $1.98 a yard. The Phillips regime was maintaining its reputation for frugality.)

In January 1981 the production was to have an engagement at London's Theatre Royal, Haymarket.

Quite a different response was kindled with the next Avon open-ing on June 11 of Tom Cone's adaptation of Goldoni's *The Servant of Two Masters*. Most critics loathed it. They hated Peter Moss's direction. They hated the performances. And they wondered why Goldoni's elegant little farce about a servant who doubles his income by working for two masters at the same time needed to be updated. Ray Conlogue's review in the *Globe and Mail* set the tone:

> Take this play and winch it unwillingly upward into the early Twentieth Century, and it will, like one of those deep sea fish that collapse when brought to the surface, present a sad sight. That is what Stratford did in commissioning a version by Tom Cone set in pre-First World War Venice. Combine that with a director who exercises too much control over his actors and thinks the audience can only understand a glacial pace, and you are in trouble. And so is Stratford with this boring production.

Despite the critical slams, the production ran for thirty perform-ances and drew a respectable 72.7 per cent in sales, but it was to be remembered as one of the major artistic failures of the decade. Still, it was a perplexing type of failure—for a number of reasons. After all, Stratford's *Servant of Two Masters* did enjoy a number of plus factors. Despite functional problems with Michael Eagan's set, it did feature witty and colourful costumes by Janice Lindsay. It also boasted an impressive cast, including such dependable company regulars as Lewis Gordon (Truffaldino, the comic servant), Graeme Campbell, Rod Beattie, and such talented newcomers as Brent Carver, Goldie Semple, and Norman Browning. Yet, as Conlogue noted in his review of the opening performance, the entire exercise seemed to be an endurance test for them.

Tom Cone was an admired playwright, but one of his traits was an original but idiosyncratic prose style which demanded particular attention to rhythm and tempo in performance. Rehearsals for *The Servant of Two Masters* had been troublesome, and on one occa-sion one of the leads stormed out of the hall, complaining that it was

Scene from the 1978/1980 Festival stage production of Titus Andronicus, *directed by Brian Bedford, designed by Desmond Heeley, music by Gabriel Charpentier, lighting by Michael J. Whitfield. L.-R.: Rod Beattie as Lucius, Domini Blythe as Lavinia (1980), William Hutt as Titus Andronicus, Max Helpmann as Marcus Andronicus. Photograph by Robert C. Ragsdale, f.r.p.s., courtesy of the Stratford Festival Archives.*

impossible to speak Cone's lines. There may well have been potential problems in assigning adaptation of a visually oriented farce to a writer with a musician's sensibility for the sound of words. How, one wondered, might Tom Cone's *Servant* have fared under a different director, for example Pamela Hawthorn, who was sensitive to his work and who had done well the year before with Stratford's production of *Stargazing*? An answer was forthcoming a couple of seasons later when this version of *Servant of Two Masters* turned up at Edmonton's Citadel Theatre. There had been adjustments to the script, but it was still very much a Tom Cone creation. And this time, it did work on stage. The discerning director was Graeme Campbell, who had foundered so badly as an actor in the Stratford original. At the time, Urjo Kareda considered *The Servant of Two Masters* perhaps the least successful of the new play projects he had initiated, and he was to find it ironic that it should later have worked well in various other productions and have become a regional theatre staple.

The revival of Brian Bedford's 1978 triumph, *Titus Andronicus*, gathered further accolades when it opened on the evening of June 11 at the Festival Theatre. William Hutt again delivered a towering performance in the title role, but there were significant changes in the supporting cast—among them a poignant Lavinia from Goldie Semple, an impressive Aaron from Errol Slue, and an astonishing Tamara from Pat Galloway, who in one critic's words turned this character into a great sensual she-tigress pawing the turf. Mark Czarnecki of *Maclean's* magazine was among those impressed with Bedford's handling of both the text and the stage:

> Bedford's lavish staging has transformed this shrill revenge tragedy into a moving Jacobean masque, a feast for the eyes and the ears. Gilt-laden funeral processions slant across the stage under eerie lighting to sinister music. Violent death lurks everywhere but treads softly—the murders are muted, all the blood is dried, the entrails are safely tucked away. The text has been cut and spliced freely, but intelligently, and when, at the end, the sibylline oracle (a Bedfordian addition) prophesies the dire fate of Rome, the play comes to rest within a historical frame, an icon frozen in time.

The public again resisted one of the most striking Stratford productions of the decade: in thirteen performances, *Titus* pulled in less than 60-per-cent attendance. Indeed, the opening performance played to only half a house, a situation lamented by Lyle Slack of the *Hamilton Spectator*:

> What those hundreds of people missed yesterday was one of the most stirring spectacles of the season. *Titus Andronicus* is, indeed, a ruthless and violent play, but it also happens to be one of Shakespeare's most brazenly theatrical. Whatever else one may say of it, it *plays* like a house on fire, particularly when William Hutt is Titus.

The presence of D. L. Coburn's Pulitzer Prize winner, *The Gin Game*, in the Avon repertoire raised some eyebrows. A few board members complained about the bad language used by Douglas Rain in his portrayal of an embittered old codger who makes the mistake of his life in inviting fellow old-folks'-home resident Kate Reid into a game of gin. A more relevant concern was why Stratford was doing the play at all. On Broadway it had been an enormously successful two-hander for Hume Cronyn and Jessica Tandy, and the promise of a Stratford production helped persuade Kate Reid to join the Festival Company after a long absence. Both she and Rain played splendidly together, but not so splendidly as to be able to conceal the play's glib, facile nature or Mel Shapiro's generally insensitive direction. *The Gin Game* played nineteen performances to 89.4 per cent of capacity.

The week came to a memorable conclusion with the opening of *Much Ado About Nothing* on June 13 at the Festival Theatre. Directed by Phillips, with costumes by Robin Fraser Paye, music by Louis Applebaum, and a pair of frolicsome performances from Maggie Smith and Brian Bedford, it was to emerge as the Festival Theatre's biggest hit, selling nearly a million dollars' worth of tickets and playing to 90.4-per-cent houses.

Harry Van Vugt of the *Windsor Star* saw it as a case of saving the best for last: "This is indeed a lovely *Much Ado*—lovely to look at and lovingly staged, performed and directed." Maureen Peterson of the Montreal *Gazette* had no hesitation in calling it "a perfect show" and in acclaiming Phillips for mastering the play's "almost unbearably keen balance between comedy and drama". Gina Mallet saw the event as a glorious hotchpotch:

> Robin Phillips has taken *Much Ado About Nothing*, which may have been written by Shakespeare but is clearly a Neil Simon potboiler concocted for the Sixteenth Century expense account crowd, given it the look of *The Three Musketeers* and peopled it with the Seventeenth Century equivalent of Katharine Hepburn and Spencer Tracy. Or, rather, Maggie Smith and Brian Bedford, who play Benedick and Beatrice fighting tooth and claw to the altar, ambiguous lovers who make every insult sound like a declaration of love. What a partnership Smith and Bedford have become, especially in this romp. What a splendid Mirabell he would make to Smith's Millamant if only *The Way of the World*, in which she appeared at Stratford in 1976, were to be revived. Here they go several rounds of the battle of the sexes without laying a glove on each other, just totting up points, a pair of champs towering over the pygmies of provincial Messina.

There were only two openings at Stratford in July, each of them aimed at showcasing the talents of one performer. Kate Reid was given the opportunity to recreate her gripping performance as a blind and crazed old mother in John Guare's *Bosoms and Neglect*. The savagery of the comedy, with its put-down of psychoanalysis and its relentless probing of familial bonds, did not make for comfortable viewing. The play, which Martin Knelman considered one of the best new dramas of the past decade, had been a personal triumph for Kate Reid in the United States—and a commercial failure. The Festival was taking a gamble in allowing Miss Reid to repeat the role at Stratford, but the production, directed by Mel Shapiro and designed by Phillip Silver, did a respectable 68.5 per cent of capacity.

The Third Stage opened on July 19 with Martha Henry directing her husband Douglas Rain in *Brief Lives*, Patrick Garland's adaptation of the outrageous writings of the seventeenth-century diarist John Aubrey. The piece had been a London and New York success with Roy Dotrice's tour-de-force performance as Aubrey, but Rain's approach to this one-man show drew mixed reviews. Doug Bale of the *London Free Press* praised Rain for the minute perception of his characterization of this ancient antiquarian wandering about his study recalling a lifetime of anecdotes about the famous and the infamous. He also was impressed with the set created by Daphne Dare and the Festival design team: "It is a fusty, dusty chaos of pots, pans, pens, papers, mortars, pestles, vials, specimen boxes, old bones, stuffed animals, innumerable books, manuscripts uncountable, overflowing every chair, table, chest, stool and stair-tread in sight." However, Ray Conlogue of the *Globe and Mail* was bothered by a lack of real drama, suggesting that "Rain's highly controlled, almost subliminal version of Aubrey may not be to everybody's taste." The production ended up doing 55.5-per-cent business.

The Stratford Festival may have seemed an unlikely venue for a folk play about the mountain people of the southern Appalachia, yet that was the subject matter of *Foxfire*, which premiered at the Avon Theatre on August 7. Even more unlikely was the inspiration for the play itself: the famed *Foxfire* books. These volumes were partly how-to-do-it, partly oral history, and had begun as a school project, with southern Appalachia students taking tape recorders to parents, grandparents, neighbours, and friends, and recording the local lore. Who would have expected viable drama from such a source, with its advice on how to cook a possum or build a log cabin? To be sure, Stratford's production did offer the spectacle of Jessica Tandy performing kitchen preliminaries on the severed head of a hog and of Hume Cronyn putting together a good, serviceable rocking chair. But the real purpose of this unusual stage play by Cronyn and British fantasy-writer Susan Cooper was to create dramatic situations which would convey the homey flavour and reflect the values of the original books. The plot has to do with the attempt of developer Prinz Carpenter (Richard Monette) to persuade widowed Annie Nations (Jessica Tandy) to sell her homestead. Further complications are caused by her guitar-strumming son (Brent Carver), who wants her to look after his children. For advice, Annie consults the shade of her late husband, Hector (Cronyn), who is given to lines like "There's nothin' like daylight between the ribs to clear a man's mind."

Foxfire had problems during rehearsals. It was a treasured project of Cronyn's and he was upset by the fact the production had two directors, Robin Phillips and Peter Moss. Moss took the lion's share of rehearsals, and Cronyn, a Phillips admirer, felt he was short-changed. Cronyn was also disturbed by some of the other casting, feeling that Brent Carver, in particular, was too young to play the son. Cronyn was under considerable pressure during this period, not only as author and performer of a new dramatic project, but as a member of the Stratford Board of Governors at a time when serious behind-the-scenes troubles were mounting.

Despite Cronyn's apprehension, the production pleased many critics and audience members when it opened. Even those whose praise was qualified felt the play had potential. *Maclean's* critic Mark Czarnecki felt *Foxfire* was "sentimental fictional drama" and concluded that its "mixture of old-time anecdotes, contemporary social issues and domestic drama" had yet to jell. "But Phillips and Moss have directed the fine cast with sure hands, and Phillips is to be commended for granting the play the early exposure it needs so that authors Cronyn and Susan Cooper can rewrite it into shape." *Foxfire* ran for twenty-three performances and averaged 77-percent attendance. In an amended version, the play was later to play Broadway.

August 8 saw the arrival at the Festival Theatre of one of the critical triumphs of the season. *The Seagull* was a happy reunion of playwright Anton Chekhov, adapter John Murrell, directors Robin Phillips and Urjo Kareda, and composer Berthold Carriere—the same team that had made *Uncle Vanya* so memorable two years previously. If anything, *The Seagull* was even better, with a cast that included Maggie Smith (Madame Arkadina), Brian Bedford (Trigorin), Roberta Maxwell (Nina), William Hutt (Dr. Dorn), Jack Wetherall (Konstantin), Pat Galloway (Masha), Graeme Campbell (Shamrayev), Lewis Gordon (Sorin), Jennifer Phipps (Polina), and Richard Curnock (Medvyenko).

Gina Mallet was so impressed by Murrell's adaptation that she gave it a separate review:

> Murrell has, after all, provided the basis for what is one of the strongest, most absorbing productions of the season, an astonishing mid-season entry when you come to think of it, and the launching pad for a performance by Roberta Maxwell as Nina which ranks with the best performances seen this year at the Festival. To most theatre-goers, the actual adaptation or translation of a foreign classic probably does not seem important—as long as the English flows smoothly. There is, however, a distinct art in the rendering of a foreign play in contemporary, idiomatic English, and Murrell has once again proved his mastery....Not only is the English pleasantly colloquial, falling on the ear easily, but it is strikingly unambiguous. The temptation with Chekhov is to interpret him to suit another's philosophy...or to

compound the complications that his all-embracing vision of life suggests. But Murrell unravels the knots miraculously without unravelling any of the play's essential mysteries. His boisterous and straightforward adaptation is the basis for the production's convincing assault on common preconceptions of Chekhov as an elusive genius.

Writing in the *New York Post*, Clive Barnes described *The Seagull* as second only to *Virginia* as being "the most talked-about and justifiably praised play" of the season. He praised designer Daphne Dare for the "attractive austerity" of the sets and for

> the way the fundamentally permanent setting can be transformed from indoors to outdoors with little more than the marked assistance of Gil Wechsler's lighting. The lighting also helps the directors' apparent concept of the play as largely a series of vignettes, almost late Victorian tableaux, mannered yet piquant, redolent of the past yet, with their certain cinematic fluidity, suggestive of the present. . . .Undoubtedly Miss Smith overplays, but at least it is an actress she is overplaying, and although she more often suggests provincial rep than an histrionic *grande dame* (sometimes her readings are almost too nervily funny) her portrayal of Madame Arkadina lacks nothing in gusto. Brian Bedford as the selfish, rakish novelist has this Stratford season been playing almost more with the audience than at the audience, but his suave presence is as effortlessly right here as his dandified offhand manner.

Barnes found Jack Wetherall's Konstantin a disappointment. "On the other hand Roberta Maxwell as Nina, the play's own symbolic bird of fate, gives the performance of her career." In the *Detroit News*, Jay Carr commented on a particular Phillips device:

> More than with any other Chekhov production I have seen, Phillips uses silences to achieve quite a cumulative effect. William Hutt as the doctor is funniest when he isn't saying a word. "You are irresistible," hisses the estate manager's wife who has loved him for years. He just sits there smiling fatuously, wallowing in smugness, and is more hilarious with each passing, pregnant second.

The Seagull played for twenty performances, but despite the rave reviews and the presence of Smith, Bedford, Hutt, and Maxwell, it only sold 77.3 per cent of capacity.

The *Henry VI* trilogy emerged at the Third Stage on August 13 in a four-hour condensation by Pam Brighton which, in Mark Czarnecki's words, did "a remarkable job of untangling the abundant treacheries that fuelled the Wars of the Roses". Parts of the play undoubtedly remained something of a marathon ordeal for playgoers, but it attracted 79-per-cent attendance for its eleven performances. Gina Mallet called it at once the best and worst of productions. It is ambitious, youthful, adventurous, risk-taking and bold. It is also endless, overcompressed, and the costumes appear to have been rented out from the circus. But what this production does prove is that among the large Stratford company there's vitality to spare and some very promising young actors. *Henry V*, now playing at the Festival Theatre, isn't one quarter as lively, nor is it offering the variety of some of the character acting to be seen in *Henry VI*.

Miss Mallet singled out two newcomers—Stephen Ouimette, "a virile, savage Clifford, and Robert LaChance, who made a striking scene as the son who kills his father"—as company members who "should be promptly promoted from the ranks of the spear carriers". She found Stephen Russell's Henry overly meek but singled out, among company veterans in the cast, none other than Nicholas Pennell:

This actor is cornering Stratford's baddies. In *Henry VI*, he first plays the Duke of Suffolk with an evil slickness that makes his courting of Queen Margaret one of the play's clearest, most enjoyable scenes, and then he limps on stage as Gloucester, the future Richard III, and very nearly hobbles away with the rest of the play. He is also one of the few actors on stage with enough technique to really make a character stick in the short time each is given on stage in this production.

The final two productions of the final Phillips season seemed almost an adjunct to the far more turbulent drama being enacted in real life behind the scenes at Stratford. As Mark Czarnecki wrote in the October 20 issue of *Maclean's*,

Tragedy begins at home, and nowhere has this been more evident than at Stratford's troubled festival. Onstage, two domestic tyrants—Shakespeare's King Lear and O'Neill's James Tyrone—sow the seeds of dissension and downfall; offstage, a third household tyrant, artistic director Robin Phillips, until recently hero-worshipped by the Festival Board for transforming the theatre into Canada's leading classical company, has resigned (again), instigating family feuds among board members, administrative staff and actors, leaving all concerned desperate for any final solution.

The events surrounding the trauma of 1980 require a chapter on their own, but Czarnecki's comments indicated how inevitable it was that they should intrude into the public's perception of what was taking place on stage.

King Lear opened its thirty-two-performance run on September 14 with Peter Ustinov delivering another fascinating performance in the title role—but also in a far less amiable frame of mind off-stage towards some of the people involved with the Festival. The production played to 97.7-per-cent houses.

On October 4, Robin Phillips's swan-song production for Stratford opened at the Avon. The reviews for *Long Day's Journey Into Night* were respectful rather than enthusiastic, despite a cast that included Jessica Tandy, William Hutt, Graeme Campbell, and Brent Carver. Robin Phillips, observed Gina Mallet, is

> going out with his quirkiness intact. This is a gothic *Long Day's Journey Into Night*, invested with doom, and played on a single and rather monotonous note of despair. It also suffers from another Phillips flaw; it is ice-cold where it should be red-hot. There are moments of majesty, notably in Jessica Tandy's Mary, but the keynote seems to be [son] Edmund's parody of Shakespeare: " We are such stuff as manure is made on, so let's drink up and forget it."

The production took in $152,770 at the box office and played to 72.2 per cent.

·C·H·A·P·T·E·R · XXVII·

The Crisis

When Robin Phillips attempted to resign in the summer of 1978, pleading artistic self-doubts, the board was able to persuade him to stay by offering him a sabbatical from the 1979 season. As it turned out, the sabbatical was only partial. The longest period that Phillips was away from the Festival was six weeks, and he ended up directing three productions. Phillips himself realized early in 1979 that the sabbatical was not going to work, and he wrote to his new board president, Toronto lawyer Robert V. Hicks, advising him of his decision to leave at the end of the 1980 season. He would meet his 1979 commitments and deliver a 1980 season, but was not prepared to continue as artistic director beyond then. The five-year contract given Phillips in 1976 was due to end at the close of the 1981 season, but it also granted him the right to withdraw on three months' notice. When Phillips wrote to Hicks early in 1979, he was in effect giving eighteen months' notice—ample time, he hoped, for a proper search for a successor to be conducted. Several months later, he was astonished to be still encountering board members who claimed to be unaware of his 1980 departure. A search committee had been established in May of 1979, but was relatively inactive for the rest of the year.

The seeds of crisis were being sown. It was a crisis that came close to destroying the Stratford Festival and convulsed the entire Canadian cultural community. It was a crisis that reached into the highest levels of government and sparked a lively debate in the editorial pages and letters columns of the nation's newspapers. It was a crisis that left a legacy of bitterness that festered for years afterwards.

(The most detailed account of these turbulent events is to be found in Canadian journalist Martin Knelman's exhaustively researched book *A Stratford Tempest*, published by McClelland and Stewart in 1982. As an account of the chaos which mounted through much of 1980, it appropriately has all the elements of a good thriller. It also caused consternation among Festival board members—an indication, one would suggest, of its importance.)

To many board members, Phillips was the wizard with the golden touch, the man who had brought the Festival the biggest commercial and artistic triumphs of its history. It was difficult for them to face the fact of his departure. Hicks, in particular, was anxious that Phillips should stay—in some capacity—with the Festival. Phillips was beset by his own ambivalent feelings. He didn't want to leave the Festival. He knew that the parting would be a wrenching experience for him. There were times, before reaching his decision, when he would drive over to the Festival Theatre in the middle of the night, park his car, and sit staring at the building that had proved so important a part of his life. But Phillips believed that he must go. He knew that the burdens of running an operation like Stratford were taking too much of a toll. His artistic self-doubts were continuing. But he also felt that it was in the Festival's best interests to have a change of command, and that if he were coaxed into staying, the Festival would ultimately be the loser.

However, the door continued to remain ajar for some future Phillips involvement with Stratford. On February 11, 1980, Phillips told a gathering of the Canadian Club in Toronto that he could not speak about the future of the Festival "as my days as its artistic director are finally being numbered". Hicks, who was also present at the luncheon meeting, confirmed that the 1980 season would be Phillips's last, but expressed the hope that Phillips would not sever all connections with Stratford and might stay on to work either on films or in the drama school. In the meantime, a committee of the board had compiled a list of possible successors, Hicks said.

But what kind of list? And what kind of "search" was the board conducting? In later months, when the board found itself under siege, it was to suggest that its search processes had, in fact, been thorough. The board's critics felt quite the reverse. The board had established criteria for potential candidates: experience in directing Shakespeare; experience in directing classical theatre; experience with a thrust stage; artistic attitude and vision; proved budgetary responsibility; fair treatment of artists; administrative experience; experience in running a large company with more than one theatre. Using these criteria, the board assessed and rejected several Canadian directors, among them some persons whose backgrounds would appear to meet the board's requirements.

The search processes, such as they were, proved secretive in nature. The position was not advertised. That the board was not functioning realistically seemed evident from the candidates it did approach during the winter of 1980. Hume Cronyn was now seventy, continuing a successful acting and writing career, and clearly not interested in a job that had taxed the stamina of a man half his age. Broadway producer Robert Whitehead was a Canadian with a respected reputation in theatre circles, and he wanted to continue being a Broadway producer. He was also in his sixties. The board tried Michael Langham, by now head of the theatre centre at New York's Juilliard School of Music, and was turned down. This type of "search" scarcely seemed serious, in view of the near-certainty that the candidates approached would not be available. Meanwhile, one obvious candidate, John Hirsch, was ignored.

There was one further approach—to John Neville, the Old Vic veteran who had come to Canada in 1972 to run the Citadel Theatre in Edmonton and who was now in charge of the Neptune Theatre in Halifax. An internationally respected actor and director, Neville could claim the experience, background, and connections to run Stratford. Against these credentials was his well-known suspicion of large "Establishment" institutions. Nevertheless, after overtures were made by board members Ronald Bryden and Arnold Edinborough, Neville did agree to go to Stratford in May for further discussions. Neville was to stress afterwards that there had only been one real basis for discussions—that he would be involved in some sort of artistic team with Phillips. The two had worked together amicably at Chichester, and had long been anxious to renew the relationship. But Neville sensed Phillips's ambivalence about staying. At that time he had absolutely no desire to end up in the position of solo artistic director. Furthermore, he was conscious of his commitments to his Halifax theatre, and was determined not to abandon it. Five days after the Stratford meetings, he informed the board he was not interested.

By May, Phillips and his company were deep into rehearsals for the 1980 season, which was shaping up as one of the major artistic and financial successes in the Festival's history. But in the background, with the issue of artistic succession undecided and without even preliminary planning under way for the 1981 season, the alarm bells were sounding.

No one was more concerned than Robin Phillips. He had not rejected the possibility of a future association with the Festival in a new capacity, but he was determined that it would not be as artistic director. A few board members, among them Barbara Ivey, had accepted the inevitability of Phillips's departure. Others, including

Hicks, had not. Phillips, frustrated, felt he was not getting through to them. On March 27 he had sent a memo to the search committee:

ATTENTION: SEARCH COMMITTEE:

The enclosed are suggestions only. First, and most important, I think you should get, if you possibly can, one person to replace me, whatever their title, so that the committee and staff are absolutely clear where the buck stops. I believe that either John Hirsch or John Neville could easily play this role with commitment, excitement and energy. . . . I stress very strongly that the Festival is in need of a change of leadership and that is what you should be working toward even if it takes another year. Much love, Robin.

Phillips was still angry with Hirsch over the latter's behaviour in 1976, but he was determined that personal feelings would not blur his professional judgment concerning what was best for the Festival. He believed that Hirsch was a candidate who could not be disregarded. He was even to hint that, under certain circumstances, he might be prepared to work on the same team as Hirsch.

Phillips accompanied his memo with two draft proposals for a restructuring of the Festival hierarchy. The first, and main, proposal suggested Neville or Hirsch as artistic director, with Douglas Rain functioning in a new capacity as "artistic liaison", plus a team of "associate directors" consisting of Urjo Kareda, William Hutt, Peter Moss, production manager Peter Roberts, treasurer Gary Thomas, and outsider June Faulkner, who would be brought in as director of production. The alternative proposal was more radical. Brian Bedford, Martha Henry, and Canadian-born Broadway star Len Cariou would be joint artistic directors. Phillips would be in charge of "future projects" and Hirsch in charge of "Toronto development". Board member Ronald Bryden would be "liaison director", and there would be the same team of associate directors as in the main proposal.

The board did not act in any meaningful way on Phillips's recommendations. This was not, however, the first time that the idea of a group directorate had been floated. In 1979, Phillips himself had suggested in media interviews that if the Festival had grown too large to be run by a single person, a group operation might well offer a solution. Several potential models existed: Britain's Royal Shakespeare Company, Manchester's Royal Exchange Theatre, and, closer to home, the Seattle Repertory Theater, where consulting artistic director John Hirsch was a member of a clearly defined artistic team.

Some Stratford board members argued that it would be impossible to run the Festival by committee. Others, including Hicks, saw merit in the plan, particularly if it meant hanging on to Phillips in some capacity. Indeed, the attractiveness of the committee idea probably helps explain the half-hearted nature of the winter "search" for a solo artistic director. The problem was that no real momentum was being established to pursue even an alternative solution.

It could be argued that the board was in paralysis over looming financial worries. Hicks was to argue cogently that the question of artistic leadership could not be separated from that of the fiscal crisis which he believed to be imminent. By the end of 1980, Hicks was to be under attack from all quarters for his handling of a complex and frightening situation, but he never wavered from his belief that the wrong kind of decision with respect to the artistic succession could have disastrous financial implications.

Furthermore, it would be doing Hicks an injustice to ignore the importance of a document he submitted to the Ontario Arts Council on February 20, 1980. Entitled "Challenge For the Eighties— Artistic Achievement or Financial Collapse", it provided a chilling appraisal of the Festival's present difficult state and clouded future.

Hicks had been disturbed by the scepticism that had greeted his warning at the 1979 annual general meeting that the 1980 season could be the last. He decided stronger words were needed. Preparing the 1980 budget, his paper said, had been an intense struggle. It was a budget that

will demand as never before a total commitment from everyone in this totally committed organization. A budget that will create an unprecedented, intense and sustained pressure to achieve dramatically increased revenue goals. A budget on the heels of two consecutive operating deficits totalling $845,000, which have left us with an accumulated deficit of $245,400. It was a budget approved with the knowledge that the gamble has become far too great, that the miracle could not be accomplished again, and that in fact it was not even rational to attempt it.

Some would say that our situation at the moment is not desperate, that our accumulated deficit is not significant, that all artistic organizations are having financial problems in which deficits are not unique. We have been told that monies are not available, that we should regard our grants as insurance, that grants are allocated on the basis of need and that there is no cause to worry. But for us to accept these statements complacently would be foolish at this time. We are acutely aware of the difficulties. We know all too well that our very survival is at stake.

The irony of the situation was that, by any standard, Stratford was a spectacularly successful operation, selling more than 500,000 tickets a year, with attendance in the 80- to 90-per-cent range. No other cultural organization in the country came anywhere near to financing so much of its budget from box office. But, Hicks warned, this success tended to blind government to Stratford's growing inability to maintain this remarkable record.

The figures he produced were revealing. From 1975 to 1979, spending had increased $2,949,000, or 81 per cent. Ticket sales had grown $2,143,000, or 84 per cent. Private-sector fund-raising was up $255,000, or 101 per cent—and this in a cultural organization with the built-in handicap of being the only one located outside a major metropolitan area. Ominously, however, public funding showed a decrease of 8 per cent during this period. One of Hicks's fundamental points was that government funding agencies were expecting the Stratford Festival to do too much in terms of balancing its budget. It was not a new situation; the Festival's remarkable box-office performance, which was so much higher than that of any other major arts group, had long encouraged a lower proportion of public funding. Now, however, things were reaching a crunch, Hicks suggested. He drew a particular bead on the Ontario Arts Council, the body to which his document was directed. "During the past five years, our grant from Council has seemed not to recognize the erosion of our dollars through inflation and not to recognize the explosion of growth and activity in our programming." In 1979, the Festival's Ontario Arts Council grant of $250,000 represented only 3.9 per cent of its total revenues. In terms of dollars, this was less than the Toronto Symphony, the National Ballet, or the Canadian Opera Company received. In terms of percentage of revenues, it was the lowest of any major arts group in the province.

Hicks saw a further danger signal: escalation of ticket prices in order to maximize Festival revenues. The top price in the Festival Theatre had jumped 60 per cent from $12.50 in 1978 to $20.00 in 1980; and at the Avon 48 per cent, from $10.50 to $15.50. How much, Hicks wondered, could the playgoing public bear?

> Obviously, with every increase built into the revenue projection, the risk of a financial disaster increases substantially. Every time we increase ticket prices, we eliminate another group of people who feel that they can no longer afford to attend. Unlike most theatres, to attend a performance at Stratford, most people must travel some distance. This involves considerable additional time and expense. Meals, travel, accommodation and other expenditures generate substantial amounts for the community, the province and the nation, but could be totally lost if the visit becomes too expensive. We also risk losing our school audience, our chief source of future audiences, as costs increase, energy continues to grow as a problem and we are forced to schedule fewer school performances in order to maximize revenues.

Hicks noted that, because of more performances and longer seasons, staff and performers were already coping with "a back-breaking load...a load that is shared by substantially the same numbers of people as were employed at the Festival several years ago.''

Bringing the 1980 budget to a break-even position had proved an "almost impossible task", which was why Hicks felt the 1981 budget would confront the Festival with its most serious financial problem in a decade:

> We cannot increase the size of our auditoriums; the season has been extended to the limit; many weeks include extra performances; and ticket prices have reached a level where, if at all possible, they should remain virtually unchanged for the next several years. Almost the entire increase in costs during the past five years has been financed from within the Festival. The next five years must provide the Festival and the public with some stability in ticket prices.

The onus, Hicks argued, was on government:

> Bluntly stated, there is at present no financial plan for the future, nor, given the circumstances, is one possible. Unbelievably, this multi-million-dollar business has proceeded from year to year with the knowledge that 9-per-cent inflation would require hundreds of thousands of dollars more to mount the next year's programming and, until the past two years, with the supreme optimism the money could be produced....Our problem with the 1981 budget exists because of our inability in the past to develop a plan for future revenues. While we could predict ticket sales and fund-raising with some confidence, government grants have been a source of confusion and disappointment to us. We are completely frustrated in our attempts to develop at the present. As has been pointed out, there are staff shortages at the Festival; we do not have the manpower to sustain the increased high level of activity. Our facilities are full to capacity. Stage One, which was intended to alleviate our space problem, has been put on hold because of the financial situation.

Hicks envisaged a scenario in which annual operating costs would continue to rise by ten per cent a year, with ticket revenues remaining relatively unchanged because of the need to stabilize prices. He saw fund-raising increasing ten per cent each year and—significantly—a substantial increase in public funding to provide the balance. He argued that by 1983 Canada Council funding should increase from its present $550,000 to $1,650,000 and Ontario Arts Council aid from $310,000 to $850,000. Without this increase, "we face an impossible challenge to respond adequately to the costs we shall surely incur....The cultural growth of this country and the development of our artists and craftsmen are at stake. Seven hundred jobs each year could be lost."

It was a frightening document and an important one. It also helped mould the thinking of Robert Hicks and other board members as they continued to wrestle with the thorny problem of who should run the Festival in 1981.

Meanwhile as spring moved into summer, there was little evidence of a concerted effort by the board to solve the problem of Phillips's successor. In May, the board examined the possibility of a three-person directorate, featuring Urjo Kareda as chairman, Peter Moss, and Peter Roberts. "We were each approached individually by the board," Kareda was to recall later. "There was also some thought that Robin might play a role in this structure. But none of the three of us ever heard back from the board. Like so many of the board's schemes, nothing came of it."

The 1980 season opened in early June, with still no 1981 action having been taken. Hicks had been conducting individual conversations with individual parties—a tactic, it was said, stemming from his experience as a labour lawyer—but had been eschewing group discussions. This led to confusion and misunderstanding as to what had actually been said in those various meetings with Hicks. Some of the people interviewed by the board president were later to argue that their responses to him had been misinterpreted. In the meantime, some board members were also starting to feel that they were not being properly informed as to what was happening.

What was lacking was any evidence of a concerted, collective effort to decide who, or what, should succeed the Phillips regime. Finally, the effort came, not from the board, but from Phillips and a number of his senior colleagues. Phillips was still determined to leave as artistic director, but he also feared for the Festival's future. Board inaction had created a vacuum, which somebody had to fill. "We cannot just sit here and do nothing," Phillips commented privately in July. The 1981 season remained a blank on the calendar; planning for it was long overdue. A sense of urgency prevailed. Among those who moved to fill the breach were Phillips, Martha Henry, Brian Bedford, and one outsider, Len Cariou, who had come to Stratford in July to take in some plays.

By this time, Phillips was accepting the probability that he would in some way be involved with the 1981 season—but not, he continued to stress, as artistic director. What was emerging in his meetings with key colleagues was the idea he had broached previously—a group directorate. In a June interview with Sid Adilman of the *Toronto Star*, Phillips had suggested this was the only basis on which he would consider returning to the Festival. "If I say, 'There's no way on God's earth that I am going to be here next year,' and if in six months I'm here doing a production, it will look crazy," he told Adilman. However, he also said the board had mixed feelings about any shared leadership proposal. "There are key board members in support of the plan, but it isn't across the board. There are at least half of them who believe that I shouldn't be here, and after seven years you can't go on with half of the people thinking that way. It has to be complete support or nothing. It's too large an organization to run any other way." Now, however, time was so short that a group directorate no longer seemed to be one possible solution; in the eyes of many, it was the only solution.

Finally, after much fine-tuning, the artists presented their proposals for a group directorate to the board at a July 24 meeting. The board in turn gave its approval subject to certain conditions and clarifications pertaining to structure and expansion plans for the Festival. The group, in offering the board a solution to the succession problem, was setting its own conditions, among them a commitment to television and film and a Toronto season for the Festival. These auxiliary activities Phillips had wanted for years, on the grounds they would broaden the Festival's income base, bring it into closer contact with the rest of the arts community, and make it easier to hang on to good people within the organization.

However, within days of the board's approval of the group directorate, roadblocks again began appearing. Phillips was troubled by the board's assumption that he would continue to be the undisputed artistic head of the restructured Festival. He was apprehensive over the board's failure to confirm the group proposal in writing. His worries accelerated when the board began fussing over the wording of the press release announcing the directorate. Hicks kept preparing fresh drafts of the release, to the exasperation of certain board members and artists. Other board members, apprehensive about the effect of expansion plans on Festival finances and the sanctity of its Stratford home-base, were privately balking at the implications of the total scenario. Phillips saw in the continued drafting and redrafting of the press release evidence of this continued waffling; when one proposed release changed the phrase "Toronto season" to a more tentative "projected Toronto season", Phillips found himself seriously doubting the strength of the board's commitment, and was close to backing out of the new arrangement completely.

Finally, on August 13, a final press release seemingly acceptable to all parties was issued:

On behalf of the Board of Governors of the Stratford Festival, R. V. Hicks, Q.C., President, today announced that with the co-operation of the Festival's company, the restructuring of its artistic administration has been completed. In order to consolidate and extend the ongoing vitality and growth of the Stratford Festival, the organization will be administered by a two-tiered committee working collectively.

The first tier, artistic directors, will consist of Brian Bedford, Len Cariou and Martha Henry. The second tier, resident directors, will consist of Pam Brighton, William Hutt, Urjo Kareda, Peter Moss and

Peter Roberts. Douglas Rain will serve as liaison chairman within the organization.

Both groups will be under the guidance of Robin Phillips, who as Festival director will be a member of each group.

The two-tiered committee will be responsible for the ongoing artistic policy of the Festival and for planning and executing each year's program in Stratford and a winter program in Toronto at a location yet to be determined. The group will also integrate the development of Stratford's connections in New York, in London, and in films and television.

It is anticipated that the contracting of the directors involved will soon be completed. By being able to draw on the exceptional range of skills and experience represented by the members of the joint committees, the Board of Governors feels that the artistic values for which the Stratford Festival has become famous will be secure. These will also be brought into play in shaping the future directions of the Stratford Festival.

Yet even as the press release went out, Phillips found his anxieties returning. He warned his colleagues in the directorate that their proposal had yet to be accepted in writing and that no contracts had been offered. He confided to certain members of the media that he doubted the board's commitment to the plan. Press reaction was guarded. The *Stratford Beacon-Herald* noted with approval that "Robin Phillips would remain in charge of the artistic organization," thereby making the very kind of emphasis that Phillips wished to discourage. The local paper was, however, apprehensive about the Toronto plans:

What is to be the future of Stage One on the Avon Theatre site? Rumors are circulating that the move to Toronto for the winter season will enable the Festival to utilize recording and film studios already in existence in Toronto, for its proposed television productions rather than going through the expensive process of building them in Stratford. . . . Stage One was conspicuous by its absence in the Festival's announcement on Tuesday. We hope that its absence does not mean that the project is dead or that Stage One will not be centred in Stratford but in Toronto. We hope too that the planned winter season in Toronto does not reduce the emphasis on the summer season here in Stratford. We hope that the announcement does not signal any move by the board to lean away from Stratford toward Toronto.

The *Beacon-Herald*'s views had many allies, among them Stratford board members who had always been uncomfortable with any type of expansionist plans that might erode the importance of the home base. It was not a favourable climate for the nurturing of the directorate idea.

Meanwhile, within days of the press release announcing its formation, the directorate itself was showing signs of disintegration. Phillips became painfully aware of what had always been obvious to everyone else: that the success or failure of the scheme depended on his presence. Two factors increased his apprehension. One was his discovery that some of the key colleagues with whom he expected to be sharing the burden of running the festival would not immediately be available. The second, even more alarming, factor was the refusal of the board to give him a new contract. The whole point of the directorate exercise was to relieve Phillips of the crushing burden of running the Festival. This was the only basis on which Phillips had been prepared to stay, and he saw it as vital that his responsibilities be legally redefined. When he realized he was expected to serve out his existing contract, his worst fears were confirmed. The new group directorate appeared to be no more than a meaningless sop; in actual fact, he would be continuing with the same responsibilities as before. As far as Phillips was concerned, his resignation as artistic director, effective at the end of the 1980 season, still stood. It had been submitted more than a year previously, and his involvement in the directorate had been an entirely separate proposition. On August 27 he decided to withdraw from the directorate; in effect, he was now severing his connection with the Festival completely. (Board member Barbara Ivey was not surprised. "The reason Robin wanted a new contract was that he needed an affirmation of the board's willingness to accept him in a new situation," she recalled. "Unfortunately, there were board members unwilling to grant him this.")

Other members of the directorate were also apprehensive. They saw the board's commitment to the Toronto plan as evidence of its good faith. "If they wanted the two-tier system," one participant recalled later, "they had to accept that expansion into Toronto was non-negotiable. We didn't mean this had to happen within the next two months—after all, one had to find the necessary money and a building. What we wanted clearly understood was that this was an inevitable aspect of the Festival's progress." The problems with the press release didn't allay the directorate's fears: it appeared that the board was supporting Toronto privately in its dealings with the directorate while seeking to hedge on the agreement in its public pronouncements. At one point, a frustrated Phillips had faced his colleagues and said: "I cannot deal with the board any more, because I don't know who I'm talking to. I don't know which face I'm talking to. I don't know which agreement I'm talking to. I just don't know." If the board was really prepared to pay no more than lip-service to this restructuring, what were its motives? By late August, some senior members of the two-tiered directorate were wondering whether some board members were exploring a new and entirely different option in which they would have no place.

Phillips's departure was not to be publicly confirmed until mid-September. In the meantime, the directorate continued to fall apart. It became clear that it had been slapped together too hastily at the eleventh hour, leaving the commitment of some key players somewhat tenuous. More significantly, the board had not appreciated the strength of Phillips's resolve to relieve himself of the burdens of artistic director as detailed in his existing contract. The board had known for many, many months that the only way to keep Phillips would be to give him different, less onerous responsibilities. It was well aware of his belief that Stratford was too big to be operated by a single artistic director and that reform of its artistic structure was long overdue. The choice facing the board should have been apparent by the end of 1979—either to go along with the proposed new formula of a group operation if it wished Phillips to retain some association with the Festival or else to bite the bullet and launch a proper, comprehensive, fully advertised search for a new artistic director. Instead, the board had made a few meaningless approaches to a few people and had dithered and procrastinated.

With Phillips out, remaining members of the directorate began reassessing their own positions. When they met the board to discuss their future, Bedford made it clear that his involvement had been conditional on Phillips's participation and that he had no desire to end up as artistic director of the Stratford Festival. He announced he was withdrawing from the group. Meanwhile, the continued involvement of Len Cariou, who had remained in New York and who was being advised of developments by telephone, seemed increasingly marginal. The board turned to the remaining members of the directorate—Urjo Kareda, Martha Henry, Douglas Rain, William Hutt, Peter Roberts, Pam Brighton, and Peter Moss—and asked them to put together a 1981 season. But in ensuing meetings, group members found themselves plagued by uncertainties. In view of the defections that had taken place from their ranks, they felt they needed clearly defined terms of reference. They wanted a written commitment from the board. They felt they could not start proper work on a 1981 season until formally empowered to do so by the board—in brief, a contract was essential, and a draft document would not be sufficient. The directorate's concern assumed additional urgency because of the imminent arrival on the scene of an unknown quantity—Englishman Peter Stevens, who had been appointed to the newly created position of executive director.

One of those most worried was William Hutt. As a quarter-century veteran of the Festival, he had seen many boards come and go. This one made him uneasy. He warned his colleagues: "I don't think they're going to offer us anything tangible. I don't trust them, and I don't think they're ever going to offer the seven of us a contract."

Not only was Hutt troubled by lack of tangible commitment from the board, he also felt that the departure of Phillips—who would have been the directorate's liaison with the board—meant that someone else would be expected by the board to fill the leadership vacuum. It was a point on which the group of seven was by no means agreed. Some felt they should be all collectively responsible to the board and that there should be no specified chairman or leader. Assuming, however, that the group continued its precarious existence and received some sort of formal mandate from the board, the latter would scarcely want all seven at its meetings. Within the directorate, sentiment favoured Kareda. Some board members saw Hutt as the ideal leader. Hutt decided that the last thing the Festival needed at this point was any sort of a power struggle within the directorate. Secondly, he now had serious doubts as to whether the directorate could work at all—even if it did receive contracts. He decided that seven people sitting around a table trying to organize a season would be chaos. He resigned—a move that stunned those board members who had counted on his statesmanlike presence—and Peter Roberts and Douglas Rain were soon to follow.

The question of artistic succession was not the only issue causing the board dismay during 1980. There were troubles over two major projects—the filming of *The Importance of Being Earnest* and the London engagement of *King Lear*.

The *Earnest* project had been the first step in fulfilling Phillips's dream for a film and television wing. Harvey Chusid had been brought in as administrator for the production, a film script was commissioned from writer Suzanne Grossman, and a contract was signed with the Toronto firm of Norfolk Communications. However, because of lack of time and resources, the scheduled 1980 production of the film never took place, and there were threats of legal action from some parties. The film became a victim of the other convulsions afflicting Stratford that year.

The tangled and terrifying problem of *King Lear*'s London engagement stemmed from Robin Phillips's personal commitment to Peter Ustinov that he would not be expected to return to Stratford for a 1980 revival of the play unless there was a West End run as well. It was the promise of a London engagement that had persuaded Ustinov to turn down some lucrative film work in favour of Stratford. To play Lear in the West End would fulfil a lifelong ambition.

Initial plans called for a package of four productions—*King Lear*, the forthcoming *Virginia*, and two triumphs from earlier seasons—to play London. Phillips was anxious that London see the Festival as a company offering a cross-section of its best work. He did not wish to see the Festival judged by a single production, particularly one as experimental as *Lear*. Furthermore, Duncan Weldon and Louis

Michaels, the operators of London's Triumph Productions and owners of the Theatre Royal, Haymarket, where the company was to perform, had made it clear that they wished the London cast to be of the same calibre as the cast in the 1979 *Lear*. In other words, they wanted Ustinov and the cream of the Stratford company; they did not want Ustinov and a pick-up cast. It was a requirement with which Phillips naturally concurred. The problem was that he became increasingly fearful of being able to fulfil it.

Negotiations respecting the London engagement continued through the winter months. Phillips was concerned that the Festival lacked the expertise to navigate its way through the shoals of a foreign engagement and strongly recommended to Hicks that he hire a London lawyer. Some board members, including Barbara Ivey, also argued that it was in the Festival's interest to have legal representation in England, but were unsuccessful in their pitch. Their fears seemed well founded when the Festival sent a proposed draft contract based on previous verbal discussions to London in April; it came back in late May containing new clauses which the board had not discussed and which would increase Stratford's share of expenses.

By now it was clear to the Stratford board that, with no special government subsidy forthcoming, it could not afford to send four productions to London. It had committed itself to raising $200,000 to help finance a West End engagement for *Lear* and *Virginia*; now even the feasibility of this truncated package seemed questionable as the board found itself involved in a transatlantic argument with Triumph over which party would be responsible for which expenses. By the end of June, it appeared that an impasse had been reached and the London tour was off. Then, following an eleventh-hour trip to Stratford by the Triumph officials, agreement was reached, and by early August a contract had been signed.

However, as far as Phillips was concerned, the situation was anything but cut and dried. His worry had been over casting. It had been so since late March when the Festival sent notices to twenty-five members of the *Lear* cast inquiring about their availability for a post-season engagement in London. Eighteen had responded affirmatively. The remaining seven were doubtful. One of them was Douglas Rain, in the vital role of the Duke of Gloucester. Phillips started to wonder whether it would be possible to guarantee a top-drawer cast for London. Furthermore, given his other commitments, he did not believe himself capable of coping with an extensive recasting of the production for London. By mid-June, with negotiations between Stratford and London reaching an apparent stalemate, his concern had increased. Aware of his promise to Ustinov, he made his first attempt to cancel the 1980 Stratford production of *Lear* but was blocked by the board. The dilemma was an intricate one. It was hazardous to line up members of the 1980 *Lear* cast for

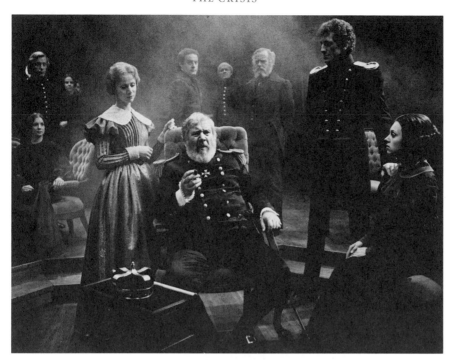

Scene from the 1979/1980 Avon stage production of King Lear, *directed by Robin Phillips, designed by Daphne Dare, music by Berthold Carriere, lighting by Michael J. Whitfield. L.-R.: Marti Maraden as Regan (1979), Ingrid Blekys as Cordelia (1979), Richard Monette as Edmund, Peter Ustinov as King Lear, Douglas Rain as Gloucester, Frank Maraden as Albany (1979), Donna Goodhand as Goneril (1979). Photograph by Robert C. Ragsdale, f.r.p.s., courtesy of the Stratford Festival Archives.*

a subsequent London engagement until that engagement was a certainty. Complicating matters further was the reluctance of some key performers to go to London at all, and the unwillingness of others to risk losing alternative work offers if the tour failed to materialize.

During the early part of August, verbal offers were made to several members of the *Lear* cast. Most were not picked up. Ustinov arrived on August 14 to begin rehearsals, and later in the month was advised by Phillips to withdraw on the grounds that casting difficulties made the London engagement unlikely. Two weeks remained before *Lear*'s Stratford engagement opened on September 14. Ustinov was not prepared to withdraw. Neither was he prepared to envisage the possibility that the London engagement would not happen. Tour plans assumed an on-again, off-again existence, with Phillips cancelling the London engagement on the grounds that the quality of the production would be endangered by recasting, and Hicks promptly resurrecting the plans. Caught in the middle was

Stratford's director of productions, Thomas Hooker, the man responsible for negotiating the London contracts. He complained to Gina Mallet of the *Toronto Star*, "I found myself at an absolute standstill. I report to Robin. He said, 'Don't talk to me, talk to Hicks.' I found myself not getting anywhere with Mr. Hicks. Then I sat down and said there's no more I can do unless I find out who's driving the train."

The *Lear* crisis was peaking at the same time that the two-tiered directorate was collapsing. Then, in early September, in the midst of the turmoil, Phillips received word of his father's death in England. He was shattered. "My focus is my family," he told the *Toronto Star*. "I come from a working class family and everybody thought it arty-crafty when I went to theatre school. But their support was colossal. With my father just gone, you feel you've lost the reason for doing it. I feel I've never repaid them." Before leaving for England for the funeral, he made a further attempt at recasting. Meanwhile, the Haymarket was being advised that *Lear*'s London tour was in jeopardy; the Haymarket's response was to remind Stratford of its contractual obligations.

Lear opened in Stratford on September 14. Phillips was back from his father's funeral. Michaels and Weldon had flown from London in a last-ditch effort to salvage the tour. Phillips continued his efforts to put together a cast. There were suggestions that, if an essentially new cast had to be found—and at this point Ustinov seemed prepared to accept any cast, provided the London run went ahead—Pamela Brighton should assume directing duties. This solution was not feasible: the contract with Triumph specified that Phillips must be director. Five days after *Lear* opened, the board finally moved and cancelled the tour. Phillips sent a note to Ustinov: "Dear Peter, I'm angry, shocked, and for you, deeply upset. I hope one day you'll understand how hard I've worked to see that you are seen in the right company. Until then, I love you, and love your Lear. I'm sorry. Love, Robin." Ustinov, still enraged, announced he would sue the Festival. In an interview with the London *Sunday Times*, he would blame Phillips for the debacle. Board member Barbara Ivey had a different perspective. "Nobody would ever give Robin credit for the amount of time he spent trying to recast the play. Michaels and Weldon insisted on the standard of production they had seen in 1979. They wouldn't accept less, nor was Robin prepared to give them less."

Ustinov was in for a further disappointment when a proposed CBC television version of *Lear* was scrapped. Once again the nationalistic Association of Canadian Television and Radio Artists was the culprit. ACTRA approved a work permit for Ustinov but refused one for Australian actress Patricia Conolly. ACTRA might have been prepared to approve Conolly had the CBC been prepared to meet its demand that it tell Canadian theatres to hire Canadians in future.

The CBC was not prepared to bow to this kind of pressure and scrapped a project that had been in the works for six months. ACTRA's tactics were not welcomed by Stratford company members, who once more saw themselves deprived of extra income. They also felt ACTRA was behaving in an insulting manner to their stage union, Equity, which had already approved the presence of Miss Conolly in Canada.

For Phillips, one of the most painful legacies of the tour fiasco was his estrangement from Peter Ustinov, an actor with whom he had developed a warm and cordial relationship. Nearly three months later, he was to rise at the Festival Foundation's stormy annual general meeting and give his account of what had happened. He said that on five separate occasions he had tried to cancel the production:

> I did it at times when I thought we could save any financial problems for the Festival before the box office opened; the only bookings received had come in by mail, and therefore we had addresses, telephone numbers and names. I did it throughout the year at times when I thought we were never going to get a contract settled with Mr. Ustinov or the Haymarket Theatre, and that the only responsible thing to do was cancel. I had given my personal word to Mr. Ustinov that he need not play at Stratford unless he also appeared in the West End. Two weeks before the production was about to open, I again cancelled the performance at Stratford because I was not sure Stratford was able to take the tour to London. I gave Mr. Ustinov the opportunity to leave Stratford and I would take the responsibility of coping with the public and refunding money. All these decisions were overturned, and when the decision finally came about over the opening day and subsequent days, I refused any further to make the decision because I could no longer protect Mr. Ustinov, and at no point from that final decision by the board would I have ever made the decision. It was in their hands.

In most years, the issue of the *King Lear* tour would alone have been sufficient to have sent an annual general meeting boiling over. However, in 1980 this embarrassment paled beside the furore which was raging over the question of artistic succession. A well-meaning but monstrously insensitive and bumbling board was by its conduct to raise doubts as to whether a 1981 season was even feasible.

To return to the month of September and the remnants of the two-tier directorate: When it became clear that Len Cariou had previous commitments which would make his services unavailable until summer, only four members of the original group remained: Urjo Kareda, Martha Henry, Peter Moss, and Pam Brighton. These people were wary of the board and bruised by the events of recent weeks. However, meetings with board representatives encouraged them to believe in the board's good faith should they be entrusted with the artistic leadership of the Festival. They were prepared to take on the job, but not on a one-year token basis. The board assured them of a three-year commitment. Ominously, no contracts were offered; nevertheless, the Gang of Four—as the group was soon to become known—decided to take the plunge.

Company members were informed of the latest arrangement at a morning meeting on September 18. Some were openly worried— among them Bedford, who was now questioning the viability of rule by committee, and Graeme Campbell, who was one of many actors concerned about the absence of Phillips from the scenario.

But Phillips was definitely out, as the press release issued at the close of the meeting made clear:

> The Board of Governors today confirmed that Robin Phillips will relinquish the position of Artistic Director of the Stratford Festival at the end of the present season. Mr. Phillips confirmed his resignation to the Board in writing in January, 1979, to become effective in 1980, and the Board respects his decision.
>
> "Robin Phillips has built the Stratford Festival into one of the most significant theatrical organizations in the world," said R. V. Hicks, president, announcing the resignation. "His dedication, talent, energy, and sheer brilliance have been an inspiration to everyone connected with the Festival Board, staff and audiences alike."
>
> The Board has now authorized an Artistic Directorate to succeed Mr. Phillips. The new Artistic Directorate, chosen from the present artistic community of the Festival, comprises: Urjo Kareda, Pam Brighton, Martha Henry and Peter Moss. They will immediately begin to plan and execute the 1981 season.
>
> "We are totally committed to this cohesive new group," said Mr. Hicks, "and it is a matter of pride that they have been chosen, and have accepted their role, from within the present Festival ranks."

When Robin Phillips finally did exit Stratford, the response of many in the arts community remained ambivalent. Ray Conlogue assessed the prevailing mentality in a widely read *Globe and Mail* post-mortem on the Phillips regime:

> Those who accuse Phillips of brain-numbingly subtle manipulation to protect his power during his six-year tenure find it easy to believe that he has orchestrated even the shock of his departure—the sudden resignation just when the board was least able to replace him and his peculiar problems in re-casting *King Lear* for London....Fresh rumors of Peter Hall departing the coveted National Theatre, and Phillips not wanting to present this quirky *Lear* as his London calling card, abounded in the fall. But extremes of self-imposed mental and physical stress are also culprits behind the resignation.
>
> Whatever the reason, he makes it seem as if Stratford didn't exist before he arrived, and can scarcely survive after he departs—an

absurd notion but a testimony to the imprint of his personality. It is not beyond imagining that he may be back. Yet even those who admire him have wearied of him. The Phillips traits that quickened and illuminated the stodgy Stratford of 1975, like a drug administered too long and in reckless dosage, have begun to undo their good work.

Working for Phillips, as Urjo Kareda had once observed, was an act of faith. For many, it was also akin to taking an exhilarating roller-coaster ride which left them drained at the end.

Phillips himself had frequently declared publicly that it was time for a change. And he would privately confess worries about a decline in his own work during the latter part of his reign. Yet many of his closest colleagues and supporters had trouble facing up to the inevitability of Phillips's departure. "They can't accept the fact that Camelot is over," said one veteran Stratford observer. "They feel they have lost their moorings."

Most members of the theatre community conceded that he would be a hard act to follow. Some meant it as a compliment; others, more grudging, meant it as further evidence of the problems his Stratford stewardship had created. A militant nationalist faction continued to resent his success.

Robin Phillips's style and personality were bound to rouse passions on both sides. His opponents on the Canadian theatre scene were always quick to seize on the shortcomings of his regime—and equally quick to ignore Phillips's own readiness to acknowledge some of these shortcomings.

He shared the problems of his predecessor, Jean Gascon, in building a great acting company. Many members of his troupe *were* bland and unexciting, and some complained that he played favourites shamelessly. Some contended that his direction was too rigid, leaving them unable to create meaningful characterizations. Others, of course, took the opposite tack and argued that Phillips gave them the freedom to grow artistically.

A number of respected Canadian actors were conspicuous by their absence from the Stratford company during the Phillips regime, but it was not always true that Phillips didn't want them. A continuing frustration on the part of the Stratford administration was its inability to attract top-flight people from the regions into the company. In many cases, it was a straightforward matter of dollars and cents: the Festival couldn't pay them enough.

Some charges against Phillips had validity. His much-touted scheme of creating associate directors from the wider theatre community never really took wing. The Young Company, which sparked such excitement when created in 1975, had basically ceased to exist by 1977. And although there was little justice in the persistent charge that Phillips had deliberately eliminated the post of general manager in order to widen his own powers, he had certainly failed to solve the administrative problems which ultimately imposed such a crushing burden on him that he felt he had to get out of the Festival. Some of his most cherished dreams—most notably Stage One and securing a Toronto base for the Festival— were never fulfilled.

However, other charges levelled at the time against Phillips had considerably less basis in fact. There was, for example, the persistent slam that he downgraded Canadian directors. Statistically, his record showed otherwise. During Phillips's six-year regime, foreign directors were involved in only seven productions. By contrast, there were twenty-eight productions which involved the talents of directors who were either Canadian, Canadian-based, or existing members of the acting company. Some of the productions were disappointing—as were some of the productions from imported directors. On the positive side, there were a number of genuine accomplishments from the likes of Peter Moss (*Henry IV, Parts I and II*), Bill Glassco (*Kennedy's Children*), John Hirsch (*The Three Sisters*), John Wood (*The Crucible*), Pamela Hawthorn (*Stargazing, The Taming of the Shrew*), Frances Hyland (*Othello*), Pam Brighton (*Henry VI*), and Brian Bedford (*Titus Andronicus*). He took gambles with some of these people, and novice director Bedford's success with *Titus* was an example of how stunningly they could pay off.

Furthermore, no male artistic director in Canadian theatre history was as hospitable to woman directors as Robin Phillips.

A further recurring myth had to do with Canadian playwrights. Phillips knew he could have taken the easy route and ignored Canadian drama entirely on the grounds it was irrelevant to Stratford's classical mandate. Instead, Canadian dramatists were involved in no fewer than twelve productions during his regime. Some created brand-new works which received major productions at the Avon. Others provided new translations or adaptations of European classics: Phillips and Urjo Kareda rightly saw that one positive way of involving good Canadian playwrights in a classically oriented theatre was to turn a Tom Cone loose on Goldoni's *The Servant of Two Masters* and entrust a John Murrell with preparing new versions of Chekhov's *The Seagull* and *Uncle Vanya*.

It was a period which also saw Canadian designers come to new prominence at Stratford and the Avon Theatre finally evolve into a productive component of the Festival organization rather than a financial drain.

If the Phillips regime was at times artistically uneven, it was certainly fiscally responsible. Despite continuing monetary pressures and the spectre of inflation, the Festival was able to sustain a period of unparalleled growth between 1975 and 1980.

Phillips's espousal of the so-called "star system" had both defenders and detractors. Yet, it was by no means as prominent a part of Festival programming as some critics suggested. Phillips was merely following a tradition first established by Guthrie and Langham when such luminaries as Alec Guinness, Irene Worth, Paul Scofield, Jason Robards, Jr., and James Mason were brought in. Robin Phillips's most stunning import was Maggie Smith, an artist who over four seasons made as devoted a commitment to Stratford as her Canadian counterparts. The Festival did something no other major classical theatre was prepared to do: it gave an internationally renowned actress the opportunity to come out of a professional limbo and find a niche for her artistry—and in the process to give some of the greatest performances of her career. Furthermore, in Brian Bedford, Smith found her ideal leading man. Indeed, Ray Conlogue, one of the most tough-minded analysts of the Phillips regime, saw the teaming of Smith and Bedford as one of the great legacies of this period. Phillips, he wrote, "rubbed Maggie Smith and Brian Bedford together like Aladdin's lamp to create theatrical magic."

It was not a regime which saw the rise of any major new Canadian acting talents. The yearning for another Christopher Plummer to emerge from the ranks of the Stratford Company continued to be unfulfilled—although many promising young talents were encouraged with important roles and did make their mark with performances which boded well for their futures. It was, however, a time which saw established performers—Maggie Smith, Brian Bedford, William Hutt, Martha Henry—continue to grow and develop. In the final analysis, the Phillips record was a most impressive one. But inevitably it would pose problems for his successors.

And, indeed, the Gang of Four *was* taking up an unenviable challenge. It was following a tough act—Robin Phillips. It was assuming its duties in an atmosphere of acrimony and apprehension. Its own credentials were being questioned openly in the media—and not without reason. Some of the most high-profile members of the original directorate were conspicuous by their absence from the revamped one. Gone was Bedford, one of the few members of the acting company with vital international connections. Gone were Cariou and Hutt, the only two with solid experience in running theatres. Kareda was the Festival's highly intelligent and capable literary manager, but he had never run a theatre and had never directed on his own. Martha Henry was a revered Canadian actress with no administrative experience. Moss had run theatres successfully in Britain, and had functioned as an associate director of the Festival, but his stock had fallen somewhat because of his disappointing 1980 productions; furthermore, Stratford would be sharing him with Toronto's Young People's Theatre, where he had just been appointed artistic director. Pam Brighton was a bright and imaginative recent arrival from Britain, but her main experience was with small alternative theatres. However, these people were dedicated. They had no illusions about their task. They were determined to put together a good 1981 season and make it work. And, besides, hadn't Robert Hicks stressed that the board was "totally committed to this cohesive new group"? Surely, with the board's support, they could make it work. Two months later, they were to be wondering at their own naivety.

The directorate had been at work a month when Peter Stevens, the Festival's new executive director, arrived on the scene to begin his $75,000-a-year job. The newly created position stemmed from the Pickering Report, a board-commissioned management study which had recommended that a chief operating officer be appointed to assume executive managerial responsibilities as opposed to artistic ones. There had been negotiations with Stevens earlier in the year, and by the start of October his appointment was set. Stevens was a Briton with impressive credentials. He had been the first administrator of the Nottingham Playhouse when it opened under the joint directorship of John Neville, Frank Dunlop, and Peter Ustinov. Later he had been general administrator of Britain's prestigious National Theatre and more recently vice-president of the Shubert Organization in New York. Stevens's duties would include responsibility for over-all budgeting as well as for negotiating contracts.

There was no doubt that Stevens was a prize catch. Nevertheless, the way in which he was hired roused resentment. As a foreigner, he required a work permit from Canadian immigration authorities. Before this happened, the latter had to be satisfied that Stratford had conducted a thorough search for a qualified Canadian before offering Stevens the job. The Immigration Department claimed such a search had been carried out. This was not the case. The so-called "search" had been a mockery—well after the board had decided to hire Stevens it had posted a notice of the job vacancy at the Stratford Manpower Office as evidence that qualified Canadians had been given a chance to apply. Barry MacGregor, who had recently resigned as company manager, felt he had the background and experience to do the job, and applied for it. Only later did he discover that Stevens had already been hired. MacGregor was angry: he felt that the Manpower posting was no more than "a joke" and that the board had been discourteous in not acknowledging his application. He became even angrier when a board member took him aside and told him to stop rocking the boat.

Another initially unhappy person was the Festival's treasurer, Gary Thomas. Until Stevens's arrival he had held the senior administrative job, although he had always been denied the title of general manager. He would have liked the board to seriously consider his candidacy for the newly created top administrative position.

Instead it hired Stevens, who took immediate steps to win the allegiance of Thomas, whom he rightly saw as a key member of the Festival organization and a person who would be invaluable in helping him adjust to the Stratford environment. Since Stevens was assuming the title of executive director, he was only too happy to comply with Thomas's wish to be renamed general manager. The move, however, shocked some board members, who felt Hicks should never have announced such a senior appointment without consulting his fellow Governors, particularly in view of the fact that the board was still supposed to be working on a possible major reorganization of the administrative structure.

Stevens proved to be a formidable presence. The Festival's director of publicity, Leonard McHardy, who had succeeded Douglas Allan in 1979, was to say later that Stevens had shown a remarkably quick grasp of the Festival operation and had excited the Stratford staff with his bold and imaginative ideas for the future. Nevertheless, Stevens saw problems looming. He had originally been lured to Stratford on the assumption that Robin Phillips would still be a major part of the team. Now Phillips wasn't there, and Stevens was dealing with a four-member directorate and the pressures of delivering a 1981 season which was being pulled together far later than was normally the case.

On October 21, the directorate presented its provisional season to the board's planning committee. The Gang of Four was to say later that its proposals had been received "with acceptance and, indeed, enthusiasm". Board member Arnold Edinborough was to write a laudatory paragraph in his *Financial Post* arts column. Nevertheless, some board members started hearing from Stevens about the inadequacies of the planned season. Meanwhile, members of the directorate were wondering why Stevens did not seem to be making any progress in contract negotiations with artists they had been busily lining up.

October 31 proved to be one of the most extraordinary days in the history of the Festival. What happened was bizarre and inexplicable. The fall-out proved appalling.

The day began with the board's executive committee perusing the Festival's submission to the Canada Council for 1981 funding. The document was remarkably detailed. Committee members went through it on a virtual line-by-line basis before approving it for forwarding to the Council. Some senior Festival officials were to argue later that the document was meaningless, a mere draft budget and season, submitted only in order to meet Canada Council deadline requirements.

The arguments were not convincing. Whereas many Canadian theatres applying for Council funding did not submit a complete production list in their initial submission, the Stratford brief spelled out the plans in unusual detail. It also projected an 80-per-cent box office for a five-play season at the Festival Theatre and 75-per-cent attendance for five other productions at the Avon Theatre. To be sure, these budget projections were traditional ones, based on previous seasons—but they were nevertheless submitted to the Council, which could only accept them in good faith.

The content of the proposed season suggested that the Gang of Four had performed surprisingly well so far. The Festival Theatre programming would include Sheridan's *The Rivals*, directed by Britain's Peter James, with a cast that would include Douglas Campbell, Pat Galloway, and Fiona Reid; Shakespeare's *The Tempest*, directed by another Briton, Colin Graham; Beverley Cross's new adaptation of Sardou's *Madame Sans-Gêne*, starring Maggie Smith and directed by John Hirsch; *The Merchant of Venice*, directed by Michael Bogdanov, a brilliant mainstay of the National Theatre of Great Britain; and Pam Brighton's production of *Hamlet*, with Stephen Ouimette, a promising young member of the Festival Company. The Avon slate included *Ring Round the Moon*, directed by Canadian Sheldon Larry, with Brent Carver, Fiona Reid, and Douglas Rain; Ibsen's *The Wild Duck*, directed by Toronto's William Lane and featuring Donald Davis, R. H. Thomson, and Clare Coulter; *Who's Afraid of Virginia Woolf*, with Kate Reid, Douglas Rain, Fiona Reid, and R. H. Thomson; Canadian playwright John Murrell's *Waiting for the Parade* with Martha Henry, Fiona Reid, Kate Reid and Jennifer Phipps; and *Colette: The Colours of Love*, a new Canadian musical, to be directed by Edmonton's talented Scott Swan.

Some of the listed participants were still provisonal. Firm commitments had been made to some directors; others had been invited but still had to work out dates before they could accept. Verbal offers had been made to several leading actors. The directorate had been cautious with some potential names. Serious discussions were under way with Jason Robards to play Shylock, but he was not mentioned in the Canada Council submission. Neither was John Neville, who had expressed willingness to direct a yet-to-be-selected play.

The Canada Council application was signed by three key Stratford officials—R. V. Hicks, Peter Stevens, and Gary Thomas—and was sent off before members of the Gang of Four had a chance to see it. Gary Thomas was subsequently to emphasize the "provisional" nature of the budget figures. This may well have been the case, but there was nothing provisional about the season. Canada Council application forms always contain a blank section allowing the arts group to list alternative plans. The Stratford submission unequivocally stated: "We shall be unable to change our plans." The irreversible nature of the proposed season was further stressed in the letter that accompanied the application.

Scene from the 1980 Avon stage production of Virginia, *by Edna O'Brien, directed by Robin Phillips, set by Phillip Silver, costumes by Ann Curtis, music by Berthold Carriere, lighting by Michael J. Whitfield, sound montage assembled by Roger Gaskell/Gie Roberts. L.-R.: Patricia Conolly as Vita, Maggie Smith as Virginia. Photograph by Robert C. Ragsdale, f.r.p.s., courtesy of the Stratford Festival Archives.*

Yet, only hours after approving the Canada Council submission, the executive committee did an about-face. Barbara Ivey chaired the meeting. Five other members were present, including Robert Hicks, the board president. Peter Stevens brought up the proposed 1981 season, and bluntly stated that it would not develop the box-office income required to support it. He warned of serious financial implications for the Festival and dependent businesses in the City of Stratford. He said attendance projections worked out with the assistance of Gary Thomas indicated a deficit of as high as $1.3 million. Committee members were staggered by the figures. Stevens then proposed an option: the directorate could be replaced by John Dexter, at this time director of production at New York's Metropolitan Opera House. The Met was currently closed because of a strike. Therefore, declared Stevens, Dexter was probably the only world-class director at present unattached. He was about to leave the Met and was prepared to come to Stratford and work with Stevens. He had a season in his head, and he had for some time considered becoming involved in a repertory company with Canadian actor Christopher Plummer.

Stevens's remarks sparked a lengthy discussion. Replying to Hicks, Stevens said Dexter would be available in another four weeks. To Hicks, who was probably more aware than any other board member of the Festival's fiscal vulnerability, Dexter's availability could not easily be disregarded. However, certain problems were immediately obvious. Assuming that the Festival embraced the Dexter option, how would it honour its commitment to the directorate? What would be the effect on the company? What would be involved in getting Dexter into the country?

The executive committee gave its support to an investigation of Stevens's recommendations. However, Barbara Ivey left the meeting convinced that there had also been agreement to confront the four members of the directorate immediately with Stevens's alarming financial projections and permit them to respond. Mrs. Ivey assumed that these duties were to be handled by those executive committee members who were already supposed to be in negotiation with the Gang of Four over its contracts. She felt the board had a clear obligation to bring the directorate into the picture immediately. "You cannot leave these people working away on their plans without keeping them informed as to what is happening," she told her colleagues. Mrs. Ivey was to contend later that fellow members of the executive committee had agreed that the directorate should be approached immediately and advised of the new developments and also be provided with more detailed income projections than those provided by Stevens. However, the Gang of Four was never approached; it continued with its plans, oblivious to the chasm opening under it.

However, some executive committee members were quick to arrange a highly secret meeting two days later with Dexter at a hotel on Toronto's airport strip.

The name of John Dexter had not exactly come out of the blue at the October 31 meeting. Despite the board's official line that the Festival had no knowledge of John Dexter's availability until October 31, some of its members were eventually to be nagged by the suspicion that some advance discussions had taken place. It was not just the groundwork laid by Stevens in discussing Stratford with Dexter in New York earlier in the autumn—although some board members were subsequently to wonder by what authority he had done this. "It was the feeling," recalled one contrite board member, "that it was all too pat, that there must have been discussions between John Dexter and somebody connected with the board long before this happened."

Suspicion and conjecture do not add up to fact. John Dexter was one of the greatest directors in the English-speaking world, with a spectacular record of successes on both sides of the Atlantic. To be sure, there were many among his admirers who wondered whether an artist of his volatile temperament would really be at home running a theatre. Nevertheless, any theatre company would give its eye teeth to have a John Dexter involved in its operations—if only as guest director. It was as a possible guest director that Dexter was apparently first touted for Stratford. The initiative had come from Hume Cronyn, who was unique among board members in having impressive connections with the international theatre hierarchy. He had been an early supporter of Peter Stevens for the Festival's new executive post. He also felt that Dexter, who happened to be a friend of Stevens, was exactly the sort of internationally renowned guest director that Stratford needed if the momentum achieved under Phillips was to be maintained.

For some reason, never to be clearly explained, Dexter's perception of the overtures made to him was that something more tangible was being offered to him than a mere guest director's stint. By February Brian Bedford had picked up rumours in New York that Dexter believed he had been offered the artistic-directorship. Later in the year, Robin Phillips had an extraordinary transatlantic telephone conversation with Dexter who was working at London's National Theatre at the time. This is how he described it at the annual general meeting in December:

> I was asked by Mr. Hicks to try to arrange for Mr. Dexter to come to Stratford as a guest director for the '81 season. I thought this was difficult for me as at that point it was unlikely I was going to be present for the '81 season. Nevertheless I was prevailed upon and I went through to Mr. Dexter. We agreed on a play, the date the production was to take place, and his staff. Later on, a phone call went through to England at the National Theatre—to ask if he would like to settle a designer. At that point, he refused to talk to me any more and said, "I do not want to come to Stratford to give an audition piece. I will only talk further when I know what my ongoing commitment to the Stratford Festival is going to be." From that point he refused my calls, and I only had contact with his agent, who asked would I please stop telling people he was going to be the next artistic director of the Stratford.

Phillips was left wondering what was happening. Similar perplexity was being experienced by Martha Henry in October. She had been trying to line up Christopher Plummer for 1981, and with him, his favourite director, John Dexter. She was prepared to go to New York to woo Dexter, and she called Plummer, an old friend and colleague, on October 15 to discuss the trip. To her surprise, Plummer was now pouring cold water on this action. As she told the annual general meeting later: "Mr. Plummer had talked to Mr. Dexter and Mr. Dexter thought it was not worth my while because a member of the board had said to him they would be back to him in three weeks. According to Chris, Dexter will not come unless it is as artistic director." When Henry referred to the mysterious board member in her remarks to the general meeting, there was an immediate interjection from Hicks, who was chairing the gathering. "I know nothing of that conversation," he declared. "The first occasion we talked to him was November 2."

At that November 2 meeting on the Toronto airport strip, Dexter made it clear that he didn't believe in rule by committee, that he was prepared to run the Festival with an all-Canadian company but only if he was sole artistic director, and that members of the directorate must be retained, although in some new capacity.

The board met in Toronto on November 5. Several important members were missing, among them Cronyn, who had been privately advised of a move to dump the directorate and who had warned Hicks of the folly of such action. Also absent were Barbara Ivey and Ronald Bryden. Urjo Kareda and Martha Henry presented their season to the board. They sensed their vulnerability when Hicks asked whether any of the artists proposed had actually been contracted. Their answer had to be no. The only person authorized to do the contracting was Peter Stevens, and they were still waiting for him to act. After they left the room, Stevens launched into a devastating assessment of their proposed season, arguing once again that it would fail to generate sufficient revenue and casting doubt on the quality and/or availability of the artists cited. It took less than half an hour for board members to approve unanimously a resolution to disband the directorate, scrap its season, and bring in Dexter. Commented one rueful board member long after the event: "We let this man take advantage of us and come in and dazzle us."

Another five days were to pass before the Gang of Four was informed. The board had to firm up its position with a visit to the Department of Immigration in Ottawa in an attempt to win assurances that Dexter would be granted a work permit. It was two days before Barbara Ivey learned what had transpired at the November 5 board meeting. She finally called fellow member John Heney and was appalled to be told that the board had voted to disband the directorate without giving it a proper opportunity to defend its season.

On Monday, November 10, Urjo Kareda and Martha Henry were invited by John Heney to meet a group of board members, ostensibly to discuss the season. When they arrived, Heney read from a prepared statement, advising them of the November 5 decision, offering each of the directorate a year's salary, and asking them to meet with Dexter in order to provide him with artistic input.

It was to become clear that most board members had no inkling that an uproar was inevitable. Kareda and Martha Henry were shattered by the events of that evening. Four years later, Kareda confessed that he still felt such emotional pain that he was unable even yet to read Martin Knelman's book on the controversy. Martha Henry, unable to forgive the board for publicly predicting that the directorate's season would have incurred a $1.3 million deficit, said she would refuse to act at Stratford again until the board apologized. It was Miss Henry who telephoned her husband Douglas Rain the night of November 10 to advise him of what had happened, and it was Rain who angrily reacted by calling newspapers in Toronto.

Public outrage was instantaneous. Even those members of the theatre community who had doubted the ability of the Gang of Four to bring off a season and who viewed Dexter as a first-class acquisition were appalled at the line of action taken by the board. Government funding bodies made it clear that the board had acted without consulting them. The Canada Council's associate director, Timothy Porteous, explained why he felt compelled to speak out. "What the board has done is not right. When things are seriously wrong with arts organizations—and that happens often, but never as badly as at Stratford—it's normally our practice to tell them in private." But this time Council was going public with a vengeance. Its chairman, Mavor Moore, an artist with Festival roots dating back nearly thirty years, was aghast. "There is a degree of irresponsibility in acting without consultation," he declared. "What I find regrettable is that Stratford acts first and talks afterwards." From England, Robin Phillips said he was appalled. "Where is the understanding of the Canadian theatrical scene which we've been struggling to support?" There was a blast from Christopher Newton, artistic director of the Shaw Festival: "Nobody fires Martha Henry. You just don't do that. It's a mess, a horrible thing to happen to the country's major theatre." The *Globe and Mail* editorial was typical of press reaction:

The events have shown that the Board is incapable of responding rationally or effectively to the challenge posed by the loss of Robin

Phillips. Losing the services of a man who was a Lord High Everything, with a prodigious capacity for work, has left the Festival
governors in a dither of uncertainty, resolved in the end by a great
pinning of faith on the miracles to be performed by a celebrated new
director. It won't wash. The action has produced anguish, dismay and
a flutter of threatened legal actions.

Not only was Pam Brighton outraged by the treatment of herself
and her colleagues, but she also, despite the fact she was a comparatively recent arrival from Britain, sensed that a nationalist uproar
was imminent. She called the board's vice-president, John Lawson,
to ask him what on earth the board had been thinking of. She was to
describe Lawson's response later: "He said, pathetically, that
Dexter had had good notices on his production of *Galileo*. I told
him we'll never have a national theatre here if you don't stop
reading notices from the English press. The board's ignorance is
unbelievable. I told him it was a parody of what a board should be."
  And, indeed, nationalism was to rear its head. On November 13,
the Council of Canadian Actors' Equity Association met in emer-
gency session in Toronto and, in effect, voted to boycott the Festival. In actual resolutions the word "boycott" was never used, but it
was clear that this was the intent of the voting. One important
resolution moved that

> Canadian Actors' Equity cease to negotiate the agreement which was
> to be effective April 1, 1981, on the grounds that the Board of
> Governors of the Stratford Festival is an unfair employer...specifi-
> cally that the president of the Board of Governors pledged full
> support to the directorate and subsequently fired the directorate
> without just cause. We require the Board to repudiate this action
> with the resignation of the members responsible and the Board's
> reconstruction in accordance with principles which would prevent a
> recurrence. Until this is done, no further negotiations will take
> place.

Equity was not prepared to recognize future contracts for services
of its members until "traditional trustworthiness" has been
restored.
  Without Equity contracts, there could be no 1981 Festival, and
members were told not to enter into any such contracts until further
notice. Some members of the Stratford board doubted the legality of
the Equity Council position, and felt it could be challenged in the
courts. But to invoke this kind of legal process could cause further
delays, which in turn could make it impossible to mount any kind of
Festival in 1981.
  There were those in the general Equity membership who were
not entirely comfortable with the way its action was being perceived. Many actors were not extreme nationalists, and they cringed

when Equity's official spokesman, Dan MacDonald, stated that the boycott would be effective until the Festival hired a Canadian or a group of Canadians. These members were as outraged as their colleagues over the shabby way the Gang of Four had been treated, but this did not mean they could subscribe to a position of hire-a-Canadian-or-else in resolving the dispute.

The board made a futile effort to reach some kind of accord with Equity, offering guarantees that it would contractually commit Dexter to ensure the development of a Canadian to succeed him, that it would consult the association when such an appointment was made, and that it would set up a joint liaison committee to facilitate more positive communications between the Festival and Equity. The board saw its action as conciliatory. Equity saw it as a further attempt to get away with behaviour that was patently wrong.

Among those Equity members most distressed by the situation were the actors in the Stratford Company. They were particularly shattered by the board's treatment of the Gang of Four. These were people they had worked with, and they respected them. They cared intensely about the way in which an institution they loved was being blackened. But they also hated to see the Festival turned into a battleground for a nationalist argument. Because of the tumult and the shouting, little attention was paid at the time to a statement issued by Rod Beattie, a spokesman for the Stratford actors. Nationalist militants resented it, but it made some significant points. It made clear that the Equity position had not received universal, unquestioning support from its membership.

> Thursday was a red-letter day for actors, indeed for all artists in Canada. Monday, the Stratford Directorate had been fired. Everyone assumed that Equity...would roll over and play dead....But Equity stood gallantly, repudiating the Board of Governors' behavior to the Directorate and refusing to recognize contracts after 31 March, 1981 (when the current agreement expires) unless the Board appoints a Canadian resident or residents to the post of Artistic Director.
>
> It's exhilarating. Many of us grew up in the '60s and will always have a soft spot for barbed wire and barricades.
>
> But the issue is too important, the stakes are too high to be careless or imprecise. The crisis at Stratford is the breakdown of communication and the flouting of ordinary principles of human decency by the Board of Governors. After a year (longer actually) of unaccepted resignations, ambivalent offers, cancelled tours (this list could be quite long), the institution's trustworthiness and competence must be restored so that artists of conscience can work there. One simply cannot function on the level of humiliating secrecy and machination which has led from moral disaster to moral disaster, culminating in the unjust firing of the directorate. We, of course, don't know what portion of the Board is to blame, or whether the entire Board should resign, but substantive changes must be made.
>
> Nowhere in the above paragraph have we mentioned the new

Artistic Director. That is intentional; that is the point. His appoint-ment is a different issue and belongs in a different discussion. Thank goodness Equity had the guts to stand by its injured members, Martha, Urjo, Pam and Peter. Huzzah. But we wish we could have stayed on topic.

Now, to the other—the nationalism thing. It's a discussion Equity has been through many, many times. Sometimes it comes up as "we don't need outsiders to teach us our craft," sometimes as "we can't work anywhere else so why should we let anyone else work here," sometimes as "are we going to let foreigners run our national theatre?"[Some Stratford Company members particularly resented the fact that some of the noisiest nationalists were people who were, themselves, foreign-born.]

Obviously, it has been much talked about at Stratford. It came up with Robin Phillips, with Michael Langham, with others. There have been disagreements within the Company but we have always found a majority position and it has always been the same. It doesn't matter where someone was born. What does matter is knowledge of and commitment to Canadian theatre and Canadian audiences. When Robin Phillips was hired he spent a year travelling in Canada, auditioning extensively and listening. After a couple of years he knew more about Canadian theatre than many native Canadians. If his kind of commitment were a requirement it would disqualify many foreigners but it would disqualify many Canadians too.

Here is our problem. If John Dexter had come in under the same sort of circumstances as Robin Phillips, there would have been hardly a ripple of protest from the Stratford Company. Conversely, if the Directorate had been fired to be replaced by a Canadian, the moral outrage would have been exactly the same as it is.

To Equity from us at Stratford: we feel as if we have made the right stand on the wrong ground. This is not to be interpreted as non-solidarity. Equity is our association and we will, of course, abide by its direction.

For board members, particularly Robert Hicks, the situation was turning into a nightmare. For one thing, a number of prominent artists whose involvement in the Gang of Four's proposed season had been questioned by the board were making it abundantly clear that discussions with the directorate had been serious. Jason Robards said publicly he had been very anxious to play Shylock. John Hirsch had been wanting to know why his contract hadn't arrived. Kate Reid made it plain that she had wanted to do *Who's Afraid of Virginia Woolf* provided a satisfactory director could be found. And Beverley Cross told the *Globe and Mail* in an interview from Paris that his wife, Maggie Smith, was more than willing to return for 1981.

The board, having hired a Toronto public relations firm, Tisdall and Clark, to ease it through its troubles, agreed to hold a press conference on November 17 in Toronto. Hicks warned reporters that it could hold out for only a few days before it would be forced to cancel the 1981 season entirely. In this warning was an implicit plea to Equity to lift its boycott, and to federal Immigration Minister Lloyd Axworthy to act quickly on Dexter's application for a work permit.

In its official statement, the board again argued that it had searched for a successor to Phillips:

> Every senior Canadian director was considered and four were interviewed. For a variety of reasons no one approached wished to assume the obligation. John Dexter had been the only non-Canadian contacted by the Board other than Michael Langham, a former artistic director of the Festival. As artistic director, John Dexter has agreed to engage in an even more aggressive search for and development of Canadian artists than the rigid standards historically demanded by the Festival and its Board. It is the Board's conviction that John Dexter will make a positive contribution to Canadian theatre through his direction of the Festival. . . .

The press conference did nothing to alleviate the hostility toward the board. There was confusion as to who, apart from Stevens, had been consulted by the board about Dexter's qualifications. When queried on this point by Ray Conlogue of the *Globe and Mail*, Hicks initially said it was a senior Canadian actor. When pressed for the actor's identity, Hicks finally said it was Roberta Maxwell. It transpired that Miss Maxwell's "endorsement" had been the casual observation to Hicks in a social situation that she had enjoyed working with Dexter and that she considered him a great director. (Maxwell had been on Dexter's list for his first season at Stratford, but when she realized the bitterness of the controversy and what had been done to friends and colleagues, she withdrew.)

There was a tendency in future years to overlook a more pertinent issue in the 1980 Stratford dispute: the public accountability of a Board of Governors of a publicly funded arts institution. Both in the manner in which it dealt with the artistic succession and in its attitude towards the public, the Stratford board was failing to fulfil its public trust. Instead, nationalism had become the key issue—and to many in the arts community the wrong issue. Some of the more militant members of Equity and the Association of Canadian Television and Radio Artists seemed close to advocating a closure of the borders to all foreign talent. They saw in the Stratford issue a high-profile opportunity to throw off the colonial yoke that they saw inherent in the continuing appointment of foreign artists to Canadian cultural institutions. There was a determination to ignore the fact that a great many foreign artists had enriched Canada's cultural life and made a substantial contribution, in a Canadian context, to its cultural identity.

Whether Dexter would have made such a contribution was to remain a matter for conjecture. The real issue was not that he, a non-Canadian, had been hired, but the *way* in which he had been hired. The irony of the situation was that, had the Stratford board conducted a proper search for an artistic director, it could well have ended up with Dexter or another capable foreigner and avoided an uproar. It was a possibility the nationalists might not have been willing to concede, but it was a genuine one. The board's "search" had clearly been inadequate, despite its protestations to the contrary at the Toronto press conference. It had known about the impending vacancy for eighteen months. It claimed to have conducted a search while also maintaining an ongoing dialogue with Phillips to see if he would, after all, stay on. But what kind of search? The position was not advertised in major Canadian newspapers or in such international trade publications as *Variety* and *The Stage*, or even in the Equity newsletter or on the notice boards of other theatres. The board had considered it sufficient to have unsuccessfully offered the job to four people whose availability was dubious from the beginning. Among those who weren't approached were John Hirsch and Douglas Campbell, former artistic director of another major classical theatre, the Guthrie in Minneapolis. Since the board had failed to do its job properly, it was scarcely surprising that xenophobic Canadians should seize on its blundering to drag in the red herring of nationalism.

When Immigration Minister Lloyd Axworthy finally announced on November 27 that he was refusing Dexter a work permit, the nationalists understandably saw this as a major victory for their cause. Internationalists feared a dangerous precedent had been created. Commented the *Globe and Mail*: "Leadership in cultural, spiritual and educational institutions cannot be reduced to mechanical specifications, and those bodies should not be denied the freedom to seek great artists on the international market."

Axworthy himself was a cultural nationalist—which left him wide open to charges from journalists like Gina Mallet that he had turned the Stratford Festival into the "Lloyd Axworthy Festival". However, other members of the cultural community saw the federal action as further evidence of the board's ultimate responsibility for everything that was happening. It was highly undesirable that government should meddle in artistic decision-making, and Axworthy was obviously leaving himself wide open to the sort of charge levelled at him by former board president Ian Lindsay: that he "had knuckled down to brute force and mass ignorance". There was no doubt that groups such as Equity had attempted to influence Axworthy. There was no doubt either that Axworthy had taken note of Canada Council guidelines which stipulating that in appointments to senior artistic posts, Canadian candidates should have prior consideration. Above all, there were the government's own immigration regulations stipulating that before a foreigner was hired, a full and proper search had to be conducted for a Canadian. Axworthy felt his department had initially been led to believe that such a search had been conducted. When this proved not to be the case, he felt he had no alternative but to act as he did in barring Dexter.

The board, by failing to do things the right way, had emerged as architect of its own misfortunes, and by its behaviour had invited the undesirable precedent of the wrong type of government intervention in artistic matters.

The board was jolted by Axworthy's decision. "I can't even contemplate what's going to happen," commented Robert Hicks. "We gave the minister exhaustive data. Just where do we turn now?" The board then asked Axworthy to reverse his decision, to which the minister replied: "The decision is made and I'm not going to change it. The sooner they quit frittering about trying to get the decision overturned, and conduct a proper search for a new director, the better off we'll all be."

The annual general meeting of the Stratford Festival Foundation took place on December 6 in the Festival Theatre. With artists, politicians, editorial writers, and concerned citizens involved in the great Stratford debate, the meeting would attract far more than its customary one or two hundred persons. The Festival had been selling an unprecedented number of $25 Foundation memberships, a sure sign that people were irate enough to ensure themselves both speaking and voting privileges at the meeting. For the first time in the Festival's twenty-eight-year history, the membership at large had nominated candidates for the Board of Governors. The board, in its turn, had been busily collecting proxy votes from members who didn't plan to attend. Concurrently, rival candidates complained of obstructionism from Festival officials in securing a list of members-at-large so they could seek proxy support as well. The Festival had hired security guards and had announced a ban on television cameras. It also attempted to bar tape recorders—but failed.

The meeting was predictably turbulent. Perhaps the one positive note was struck when Hicks, who was chairing the meeting despite an agonizing back problem, announced that the 1980 Festival had made a surplus of $319,668. This had wiped out the accumulated deficit of $245,398, leaving a surplus for the 1981 season of $74,270. However, the over-all atmosphere of the meeting, attended by some 1,000 persons, was hostile to the board.

The tone was set early on when Gregory Wanless, a company member, read an open letter to the board from the four dismissed members of the directorate. The letter was blistering:

We have stood by until now without a formal public statement because we knew perfectly well that not every member of the Board was responsible for this decision. However, they continue to present themselves as a complete entity with a right to slander our professional reputations. The continual and constant media coverage since November 10 has summarized the events leading up to that date in a misleading and often totally inaccurate fashion. Not one member of the Board has spoken on our behalf. We can no longer allow this situation to continue.

On the CBC on November 11, John Lawson of the Board said, "It comes back to maintaining a financially viable theatre. If the artistic directorate could have done that, then fine. Unfortunately, they were not able to, in the Board's opinion."

Peter Trueman on the Global TV news on November 27 said, "The Stratford Board hired Dexter two weeks after the firing of its four-person artistic directorate for coming up with a financially unviable season."

These statements are false.

We were given the go-ahead by the Board, in a letter of intent signed by R. V. Hicks at 3 p.m. on Saturday, September 13, 1980. We were fired at 8.15 p.m. on Monday, November 10, 1980. Between these two dates, working swiftly and with the total support of a highly efficient and gifted production staff, we were able to plan a 1981 season.

We had made commitments to five Canadian directors, not counting Pam Brighton herself; seven of these eleven productions were to have been directed by Canadians, and three directors were invited from England. We had actually made verbal offers to seventeen leading actors, and on Monday afternoon, November 10, we had drawn up the basic construction of the rest of the Company, which would have reached a total of approximately seventy-five actors. We had scheduled auditions in Vancouver. We were in the process of constructing a workshop and teaching situation which would have involved permanent movement, voice, fencing and Alexander technique instructors working within the Company, as well as text, improvisation and music sessions taught by senior members of the acting Company and the artistic staff. . . .

Although we had within the building no person empowered to draw up any contracts for the actors, directors and playwrights—no person other than the Executive Director, Peter Stevens, and therefore we have not one signed contract for the 1981 season—we do have documented proof of our work. This is a documentation in the form of commitments in the form of notes, memos, letters, telegrams, and verifiable telephone conversations to prove that every word of the above is true and factual. We have not included the names of artists from whom we have not yet heard, nor of artists who turned down our invitation. We have not included the many thoughts and plans which were only in our heads or in private notes. Everything stated above was actually in the works.

The Gang of Four, clearly infuriated at recurring charges that their season would have generated insufficient box office, told the meeting that it had consulted ticket figures for the previous twenty-eight seasons in preparing for 1981. For example: the consistent success of *The Merchant of Venice* in doing 85 to 95 per cent; the fact that *Hamlet*, without an international star, had drawn 93 per cent in 1969; the perennial popularity of classic comedies like *The Rivals*:

> If the Board of Governors had wished to fire us because they were more impressed with someone else's biography, then fine: let them do it. But let them do it cleanly and let them have the courage to say that's why they are doing it. We might be angry or wish to jump on a nationalist bandwagon, but basically we would have had no recourse. The Board runs the theatre, and has the final say, much as we might disagree with their decision.
>
> But for the Board to try and discredit us artistically and financially in order to justify their decision is intolerable. For a building contractor, the vice-president of a furniture company and an insurance man to sit in front of us [as Oliver Gaffney, John Heney, and John Lawson had done] and tell us that our season was not artistically viable is a ludicrous, craven and intolerable insult.

The knives were out. "The strategy," wrote Gina Mallet a few days later, "was clearly to prove the board dumb, incompetent, cruel, and philistine. Tactics included class warfare, xenophobia and insults." Mallet had found herself at loggerheads with many of her journalistic colleagues because of her belief that John Dexter could work wonders for the Festival. (Indeed, she had interviewed Dexter in New York about his plans for 1981.) At the same time, she had also questioned the board's handling of the situation. Nevertheless, she disliked the "gang-up" atmosphere prevailing at the annual general meeting. The mood was ugly, making it easy to forget that the board genuinely believed it had acted in the best interests of the Festival. The members of the directorate had a case, but it was an unfortunate measure of their anger that they should have felt driven into attacking the personal background of a man like Gaffney, who twenty-eight years before had staked his reputation and his company on getting the tent foundation built in time for the opening. And it was an indication of the atmosphere within the theatre that Saturday afternoon that remarks like this should have won warm applause. But, as Mallet also noted, the board's tactic was to stonewall, and "when it opened its mouth it tended to put its foot in it."

In his reply to the Gang of Four's statement, Hicks claimed that the board had acted "in all honesty, and in all integrity, and in the best interests, long term, short term, of this marvellous Festival". He contended that the decision to reject the Gang of Four's plans was an independent action, "unrelated to the possibility of Mr. Dexter or anyone else". He reiterated that the board "had not heard about John Dexter and his availability until after this decision was

taken'', and contended that it wasn't until November 2 that any
consideration was given to hiring a non-Canadian.

In view of revelations already made in the media concerning the
processes under which Dexter was hired, Hicks's comments didn't
seem to make any sense at all. It was difficult for the general
membership to accept the contention that there was no relationship
between the decision to dump the directorate and scrap its season
and the decision to approach Dexter. Some board members present
at the meeting were also confused. As president, Hicks had been
very much a solo performer, and for many board members, that
December meeting of the membership marked the first occasion a
real pattern began emerging. Yet they continued to maintain closed
ranks in the face of a major onslaught from the membership.

It was Jeffrey Macdonald, one of the membership's rival board
candidates and for eighteen years the Festival's unofficial doctor,
who rose to make the inevitable motion. ''I have been associated as
physician with the Stratford Festival since 1957. It is a sad afternoon
for me, sir, when I have to move a motion of non-confidence in this
board.'' His seconder was Douglas Campbell, who had earlier told
the board that, whether its actions were sincere or not, they had
been ''objectionable and ill-advised''.

If a motion of non-confidence was inevitable, so was the outcome
of the vote. The board survived Macdonald's non-confidence
motion by a vote of 874 to 305. But it survived only because it had
come equipped with 628 proxy votes from absent Foundation
members. Without those proxies, the non-confidence motion
would have carried. The proxy may have been a perfectly legal
device, and the board was within its rights in using it, but to many of
those present at the meeting, the resort to proxies on this occasion
seemed another example of the board's arrogant attitude toward its
constituents and of a refusal to acknowledge its accountability as a
public trustee of the Festival. These sentiments were further
inflamed when Hicks, as chairman, refused even to allow a show-of-
hands vote.

Confusion in the voting halls did not relieve the tensions. Many
members were to claim later they had never managed to vote on the
non-confidence issue because they had not been advised on proper
procedures. There were also complaints that ballot boxes containing votes sat unattended for three hours.

The board again wielded proxies to re-elect its own slate of
candidates, including Hicks, and to beat back an opposition slate
which included such respected individuals as former general manager Bruce Swerdfager, former executive producer John Hayes, and
former city mayor Betty Macmillan. With twenty-seven incumbent
board members returned, resentment intensified. Art-shop owner
Beverly Nye rose and questioned the ''fairness and morality of the
proxy system'' and attacked the board for refusing dissident candi-

dates access to the Foundation's membership list.

By this time it was evening, and the board was anxious to adjourn the meeting. Earlier in the long day, microphones placed on the floor had been mysteriously turned off, and this was about to happen again.

However, there was provision on the agenda for unfinished business, and there was one obvious item in this category that really hadn't been dealt with. What was to happen next? What was to happen in 1981? Who was to run the Festival? Several hundred members had come out for this meeting. They knew that it had been preceded by a meeting of the outgoing board, which, save for three changes, was also the incoming board. As members, they believed they had a right to know what actions would be taken, particularly in view of Ottawa's barring of Dexter. They also believed they had the right to make their views known in the form of resolutions, and they feared the board was determined to block any eleventh-hour resolution that might, for example, require it to reconsider the fired directorate. The board by this time had decided there would be a press conference—after the general meeting had adjourned and after it had met in brief closed session—and that if there were any new announcements to be made, they would be made then. In other words, the voting membership would be denied input. Replying to a question from the floor in the dying moments of the meeting, Hicks conceded that a press announcement could be forthcoming later in the evening. At this point, the meeting exploded into chaos, with company member Richard Monette leaping to his feet and screaming "You pig" at Hicks. "We have spent our life in this theatre. We have given our time, and we care about art, not about money all the time. You have no morals. I don't know how you can sleep. I care passionately about this place and you must address yourselves to your consciences and to your hearts."

Hicks, red-faced and shaken by the outburst, declared, "This meeting is adjourned," and started to leave the platform. He was not fast enough for Amelia Hall, the first actress ever to have spoken from that historic stage. Her voice rang out through the theatre:

I want to say something to you this afternoon and my subject is theatre, not this theatre but theatre. Back before 1952, when there were no arts councils and no corporations giving money to theatres, I happened to belong to a non-profit professional theatre, and I remember meeting one day on the street a businessman who was the president of our board of directors, and he said to me, "Well, Amelia, we dropped a thousand dollars on that production last week but by God we can be proud of ourselves." I'll tell you something: it isn't the building, it isn't the foundation, it isn't the balance sheet, it's heart and spirit. And in 1953 when this theatre went up like a great rocket it was the heart and spirit that did it.

Where was the heart and spirit now? Hicks was off the platform. The meeting, seemingly, was "adjourned". Jeffrey Macdonald said afterwards that the membership "should have challenged the chair's ruling to close that meeting. Not only did they walk off-stage without completing the meeting's published agenda, they also should have been prepared to give the membership the information they were later prepared to give the media."

But it was too late. Essentially the same board was in power. One Governor who was not was Barbara Ivey. Initially, as first vice-president, she had been slated to succeed Hicks. But she had also set a deadline for her decision, and when the deadline passed without a nominating committee having been convened, she made it clear she was no longer available. Furthermore, her personal unhappiness with the way some of her board colleagues, particularly Hicks, had been functioning had soured her feelings. In November, when the Gang of Four's dimissal blew up in the board's face, she had resigned as chairman of the executive committee because she felt Hicks was making too many decisions on his own and giving questionable statements to the press. However, at the final meeting of the old board just before the general meeting, she came armed with a carefully prepared statement. Because of shortage of time, she was not allowed to give it. Among her most pertinent points:

> We have all been present at a strange time in the Festival's history. It is the end of an era, and it is also a time of great difficulty. You are all going to be part of a new period, hopefully a strong and valuable one. As this is my last meeting after thirteen years on this Board, I would like to leave you some words of advice and encouragement.

· · ·

> There is a cardinal rule in the entertainment business that if an actor or personality begins believing his own P.R. he is heading for trouble. I suggest that this Board is in that danger. It is very easy when trying to qualify a position to begin to believe in it completely. One's ability to make an open and honest assessment of a point or position becomes difficult without one realizing it. Again, I suggest that the Board is in that danger.
>
> As a new year begins, I beg you to look inward, make an honest assessment of the way the Board is functioning and your position in it. At the present moment, the credibility of the Board is deeply suspect. Never mind whether that is fair. It is fact. It is suspect with some of the individual contributing members of the Festival, some corporate members, the Arts Councils, the Ministries, the Stratford company. Our credibility has been questioned in Parliament. Because of all this, the autonomy of our Board is at risk, and that is very dangerous indeed. The time has come for a return to a basic but solid method of Board function. There should be an immediate return to the system of

regularly scheduled meetings, of all committees. For additional non-scheduled meetings, every member of that committee should be notified regardless of the length of notice possible. All this is imperative for the proper recording of business. Telephone conversations to keep one informed, while necessary on occasion, can never equal the give and take of opinion at a meeting. They deprive one of the opportunity of making one's own decisions based on all available information, for without regular meetings, one can only get the information and opinion given. Assuming that of course the information is accurate, it is still subject to the natural bias of the person transmitting it.

I urge each board member to remember that you are not here to rubber-stamp the decisions or actions of the executive or any other committee. Each of you has a responsibility to make your decisions based on all the information you can get. (Incidentally, in this regard, I still find it astounding that only two members of the Board took up Mr. Phillips' offer to explain in person his reasons for not continuing as Festival Director. I also find it somewhat astounding that not one member has asked me why I resigned as chairman of the executive committee. Contrary to what I am told a senior staff member told the press, it had nothing to do with the financial settlement of Mr. Phillips' contract.)

In my view, the key to the whole board function is the Nominating Committee. I believe in the principle of a self-perpetuating board, but with that comes enormous responsibility for the nominating committee. Prospective members should be considered for what strength they can bring to the board. They should be clearly informed of the responsibility one assumes when joining the Board, the commitment required, the importance of board confidentiality. A balance of individual abilities should be maintained as far as is possible. Regional balance is important too, for it brings a variety of points of view. But the Stratford Festival deserves nothing less than the best qualified people for its Board, and the best qualified members for its officers. Its record over the years shows that it can attract them. I have said many times during the past year that this is a good board with some of the most able people I have ever worked with. I will continue to say it because it is true. But the sad but true fact about boards is that, in ten years, few but those of us here at the time will remember who we were.

What is remembered, and will be remembered is what this place is, and what it stands for. . .what it has contributed to the quality of life in this country. . .to the standards of theatre in this country. . .that is, what has happened on its stages, what has been seen here. This theatre has a heart and soul, come from all the people who have worked in it, their triumphs and disappointments, their giving of their individual talents to make this wonderful whole. The Board's job is protect this place, its heart, its soul. Our reward is to be associated with its glory.

Epilogue and Prologue 1980-82

When Robert Hicks abruptly adjourned the annual general meeting, his action did not mark an end to the evening. The "new" board adjourned for its meeting, while famished members of the media replenished themselves with take-out pizzas. Later, incoming president John Lawson faced the press to announce the formation of a search committee to find a Canadian successor to former artistic director Robin Phillips. To those present, it seemed a curious sort of "search". The committee was to be chaired by one of the board's new additions, prominent Toronto lawyer Julian Porter. Lawson admitted that Porter's committee had been given a list of five candidates to be contacted. The artistic director's position would not be advertised, nor would applications be sought.

The information provided by Lawson was, at best, limited. Had it been given out at the general meeting, the membership would clearly have considered it inadequate and asked for more details. But the meeting was over and Lawson, although visibly shaken by the day's ordeal, maintained a stiff resistance to some of the more probing questions. As far as many media members were concerned, there remained one unanswered question. What about John Dexter? Despite a ten-minute grilling by reporters, Lawson refused to say unequivocally that the board had withdrawn its offer to Dexter. "Mr. Axworthy has said Mr. Dexter can't come in," he hedged. "In the light of Mr. Axworthy's decision I'm not really sure there is an offer in to Mr. Dexter." Reporters found Lawson's response unsatisfactory. Repeatedly he was asked to answer a simple yes or no as to whether the board had withdrawn its offer to Dexter. Repeatedly he refused.

A far more decisive response came from Porter. "My present mandate and my present intention is to find a Stratford director among these five Canadians," he emphasized. Two days later, perhaps sensing media cynicism, he phoned a reporter to stress that he would not be a party to a sham search.

Porter's concern was understandable, particularly in view of the sentiments prevailing at the final session of the old board, just prior to the annual general meeting. It was at this gathering—although the information was to be kept later that day from the membership —that the actual search strategy was evolved. Donald MacLeod moved and Robert Heneault seconded

> that the 1980 Board of Governors recommend to the 1981 Board of Governors that a search committee be established immediately in accordance with Lloyd Axworthy's request that a new search be undertaken by the Board to ascertain the availability or otherwise of a suitable Canadian to fill the position of Artistic Director, and to make recommendations to the Board.

It was a cautiously worded resolution. The phrase "availability or otherwise" might have raised questions as to how committed the search would be. The morning meeting also went through a list of possible candidates. It included the names of John Hirsch, William Hutt, Peter Coe (who had recently resigned from Edmonton's Citadel Theatre), John Neville, Robin Phillips, Hume Cronyn, Jean Gascon, Douglas Campbell, and Robert Whitehead. There were potential artistic directors on that list: Hirsch, obviously, plus Douglas Campbell, with his Guthrie experience, and William Hutt, who was by this time looming as the dark-horse choice of Stratford citizens. During discussions, the list was narrowed down to five names—Hirsch, Gascon, Cronyn, Whitehead, and Neville. A board member scribbled down the tenor of the discussion in a notebook: if these five candidates turned down the job, the board could go back to Axworthy saying another unsuccessful search had been conducted, and Dexter would be in.

This kind of list could only deliver a blow once again to the credibility of the Festival's search processes. It had deliberately included the names of Cronyn, Whitehead, and Neville, who had already made it clear they didn't want the job. (From Halifax, Neville tartly commented that the board had painted itself into a corner, again reiterated his priority commitment to the Neptune Theatre, and expressed astonishment that Hutt wasn't on the short list.) Jean Gascon was very much of a long shot because he was deeply involved with the National Arts Centre in Ottawa. As for Hirsch, he had an ongoing commitment with the Seattle Repertory Theater.

Whatever his colleagues may have thought, Julian Porter took his search duties seriously. He knew time was of the essence. Less than twenty-four hours after the general meeting, he was at Hirsch's Toronto home offering him the job.

While Hirsch pondered the offer, there was a movement afoot in the City of Stratford to recruit William Hutt. Eleanor Kane, a local restaurant owner, had formed a Festival Action Committee of Stratford with the aim of forcing the board to become more accountable to its constituency. However, the group also put forward Hutt's name as a possible artistic director.

Hutt, as the Festival's elder statesman, had been appalled by what had transpired since he had left the two-tier directorate and resigned as Festival associate director (a resignation that has never been formally accepted to this day). He felt disturbed that nationalism had become such a major issue. "It had nothing to do with nationalism," he was to say later.

> It was the fact that four Equity members who were highly respected within their profession in this country were summarily fired. I don't care what the board said—they were fired. Now, in the first place you don't fire a Martha Henry any more than you fire anybody who is in the public eye. You give them a chance to resign. The first thing the board neglected to do was to try to save the face of any of these four people. We're not discussing right and wrong. We're discussing something more fundamental—that when you're dealing with a Martha Henry, for example, you give that person, that wonderful performer, at least the opportunity to respond to any doubts which had been expressed about the directorate's season. This was the second thing which affronted the theatre profession. The profession knew the correct mechanism to be followed. It knew those four people were not given the opportunity to use this mechanism and respond to the financial assessment of the season and if necessary revise their plans.

It was because of Hutt's rage over the treatment of his colleagues and because of his deep feeling for the Festival that he was reluctant to have any dealings with this board. Shortly after the general meeting, Hutt had a highly unofficial visit from John Lawson and two other board members to see if he would take over the Festival for one year. Hutt decided he didn't want to be anybody's surrogate. He didn't wish to be regarded as a caretaker artistic director until a permanent one was in place. He was flattered by the suggestion that he was the one person capable of binding up the wounds, but he knew these kinds of wounds couldn't be healed in one season. "You folks are going to have to bite the bullet," he told his visitors. "At some point you're going to have to make a public apology to the Gang of Four."

Later, Hutt attended a meeting of the local action committee.

Those present asked if they could propose his name as a possible artistic director. "I don't mind you proposing me," Hutt replied, "but you must understand that I did not attend this meeting with the intention of lobbying for myself."

By this time Hutt was not interested in taking over the Festival, but he was not prepared to abandon the institution completely. When news broke of the committee's endorsement of him, he issued a statement: "I have always indicated my willingness to help but my response to the artistic directorship of Stratford would depend entirely on the nature of the proposals if and when such proposals are made at all." In other words, Hutt would have to be approached by the board—properly. Cynics said privately that the board would never make such a move for fear that Hutt would actually accept.

In the meantime, talks continued with Hirsch. Some board members had initially hoped for a "fast" search of no more than forty-eight hours' duration, but Porter had no intention of being rushed that quickly despite the urgency of the situation. Hirsch had other commitments; the Stratford offer had come with startling abruptness; he needed time to consider all aspects of the situation.

By December 13 the news broke that Hirsch had conditionally agreed to take the job. "I have said yes, depending on certain negotiations," Hirsch was quoted as saying in a Canadian Press dispatch. The fifty-year-old Hirsch had sent a memorandum to Porter explaining his current theatrical commitments and future requirements if he were to take on Stratford. The public revelation that Hirsch had been offered the Festival and was prepared to accept it helped legitimize his candidacy at a time when certain factions within the Festival were still eyeing John Dexter hopefully. There were those who felt Porter had overstepped his authority as search committee chairman. In the first meeting with Hirsch, the latter had interpreted Porter's words as a direct offer. Stevens, in contrast, suggested it was a mere check to see whether he would be available. When news of Hirsch's conditional acceptance finally broke in the *Star*, John Lawson was quick to respond with the warning that "the Board has to approve what the search committee comes up with before any offer is made."

The die, however, was cast. Peter Stevens had protested that no appointment could be made without the approval of the Board of Governors—but it was becoming clear that if the board balked, it would be risking another uproar and a potential sabotaging of the 1981 season. Initially, when this latest search had been launched, it had appeared to be a cut-and-dried matter to most board members: either a candidate was available or he wasn't. Hirsch and Porter had introduced an unexpected wrinkle: a candidate who would be partially available at the outset and fully available later. The assumption by some that Hirsch could not possibly accept the job under any circumstances proved misplaced. Hirsch himself was scrupulously candid in his public pronouncements once news of his availability broke. "They asked me to start straight away," he told the *Globe and Mail*, "and I said, sorry, I can't. I'm committed to July and even beyond. I told them the best I can do is to supervise the '81 season or act as consultant, and then I would be fully available for the '82 season....I'm not doing a savior act. I've always said you can't walk on water at Stratford unless you have a hundred people standing on water for you to walk on."

On January 5, 1981, Hirsch signed a three-year contract to be artistic director of the Stratford Festival. The board had finally agreed unanimously to offer him the job and had accepted his conditions. Although he would be available only as "consulting Artistic Director" until July, he would be assuming full responsibility for the planning and execution of the 1981 season.

Hirsch had to move swiftly. A key component in his 1981 strategy was the appointment of a producer to share responsibility with him for his first season. His choice was Muriel Sherrin, a former general manager of the Shaw Festival and one of Hirsch's most trusted colleagues during the years he was head of CBC Television Drama. A further significant appointment was that of Michal Schonberg, an assistant professor of drama at the University of Toronto, as his new literary manager.

Hirsch and Sherrin faced a horrendous task. It was painfully late to be programming a major season which was only four months away and to be contracting actors, directors, and designers. Some possibilities were quickly examined and dropped, among them a double bill of Sean O'Casey's plays and a major production of Gordon Pinsent's *John and The Missus*. Several major performers were contacted but proved unavailable—Martha Henry and Douglas Rain (who insisted they would not return until the board had apologized for its 1980 actions), Hume Cronyn (who had left the board in 1980 because of its treatment of the Gang of Four), Jessica Tandy, Frank Langella, and Peggy Ashcroft. Nevertheless, a season took shape in astonishingly short order. Jean Gascon would return to direct Molière's *The Misanthrope* and Friedrich Dürrenmatt's *The Visit*. Britain's Peter Dews, who had demonstrated his ease with the Festival stage many years before during his production of *King John*, was contracted to direct *The Taming of the Shrew* and *The Comedy of Errors*. Leon Major would direct Gilbert and Sullivan's H.M.S. *Pinafore*, and Derek Goldby, the British director who had scored some spectacular successes at the Shaw Festival, was signed to stage a late-season production of John O'Keeffe's *Wild Oats*.

A major coup was the contracting of Brian Bedford, who had decided to pursue other career interests in 1981 but was drawn back to Stratford because he knew the institution was in trouble.

Bedford would play the title role in *The Misanthrope* and direct two productions—*Coriolanus* and *The Rivals*. A further coup was the signing of Len Cariou, who some twenty years previously had received his first professional job from Hirsch. Cariou had done supporting work for the Festival in the 1960s; now, a major star of both Broadway musicals and classical theatre at the Guthrie, he was returning to play Petruchio in *The Taming of the Shrew* and the title role in *Coriolanus*. Hirsch, because of other pressing commitments, would not direct in 1981.

What Hirsch did do, however, was to speak eloquently whenever possible of his vision of the Festival. Outspoken, acerbic, often outrageous, he had good reason to feel ambivalent about Stratford. He had never in the past been comfortable with its Establishment atmosphere, and although he had his own pronounced internationalist views (which often made his nationalist fans uncomfortable), they did not necessarily reflect the type of internationalism embraced by Stratford boards. The "send for the colonial governor" philosophy was not one to which he subscribed, yet once again it had been given utterance in the attempt to bring in John Dexter. Canadian arts boards, he said early in 1981, "have been conditioned. It's not their fault. It's hundreds of years of conditioning where you are taught that quality is always associated with somebody from Britain, not even from America. Americans are vulgar and commercial and crass, and the British are the representatives of high culture and truth. This is the kind of mentality." (Commented a board member who knew both Phillips and Hirsch well: "John has always been very emotionally involved with the American stage. Robin's background is the English stage. The flaw in John's thinking is that there's no real classical tradition in the American stage.") On the other hand, there was absolutely no doubt of Hirsch's belief in the Festival as the one genuinely credible guardian of the classical tradition in North America. He never tired of reiterating this argument, and he stated the case for Stratford with passion and eloquence:

Stratford has a continental mandate. Everybody in the United States looks at it as the premier theatre on this continent. It is a continental resource. Perhaps Americans understand more acutely than we do how important the survival of this place is—provided it keeps doing what it has always done, which is to set standards. There is no other place on the continent where a young actor or director can see these plays done on this scale with these resources at this level. This festival provides a service to this nation, to this continent, which is still valuable. By service, I mean a classical repertory company which occupies itself with the articulation and display in dramatic form of certain values which are central to the existence of this society. But to have an institution where these values are articulated, displayed, examined, and communicated, you have to realize that there are certain skills and crafts involved and that a certain size is involved. You cannot do *Hamlet* with ten people on this stage. You have to do it with a minimum of thirty and you have to retain actors, craftsmen, carpenters, wig makers, prop experts—all special people whose training is more and more endangered by virtue of a society that cannot afford these things any more.

Hirsch felt it necessary to hammer home these points because of the Festival's financial vulnerability and because of the continuing fall-out from the 1980 crisis. "It took thirty years to build this place. It could take a minute to die. It could take maybe 150 or 200 years to build it up again."

He was, he admitted to Gina Mallet in an interview, expecting "to get flak from everyone. . . . I got flak from everyone at the CBC for four years, I don't expect anything else. There will always be bitterness towards institutions. Stratford's a very exclusive club, you know, and you have to be discriminating in the right way. Its primary responsibility is to provide the highest quality of theatre in this country." He told Miss Mallet that the Festival currently lacked the creative resources to go after a Toronto home. He also vetoed Stage One, which had yet to get off the ground: "I don't believe in real estate. A smart producer works out of a very small office." But he was determined to follow through on Phillips's plans to film Stratford productions and to start a school. Although the darling of the nationalists, he was clear in his feelings about new Canadian drama: Stratford was a classical theatre, he said, and it did not have a mandate to do new Canadian plays.

One of his biggest frustrations was the tendency of so many around him to relive repeatedly the agonies of 1980. He felt this preoccupation with the past could only obscure the more immediate problem of Stratford's present and future. On May 19, at a discussion gathering organized by the Toronto Theatre Festival, he made clear his feelings on the subject:

> This country, the media, unions, can go on for ten years talking about the troubles, and they'll do nothing but further weaken the place. Whatever mistakes were made must be closely examined, and remedies must be found, but at this point in time what the place needs is the support, the love, the care, the concern of every single person who cares about theatre in this country. Institutions are incredibly precious and weak as human beings. They can get weak, die and disappear. We must stop in this country rejoicing in troubles and difficulties. . . . The essential thing is to ensure that good things go on.

But Hirsch got into trouble with another section of his comments when he gave an analysis of why 1980 had happened:

> For the past seven years, in my opinion, the Festival became more and more dependent on stars until last season we had Maggie Smith, Brian

Bedford, Peter Ustinov, Jessica Tandy, Hume Cronyn, Kate Reid, and Roberta Maxwell sitting like a crown on the company. The reputation of Stratford was gained by the existence of a strong company. People went to see *this company* doing Shakespeare. Over the past seven years, there was a slight shift, and in my opinion to some extent the shift has proven to be disastrous. I don't know why this happened, whether it was necessitated by economic demands and needs. The Festival got longer and longer; it was a way for the town to get a lot of income as fall-out. Times have changed. It's more difficult to get people to Stratford. Somehow the mandate of that place got diluted or slightly corrupted, and that was one of the reasons why the place collapsed.

Hirsch's words were widely viewed as an attack on Robin Phillips. Hirsch was upset by press reports emphasizing his observations on the Phillips years and interpreting them as criticisms of his predecessor's policies. "I have no quarrel with the man whatsoever," he said two days later. "I feel very positively about the theatre's future and am working hard to turn it around. What can I do when people insist on representing me this way?" Hirsch was not uncomfortable with the idea of using international stars; indeed, he was to make an unsuccessful bid to get Maggie Smith back. What concerned him was what he saw as a dangerous dependence on stars to make the Festival work. Indeed, in a subsequent interview with Southam News, Hirsch emphasized that the longer he was at the Festival, the more he understood the problems Phillips had faced. He felt that rising production costs, coupled with the nightmare of escalating seat prices, increased the pressure to ensure good audiences by emphasizing the star system. Given the circumstances, he suggested, what else could Phillips do? "I don't blame the guy because I see what is going on now. You bring in Peter Ustinov to play King Lear at twenty dollars a seat because you know it will sell out. I understand exactly what Robin was doing." However, he added, he would resist being forced to follow the same route. A different formula for survival, he insisted, had to be found.

By his own admission, Hirsch had a volatile temperament. That factor, plus the pressures of putting together a season on short notice, helped generate tension within the Festival office. Employees, some of whom had been with the Festival since the Gascon years, started feeling isolated from the ongoing processes of preparing a season. "People weren't brought together," recalled one staffer. "They tended to be spoken to on an individual basis. There was a lack of community. Furthermore, the new regime didn't really seem interested in knowing how and why things had been done in the past." Over the next two years there were to be significant departures. One of the earliest was publicity director Leonard McHardy, who had initially been excited by Hirsch's vision, only to be later disappointed.

Another departure was Peter Stevens, and his exit caused international reverberations. Before the board decided to hire Hirsch, Stevens had made a last-ditch effort to persuade the board to reconsider Dexter. He felt that the board had a moral commitment to Dexter to bring him in if at all possible. The board rejected Stevens's plea. By March, after two months of growing friction between Stevens and the Hirsch-Sherrin team, Stevens quit. Stevens was in England visiting a dying parent when the news of his departure found its way into the papers. From England he issued a statement, contending that "the Canadianization of the control and the direction of the performing arts in this country renders my position untenable." *The Times* of London interviewed Stevens, who accused the Canada Council of telling the Festival that it couldn't entertain any grant application as long as he was part of the organization. Stevens's blast, which came only a week after John Dexter gave a *Times* interview describing the board as "outstandingly incompetent", sparked a fast response from Canada Council chairman Mavor Moore. "Any suggestion that the Canada Council's grant was dependent on Mr. Stevens' leaving is extremely mistaken." he declared. However, the Council had earlier rebuked the board for failing to conduct a proper search before hiring Stevens and attempting to bring in Dexter. The Council had also rejected pressures to increase Festival funding substantially, but instead froze its 1981 grant at the 1980 level of $550,000, on the legitimate grounds that Council finances were tight and the Festival season was reduced in size from the previous year. Stevens had felt increasingly isolated since the New Year. As an internationalist, he was upset by pressures for a Canada First policy in the country's cultural life, and his failure to win landed-immigrant status had dismayed him further. Feeling his usefulness was over, he asked the board to come to a mutually agreeable arrangement over termination of his contract.

There were veteran staff members who regretted Stevens's departure. They may have had mixed feelings about his role in the John Dexter controversy, but they also felt he could have made a significant contribution to the Festival. "I was very impressed with his abilities," said one colleague. "He understood the weaknesses and strengths of the institution and how they could be dealt with. He believed in creative management and in the importance of marketing. He was a loss."

Whatever Hirsch may have thought of Stevens, he did believe in marketing. Although Stevens had left, one of the latter's major appointments, John Uren, remained as director of marketing. Uren, whose background included a successful stint with the Charlottetown Festival, had the drive and ability to meet Hirsch's demand for more aggressive marketing of the season. However, some of the early advertising pushed by Hirsch was later to be denounced by some company members as tacky and tasteless.

Hirsch, however, was unrepentant about such methods. He had a season to sell. He was still picking his way through the debris of 1980. He and Muriel Sherrin had done a remarkable job in putting a season together at a time when the very credibility of the institution was continuing to be questioned. The financial costs were substantial: in a controversial effort to ensure that the Festival did have a capable company for 1981, astonishingly high salaries had been offered. (Hirsch had no apologies to make about this beneficence. Stage actors, he felt, were notoriously underpaid. "Actors can get $4,000 for a commercial pretending to be a banana and $10,000 for five days' work on a film. In the theatre you get $400 to $500. It's like running a monastery on 42nd Street." He scandalized his board in early June by publicly warning of a possible $2 million deficit, and echoed Phillips's plea for a substantial increase in government funding.

In preparing for the 1981 season, Hirsch ordered structural changes at both the Festival and the Avon theatres.

Construction at the Festival Theatre restored the original floor of the stage, thereby reversing a major change made by Robin Phillips in 1975. However, Phillips's other innovation, a movable stage balcony, was retained.

At the Avon, the auditorium was redecorated, the stage rebuilt, and the original proscenium arch restored.

H.M.S. *Pinafore*, which officially opened the 1981 season the afternoon of June 15 at the Avon Theatre, proved to be the only offering to exceed 90 per cent of capacity. Grossing $879,599 over fifty-nine performances, it was an undeniable commercial hit. However, it was not judged an artistic success. "Draw up papers to court-martial director Leon Major for steering his H.M.S. *Pinafore* by a compass setting that has it sinking with all hands," wrote the *Windsor Star*'s Harry Van Vugt. The critic liked the "ingenious riggings" of Murray Laufer's set and the imaginativeness of Astrid Janson's costumes, but he chastised Major and choreographer Judith Marcuse for "a fidgety, overwrought *Pinafore* that has no intention of standing still whenever the slightest occasion for additional dancing and prancing presents itself. The consequence is a manipulative *Pinafore*, in which characters are shoved about like pieces on a chessboard."

Gina Mallet found *Pinafore* "about as eclectic as a church service" and she didn't like the look of the show either:

> The theatre's brick facade has been blanketed with vulgar decorations of a vaguely nautical kind, while inside the theatre the huge aft deck of a barque, snarled in a million knots no sailor ever knew, is filled with costumes designed in Dayglo colors. If, in fact, Gilbert

237

Scene from the 1981 Festival stage production of The Misanthrope, *by Molière, translated in English verse by Richard Wilbur, directed by Jean Gascon, designed by Desmond Heeley, music by Alan Laing, lighting by David F. Segal. L.-R.: Brian Bedford as Alceste, Nicholas Pennell as Philinte. Photograph by Robert C. Ragsdale, f.r.p.s., courtesy of the Stratford Festival Archives.*

and Sullivan's H.M.S. *Pinafore* were not so well-known and the score not so precisely and affectionately rendered by music director Berthold Carriere and a splendid cast of singers, the show might be mistaken for Shirley Temple's Good Ship Lollipop.

Reviewers, although acclaiming the singing of Michael Burgess (the Captain), Katherine Terrell (Josephine), and James McLean (Ralph Rackstraw), were far less happy with the acting. Faring best was veteran Eric Donkin as the admiral. "He has a pleasant voice but is in no way equal to the demands of the music," admitted Ray Conlogue in the *Globe and Mail*. "Happily, however, in this case, the director has traded off musical excellence for a genteel, lightly daffy performance which is essential to counteract the prettiness of the rest of the cast."

Major critics were generally unhappy with the Festival Theatre's evening opening of *The Misanthrope* as well. There were really three areas of disappointment. One was the stolid, unimaginative direction of Jean Gascon, normally one of the continent's leading Molière interpreters. A further disappointment was the presence of Brian Bedford, whose Alceste was regarded by many as the least interesting performance of his Stratford years. The third disappointment was Desmond Heeley's set design: what appeared to be green artificial turf covered the stage, which in turn was garnished with artificial Christmas trees and flowers. In fairness to Heeley, however, it is only fair to record that he himself was unhappy with the way his design concepts looked, and had objected to the contribution of lighting designer David Segal, an American import. Segal's lighting was so harsh it made most characters look fatally ill.

Ray Conlogue was the production's strongest champion, praising the Alceste of Bedford and the Philinte of Nicholas Pennell for the comic purity of their opening scenes in particular. Although aware of a lack of stylistic consistency, he was none the less impressed by the work of Pat Galloway as the shrew Arsinoé—"like Bedford and Pennell she brought a depth of confidence to the role that established its authority without for a moment embalming it"—as well as Susan Wright's Eliante and Scott Hylands's Oronte. For Conlogue, the disappointment was the Célimène of Sharry Flett, a Festival newcomer with a solid list of credentials from the Charlottetown Festival and various regional theatres. Conlogue felt it "was all she could do to project her voice and the first layer of Celimene's personality...."

Lawrence DeVine of the *Detroit Free Press* found *Misanthrope* "a dramatic drop-off from the heights of recent Stratford seasons". He found Gascon's direction "bloodless" but felt that Bedford was still "a prince to watch. Even standing on the outside of the production, Bedford's Alceste is a virtuoso turn. He zips through the two-beat rhyming couplets of Richard Wilbur's generally admired translation as if they were everyday speech with an accidentally charming melody to them." But Gina Mallet thought Bedford "unbelievably lacklustre"—the result, she judged, of "working without a context". Sharry Flett, "a truly delightful actress", was, she suggested, a victim of miscasting: "she is far too soft and gentle and yielding to ever play Celimene, a lady who is adept at sado-masochism." Miss Mallet's real wrath was reserved for what she deemed misuse of performers who should have been ideally suited to their roles:

There is something wholly debilitating and even infuriating in watching actors such as Pat Galloway, Brian Bedford, Nicholas Pennell and Susan Wright promenade around the Festival stage like a room-full of mannequins, adopting elaborately artificial poses as they throw off the rhyming couplets of Richard Wilbur's excellent translation without appearing to have connected any of the words to their own feelings.

The Misanthrope played thirty-four performances and did 73.6 per cent at the box office.

An even more disappointing figure—61 per cent—was registered by *Coriolanus*, despite the fact that Brian Bedford's production of this intimidating Shakespearean play was the critical success of opening week. With Michael Whitfield's memorable lighting, starkly effective costumes by Desmond Heeley, and a pulsating soundscape by composer Gabriel Charpentier, the production aimed for strong theatrical impact.

What sparked most press enthusiasm was the power of Bedford's staging and the excitement of some of the individual performances. Lyle Slack of the *Hamilton Spectator* said that with the title role Len Cariou had fashioned

> the most stirring and masculine performance the Festival has seen in years. It is hard to conjure enough radiant adjectives to describe the doomed man he has created—commanding, high-minded, dignified, princely in the very best sense of a man whose bearing and values represent the noblest instincts in men. . . .

Gina Mallet felt it took time for Cariou to warm up to the role:

> He begins so rigidly that one wonders where he can go from there. But by the time Coriolanus is forced to try to play politics with the mob, he has fragmented into ambition, pride and conviction. After he has succumbed to his mother's pleas, Cariou's Coriolanus essays a pathos that further complicates and enriches his performance.

The *Toronto Star* critic also lauded the staging, contending that the Festival Theatre had not been used as well since the historic *Richard III* in 1977:

> Bedford plunges us immediately into the heart of Coriolanus's tumult with a singular effect. In the dark we hear the sound of the mob panting. The lights go up on a starving Rome deprived of food by the apparently callous ruling class.

There was some praise for Max Helpmann (Sicinius), Lewis Gordon (Menenius) and Lynne Griffin as Coriolanus's pathetic and complacent wife. But Barbara Chilcott's Volumnia was judged to be not overbearing enough. There were, however, raves for the work of Scott Hylands, a West Coast actor brought back for this season from the United States, where he had been pursuing a stage and screen career. Ray Conlogue, who didn't care much for the production, was impressed with Hylands, judging him one of the Festival's lucky new catches. "He is muscled like a whippet, menacing as a gila monster and perhaps the only actor who could make the 'shredded' savagery of Desmond Heeley's costumes look actually savage."

It was a measure of the 1981 Festival's disturbing box-office showing that a normally sure-fire hit like *The Taming of the Shrew* played to only 77.1-per-cent attendance. It had the longest run— forty-three performances—of any Festival Theatre offering, and had seemed a good choice for a season that needed traditional favourites in order to generate maximum income. Yet it fared disappointingly —although the fifteen school performances did attract a more satisfactory 85 per cent.

Reviews were mixed. Some critics felt that Peter Dews had delivered an engaging, straightforward production and that Len Cariou and Sharry Flett had been a diverting Petruchio and Katharina. "This is Cariou at his most enjoyable," wrote Ray Conlogue, "the macho lout softened by supreme self-confidence to the point where he can't be roused to anger." As for Sharry Flett, after too grim a start she emerged

> as an actress with comic ability. She agrees to call the sun the moon at Petruchio's command, but does it with agreeable gamefulness. . . . This production won't please those who see Shakespeare wrestling with dark questions of the battle of the sexes in this play; but it will delight those who think the issue has been beaten to death and could bear a little laughter.

On the opposing side, Gina Mallet saw the production as painfully earnest and lacking in insight—so why, she asked, do it? She disliked some of the casting—"Poor Sharry Flett, once again cast entirely against her charm, her style and her talent, can no more stand up to Mr. Macho than a mouse could roar at a lion"—and found that some actors seemed not only unfamiliar with the Festival stage but with Shakespeare as well. As far as she was concerned, a minor character stole the show, thanks to Max Helpmann:

> When a Company member whisks off with a show right under the nose of Len Cariou, it does seem like an underdog has won. Not that Helpmann behaves like an underdog. On the contrary, he commands the stage with the authority of an Olivier. Even though he only has a tiny role, that of Vincentio, father to Lucentio, who is part of one of the most convoluted love tangles in dramatic literature, Helpmann creates with marvellous economy the most enduring character to be seen on stage all evening; an honest, bewildered and grumpy father who refuses to be made fun of.

Peter Dews's second production of the season was *The Comedy of Errors*, which opened on August 14 to another round of mixed reviews. Mark Czarnecki of *Maclean's* found it surprisingly rich:

Dews has a knack, gently demonstrated in *Shrew*, for dressing these comedies in pastoral hues, and in *Errors* the results are once again more than merely decorative. The misfortunes of Ægeon, condemned to death as he searches for his lost twin sons, and the often cruel misunderstanding precipitated by multiple incidents of mistaken identity have been treated seriously enough to move the heart as well as tickle the ribs. The production breathes an air of bewitched illusion, at times deceiving the audience into thinking that this is not the city of Ephesus they have landed in but the island of Prospero. Susan Benson's filigree set and brightly hued costumes, Stanley Silverman's haunting music and Michael J. Whitfield's subtle lighting sensuously counterpoint the plot's inanities by conjuring up a vivid time and place (the play has been set in 1820). But the cast takes top honors, especially Stratford newcomers Fiona Reid as the aggrieved wife of one Antipholus and Susan Wright as her sister and confidante. The Dromios are superb, again played by Stratford rookies: John Jarvis could easily strengthen his hyperactive *commedia* approach by slowing down both verbally and physically, but Miles Potter has created a masterpiece of timing and invention which hurtles him into the front ranks of Canada's comic actors.

Other critics were less effusive. Ray Conlogue found the production "harsh, jarring...frenetic and yet flat, energetic yet almost empty of laughter". Conlogue chastised Dews for allowing Potter and Jarvis to practise "wildly different styles of comedy" and for not exerting a tighter rein over the latter's antics. Gina Mallet felt the play had been directed with "commendable clarity" but wondered why the 1981 season featured so many plays (four) about mistaken identity. Fiona Reid's Stratford debut she found to be "as pallid as the poor puzzled wife she plays". The production drew a disappointing 69.4-per-cent attendance.

Sheridan's *The Rivals*, which opened at the Avon on August 8, suggested that Brian Bedford, a masterful comedy actor, was less masterful when it came to directing the genre. Many critics thought the first night a disaster, redeemed only by British actor David Langton's gruffly endearing portrayal of the frustrated Sir Anthony Absolute and by Pat Galloway's comic adeptness as the language-mangling Mrs. Malaprop. A production that failed to generate a single laugh in the first forty minutes seemed a production patently in trouble. As Gina Mallet reported,

> *The Rivals*, usually held aloft by the helium of laughter, was punctured by a production which has the finesse of an armored tank. It isn't as if this were a cut-rate production. Obviously, no expense has been spared. A small orchestra is on hand to play Berthold Carriere's arrangement of William Boyce; David Walker's elaborate architectural set, with many time-consuming changes, features a truly astonishing secretary of the most intricate inlay. The costumes are dashing. But all this adds up to is some very lavish window-dressing that fails to disguise the overwhelming inadequacy of the main production.

Miss Mallet found several of the supporting performances unintelligible, felt that Nicholas Pennell's love-struck Faulkland was played with such seriousness that it denied the play its wit, and judged Margot Dionne's Julia inordinately glum. She was also disappointed in other performances:

> Young love is what keeps *The Rivals* sweet, but whose idea was it to cast Richard Monette as that scamp, Jack Absolute? Monette is never at home in a period part, and light comedy is hardly his forte. . . .Are we really to believe that Jack and Lydia Languish are swooning for each other? No such luck when Monette is partnered with a Mary Rutherford so scornful that she could shoot down a glance of love at a hundred paces.

Miss Mallet, along with other critics, was not enamoured to discover that the production's lighting designer was the controversial David Segal. "As for youth it is banished by David F. Segal whose idea of lighting appears to have been inspired by the embalming chambers at Forest Lawn, and who once again, as he did in *The Misanthrope*, bathes the stage in such harsh light that the entire cast seems prematurely aged." What, this critic wondered, had Brian Bedford been doing? "Sheridan requires a director with a jeweller's precision and patience if his plays are to be set right. Bedford has directed *The Rivals* more in the style of a sit-com than a sophisticated comedy, going for individual laughs rather than a bubbling stream of nuance and wordplay. . . ." *The Rivals* ran for thirty-three performances, and did 79.5-per-cent business, the season's highest attendance percentage after *Pinafore*.

Jean Gascon's production of *The Visit* marked William Hutt's single appearance with the Festival that season. Hutt had agreed to do the role only if the Festival provided him with an actress of international stature as his co-star. Muriel Sherrin felt she had lined up French actress Danielle Darrieux. A letter from the latter's agent appeared to have clinched the deal, and the Festival in good faith advertised Darrieux's presence in its publicity for the forthcoming season. Then Darrieux pulled out before a contract had been signed and failed to give the Festival an explanation for her action. In desperation, Muriel Sherrin looked elsewhere and finally signed Alexis Smith, the Canadian-born actress who had been a major Warner Brothers film star in the 1940s and who in recent years had concentrated on stage-work—examples being Stephen Sondheim's Broadway musical *Follies* and a touring production of *The Best Little Whorehouse in Texas*.

The production that opened on August 15 seemed like the curate's egg—good in parts. There were those who argued that Dürrenmatt's relentlessly simplistic parable of greed had dated and that its reputation within the English-speaking world was due to the fact that it had been the farewell stage vehicle before retirement of the legendary Alfred Lunt and Lynn Fontanne and had been directed by the equally legendary Peter Brook.

The story was flamboyant and had great theatrical potential—with Clare Zachanassian, the richest woman in the world, returning to her birthplace to wreak revenge on the man who had wronged her years before. Her method: to promise to restore the impoverished community's fortunes provided that the townsfolk execute Anton Schill, who, although the most popular man in town, is also the person who disgraced her in her youth.

Perhaps the most positive review came from Ray Conlogue, who, although acknowledging shortcomings in certain acting performances, heralded *The Visit* as a blockbuster, "a vindication of Gascon's ability as a director" and "a portent of Stratford productions to come".

The production also gave the Avon one of the most dazzling set designs in its history. However, even with the removal of Daphne Dare's old and economical basic set, the stage was not large enough to accommodate all of John Ferguson's original design concept. What remained was striking. Commented Conlogue:

> *The Visit* happens in an artificial world which the designer brings to life with painted sets. The streets are painted ajumble on a backdrop and the nearer houses painted on flats rolled out on stage. It's meant to look like those children's books in which the pictures fold out when the page is opened. The quaint yet menacing style is inspired by the Swiss artist Schiele. When the trains go by, an old-fashioned wooden clamper atop a post flops idiotically up and down. A cut-out sun and moon drop in and fly out as necessary. Behind the backdrop painting, as the white-gloved council decides Schill's fate, little lights wink on in the windows. When the grotesque adventure is over, smudges of fireworks appear behind the canvas sky.

The Visit's author had once described his play as a comedy with a tragic end. Gina Mallet felt Stratford's treatment was neither funny nor tragic. "One minute it is distanced and Brechtian, the next naturalistic, and the next minute Gothic. Lacking a consistent style it seems to say only the obvious. To be told baldly that we all have our price is nothing new." The *Toronto Star* critic gave highest marks to Max Helpmann, whose "butler, in round dark glasses and wearing a mien of shameless corruption, establishes his authority before he opens his mouth." She was troubled by the two high-powered leads:

> Such shameless evil should produce a thrill of horror. And perhaps if Alexis Smith, a most glittering monster in a wig the color of red peppers, did not signal so soon that her visit was going to be lethal, there might have been one. Almost as soon as she steps off the train, Smith ices her charm, allows her smile to harden, and does a few

claw-stretching exercises that indicate a very mean jungle cat has come to town. Very nice. If only, however, she would delay showing her claws until she actually pounced, how much more effective a predator she would be....William Hutt has the beginnings of a masterful performance; perhaps his Anton is a little too meek at the beginning, but the lines are there for the development of a truly tragic figure. The trouble is that he is prevented from going the whole way by the collapse of the play's context.

The Visit attracted 75.7-per-cent attendance and the autumn Avon attraction, *Wild Oats*, 58.1-per-cent. John O'Keeffe's eighteenth-century comedy had recently become a twentieth-century rediscovery—thanks to Stratford board member Ronald Bryden, who had stumbled on the play during his years as literary advisor to Britain's Royal Shakespeare Company. Stratford hoped to match the success of the RSC production. There were those who found Stratford's *Wild Oats* to be cold porridge, but there was virtually unanimous acclaim for Nicholas Pennell's cawing, yellow-visaged portrayal of one of the most delicious hypocrites in the annals of theatre. *London Free Press* critic Doug Bale, who found Derek Goldby's production both "brilliant and endearing", was fascinated by the normally handsome and hardy Pennell's transformation into "Ephraim Smooth...a most amazingly mean little man with a codfish eye and the mouth of a hungry pike". Scott Hylands had the pivotal role of Rover. Bale found him "larger than life and twice as splendid in the role of Rover, the generous-hearted, madly romantic and incurably stage-struck actor who can't help talking in quotations from every play he's ever read. He lights up the stage every time he walks on."

It was a season overshadowed by the turbulent events of 1980— too much overshadowed in the opinion of some Festival officials who felt the press was showing a lamentable tendency to fight the battles of the past instead of looking at the present. Hirsch was angered at one media suggestion that, if he was really serious about staying only three years, a search for a successor should be launched immediately in order to avoid the chaotic events that had ushered him into power. He also took to denouncing certain members of the media in both newspaper interviews and meetings with the company, questioning their motivations for writing as they did.

The season had at best been a mixed success artistically, and the reviews reflected that fact. Yet Hirsch and Muriel Sherrin had done a remarkable job in bringing it off at all. Mrs. Sherrin, in particular, had ruffled many members of the company in her single-minded drive to get a season of plays on the stage, but the Festival owed her a great debt for her one-year contribution to its continuing survival. Ultimately, however, the finished product was what counted. Ticket prices reached a high of $22.50 in 1981, and journalists who wished to be supportive and charitable nevertheless felt they had a duty to tell readers whether a production was worth that kind of outlay. Considering the solid calibre of talent the Festival had been able to round up, there were limits to which one could blame the 1981 season's deficiencies on the problems of 1980. Some members of the new Stratford regime had announced publicly that if the season proved a disaster, it wouldn't be their fault—it would be the fault of the 1980 crisis. Yet could past problems get them off the hook completely? After all, the Festival was mounting a 1981 season of eight productions, half the number offered in 1980, but with virtually the same-size company and a $7.8-million spending budget which was actually $400,000 more than the previous year.

The season had certainly been disappointing artistically on occasion, but it could scarcely be termed a full-scale disaster. Robert Cushman of the London *Observer* visited the Festival in late summer. He found Dews's *Comedy of Errors* "fair", Gascon's *The Visit* "first-rate", Bedford's production of *Coriolanus* "disappointing" for its failure to clarify the impact of the mob scenes, and concluded: "This hastily prepared season is turning out better than many people expected—or, in some cases, hoped." It seemed a fair appraisal, although scarcely the international rave some members of the Festival office later claimed it to be.

It had been a crisis season and it produced a year-end financial crisis. Board president John Lawson faced a conspicuously subdued annual general meeting on November 28 and reported a net loss for the season of $1,077,639. Hirsch was not blamed for the loss. "By the time the season was set," Lawson contended, "no opportunity existed to arrive at a break-even position. Although there is a final shortfall, the Board is aware of the reasons for it and fully expects its responsibility to find solutions to the financial problems we face." The Festival had also been faced with some extraordinary expenses in the form of pay-offs stemming from the 1980 fiasco. These included legal settlements with Ustinov, Stevens, and London's Triumph Productions. Hirsch had ordered a press release to be issued stating that the $5.2-million ticket gross had made the season the second-best in Stratford's history. The media were quick to respond that this was misleading; revenues over the twenty-two-week season were certainly the second-highest in history, but this was due to increased ticket prices; furthermore, the total attendance figure of 422,818 was the lowest since 1974.

Nevertheless, the Festival was looking with surprising and reassuring confidence into the future. Fall-out from the 1980 crisis had tended to obscure the fact that, even though Hirsch had been burdened with other commitments in 1981, he had started to make his imprint on Stratford.

Thanks to Hirsch's influence, the board was strengthened with the addition of some important new names with significant connections in the larger cultural arena. The presence of CBC vice-president Peter Herrndorf, Toronto arts bureaucrat David Silcox, writer and broadcaster Donald Harron, and former Tory Secretary of State David MacDonald gave some degree of balance to a board that had been condemned for its preoccupation with fund-raising and its ignorance of cultural matters. But these worthy individuals were part of the board nominating committee's official slate; once again the board invoked its proxy power to block nominations made by the general membership.

Under Hirsch, the Festival also sought a strengthening of its senior staff. Gerry Eldred, a former general manager of the National Ballet of Canada and the Manitoba Theatre Centre, was brought in as executive director. Another major coup was the signing of Mary Jolliffe, a legendary figure from the Festival's past. Since her early years as a member of the Guthrie team, she had gone on to major positions with the National Ballet, Expo 67, and the National Arts Centre and had become one of the most revered arts publicists on the continent. She took over the crucial post of director of communications, with responsibility for supervising and co-ordinating the marketing, publicity, and public-relations departments of the Festival.

Mary Jolliffe's relationship with Hirsch was to prove a stormy one. She was arriving back at an institution which had changed greatly from the Guthrie era. The legacy of 1980 still lingered, and one of the first tasks Miss Jolliffe set herself was to read Martin Knelman's book. She found herself plunged into a deteriorating media-relations situation with an artistic director who refused to speak to some members of the press. Mary Jolliffe was to be gone from the Festival by the summer of 1983, and, in keeping with other departures that were occurring at that time, the atmosphere was bitter.

The sad irony was that Mary Jolliffe felt she whole-heartedly shared Hirsch's vision for the future and was prepared to do all she could to help him bring it to fruition. Hirsch in 1982 was giving high priority to reaffirming the Festival mandate and setting down a fundamental list of aims and objectives for the 1980s. The Festival would mark its thirtieth season in 1982—a good time, Jolliffe felt, for proceeding with the difficult task of articulating the mandate. She stressed this point in a June 6 memo to the board:

> From the point of public perception this season, all the elements are moving with the Festival in terms of the anniversary, the realization of John Hirsch's enunciated plans, the strength of the productions, the health of advance sales, the endorsement by government support. The timing is *now* for the Festival to underline a strong public position. The occasion is appropriate and the opportunity ripe for

the Board to publicly reaffirm the Festival's mandate and purpose for Stratford in the Eighties.

Properly expressed and communicated, such a statement should generate reassurance in the solidarity of the Board's leadership— underlining its support of the three decades past which have sustained in spite of trial, and demonstrated through its repeated commitment, a confidence in the Festival's future. Such a statement should be supported by an appropriate communications campaign aimed at the target publics of government at all levels, the national and international theatre communities, the educational institutions, the corporate and individual donors. A properly structured educational campaign designed to make a sustained impact, supporting the strength of the artistic season, will do much to lift the Festival from the victim position to which it was reduced.

Hirsch's mandate stated the vital importance of Stratford, and set down the organization's aims and objectives for the 1980s. Highlights of it were to be contained in *The Stratford Festival Story*, the annual background booklet made available free to playgoers:

> The Stratford Festival is a classical repertory theatre, created to perform the plays of Shakespeare and other major dramatists of the world....
>
> This obliges the Festival to present the best, without undue regard to fashion, popularity and instant topicality....
>
> It is committed, for the sake of its audiences and its actors, to the repertory system....
>
> In order to perform a classical repertoire, the Festival needs to train its actors in the skills of classical performance....
>
> The sum of these skills is ensemble playing. To achieve such playing, the Festival must attract actors to return season after season....
>
> For the same reasons that Stratford needs to train and hold on to actors, it needs to train and hold on to directors and designers....
>
> The Festival recognizes that it cannot achieve all these declared aims from the proceeds of the box office alone while making its plays available to the widest possible audience. It must therefore depend on both private and public support....
>
> If the Festival is to claim support as a public repository of drama, it must endeavour to make classic drama something that a majority, not a minority, of the public wish to support....
>
> Finally, above all, the Festival should see itself, and ensure that it is seen, as a cultural and educational resource of irreplaceable public value to Canada and North America....

Many of the principles stressed were already familiar. Others heeded the new challenge of communications technology, previously invoked by Phillips, and the need for the Festival to take advantage of it. But the overriding purpose of the mandate was to reaffirm the vital importance to North American life of an institution which Hirsch saw as a bastion against the possible approach of a new cultural Dark Ages. He also was determined to remind people that to maintain the Festival's particular standards of excellence and to meet its ongoing commitments would cost money.

Two of Hirsch's big concerns were to find expression during the winter of 1982. One was the creation of a new theatre-training program at the Third Stage. The other was the CBC release of television versions of the 1981 productions of H.M.S. *Pinafore* and *The Taming of the Shrew*.

The training program was announced in early March at a press conference in Toronto. Hirsch called the new "Shakespeare Three" company "one of the most extraordinary and productive" innovations in the history of Canadian theatre, saying that during his years as artistic director of the Manitoba Theatre Centre and during his later period at the CBC, he had always maintained a training program as "a means of taking care of the future". When he took over Stratford, he said, he immediately saw the need for a program there.

The training program, which would operate out of the Third Stage, was supervised by Kristin Linklater, an internationally renowned voice coach and a founder of Shakespeare and Company in the United States. A young, twelve-member acting company would undergo intensive training for three weeks in April before beginning rehearsals for summer productions of *A Midsummer Night's Dream* and *All's Well That Ends Well*. Four senior actors— Charmion King, Joseph Shaw, Paul Massie, and Nicholas Simons— would join the company to contribute their classical theatre experience.

At the same Toronto press conference, Imperial Oil Limited announced it was contributing $200,000 to the young company over the next two years. The contribution provoked a negative reaction from Doug Bale of the *London Free Press*:

> The arts are desperate indeed when our greatest theatre must fawn on a multi-million-dollar oil conglomerate for donating less than the price of two oil trucks. The Stratford Festival sent at least a score of representatives to bow and smile at a Toronto press conference Monday while Imperial announced a grant that amounted to less than .03 per cent of the $682 million profit Imperial reported in 1982.

Bale admitted the company deserved credit for helping:

> But, keeping things in proportion, $200,000 is not an extravagantly

generous gift for a money-spinning giant to make to North America's foremost classical theatre. Especially not when one considers that the company's getting a tax break and a pile of publicity out of it. Imperial got a bargain.

The CBC productions of *Pinafore* and *The Taming of the Shrew* won large viewing audiences and a mixed critical response. Many wondered why *Pinafore*, which had not received good reviews the previous summer, should have had a CBC production at all. There were also misgivings about *Shrew*—particularly its manner of television presentation. When Robin Phillips had been promoting a television role for the Festival, he had argued that only the best should be preserved and that more than merely a photographed stage performance was necessary if Stratford was to win a place in the international marketplace against such formidable competition as the BBC Shakespeare series. Had *King Lear* gone ahead in 1980, it would have been a proper studio treatment of the Stratford production. *Shrew*, on the other hand, was most definitely a photographed stage performance—with all the accompanying limitations. Award-winning director Norman Campbell tried to be fluid in his use of the camera, employing such basic devices as the close-up and cross-cutting whenever possible. But in moments of fast stage action involving groups, the camera was forced to fall back on the type of long shot that killed dramatic immediacy and gave the viewer the impression of viewing proceedings through the wrong end of a telescope. There were times when the tops of performers' heads were cut off and when the viewer was uncomfortably aware of audience members seated behind the performers on the other side of the Festival Theatre's famous thrust stage. Finally, because this was a live taping in front of an audience of 2,500, everybody seemed to be projecting like mad. Within the acoustical context of the actual theatre, this may have sounded normal, but when it was picked up by microphones and transferred to the TV set, the result was strident.

The Stratford Festival's thirtieth season officially opened on June 6 after two weeks of previews for schools and general audiences. (Since 1953, more than 1.5 million students had participated.) The spring months had seen Hirsch start to impose his own personal style on the Festival. It was reflected most significantly in the new popular image which supported Hirsch's fervent belief that Stratford must serve as wide and varied an audience as possible.

Opening-week visitors were to be greeted by a redesigned foyer area in the Festival Theatre featuring exhibits of props and costumes from past seasons. The popular book-and-gift store had been moved into a building across from the front entrance. There were plans to turn part of the second level into a restaurant offering snacks and light refreshments (a move that enraged local restaurant owners when news of it was sprung on them without warning). The traditional rectangular house program, the classic simplicity of which had epitomized Stratford's image for so many years, had given way to a fat thirty-eight-page booklet, similar to those issued by other theatres across the country and stuffed full of paid advertising.

The Festival's own promotion had become jazzier. One early newspaper ad promised a "free gift" if the reader filled out a coupon and answered a series of "skill-testing questions". Typical questions: "What is your name? What is your street address?" The free gift turned out to be the Festival's 1982 brochure.

Some critics complained about tacky, gimmicky promotions, but Festival marketing consultant John Uren had some powerful arguments in rebuttal—mail-room cartons overflowing with returned coupons. Uren believed that a new populist approach was vital if the Festival was to build and maintain audiences. "We are not exempt from the recession or from market forces," he stressed in interviews. "We're talking about survival. We are labour-intensive. We're located in a small centre. We have to generate visitors from afar. I'll resort to anything to get people through those doors." But Uren also stressed he couldn't promote material that wasn't good. "What happens on stage remains most important. We may want to broaden the appeal of what this theatre is about. We can go in for jazzy advertising, and we're prepared to spend up to $500,000 for that."

There were times when opening week seemed as notable for what was happening off-stage as for what was taking place in performance. There were problems with the press. Hirsch was refusing interviews to most journalists in the weeks preceding the opening, and continued to do so the week of June 6, apart from submitting to a session with Canadian Press's James Nelson, a writer he considered neutral and unbiased. There was a row going on between the Festival and the *Beacon-Herald*, which had publicized Hirsch's decision to dump a Stratford graphics firm in favour of a Toronto company; Festival officials complained to the local daily about its coverage. The weekend the season opened, there was a book-launching party in Stratford for Martin Knelman's *A Stratford Tempest*—an event that reportedly reduced some board members to near-apoplexy and prompted demands that such an unflattering volume be barred from the Festival shop. Actor Jack Medley, who had the title role in *Julius Caesar*, was in hospital after a rib was broken and a lung punctured at the play's final preview. (James Bradford took over the role.)

The *Toronto Star* continued its watchdog function. It entertainment columnist, Sid Adilman, had some devastating comments about opening-week socializing:

While Canada suffers through its worst depression in six decades, the

Stratford Board of Governors are partying again the way they did in the high-flying days of the 1960s and early '70s. Imported wine and rich foods load buffet tables at board parties before and after most of the performances this week. Such a heady round, in fact, that one barely has time to change for the show.

"There are more parties crowded into four days this year than there has been for years, and the 30th anniversary might have something to do with it," says a long-time Festival staffer. But, of course, these parties at restaurants and large homes are for board members and VIP guests only. No press, and certainly no members of the general public.

The fact that board members may have been entertaining out of their own pockets was not the relevant factor to Adilman. It was the contrast between this elitist merry-making and the so-called public partying:

So what does the ordinary theatre-goer get on opening week? Crumbs in a roller rink. Opening day Sunday, after federal and provincial politicians had gone out of their way to praise the Festival's key position in Canadian and international theatre, and applauded its thirtieth anniversary, the Board pulled a major social blunder. It arranged a post-show anniversary party at the chilly Stratford Coliseum and charged $7.50 for what turned out to be a miserable collection of watery canapes, soggy quiches, cubes of stale cheese, squashed devilled eggs, and $2.50 for alcoholic drinks served in plastic cups. An infuriated actor claimed that bartenders were "skimming" the drinks—failing to pour in the right amount.

While 1,000 dismayed guests wandered around trying to locate friends, the din from a five-man showband was deafening. "This is where we come to roller-skate," complained actress Patricia Collins, shouting to be heard. "This is no way for the Festival to fight its way back into making itself popular again with its most loyal supporters," groaned a long-time supporter from Toronto.

Wiser Board members and many arts VIPs ducked out quickly. They, at least, had their own private parties to attend. "Appalling," is how one Festival staffer described the Coliseum affair. "The Board did this one on its own and it should be ashamed of itself!"

Adilman's opening-week column infuriated several board members, who felt that once again they were being unfairly treated. But some Stratfordites saw the fiasco of the opening-night party as just another example of board insensitivity to its constituency—and they may have had a point. (Two years after the horrors of 1980, a veteran board member could still speak to a reporter and say, "I still don't understand what all the fuss was about. After all, we did nothing wrong.")

The board was also to see its proudest opening-week achievement —the announcement of $300,000 in Ontario government grants and a total of $318,000 in federal grants—blow up in its face. Board members with political connections had pulled strings to get the money—and other members of the arts community were unhappy. For anyone who genuinely cared about the state of the arts in Canada, the Festival's financial problems were a matter of grave concern. However, many felt that the problems were essentially of the Festival's own making because of the bungled 1980 crisis, and that it did not deserve to be automatically bailed out—especially at a time when other Ontario arts organizations, among them the Shaw Festival and the National Ballet, were facing serious financial problems.

It was this latter consideration that prompted some sharp public comments from Walter Pitman, director of the Ontario Arts Council. Pitman said he was shocked to learn from the newspaper that Ontario Culture Minister Bruce McCaffrey had announced a special one-time grant of $300,000 to the Festival in recognition of its contribution over the past thirty years. The reason for Pitman's chagrin: his agency had been completely bypassed in the negotiations that led to the grant.

Pitman feared that a dangerous precedent had been set in circumventing the Arts Council, an autonomous agency with a responsibility for awarding public money to arts groups throughout the province, and operating free of political interference. The Canada Council's retiring theatre officer, Walter Learning, also was concerned about this type of direct government grant. "This kind of thing points out the danger of distributing arts funds on any sort of political basis," he declared. "Those like Stratford, which have the clout, have the greater chance of getting special consideration when they can deal directly with the politicians rather than council."

Derek Goldby's opening-night production of *Julius Caesar* offended many critics with its harsh violence and its forceful but simplistic treatment of mob psychology. Goldby, a director whose pile-driver style had worked well in Shaw Festival productions of vintage farce, used a similar approach in *Caesar*, and there wasn't much in his treatment to remind viewers that the play's vital human dimension rested on the tragedy of two men—Caesar and Brutus. Nevertheless, Goldby's production could compel with its vision of a system tearing itself apart and with its final despairing image of a victorious Mark Antony mourning the death of his enemy Brutus and cringing in anticipation of the carnage yet to come. Furthermore, some initially hostile first-nighters were later to feel somewhat more tolerant towards the production after having experienced some of the week's other fare.

Gina Mallet wasn't surprised that Jack Medley had been injured during previews:

This *Julius Caesar* is noisy, violent and fast, and definitely means

business. . . .Caesar spouts blood which the conspirators ritualisti-
cally dip their hands into. Antony hauls the punctured body of Caesar
from the bier to display it to the crowd, which maddened, goes
screaming into the streets to tear Cinna the poet literally, or so it
seemed, from limb to limb.

Strong stuff. As the gentleman in the seat in front of me cried
jovially to a friend, "Couldn't sleep through this, eh?" A very important point. Opening night at the Festival is often down-time for first-
night party-goers. Scheduling *Julius Caesar* may be considered a
master stroke. But once awake, the mind may be too alert. What is
going on under all the blood and thunder? As usual not very much.

Miss Mallet was a critic who considered *Julius Caesar* to be a play
more interesting in its potential than in its actual fulfilment. She
faulted Stratford's new production for lacking true conflict among
the three leading characters. Len Cariou's Brutus she found inappropriately "cross" and "testy", at best "an ambitious vice-president of a large corporation, not a worried republican of ancient
Rome". R. H. Thomson, a gifted Toronto actor making his Festival
debut as Antony, overdid the sensitivity and gentleness: "Antony is
not sensitive and gentle; he is an impetuous sportsman of a general
with a shark's intuition. . . ." She was happier with Nicholas Pennell's performance of Cassius—a "persuasive second-rater"—and
Richard Monette's harrowing cameo as Cinna. John Pennoyer's
costumes she considered "a job lot".

In the *London Free Press*, Doug Bale complained of too much
ranting:

> Len Cariou. . .booms out his lines as if the audience were miles away
> —although only their attention is. . . .R. H. Thomson. . .dodges inde-
> cisively around the stage with his mouth open, running his hands
> through his hair and doing a presumably unintentional imitation of a
> young James Stewart vowing to get even with the no-good owl-hoots
> that kilt his pa.

Julius Caesar's $965,965 box-office gross would have given it
hit status a few seasons before, but prices had risen substantially at
Stratford in recent years, and the figure translated into only 70.5-
per-cent attendance.

After the blood-letting of *Caesar*, first-nighters needed a respite,
and they received it the following evening in the most delightful
fashion imaginable. Brian Macdonald's imaginative, lively, and
irresistible production of *The Mikado* ushered in a glorious new era
for Gilbert and Sullivan at the Stratford Festival. Macdonald's treatment, which could deservedly be mentioned in the same breath as
Guthrie's historic productions of the Savoy operas two decades
earlier, would be the only one that season to break through the
magic 90-per-cent-attendance barrier. It did 96.4 per cent, an

Scene from the 1982/1984 Avon stage production of The Mikado, *book by W. S. Gilbert, music by Arthur Sullivan, direction and choreography by Brian Macdonald, musical direction by Berthold Carriere, set design by Susan Benson and Douglas McLean, costumes by Susan Benson, lighting by Michael J. Whitfield. L.-R.: Henry Ingram as Nanki-Poo (1982), Marie Baron as Yum-Yum, Eric Donkin as Ko-Ko. Photograph by Robert C. Ragsdale, f.r.p.s., courtesy of the Stratford Festival Archives.*

achievement that helped compensate for the disappointing box office of some other offerings.

Gina Mallet admitted that the spirit of this *Mikado* was so sweet it occasionally gave the viewer tooth-ache and wondered whether its Japanese stereotypes might be considered to have racist connotations in the Canada of the 1980s. But she confessed it was a difficult production to dislike and she had high praise for the visual quality:

> Never has Titipu looked so sumptuously, so extravagantly, so expensively beautiful. Susan Benson and Douglas McLean have provided a Cook's tour of Japanese design at the Avon Theatre. *The Mikado* is unfolded from a giant gold screen. A giant bonsai is Ko-Ko's perch while he sings Tit-Willow and a huge fan is half-opened as a backdrop to musical numbers. And never have Pish-Tush, Yum-Yum, Pitti-Sing, Peep-Bo and Nanki-Poo been given such handsome wardrobes, courtesy of Susan Benson. They look like a stage-full of cute Japanese dolls, all bound up in iridescent silks.

The production's musical values were excellent, thanks to the dependable presence of musical director Berthold Carriere. The cast included a delectable Yum-Yum (Marie Baron), an imposing Mikado (Gidon Saks), a Katisha (Christina James) who sounded eerily like British Prime Minister Margaret Thatcher, and two show-stopping performances from the ever-dependable Eric Donkin as a lovable Ko-Ko, and Richard McMillan, who played Pooh-Bah with a virtuoso flourish.

June 9 brought the opening of a generally tedious production of *The Merry Wives of Windsor*, with Douglas Campbell failing to generate much comic excitement in the role of Sir John Falstaff. The production had suffered from a troubled rehearsal period, owing to friction between Campbell and Robert Beard, the young American director who had assisted Brian Bedford with 1981's production of *Coriolanus*. The production afforded some peripheral pleasures: Max Helpmann's magnificent dried prune of a Nym, Amelia Hall's bouncing Mistress Quickly, R. H. Thomson's loping hillbilly of a Slender, and Richard Monette's mustache-twirling Dr. Caius. But Pat Galloway's Mistress Ford seemed as perversely glum a merry wife as had ever appeared on stage, and Nicholas Pennell was a disappointingly damp Mr. Ford. The production, which had more performances (forty-two) than any other Festival Theatre offering that season, did only 70.1-per-cent business, and also raised questions about the wisdom of confronting a relatively inexperienced visiting director with the frightening challenges of the thrust stage —particularly when the play in question was by no means foolproof.

The week's most controversial opening was *The Tempest*, which marked John Hirsch's first Festival production since becoming artistic director. It provoked the week's most blistering reviews, sending even B. A. Young, the normally mild-mannered critic of Britain's *Financial Times*, into a denunciation of it as "one of the most extravagantly vulgar things I've ever seen". Featuring Len Cariou as Prospero, Sharry Flett as Miranda, Ian Deakin as Ariel, Jim Mezon as Ferdinand, and Miles Potter as Caliban, it was dominated by Desmond Heeley's metallic visual concepts and the grinding of stage machinery.

One of the most devastating reviews was penned by Reg Skene, the *Winnipeg Free Press* critic, who had first seen Hirsch's work more than a quarter of a century previously. Skene bluntly called it "an artistic disaster", and he drew unflattering comparisons with a penny-pinching warehouse treatment of the same play staged by the Manitoba Theatre Centre's Richard Ouzounian a few months previously in Winnipeg. Whereas Ouzounian's actors had managed a clear, modulated, conversational style, Hirsch's Stratford performers offered quite the opposite. "Len Cariou as Prospero reduces one

Scene from the 1982 Festival stage production of The Tempest, *directed by John Hirsch, designed by Desmond Heeley, music by Stanley Silverman, lighting by Michael J. Whitfield. L.-R.: Jim Mezon as Ferdinand, Len Cariou as Prospero, and Sharry Flett as Miranda. Photograph by Robert C. Ragsdale, f.r.p.s., courtesy of the Stratford Festival Archives.*

of Shakespeare's most complex characters into an insensitive, ranting bully. . . . The role is played without irony and without a clear definition of emotional relationships.'' Skene found that Sharry Flett as Miranda couldn't handle the verse, but that Deakin, Potter, and Nicholas Pennell as Stephano offered masterful performances which offered a glimpse of *The Tempest* that might have been.

257

Skene was angered by the speaking of the verse and found the expensive visual spectacle irrelevant:

> The huge insects attendant on the banquet scene add a grotesque horror which, considered in isolation, is highly effective. The wedding masque, with its swirling lights and changing images, is breathtakingly beautiful. All of this would be worth what it cost if it had contributed to our understanding of the play—if we had seen the bizarre images as issuing from Prospero's imagination or resulting from some clash of cosmic forces. As it is, they merely confirm John Hirsch as undisputed king of kitsch.

Vancouver *Province* critic Bob Allen credited Hirsch for his brilliance with visual spectacle but regretted that the director had been more interested in impressing viewers than in moving them. "The opening shipwreck scene is utterly stunning theatre. Unfortunately he doesn't seem to understand that even magic must have its limits. Gimmicks are piled onto gimmicks to the point of the near-ridiculous, including enough technical hardware and machinery to launch a moonshoot." In the *London Free Press* Doug Bale decided that most performers "made as much hubbub as a hurricane and just about as much sense."

The production had its defenders among senior critics, one of whom, Ray Conlogue, felt the play reasonably well performed and genuinely deserving of praise for its visual glories. But *The Tempest*'s most spirited defence occurred two months later when Robert Fulford, the editor of *Saturday Night* magazine, turned over one of his weekly *Toronto Star* columns to a discussion of the production. Whereas other critics had hated it for its vulgarity, Fulford found this one of the production's most appealing traits:

> When it opened in June, the reviews were tepid or worse, and when I went to see it (two weeks after the opening, which may have some bearing on what I'm saying) I expected nothing extraordinary. It would be good, certainly—John Hirsch is always good, in some way or other—but clearly it wouldn't be sensational. In fact, it turns out to be a wonder, startling in a dozen different ways. . . . The audiences have caught on (word of mouth must have offset the reviews) and the box-office is running good to excellent. The night I went there was a sense of surprised joy in the house, and an excited standing ovation. Half a dozen people have since told me they have gone to see it several times. I sense that it's becoming a legend. . . .
>
> This is not a Shakespearean scholar's *Tempest*, nor is it a star's *Tempest*. It's a showman's *Tempest*. Among other qualities, it exhibits the side of Hirsch that is at home with burlesque or musical comedy or night club acts. Hirsch has taken that part of his artistic personality that responds to show-business dazzle and applied it to Shakespeare's most graceful, delicate and eloquent magic play. And somehow he's made that magic work.

The Tempest ended up grossing $1.1 million—80.4 per cent of capacity.

Mid-July openings included the two productions of the new Shakespeare Three training company and the Canadian première of *Translations*, Brian Friel's play about a nineteenth-century Ireland in which map-makers fulfilled the law by changing local Gaelic place names into English. *Translations*, which opened at the Avon on July 17, was directed by Guy Sprung, a talented Torontonian who had scored major successes with productions elsewhere of new Canadian plays by W. O. Mitchell and David Fennario. Sprung's Stratford directing debut resulted in some particularly glowing reviews. Writing in the *Globe and Mail*, Ray Conlogue praised the director for weaving a complex play

> into a production of striking unity and beauty. In this he is helped by Phillip Silver's set, which at first appears to be the inside of a barn in the style of a dated Synge production, but which has a number of levels and perspectives that suggest what is going on inside as well as outside. Harry Frehner's lighting, which creates the illusion of an entire second set for a scene on the heath, also deserves mention.

Conlogue felt that Sprung's concern with unity of tone had deprived the play of an important emotional build-up, with the result that its vitality was "repeatedly siphoned off".

> Nevertheless, the acting is fine and the direction such that the characters support each other and the script. There are no star turns which would have been fatal to the mechanism of the play. Biff McGuire as Hugh (the teacher) is the "star" name in the cast, but his character's job is really to depict the ancient sensibility over which the younger antagonists struggle. McGuire understands this, and his portrait is rich and detailed but not obtrusive.

In contrast to his campy Pooh-Bah in *The Mikado*, Richard McMillan played the womanizing farmer, Doalty, unleashing "his considerable physical power as well as his customary wry persona". Conlogue praised newcomer John Jarvis for sublimating his normal clowning instincts into a performance of "ragged vulnerability" in the role of the teacher's doomed son, and Kate Trotter for a "peremptory and commanding" characterization of a girl who falls in love with an English cartographer.

Conlogue had special praise for Sharry Flett, an actress many critics felt was being misused by the Festival:

> A special commendation for Sharry Flett, who has mistakenly been hurled more than once into the role of scintillating ingenue. Here she is Sarah, a mute whose tentative success in speech is abruptly ended by the terrorism of the British. The character as written is a

pathetic fallacy, but she makes the girl's struggle more believable than it deserves to be.

Among the negative votes for play and production was that cast by Lyle Slack in the *Hamilton Spectator*. Slack admitted that Kate Trotter's performance was fetching and that as her suitor Jim Mezon had the "sour, gentlemanly mien of Leslie Howard". But he still considered *Translations* a non-play, a mere reverie. "*Translations* is...not a piece of theatre but a heartfelt piece of research—although admittedly Guy Sprung has not helped matters by directing the play with a generally stolid, literal hand."

Hirsch's inclusion of *Translations* in the Festival season was a commendable move, reflecting a determination to offer Festival-goers distinguished new international fare. Despite the mixed reviews, the play's unusual subject matter and good cast should surely have generated more box-office attention than a miserable 44.3 per cent.

There were high hopes for *A Midsummer Night's Dream*, which opened on July 16 at the Third Stage, and for *All's Well That Ends Well*, which premiered July 17. But the end product suggested that all was not quite well with the Shakespeare Three training program in this first year of operation. *Dream*, which was directed by Peter Froehlich, suggested that the chief purpose of the training program was to give elocution exercises. Cast members spoke their lines clearly and often beautifully; what was lacking was any sense of emotional and intellectual connection with the speeches. Some of the performers, who had done good classical work in previous years in regional theatres, seemed to have merely regressed by taking part in this allegedly superior training program. It almost seemed as though the company's idea of fulfilling its training mandate was to reduce its performances to the generally tedious level of classroom exercises.

Ray Conlogue's assessment of *Dream* was that several of the young performers showed promise but that the production disappointed with its glacial pace. He also noted the "mellifluous foghorn voices of some of the actors. This is the signature tune of Kristin Linklater who drives out the old shallow-breathing chattiness of North American actors by teaching them to deliver Shakespeare as if their bodies were vertical fireplace bellows. It makes the sounds so delicious one forgets they are supposed to mean something too." Conlogue suggested a major decision faced Shakespeare Three: "whether it is inviting us to see a completed production of a play, or the audition pieces of promising actors. This appears to be more the latter."

The following night's *All's Well*, staged by veteran British director Richard Cottrell in an eccentric 1930s setting, offered Conlogue further puzzlement concerning the youth company's aim. "*All's*

Well is a difficult play that can only work with a faultless cast. That was far from being the case Saturday on the Third Stage.'' (The training program was to be revamped the following year when Michael Langham was placed in charge.)

Dream drew 94.4 per cent to the Third Stage and *All's Well* a respectable 72.2 per cent. The Festival's smallest theatre also offered two solo productions: Nicholas Pennell's *A Variable Passion*, a pot-pourri of prose and poetry about personal relations, which played to 93.5-per-cent capacity over six performances; and Aldyth Morris's *Damien*, in which Lewis Gordon delivered a much-praised performance as a devoted Belgian priest; it attracted 84.7 per cent.

John Hirsch's other production of the season was Friedrich Schiller's *Mary Stuart*, which opened a thirty-six-performance run on August 6 at the Avon and which was to end up playing to 56.7-per-cent capacity. It was an expensive production, the likes of which would never have been possible in the old days when the Avon was equipped with a money-saving basic set. Hirsch had imported the brilliant American designer Ming Cho Lee to design a highly controversial slab-like set so enormous that there were difficulties in storing it within the Avon prior to the opening of the production. Hirsch brought back Tanya Moiseiwitsch from England to design the costumes, and again hired U.S. theatre composer Stanley Silverman to supply music (Silverman was also composer for the earlier production of *The Tempest*); he hired another American designer, Beverly Emmons, to work with the new lighting especially installed for this production. The well-known Stephen Spender translation was not used. Instead, Hirsch turned to a version by American Joe McClinton—a version reworked for this production by the Festival's Michal Schonberg. Heading the cast were Margot Dionne as Mary Stuart and Pat Galloway as Elizabeth I.

The production did have its supporters. Others thought it one of the worst offerings in the Festival's history. Ray Conlogue felt that Hirsch's production grew more and more compelling as it unfolded:

> Joe McClinton's free-verse translation (which Michal Schonberg also worked on) is something of a break-through. The language is spare and contemporary, although it sometimes springs like a broken wing into flights of poetic fancy. But it does the job. It brings Schiller to us. In Ming Cho Lee's set, we have Mary imprisoned in a room with towering grey walls and tiny sticks of Puritan furniture. The lungs hardly want to draw breath in it. But a single backdrop, a wall with a fireplace across the back of it, transforms it into Elizabeth's equally spartan chamber. Puritanism chokes the life out of both practitioner and victim.

Along with many critics, Conlogue was unhappy with R. H.

Scene from the 1982 Avon stage production of Mary Stuart, *by Friedrich Schiller, translated and adapted by Joe McClinton, Stratford version by Joe McClinton and Michal Schonberg, directed by John Hirsch, set design by Ming Cho Lee, costumes designed by Tanya Moiseiwitsch, music by Stanley Silverman, lighting by Beverly Emmons. L.-R.: Graeme Campbell as Burleigh, Pat Galloway as Elizabeth I, Stephen Russell as Leicester, Colm Feore as Davison, William Needles as Shrewsbury, and Joel Kenyon as Kent. Photograph by Robert C. Ragsdale, f.r.p.s., courtesy of the Stratford Festival Archives.*

Thomson's Mortimer and also with Dionne's early scenes:

> In the early exposition scenes, Margot Dionne's Mary rushed through her speeches like one of those breathless heroines of bad historical movies. And R. H. Thomson's Mortimer, inflating the character's youthful impetuousness, almost started a localized hurricane onstage with his lung-stopping delivery.
>
> He never got past it, even to the point of killing himself with a gratuitous backflip, but she thankfully did; showing herself a young actress of considerable and growing power. The scenes where she takes confession, and especially where she goes to execution, are remarkably concentrated and moving.

As for Pat Galloway, Conlogue judged her Elizabeth one of this Stratford veteran's finest performances.

Other critics were less enthusiastic. The translation sparked controversy. "Go to hell!" bellowed one character. "Stop it, sister," declared another. "She won all the men by just being a woman!" sputtered Elizabeth. "Cool air floods over my thighs. I can see heaven's arms reaching down to embrace me," intoned Mary. Dialogue like this prompted Gina Mallet to suggest that "at best, this *Mary Stuart* sounds like a Barbara Cartland romance". The *Toronto Star* critic also questioned the whole philosophy of the production:

> Schiller's ideas, including the argument over the legitimacy of Mary's execution, are absorbed into padded-costume drama of an only too familiar kind. More sinisterly, John Hirsch has directed the play as just this side of Catholic propaganda. . . . Revisionist history is incendiary material. The establishment of the Church of England is still a potent fact. It seems to me that the play must be projected on an altogether different plane than one of sectarian strife that still continues today. Instead the play's tone here is angry and persecutes a poor little pure Mary against wicked, worldly Elizabeth. Margot Dionne's Mary is a saint—demure, noble, suffering, forgiving—who goes to her death yearning to have shared mass with her co-religionists rather than having to be slipped the wafer on the sly.
>
> Ming Cho Lee's vast marbled sets appear to have been designed by Albert Speer after his plans for Hitler's Berlin. They bring to mind the art historian Kenneth Clark's contention that no great thought was ever conceived in a huge room; ditto theatre. And while the style of Schiller's theatre was operatic, why should this be the case with a contemporary production, particularly one that is not using a verse translation? . . . The play is mostly conducted in a series of staccato shrieks that renders Schiller ridiculous and turns Mary and Elizabeth into harpies.

Miss Mallet expected Pat Galloway to show Elizabeth's qualities as "a fascinator" but was disappointed. "Here she is a frustrated old maid with a touch of Winston Churchill in drag. Frantic and incoherent is the only way to describe most of the rest of the cast." The *Star* critic has good words for Graeme Campbell's authoritative Burleigh and the compassion and humanity of Amelia Hall's performance as Mary's companion:

> There were moments when the ponderous staging looked like a devout high school production. A woman and child were shifted around from scene to scene like tear-jerking icons. Stanley Silverman's music is incidental and that is the best that can be said for it. And someone up there was not pleased. The lights, bought especially for this production, had a mind of their own, abruptly and portentously flooding the stage with bright white light that revealed all too soon the barrenness of it.

There was a far more positive reaction to Bernard Shaw's *Arms and the Man*, which marked Michael Langham's triumphant return to the Festival he had directed for so long. It played twenty-eight performances, grossed $871,757, and played to 81.5-per-cent houses. Langham turned the Festival Theatre stage into a surprisingly effective locale for what was essentially a proscenium play, aided by Desmond Heeley's robust designs.

It had a spectacular cast: Brian Bedford as Bluntschli, the pragmatic Swiss mercenary with the unromantic view of war; Helen Carey as Raina, the dewy-eyed young lady in whose bedchamber this soldier takes refuge; Douglas Campbell as her thick-headed father; Carole Shelley as her posturing mother; Susan Wright and Colin Fox as two rebellious servants; and Len Cariou giving his best performance of the season as Raina's absurdly militaristic suitor, Major Sergius Saranoff.

The atmosphere was cosily operettish. The designated setting of the play was Bulgaria in the 1880s, but the heart and soul of the production belonged in a never-never land of Ruritania, where heroines fluttered and palpitated and officers like Sergius twirled their mustaches and declaimed that they would *never* surrender. In keeping with the mood, Heeley turned the Festival stage's legendary centre balcony into a conglomeration of rustic woodwork complete with dovecot, and clothed his characters in picture-book costumes.

The reaction of Trish Wilson of the *Kitchener-Waterloo Record* was typical of the critical raves: "*Arms and the Man* brings triumphantly back some of the values that have been missing from the Festival stage too often lately. It's just unfortunate that opening late in the season will make the production's life comparatively brief."

An even later opening was that of Noel Coward's *Blithe Spirit*, which arrived at the Avon on September 10 and then moved to Toronto's Royal Alexandra Theatre after it closed its Stratford run on October 23. Despite a cast that included Tammy Grimes, Carole Shelley, and Brian Bedford (who also directed), the Stratford run did only 70.7-per-cent business, which raised questions about the wisdom of taking it into Toronto for an engagement that undoubtedly siphoned away potential theatre-goers from the Avon performances.

A number of critics felt the production untidy, lacking in accurately conceived characterizations, and conspicuous in its failure to take full advantage of Coward's witty dialogue. Reviews improved with the play's move to Toronto.

In retrospect, *Blithe Spirit* almost seemed a mere coda to a season which had proved uneven but, in the final analysis, stimulating. The box-office returns continued to be ominous, with few of the spectacular attendance figures so prevalent a few seasons back, and raised questions once again about the impact of spiralling ticket prices on Festival visitors. But few would suggest that those involved in the 1982 season had proceeded with anything other than love and dedication.

At the annual general meeting on December 4, Board President John Lawson was able to report that some 500,000 persons had attended performances and that some 100,000 of them had come for the first time. Hirsch's marketing commitment was obviously paying off. Furthermore, Lawson was able to show that the Festival was again becoming a well-functioning machine. Company workshop productions were again taking place behind the scenes, allowing artists and technicians to confront new challenges. Special programs were in effect for assistant designers and assistant lighting designers. Twenty-five individuals had been brought in to work in various Festival departments under the auspices of Canada Manpower. Michal Schonberg had initiated a Sunday morning Celebrity Lecture series featuring such speakers as Hugh MacLennan and Northrop Frye. The Shakespeare Three Company had made a beginning.

There was also good financial news. The season ended with an operating surplus of $689,366, thereby reducing the accumulated deficit to $363,324. Performance revenues were $2 million over 1981, topping the $7-million mark. There was an ominous note in the fact the Festival's operating surplus for the season would have been minuscule without the controversial bail-out money from the provincial and federal governments. But very much on the plus side was the Festival's remarkable private-sector fund-raising performance, which brought in more than $1 million. By taking advantage of the Ontario government's Wintario Arts Challenge fund with its two-for-one matching-grant formula, the Festival was able to project an endowment fund valued at just over $3.4 million.

As Lawson told the meeting:

Many contributed to this year's successful fund-raising. The Festival's Board of Governors initiated many special fund-raising programs and were assisted to a great degree by our fund-raising and administrative staffs, as well as a number of individual Festival members. In addition, certain fund-raising events involved the participation of John Hirsch, as well as members of the acting company—Len Cariou, Sharry Flett, Nicholas Pennell, Amelia Hall, Eric Donkin—to all these people I would say thank you.

The most important group, however, are those who gave so generously to the various fund-raising programs. I would like to thank the corporate sponsors whose contributions increased significantly in 1982 over 1981. Our seat endowment program was generously supported by many corporations and individuals with a total of 261 seats endowed since the program began. In addition, members of the Festival have continued their support and, in many cases, increased their financial contribution. With the addition of new members this year, our total membership now stands at just over 9,000. This broad base on which our support is drawn is one of the strengths of the Festival, and I would like to thank you, the members, for your continued support. . . .

Lawson stressed the teamwork and commitment that had helped bring the Festival out of the uncertainties of the recent past. He warned of a difficult future and of solutions that were increasingly complex. But there was an undeniable note of optimism in his tone.

For John Hirsch, it had been a difficult two years. He had fought, successfully, to keep the Festival alive artistically. He had unrepentantly been prepared to court unpopularity in the process. He had been single-minded in pursuit of his vision. And he had felt understandably hurt at those who suggested he wanted anything less than the best for the Stratford Festival. He was to continue as artistic director into the Festival's fourth decade—a decade that promised to be the most challenging in Stratford's history. He, along with all his colleagues, was becoming part of the legend and tradition that were so much of the Festival's sustaining forces over the years. By temperament, Hirsch shrank from running institutions. But Stratford, he was always to declare, was "a special situation".

"I'm doing what could be called a national service," he once said. "Your country calls, and you go. I love this country, you see. And I don't see why I shouldn't say I love it or that I'm proud of it. I have no problems having strong emotions about anything or anyone."

Service. That was really the characteristic feature of those who had toiled for Stratford over the years—from the early visionaries like Patterson and Showalter and Guthrie through to Robin Phillips, John Hirsch, and the troubled eighties. It was again to be the salvation of Stratford as it embarked on its next thirty years.

·A·P·P·E·N·D·I·X · I·

The Seasons 1953-1982

1953

Richard III — directed by Tyrone Guthrie, designed by Tanya Moiseiwitsch, music by Louis Applebaum.

All's Well That Ends Well — directed by Tyrone Guthrie, designed by Tanya Moiseiwitsch, music by Louis Applebaum.

Members of the Company: George Alexander, Michael Bates, Lloyd Bochner, Douglas Campbell, Robert Christie, Richard Easton, Robert Goodier, Alec Guinness, Amelia Hall, Donald Harron, Eric House, William Hutt, Betty Leighton, Peter Mews, William Needles, Douglas Rain, Eleanor Stuart, Bruce Swerdfager, Irene Worth.

Music

Sixteen afternoon concerts were presented in the Tent Theatre with Glenn Gould, Jan Rubes, Lois Marshall, Gerhard Kander, Albert Pratz, Ed McCurdy, John Knight and James Milligan as featured guest artists.

1954

Measure for Measure — directed by Cecil Clarke, designed by Tanya Moiseiwitsch, music by Louis Applebaum.

The Taming of the Shrew — directed by Tyrone Guthrie, designed by Tanya Moiseiwitsch, music by Louis Applebaum.

Oedipus Rex — by Sophocles, directed by Tyrone Guthrie, designed by Tanya Moiseiwitsch, music by Cedric Thorpe Davie.

Members of the Company: Lloyd Bochner, Douglas Campbell, Barbara Chilcott, Robert Christie, Donald Davis, Bruno Gerussi, Robert Goodier, Dawn Greenhalgh, Donald Harron, John Hayes, Eric House, William Hutt, Frances Hyland, Marionne Johnston, James Mason, Jack Merigold, Peter Mews, Mavor Moore, William Needles, Douglas Rain, Toby Robins, William Shatner, Eleanor Stuart, Bruce Swerdfager, Neil Vipond.

Music

One Sunday afternoon concert in the Tent Theatre by the Elizabethan Singers of Stratford.

Other Activities

Richard Southern Theatre Exhibit;

*Appendices I and II are reprinted with the kind permission of the Stratford Festival from their publication *The Stratford Festival Story*.

267

Exhibition of Canadian Sculpture and Fine Art. A short Drama Course.

1955

The Merchant of Venice — directed by Tyrone Guthrie, designed by Tanya Moiseiwitsch, music by John Cook.

Julius Caesar — directed by Michael Langham, designed by Tanya Moiseiwitsch, music by Louis Applebaum.

King Oedipus — by Sophocles, directed by Tyrone Guthrie, designed by Tanya Moiseiwitsch, music by Cedric Thorpe Davie.

Members of the Company: Lloyd Bochner, Helen Burns, Douglas Campbell, Barbara Chilcott, Robert Christie, Donald Davis, Robert Goodier, Ted Follows, David Gardner, Bruno Gerussi, Lorne Greene, Donald Harron, John Hayes, Roland Hewgill, Eric House, William Hutt, Frances Hyland, Douglas Rain, Charlotte Schrager, William Shatner, Eleanor Stuart, Bruce Swerdfager, Frederick Valk, Tony van Bridge.

Music

A Soldier's Tale — by Stravinsky and C. F. Ramuz, directed by Douglas Campbell, conducted by Paul Scherman, designed by Clarence Wilson.

Members of the Company: Lilian Jarvis, Marcel Marceau, William Needles, Douglas Rain.

The Hart House Orchestra — conducted by Boyd Neel.

The Festival Chorus — conducted by Elmer Iseler.

Soloists including: Maureen Forrester, Glenn Gould, Eugene Kash, Lois Marshall, Alexander Schneider, Elisabeth Schwarzkopf, Isaac Stern.

A Program of Solo Mime — by Marcel Marceau.

Other Activities

Canadian Art from the National Gallery; Richard Southern Theatre Exhibit; Canadian Films; Exhibit of Books by the Book Publishers' Association of Canada.

1956

Henry V — directed by Michael Langham, designed by Tanya Moiseiwitsch, music by Louis Applebaum.

The Merry Wives of Windsor — directed by Michael Langham, designed by Tanya Moiseiwitsch, music by John Cook.

Members of the Company: Sharon Acker, Lloyd Bochner, Helen Burns, Douglas Campbell, Robert Christie, Donald Davis, Richard Easton, Ted Follows, Roger Garceau, Gabriel Gascon, Jean Gascon, Gratien Gélinas, Bruno Gerussi, Robert Goodier, Amelia Hall, Max Helpmann, Roland Hewgill, Guy Hoffman, Eric House, William Hutt, Pauline Jameson, Ginette Letondal, William Needles, Christopher Plummer, Douglas Rain, Jean-Louis Roux, William Shatner, Eleanor Stuart, Bruce Swerdfager, Tony van Bridge, Helene Winston.

Music

The Rape of Lucretia — by Benjamin Britten, directed by Herman Geiger-Torel, conducted by Thomas Mayer, designed by Marie Day.

Members of the Company: Adelaide Bishop, Harry Mossfield, Regina Resnik, Patricia Rideout, Jan Rubes, Jennie Tourel, Bernard Turgeon, Jon Vickers.

The Festival Orchestra — conducted by Reginald Stewart, Thomas Mayer, Heinz Unger.

The Festival Chorus — conducted by Elmer Iseler.

Concert Soloists: Claudio Arrau, Inge Borkh, Maureen Forrester, Glenn Gould, Rudolf Serkin, Martial Singher.

Jazz Concerts — Wilbur de Paris, Paul Draper, Duke Ellington, Calvin Jackson, Oscar Peterson, Dave Brubeck, Modern Jazz Quartet, Phil Nimmons, Norm Symonds Octette.

Other Activities

Three Farces by Molière with Le Théâtre du Nouveau Monde; Richard Southern Theatre Exhibit; Exhibit of Books by the Book Publishers' Association of Canada; Canadian Graphic Art; An Exhibit of Shakespeare Books from the collection of Sidney Fisher; Paintings by Pavel Tchelitchew and Leslie Hurry — arranged by the National Gallery; Film Festival.

International Film Festival

1957

Hamlet — directed by Michael Langham, designed by Desmond Heeley, music by Louis Applebaum.

Twelfth Night — directed by Tyrone Guthrie, designed by Tanya Moiseiwitsch, music by John Cook.

Members of the Company: Mervyn Blake, Lloyd Bochner, Douglas Campbell, Eric Christmas, Ted Follows, Bruno Gerussi, Amelia Hall, Max Helpmann, Roland Hewgill, John Horton, William Hutt, Frances Hyland, Michael Kane, Joy Lafleur, George McCowan, Siobhan McKenna, Alan Nunn, Christopher Plummer, Douglas Rain, Powys Thomas, Tony van Bridge, Neil Vipond.

Music

The Turn of the Screw — by Benjamin Britten, directed by Basil Coleman, conducted by Benjamin Britten, designed by John Piper (Presented by the English Opera Group).

Members of the Company: Peter Pears, Jennifer Vyvyan, Judith Pierce, Olive Dyer, Michael Hartnett, Arda Mandikian.

CBC Symphony Orchestra — conducted by Thomas Mayer, Walter Susskind, Heinz Unger, Geoffrey Waddington.

Soloists: John Boyden, Betty-Jean Hagen, Lois Marshall.

Jazz Concerts — Count Basie, Ron Collier, Duke Ellington, Billie Holliday, Gerry Mulligan Quartet, Teddy Wilson Trio.

Other Activities

International Film Festival

Richard Southern Theatre Exhibit; Exhibit of Books by the Book Publishers' Association of Canada; An Exhibit of Shakespeare Books from the collection of Sidney Fisher; Photographs of Shakespearean Productions; Painting and Sculpture by Art Price; National Gallery of Canada Exhibition of Contemporary American Painting.

1958

Henry IV, Part I — directed by Michael Langham and George McCowan, designed by Tanya Moiseiwitsch and Marie Day, music by John Cook.

The Winter's Tale — directed by Douglas Campbell, designed by Tanya Moiseiwitsch, music by John Cook.

Much Ado About Nothing — directed by Michael Langham, designed by Desmond Heeley, music by Louis Applebaum.

Members of the Company: Conrad Bain, Mervyn Blake, Douglas Campbell, Eric Christmas, Peter Donat, Ted Follows, Bruno Gerussi, Tammy Grimes, Max Helpmann, Eileen Herlie, John Horton, William Hutt, Frances Hyland, Charmion King, Diana Maddox, Roberta Maxwell, George McCowan, Ann Morrish, Alan Nunn, James Peddie, Christopher Plummer, Douglas Rain, Jason Robards Jr., Powys Thomas, Tony van Bridge, Jeremy Wilkin.

Music

The Beggar's Opera — by John Gay, directed by Tom Brown, conducted by Louis Applebaum, designed by Brian Jackson.

Members of the Company: Helen Burns, Ann Casson, Robert Christie, Marie Gauley, Robert Goulet, Maxine Miller, Chester Waton.

The Festival Singers — conducted by Elmer Iseler.

The New York Pro Musica — directed by Noah Greenberg.

Little Carib Dancers — directed by Beryl McBurnie.

Folk Music — Emma Caslor, Richard Dyer-Bennet, Jacques Labreque, Marais and Miranda.

Jazz Concerts — Henry "Red" Allen, Maynard Ferguson, Wilbur de Paris, Dizzy Gillespie, Carmen McRae, Moe Koffman Quartet, Billy Taylor Trio.

Other Activities

International Film Festival

Le Malade Imaginaire by Molière, with Le Théâtre du Nouveau Monde.

Marcel Marceau in Mime Performances

Second Biennial Exhibition of Canadian Painting from the National Gallery of Canada; Canadian Guild of Potters Display; Woodcuts by Gordon Craig; Exhibit of Books by the Book Publishers' Association of Canada; An Exhibit of Shakespeare Books from the collection of Sidney Fisher; Costumes, Sketches and Properties from the Festival Theatre.

1959

Othello — directed by Jean Gascon and George McCowan, designed by Robert

Prévost, music by Louis Applebaum.

As You Like It — directed by Peter Wood, designed by Desmond Heeley, music by John Cook.

Members of the Company: Bernard Behrens, Mervyn Blake, Douglas Campbell, Eric Christmas, Ted Follows, John Gardiner, Dawn Greenhalgh, Max Helpmann, John Horton, William Hutt, Frances Hyland, Roberta Maxwell, Ann Morrish, William Needles, James Peddie, Douglas Rain, Kate Reid, William Sylvester, Powys Thomas, Tony van Bridge, John Vernon, Jeremy Wilkin, Irene Worth.

Music

Orpheus in the Underworld — by Offenbach, adapted by Robert Fulford and James Knight, directed by Tom Brown, conducted by Louis Applebaum, designed by Brian Jackson.

Members of the Company: Alan Crofoot, Eric House, Irene Jordan, John McCollum, Jan Rubes, Martial Singher.

National Festival Orchestra — conducted by Louis Applebaum, Alexander Brott, Oscar Shumsky, Leonard Rose, Ernesto Barbini.

Soloists including: Julius Baker, Robert Bloom, Lois Marshall, Leonard Rose, Oscar Shumsky.

Folk Music — Ed McCurdy, Pete Seeger.

Other Activities

Shakespeare and Music — with Michael Langham, Martial Singher, Irene Jordan and the Elizabethan Singers.

After Hours — a revue directed by Norman Jewison.

The Heart Is Highland — a Scottish fantasy with Lennox Milne.

International Film Festival

Exhibit of Eskimo Life in the Arctic; Exhibit of Paintings by Ten Canadian Artists; The Merten Puppet Theatre; Exhibit of Books by the Book Publishers' Association of Canada; Canadian Handicrafts; An Exhibit of Shakespeare Books from the collection of Sidney Fisher; Costumes, Sketches and Properties from the Festival Theatre.

1960

King John — directed by Douglas Seale, designed by Tanya Moiseiwitsch, music by John Cook.

A Midsummer Night's Dream — directed by Douglas Campbell, designed by Brian Jackson, music by Harry Somers.

Romeo and Juliet — directed by Michael Langham, designed by Tanya Moiseiwitsch, music by Louis Applebaum.

Members of the Company: Bernard Behrens, Mervyn Blake, Helen Burns, Deborah Cass, Ann Casson, Dinah Christie, Eric Christmas, Leo Ciceri, Jack Creley, Jake Dengel, Peter Donat, Pat Galloway, Robin Gammell, Bruno Gerussi, Robert Goodier, Lewis Gordon, Julie Harris, Max Helpmann, John Horton, Alexis Kanner, Hayward Morse, Peter Needham, William Needles, Christopher Plummer, Douglas Rain, Kate Reid, Sydney Sturgess, Tony van Bridge, John Vernon, Chris Wiggins.

Music

H.M.S. Pinafore — by Gilbert and Sullivan, directed by Tyrone Guthrie, conducted by Louis Applebaum, designed by Brian Jackson.

Members of the Company: Irene Byatt, Douglas Campbell, Andrew Downie, Eric House, Elizabeth Mawson, Howard Mawson, Harry Mossfield, Marion Studholme.

Festival Concerts with soloists Douglas Campbell, Glenn Gould, Julie Harris, Leonard Rose, Oscar Shumsky, Walter Susskind.

The National Festival Orchestra.

Three Saturday morning chamber music concerts.

International Conference of Composers including concerts by the CBC Symphony Orchestra conducted by Walter Susskind, Otar Taktakishvili; National Festival Orchestra conducted by Victor Feldbrill; International String Congress conducted by Roy Harris.

Other Activities

International Film Festival

Two Canadian Plays from THE GLOBE AND MAIL — STRATFORD FESTIVAL COMPETITION — *The Teacher* by John Gray and *Blind Man's Buff* by Alfred Euringer.

Shakespeare Seminar — conducted by McMaster University, Hamilton.

A Panorama of the Western Canadian Indian — Collection of Paintings by Emily Carr; Paintings by Ten Contemporary British Columbia Artists.
Canadian Handicrafts; Art and Theatre Display; Displays by the Book Publishers' Association of Canada and the Canadian Music Publishers' Association; An Exhibit of Shakespeare Books from the collection of Sidney Fisher; The Henry Osborne Collection of Early Children's Books.

1961

Coriolanus — directed by Michael Langham, designed by Tanya Moiseiwitsch, music by Louis Applebaum.
Henry VIII — directed by George McCowan, designed by Brian Jackson, music by Louis Applebaum.
Love's Labour's Lost — directed by Michael Langham, designed by Tanya Moiseiwitsch, music by John Cook.
The Canvas Barricade — a contemporary Canadian comedy by Donald Lamont Jack. Directed by George McCowan, designed by Mark Negin, music by Harry Freedman.
Members of the Company: Mia Anderson, Claude Bede, Bernard Behrens, Christine Bennett, Mervyn Blake, Zoe Caldwell, Douglas Campbell, Douglas Chamberlain, Dinah Christie, Eric Christmas, Leo Ciceri, John Colicos, Jack Creley, Peter Donat, Maureen Fitzgerald, Pat Galloway, Robin Gammell, Bruno Gerussi, Robert Goodier, Lewis Gordon, Amelia Hall, Max Helpmann, Edward Holmes, Michael Learned, Peter Needham, William Needles, Louis Negin, Joy Parker, James Peddie, Douglas Rain, Kate Reid, Joseph Rutten, Paul Scofield, Eleanor Stuart, John Vernon.
Music
The Pirates of Penzance — by Gilbert and Sullivan, directed by Tyrone Guthrie, designed by Brian Jackson, conducted by Louis Applebaum.
Members of the Company: Irene Byatt, Andrew Downie, Marie Gauley, Howell Glynne, Genevieve Gordon, Alexander Gray, Darlene Hirst, Eric House, Harry Mossfield, Marion Studholme.

Festival Concerts with soloists Victor Braun, Oscar Shumsky, Glenn Gould, Leonard Rose, Lois Marshall, Maureen Forrester, Ellen Faull and members of the National Festival Orchestra.
The National Youth Orchestra directed by Walter Susskind.
Four Saturday morning chamber music concerts.
Other Activities
International Film Festival
Two Shakespeare Seminars of one week each conducted by McMaster University, Hamilton.
The Arts of French Canada — Paintings by twenty-five contemporary Quebec artists.
Canadian Handicrafts; Art and Theatre Display; Displays by the Book Publishers' Association of Canada and the Canadian Music Publishers' Association; An Exhibit of Shakespeare Books from the collection of Sidney Fisher.

1962

Macbeth — directed by Peter Coe, designed by Brian Jackson.
The Taming of the Shrew — directed by Michael Langham, designed by Tanya Moiseiwitsch, music by John Cook.
The Tempest — directed by George McCowan, designed by Desmond Heeley, music by John Cook.
Cyrano de Bergerac — by Edmond Rostand, translated by Brian Hooker, adapted and directed by Michael Langham, designed by Tanya Moiseiwitsch and Desmond Heeley, music by Louis Applebaum.
Members of the Company: Karen Austin, Claude Bede, Bernard Behrens, Len Birman, Mervyn Blake, Len Cariou, Dinah Christie, Eric Christmas, Leo Ciceri, John Colicos, Peter Donat, Pat Galloway, Bruno Gerussi, Lewis Gordon, Garrick Hagon, Amelia Hall, Max Helpmann, Martha Henry, John Horton, William Hutt, Al Kozlik, William Needles, Adrian Pecknold, James Peddie, Gordon Pinsent, Christopher Plummer, Douglas Rain, Kate Reid, Toby Robins, Joseph Rutten, Mary Savidge, Joseph Shaw, John Vernon, Hugh Webster, William Webster, Norman Welsh, Anthony Zerbe.

Music

The Gondoliers — by Gilbert and Sullivan, directed by Leon Major, designed by Mark Negin, music direction by Louis Applebaum, conducted by John Cook.

Members of the Company: John Arab, Victor Braun, Douglas Campbell, Ann Casson, Jack Creley, Alexander Gray, Darlene Hirst, Ilona Kombrink, Dodi Protero.

Festival Concerts with soloists Glenn Gould, Leonard Rose, Oscar Shumsky, Lois Marshall, Maureen Forrester, Leopold Simoneau, Grace-Lynne Martin, Lukas Foss and Soloists of the National Ballet of Canada.

Five Saturday morning chamber music concerts.

Other Activities

Two Shakespeare Seminars of one week each, conducted by McMaster University, Hamilton.

Tenth Season Theatre and Art Exhibit — Paintings by Nine Prairie Province Artists and an exhibit reviewing the first ten seasons of the Festival; Displays by the Book Publishers' Association of Canada and the Canadian Music Publishers' Association; An Exhibit of Shakespeare Books from the collection of Sidney Fisher; Canadian Handicrafts. On July 23 the CBC televised a portion of *Macbeth* for the first intercontinental Telstar broadcast, seen simultaneously on this continent and in Europe.

1963

Troilus and Cressida — directed by Michael Langham, designed by Desmond Heeley, music by Louis Applebaum.

Cyrano de Bergerac — by Edmond Rostand, directed by Michael Langham, designed by Tanya Moiseiwitsch and Desmond Heeley, music by Louis Applebaum.

The Comedy of Errors — directed by Jean Gascon, designed by Robert Prévost and Mark Negin, music by Gabriel Charpentier.

Timon of Athens — directed by Michael Langham, designed by Brian Jackson, music by Duke Ellington.

Members of the Company: Claude Bede, Christine Bennett, Len Birman,

Mervyn Blake, Len Cariou, Eric Christmas, Leo Ciceri, John Colicos, Clare Coulter, Jake Dengel, Peter Donat, James Douglas, Fred Euringer, Lewis Gordon, Garrick Hagon, Amelia Hall, Max Helpmann, Martha Henry, Rita Howell, William Hutt, Al Kozlik, Diana Maddox, William Needles, Adrian Pecknold, Douglas Rain, Kate Reid, Donnelly Rhodes, Joseph Rutten, Joseph Shaw, Tony van Bridge, Hugh Webster.

Music

The Mikado — by Gilbert and Sullivan, directed by Norman Campbell, music numbers staged by Alan Lund, designed by Brian Jackson, music direction by Louis Applebaum, conducted by Mario Bernardi.

Members of the Company: Maurice Brown, Irene Byatt, Andrew Downie, Howell Glynne, Eric House, Anne Linden, Kathryn Newman, Arthur Sclater, Heather Thomson.

Festival Concerts with Robert Craft, Glenn Gould, Lois Marshall, Oscar Shumsky, Carolyn Stanford, Elizabeth Benson Guy, John Boyden, Adele Addison, Greta Kraus, Jon Vickers, Shirley Verrett, Sol Schoenbach, Avraham Sternklar, Lillian Fuchs, Mario Bernardi, William Aide, The Fine Arts String Quartet, Leslie Parnas, Rudolf Serkin, Phyllis Curtin, Hans Kohlund, Maurice Brown, the Festival Singers conducted by Elmer Iseler, the National Youth Orchestra conducted by Walter Susskind, the National Festival Orchestra, The Canadian String Quartet.

Choral programme by the Festival Choral Workshop directed by Elmer Iseler. Five Saturday morning chamber music concerts with solo artists and members of the National Festival Orchestra Workshop.

The National Dance Theatre Company of Jamaica

Other Activities

Art and Theatre Exhibits — *Canada on Canvas*, a showing of Canadian landscape painting from 1900 to the present, arranged by Alan Jarvis; the Sidney Fisher Collection of Rare Books and Shakespeareana; Displays by the Book Publishers' Association of Canada and the Canadian Music Publishers' Association; Handicrafts by the Canadian Handicraft Guild; Costumes and Properties from the Festival Theatre.

Two Shakespeare Seminars of one week each, conducted by McMaster University, Hamilton.

1964

Richard II — directed by Stuart Burge, designed by Desmond Heeley, music by John Cook.

Le Bourgeois Gentilhomme — by Molière, directed by Jean Gascon, designed by Robert Prévost, music by Gabriel Charpentier, dances staged by Alan Lund.

King Lear — directed by Michael Langham, designed by Leslie Hurry, music by Louis Applebaum.

The Country Wife — by William Wycherley, directed by Michael Langham, designed by Desmond Heeley, music by Godfrey Ridout.

Members of the Company: Claude Bede, Len Birman, Mervyn Blake, Patrick Boxill, Helen Burns, Jackie Burroughs, Len Cariou, Eric Christmas, Leo Ciceri, John Colicos, Clare Coulter, Patrick Crean, Bruno Gerussi, Lewis Gordon, Suzanne Grossmann, Garrick Hagon, Amelia Hall, Max Helpmann, Martha Henry, Eric House, William Hutt, Frances Hyland, Al Kozlik, Heath Lamberts, Diana Maddox, Leslie Mulholland, William Needles, Ken Pogue, Leon Pownall, Douglas Rain, Joseph Rutten, Mary Savidge, Joseph Shaw, Cedric Smith, Tony van Bridge, Hugh Webster.

Music

The Yeomen of the Guard — by Gilbert and Sullivan, directed by William Ball, music direction by Louis Applebaum, conducted by John Cook, designed by Mark Negin.

The Marriage of Figaro — by Mozart; directed by Jean Gascon, music direction by Richard Bonynge, designed by Mark Negin.

Members of the Company: Jack Bittner, Jean Bonhomme, Garnet Brooks, Maurice Brown, Rita Gardner, Howell Glynne, Muriel Greenspon, Caroline Guay, Laurel Hurley, Ilona Kombrink, Anne Linden, Barry MacGregor, Elizabeth Mawson, Kathryn Newman, Cornelis Opthof, Thomas Park, Robert Peters, Jan Rubes, Huguette Tourangeau.

Festival Concerts with Israel Baker, Artur Balsam, Perry Bauman, Elizabeth Benson Guy, E. Power Biggs, Shannon Bolin, Jean Bonhomme, John Boyden, Charles Bressler, Maurice Brown, Rudolf Firkusny, Leon Fleisher, Robert Koff, David Mankowitz, Paul Makanowitzky, Lois Marshall, David Nadien, Robert Oades, Patricia Parr, Patricia Rideout, Leonard Rose, Charles Rosen, Sol Schoenbach, Eudice Shapiro, Oscar Shumsky, Mary Simmons, Walter Susskind, Soloists of the National Ballet of Canada with Arthur Mitchell, the Festival Singers conducted by Elmer Iseler, the National Festival Orchestra.

Six Saturday morning chamber music concerts with solo artists and members of the National Festival Orchestra.

Choral programme by the Festival Choral Workshop directed by Elmer Iseler.

Other Activities

Art and Theatre Exhibits — *The Faces of Canada*, a showing of portraiture arranged by Alan Jarvis; the Sidney Fisher Collection of Rare Books and Shakespeareana; Displays by the Book Publishers' Association of Canada and the Canadian Music Publishers' Association; Artist-Craftsmen, and the Students of the National Theatre School; Costumes and Properties from the Festival Theatre.

Two Shakespeare Seminars of one week each, conducted by McMaster University, Hamilton.

1965

Henry IV (*Henry IV, Part One*) — directed by Stuart Burge, designed by Desmond Heeley, music by John Cook.

Falstaff (*Henry IV, Part Two*) — directed by Stuart Burge, designed by Desmond Heeley, music by John Cook.

Julius Caesar — directed by Douglas Campbell, designed by Leslie Hurry.

The Cherry Orchard — by Anton Chekhov, translated by Tyrone Guthrie and Leonid Kipnis, directed by John Hirsch, designed by Brian Jackson, music by Louis Applebaum.

Members of the Company: Claude Bede, Mervyn Blake, Douglas Campbell, Eric Christmas, Leo Ciceri, Patrick Crean, Peter Donat, Maureen Fitzgerald, Bruno Gerussi, Lewis Gordon, Max Helpmann, Martha Henry, Roland Hewgill, Henry Hovenkamp, William Hutt, Frances Hyland, Ken James, J. C. Juliani, Joan Karasevich, Al Kozlik, Heath Lamberts, Paul Massie, Richard Monette, William Needles, Briain Petchey, Kenneth Pogue, Leon Pownall, Douglas Rain, Kate Reid, Mary Savidge, Joseph Shaw, Powys Thomas, Tony van Bridge, Hugh Webster.

Music

The Rise and Fall of the City of Mahagonny — by Bertolt Brecht and Kurt Weill, directed by Jean Gascon, music direction by Louis Applebaum, designed by Brian Jackson.

The Marriage of Figaro — by Mozart, directed by Jean Gascon, music direction by Mario Bernardi, designed by Mark Negin.

Members of the Company: Jean Bonhomme, Maurice Brown, Len Cariou, Carrol Anne Curry, Muriel Greenspon, Yoland Guérard, Mona Kelly, Gwenlynn Little, Elizabeth Mawson, Daniel McCaughna, James McCray, Helen Murray, Thomas O'Leary, Joan Patenaude, Roxolana Roslak, Jan Rubes, Donald Saunders, Martha Schlamme, Phil Stark, Lilian Sukis, Danny Tait, Bernard Turgeon, Marcelle Zonta.

Festival Concerts with Claudio Arrau, Mario Bernardi, Charles Bressler, Dave Brubeck, Barbara Collier, John Covearts, Norman Farrow, Leon Fleisher, Benny Goodman, Elizabeth Benson Guy, Weldon Kilburn, Stephen Kondaks, Judy Loman, Lois Marshall, Jean-Pierre Rampal, Leonard Rose, Oscar Shumsky, Beveridge Webster, the Festival Singers of Toronto conducted by Elmer Iseler, members of the Toronto Mendelssohn Choir, National Youth Orchestra of Canada conducted by Franz Paul Decker, the Dave Brubeck Quartet, the Benny Goodman Quartet, the National Festival Orchestra.

Six Saturday morning chamber music concerts with solo artists Walter Buczynski, John de Lancie, Oscar Shumsky and members of the National Festival Orchestra.

Commentators: Tony van Bridge, Douglas Campbell, Leo Ciceri, Peter Donat, Frances Hyland.

Guest Instructors for the Workshop: John de Lancie, Jean-Pierre Rampal, Paul Stassevitch.

Choral programme by the Festival Choral Workshop directed by Elmer Iseler.

Master Classes

The National Ballet of Canada.

Other Activities

Art and Theatre Exhibits — *Canadian Ceramic '65* under the auspices of the Canadian Guild of Potters; Sculpture Exhibition by the Sculptors' Society of Canada (Ontario Chapter); Displays by the Book Publishers' Association of Canada, the Canadian Music Publishers' Association and the students of the National Theatre School; Costumes and Properties from the Festival Theatre.

Two Shakespeare Seminars of one week each, conducted by McMaster University, Hamilton.

1966

Henry V — directed by Michael Langham, designed by Desmond Heeley, music by John Cook.

Henry VI* — directed by John Hirsch, designed by Desmond Heeley, music by John Cook (*adapted by John Barton for Peter Hall's production of *The Wars of the Roses* for the Royal Shakespeare Company).

Twelfth Night — directed by David William, designed by Brian Jackson, music by Louis Applebaum.

The Last of the Tsars — an original play about the Russian Revolution by Michael Bawtree. Directed by Michael Langham, designed by Leslie Hurry, music by Louis Applebaum.

The Dance of Death — by August Strindberg, directed by Jean Gascon, designed by Mark Negin.

Members of the Company: Claude Bede, Bernard Behrens, Mervyn Blake, Barbara Bryne, John Byron, Eric Christmas, Leo Ciceri, Eric Donkin, Colin Fox, Angelo Fusco, Jacques Galipeau, Jean Gascon, Lewis Gordon, Amelia

Hall, Max Helpmann, Martha Henry, Dominic Hogan, William Hutt, Frances Hyland, Al Kozlik, Gaitan Labreche, Heath Lamberts, Diana Leblanc, Guy L'Ecuyer, Barry MacGregor, Roberta Maxwell, Richard Monette, William Needles, Christopher Newton, Michael O'Regan, Jérôme Tiberghien, Powys Thomas, Hans Werner Tolle, Tony van Bridge, Kenneth Welsh, Kim Yaroshevskaya.

Music

Don Giovanni — by Mozart, directed by Jean Gascon, music direction by Mario Bernardi, designed by Robert Prévost.

Members of the Stratford Festival Opera Company: Maurice Brown, Carrol Anne Curry, Howell Glynne, Sylvia Grant, Mona Kelly, Gwenlynn Little, Cornelis Opthof, Roxolana Roslak, Jan Rubes, Irene Salemka, Sylvia Saurette, Jerold Siena.

Festival Concerts with Leonard Pennario, Oscar Shumsky, José Iturbi, Mary Simmons, Mario Bernardi, Jean-Pierre Rampal, Phyllis Curtin, Leonard Rose, Walter Susskind, the Festival Singers of Toronto conducted by Elmer Iseler, National Youth Orchestra, conducted by Walter Susskind, Duke Ellington and his Orchestra, the George Shearing Quintet, the National Festival Orchestra.

Six Saturday morning chamber music concerts with members of the National Festival Orchestra and solo artists Ray Still, Sheila Henig, Phyllis Mailing, Jean-Pierre Rampal, James Chambers, Marcel Moyse, Sol Schoenbach, Tibor Serly.

Commentators: Jean Gascon, Powys Thomas, Martha Henry, Leo Ciceri, Tony van Bridge, Frances Hyland.

Guest Instructors for the Workshop: Ray Still, Tibor Serly, Jean-Pierre Rampal, James Chambers.

Ballet

Rose Latulippe — world première of a new ballet choreographed by Brian Macdonald, designed by Robert Prévost and music by Harry Freedman, performed by the Royal Winnipeg Ballet.

Other Activities

Art and Theatre Exhibits — Sculpture Exhibitions by the Sculptors' Society of Canada (Quebec Chapter); Displays by the Book Publishers' Association of Canada, The Canadian Music Publishers' Association and students of the National Theatre School; Costumes and Properties from the Festival Theatre.

Two Shakespeare Seminars of one week each, conducted by McMaster University, Hamilton.

1967

Antony and Cleopatra — directed by Michael Langham, designed by Tanya Moiseiwitsch, music by Louis Applebaum.

Richard III — directed by John Hirsch, designed by Desmond Heeley, music by Stanley Silverman.

The Merry Wives of Windsor — directed by David William, designed by Brian Jackson, music by Louis Applebaum.

The Government Inspector — by Nikolai Gogol, adapted by Peter Raby, directed by Michael Langham, designed by Leslie Hurry, music by Raymond Pannell.

Colours in the Dark — an original play by James Reaney, directed by John Hirsch, designed by Eoin Sprott and Don Lewis, music by Alan Laing.

Members of the Company: Alan Bates, Bernard Behrens, Mervyn Blake, James Blendick, Garnet Brooks, Barbara Bryne, Zoe Caldwell, Jane Casson, Eric Christmas, Leo Ciceri, Patrick Crean, Neil Dainard, Eric Donkin, Ann Firbank, Michael Fletcher, Colin Fox, Jean Gascon, Dawn Greenhalgh, Amelia Hall, Max Helpmann, Martha Henry, Dominic Hogan, William Hutt, Frances Hyland, Peter Jobin, Joel Kenyon, Al Kozlik, Heath Lamberts, Marilyn Lightstone, Barry MacGregor, Roberta Maxwell, Richard Monette, Christopher Newton, Blaine Parker, Briain Petchey, Christopher Plummer, Kenneth Pogue, Leon Pownall, Douglas Rain, August Schellenberg, Joseph Shaw, Cedric Smith, Tony van Bridge, Sandy Webster, Kenneth Welsh, Anna Wing, Jonathan White.

Music
Cosi Fan Tutte — by Mozart, directed by Jean Gascon, music direction by Mario Bernardi and John Matheson, designed by Desmond Heeley.

Albert Herring — by Benjamin Britten, directed by David William, music direction by John Matheson, designed by Leslie Hurry.

Members of the Stratford Festival Opera Company: Ernest Atkinson, Corinne Curry, Carrol Anne Curry, Gregory Dempsey, Sylvia Fisher, Howell Glynne, Alexander Gray, Muriel Greenspon, Muriel James, Mona Kelly, Gwenlynn Little, Peter Milne, Mary Munroe, Cornelis Opthof, Patricia Rideout, Roxolana Roslak, Jan Rubes, Elsie Sawchuk, Jerold Siena, Peter Young, Jeannette Zarou.

Festival Concerts with Julian Bream, Lois Marshall, Mario Bernardi, Maureen Forrester, José Iturbi, Louis Quilico, Mstislav Rostropovich, Oscar Shumsky, Jean-Pierre Rampal, Yehudi Menuhin and the Bath Festival Orchestra, Festival Singers of Toronto, Members of the Toronto Mendelssohn Choir with conductor Elmer Iseler, The Modern Jazz Quartet, Wilbur de Paris and his Traditional Jazz, National Festival Orchestra. Six Saturday morning Chamber Music Concerts with members of the Stratford Festival Orchestra and solo artists John Barrows, Oscar Shumsky, Mario Bernardi, Ray Still, Jean-Pierre Rampal.

Guest Instructors for the Workshop: John Barrows, Jean-Pierre Rampal, Ray Still.

Other Activities
Art and Theatre Exhibits — *One Hundred Years of Theatre in Canada*: An exhibit of Shakespeare Books from the collection of Sidney Fisher; Costumes and Properties from the Festival Theatre; Paintings of various eras at the Rothmans Art Gallery; Displays by the Book Publishers' Association of Canada, and the Canadian Music Publishers' Association.

Two Shakespeare Seminars of one week each, conducted by McMaster University, Hamilton.

1968
Romeo and Juliet — directed by Douglas Campbell, designed by Carolyn Parker, music by Louis Applebaum.

A Midsummer Night's Dream — directed by John Hirsch, designed by Leslie Hurry, music by Stanley Silverman.

Tartuffe — by Molière, translation by Richard Wilbur, directed by Jean Gascon, designed by Robert Prévost, music by Gabriel Charpentier.

The Three Musketeers — adapted by Peter Raby from the Dumas novel, directed by John Hirsch, designed by Desmond Heeley, music by Raymond Pannell.

The Seagull — by Anton Chekhov, directed by Jean Gascon, designed by Brian Jackson.

Waiting for Godot — by Samuel Beckett, directed by William Hutt, designed by Brian Jackson.

Members of the Company: Mia Anderson, Anne Anglin, Malcolm Armstrong, Guy Bannerman, Bernard Behrens, Lawrence Benedict, Christopher Bernau, Mervyn Blake, James Blendick, Barbara Bryne, Northern Calloway, Joyce Campion, Deborah Cass, Jane Casson, Leo Ciceri, Patrick Crean, Neil Dainard, Eric Donkin, David Foster, Pat Galloway, John Gardiner, Pamela Gruen, Amelia Hall, Max Helpmann, Martha Henry, Mary Hitch, William Hutt, Terry Judd, Joel Kenyon, Nancy Kerr, Leo Leyden, Marilyn Lightstone, Louise Marleau, Robin Marshall, Tedde Moore, Neil Munro, Christopher Newton, Adrian Pecknold, Denise Pelletier, Kenneth Pogue, Leon Pownall, Douglas Rain, Peter Scupham, Powys Thomas, Louis Thompson, Jérôme Tiberghien, John Turner, Christopher Walken, Sandy Webster, Kenneth Welsh.

Music
Cinderella (La Cenerentola) — by Rossini, directed by Douglas Campbell, music direction by Lawrence Smith, designed by Leslie Hurry.

Members of the Stratford Festival Opera Company: Anne Marie Clark, Howell Glynne, Nancy Gottschalk, Muriel Greenspon, Muriel James, Patricia Kern, Gwenlynn Little, Peter Milne, Jean-Louis Pellerin, Danielle Pilon, Oscar Raulfs, Herman Rombouts, Donald Rutherford, Robert Savoie,

Daniel Tait, Peter van Ginkel, Leslie Wertman.

Festival Concerts with the New York Pro Musica, conducted by Lawrence Smith; Ravi Shankar; Duke Ellington and his Orchestra; the English Chamber Orchestra, conducted by Daniel Barenboim, with Jacqueline du Pré; Van Cliburn; Stratford Festival Orchestra with guest artists David Nadien, Gunther Schuller, John Ogdon, Harvey Phillips, Judith Raskin, George Schick, Ruggiero Ricci, Lawrence Smith and Walter Susskind.

Six Saturday morning Chamber Music Concerts with members of the Stratford Festival Orchestra, featuring the première performances of commissioned works by Canadian composers Serge Garant, Bruce Mather, Gabriel Charpentier and Steve Gellman. Orchestra under the direction of Robert Koff, Charles Libove, David Nadien, John Barrows, Ray Still and Harvey Phillips. Special programmes featured The Lenox Quartet and a talk by Ravi Shankar on Indian music.

Four Music at Midnight after-theatre concerts, presented at the Rothmans Art Gallery in cooperation with the Stratford Art Association, and featuring guest artists and resident musicians of the Festival Orchestra.

Ballet

The Royal Winnipeg Ballet — Arnold Spohr, Artistic Director. Four works performed: *Pastiche*, choreographed by José Ferran; *While the Spider Slept*, choreographed by Brian Macdonald; *The Black Swan Pas de Deux*, choreographed by Petipa; *The Golden Age*, choreographed by Agnes de Mille.

Other Activities

Workshop — The Drama Workshop, under the direction of Powys Thomas, presented two groups of presentations: (a) Actors Off-Duty—eighteen informal poetry and prose readings given by members of the Company, with musicians from the Drama orchestra occasionally participating. These were held Saturday evenings in the Rehearsal Hall of the Festival Theatre and were open to the public; (b) productions which were planned initially to be shown only to the Company, but four of which were given public performances—Scenes in French from *Richard III*; an adaptation of Faulkner's *As I Lay Dying*; a Mime production; and Pirandello's *The Man with a Flower in His Mouth*.

Art and Theatre Exhibits — *Art in Theatre* at the Exhibition Hall. Exhibits included: contemporary and turn-of-the-century theatre posters; a collection of Shakespeare's plays on film; costume designs of the 1968 season; props and costumes; and a revised exhibit of the 1967 presentation—*100 Years of Theatre in Canada*.

At the Rothmans Art Gallery in Centennial Park, the Peter Stuyvesant Collection and a contemporary tapestry exhibit were presented. Outside the Gallery, Dorothy Cameron's new sculpture exhibit was on display throughout the season.

A Photographic Display by Desmond Heeley, Brian Jackson and Don Lewis.

Two Shakespeare Seminars of one week each, conducted by McMaster University, Hamilton.

1969

Hamlet — directed by John Hirsch, designed by Sam Kirkpatrick, music by Louis Applebaum.

The Alchemist — by Ben Jonson, directed by Jean Gascon, designed by James Hart Stearns, music by Gabriel Charpentier, textual revisions by Jack Ludwig.

Measure for Measure — directed by David Giles, designed by Kenneth Mellor, music by Raymond Pannell.

Tartuffe — by Molière, translation by Richard Wilbur, directed by Jean Gascon, designed by Robert Prévost, music by Gabriel Charpentier.

Hadrian VII — by Peter Luke, based on the novel and other works by Fr. Rolfe (Baron Corvo), directed by Jean Gascon, designed by Robert Fletcher.

Members of the Company: Thomas Alway, Douglas Anderson, Anne Anglin, Malcolm Armstrong, Guy Bannerman, Diana Barrington, Bernard Behrens, Lawrence Benedict, Mervyn Blake, James Blendick, Margaret Braidwood, Clyde Burton, Joyce Campion, Jane Casson, Tyrus Cheney, Patrick Christopher, Leo Ciceri, Alan Clarey, Paul

Craig, Patrick Crean, Hume Cronyn, John Cutts, Neil Dainard, Donald Davis, Eric Donkin, Ronald East, Donald Ewer, Karin Fernald, Pat Galloway, John Gardiner, Ian Gaskell, Edmund Glover, Louis Guss, Amelia Hall, Paul Harding, Mary Hitch, D. M. Hughes, William Hutt, Richard Kelley, Joel Kenyon, David Lindsay, John Maddison, Stephen McHattie, Edward McPhillips, Stephen Markle, Robin Marshall, Alain Monpetit, Tedde Moore, George Neilson, P. L. Pfeiffer, Jennifer Phipps, Leo Phillips, Kenneth Pogue, Gary Reineke, Linda Rice, Jason Robards, Jack Roberts, Reginald Rowland Jr., Saul Rubinek, Joseph Rutten, Jack Saunders, Peter Scupham, Wendell Smith, Peter Sturgess, Don Sutherland, Powys Thomas, Joseph Totaro, Ratch Wallace, Kenneth Welsh, Hans Werner, Angela Wood, Elaine Wood, Joseph Wynn, David Yanovitz.

Music

The Satyricon — book and lyrics by Tom Hendry, music by Stanley Silverman (based on the writings of Petronius), directed by John Hirsch, music direction by Lawrence Smith, designed by Michael Annals, staging of musical numbers and choreography by Marvin Gordon, projections by Eoin Sprott, lighting by Gil Wechsler.

Members of The Satyricon Company: Jeri Archer, James Blendick, Diana Broderick, Marcia Brooks, Jane Casson, Dinah Christie, Robert Christie, Johnny Christopher, Jack Creley, Alan Crofoot, Martha Cutrufello, Birdie Davis, Eric Donkin, David Drummond, Ray Edwards, Stephen Foster, Marilyn Gardner, Irving Harmon, Kevin Kamis, Sanford Levitt, Marc Mantell, Nancilou Moretti, Al Perryman, Margaret Rowan, Arnold Soboloff, Don Sutherland, Powys Thomas, James Tolkan, Christina Wachowiak, Robert Weil, Diane Young.

Festival Theatre Concerts featuring The Procol Harum with the Stratford Festival Orchestra; Canadian sopranos Colette Boky and Clarice Carson, tenors Leopold Simoneau and Bernard Fitch, baritone John Macurdy, narrator Powys Thomas and the Stratford Festival Orchestra in a concert version of Mozart's *The Abduction from the Seraglio*; Leonard Rose, cello, and Eugene Istomin, piano; Peter Nero, piano; National Youth Orchestra of Canada with Victor Feldbrill, conductor, and David Nadien, violin; Julian Bream, guitar; Elisabeth Schwarzkopf, soprano; Ravi Shankar.

Eight Saturday morning Chamber Music Concerts with members of the Stratford Festival Orchestra, featuring première performances of commissioned works by Canadian composers John Hawkins, Brian Cherney and Gilles Tremblay. Special programs featured The Guarneri String Quartet; the Beaux-Arts String Quartet, Nina Lugovoy, piano; the Orford String Quartet, Stanley McCartney, clarinet; a guitar recital with guitarists from the Julian Bream master class; and a talk by Ravi Shankar on Indian Music.

The Avon Concerts featured the Stratford Festival Orchestra with Lawrence Smith conducting and guest artists George Schick, conductor; Leonard Rose, cello; David Nadien, violin; Aaron Copland, composer-conductor; Mario Bernardi, conductor; and Patricia Kern, mezzo-soprano. Also at the Avon Theatre a special Contemporary Trends series featured Canadian folk composer-singers Joni Mitchell, Ian & Sylvia and Gordon Lightfoot. Other guests were Peter Serkin, piano, Peter Milne, baritone, and Stanley Silverman and Lawrence Smith, who jointly organized a contemporary music program.

Eight Music at Midnight after-theatre concerts were presented at the Rothmans Art Gallery in cooperation with the Stratford Art Association, featuring guest artists and resident musicians of the Festival Orchestra.

Julian Bream conducted a master class in guitar; outdoor programs of woodwind and brass music were performed by resident musicians; and military service band concerts were given in the park between Festival performances on Wednesdays and Saturdays.

Other Activities

Workshops — The Drama Workshop held classes in voice, movement, fencing, improvisation, texts, masks, period movement, modern jazz dance, mime and yoga. These were taken voluntarily by members of the company and staff.

Under the direction of Powys Thomas, the Workshop presented informal poetry readings, plays and films to the company and staff. Some plays and poetry readings were also given public performances during the 15-week Workshop season. Each "project" was presented by members of the acting company or production staff. Three productions were broadcast on CBC radio: *The Bard Meets the Beats*, presented by Kenneth Pogue; *Words of Love; An Infinite Variety*, a recital given by Donald Davis; *Tub* by J. W. Nichol, directed by Powys Thomas.

Art and Theatre Exhibits — *The Stratford Festival Exhibit* — The Festival and the Rothmans Art Gallery jointly produced a display of costumes and properties, costume designs and photographs shown at the Gallery.

Also shown throughout the season at Rothmans Art Gallery in Centennial Park, Gaspero del Corso's 60 pieces of Italian sculpture produced in the mid 1960's. This showing was entitled *Scultura Italiana*. Canadian figurative sculpture of the past decade was exhibited in the park outside the gallery and was entitled *People in the Park*.

Two Shakespeare Seminars of one week each were conducted by McMaster University, Hamilton.

1970

The Merchant of Venice — directed by Jean Gascon, designed by Desmond Heeley, music by Gabriel Charpentier, lighting by Gil Wechsler.

The School for Scandal — by Richard Sheridan, directed by Michael Langham, designed by Leslie Hurry and assistant designer Jack King, music by Stanley Silverman, lighting by Gil Wechsler.

Hedda Gabler — by Henrik Ibsen (a new version by Christopher Hampton), directed by Peter Gill, designed by Deirdre Clancy, lighting by Gil Wechsler.

Cymbeline — directed by Jean Gascon, designed by Tanya Moiseiwitsch, music by Gabriel Charpentier, lighting by Gil Wechsler.

The Architect and The Emperor of Assyria — by Fernando Arrabal, translated by Everard d'Harnoncourt and Adele Edlings, directed by Chattie Salaman, designed by Jean Baptiste Manessier, music by Louis Applebaum, lighting by Gil Wechsler.

The Friends — by Arnold Wesker, directed by Kurt Reis, designed by Peter Wingate, lighting by Gil Wechsler.

Vatzlav — by Slawomir Mrozek, translated by Ralph Manheim, directed by Colin George, designed by Brian Jackson, lighting by Gil Wechsler, music by Louis Applebaum.

The Sun Never Sets — devised and performed by Patrick Crean, directed by Powys Thomas, lighting by Gil Wechsler.

Marcel Marceau

Members of the Company: Malcolm Armstrong, Bernard Behrens, Christine Bennett, Colin Bernhardt, Mervyn Blake, Roger Blay, James Blendick, Pamela Brook, Blair Brown, Douglas Campbell, Joyce Campion, Helen Carey, Jane Casson, Eric Christmas, Leo Ciceri, Stanley Coles, Patrick Crean, Richard Curnock, Donald Davis, Zulema Dene, Eric Donkin, Ronald East, James Edmond, Bernerd Engel, Donald Ewer, Alfred Gallagher, Pat Galloway, Robin Gammell, John Gardiner, Roland Hewgill, Mary Hitch, Dominic Hogan, Eric House, James Hurdle, Anne Ives, Gordon Jackson, Joel Kenyon, Salem Ludwig, Barry MacGregor, Stephen Markle, Robin Marshall, Gillian Martell, Elizabeth Milne, Melanie Morse, Stephen Murray, William Needles, Maureen O'Brien, Bette Oliver, Leon Pownall, Kate Reid, Joseph Rutten, Arnold Soboloff, Don Sutherland, Dolores Sutton, Powys Thomas, Joseph Totaro, Kenneth Welsh, Irene Worth, Carolyn Younger.

Music

Festival Theatre Concerts with Tim Hardin, folk singer; The Romeros, classical guitarists; Louis Quilico, baritone and Lois Marshall, soprano, Paul Tortelier, cellist, Karl Engel, pianist; Claudio Arrau; The National Youth Orchestra; Lili Kraus, pianist; Itzhak Perlman, violinist; Hans Richter-Hauser, pianist; and José Feliciano.

Eight Saturday Morning Chamber Music concerts with the Philharmonia Trio, the Orford Quartet (3 appearances); the Beaux-Arts Quartet (2 appearances); Paul Tortelier, cellist, and Karl Engel, pianist; and John Boyden, baritone.

Eight Music at Midnight after-theatre concerts were presented at Rothmans Art Gallery in cooperation with the Stratford Art Association, featuring guest artists.

Other Activities

Workshops — The Drama Workshop held classes in voice, movement, historical dance, mask, mime, improvisations, fencing, Shakespeare text, makeup, film making and use of video tape equipment as well as master classes given by senior members of the company. These were taken voluntarily by members of the company and staff. Under the direction of Ron Singer, the Workshop presented informal revues, poetry readings, plays and films to the company and staff, and on certain occasions, to the general public. Guest directors and playwrights were invited to participate with members of the acting company and production staff in the Workshop projects. Two productions were broadcast on CBC radio: *I See You, I See You* by B. J. Wylie, directed by Clarke Rogers; and *Jon Jon* by David Windsor, directed by Ron Singer.

Art and Theatre Exhibits — *The Stratford Festival Exhibit* — The Festival and the Rothmans Art Gallery jointly produced a display of costumes, properties, costume designs and photographs shown at the Gallery. Rothmans Art Gallery also presented three other exhibitions throughout the season, *Rodin and his Contemporaries, Cross-section '70* (displaying the works of Contemporary Canadian artists in form segments) and an Outdoor Exhibit by Intermedia of Vancouver.

Two Shakespeare Seminars of one week each were conducted by McMaster University, Hamilton.

The University of Western Ontario conducted summer courses in Fine Art and Music at Stratford Teachers' College.

1971

Much Ado About Nothing — directed by William Hutt, designed by Alan Barlow, music by Harry Freedman, lighting by Gil Wechsler.

The Duchess of Malfi — by John Webster, directed by Jean Gascon, designed by Desmond Heeley, music by Gabriel Charpentier, lighting by Gil Wechsler.

Macbeth — directed by Peter Gill, designed by Dierdre Clancy, sound by Alan Laing, lighting by Gil Wechsler.

Volpone — by Ben Jonson, directed by David William, designed by Annena Stubbs, music by Louis Applebaum, lighting by Gil Wechsler.

An Italian Straw Hat — by Eugène Labiche and Marc-Michel, translated by Michael Bawtree, directed by Stephen Porter, designed by Lewis Brown, lighting by Gil Wechsler, music by Pierre Philippe.

There's One in Every Marriage — by Georges Feydeau, translated and adapted by Suzanne Grossman and Paxton Whitehead, directed by Jean Gascon, designed by Alan Barlow, lighting by Gil Wechsler.

The Red Convertible — by Enrique Buenaventura, translated and adapted by Michael Bawtree and Antony Sampson, directed by Michael Bawtree, designed by Art Penson.

America's National Theatre of Puppet Arts — *Excerpts from Shakespeare.*

The Montreal Marionettes — *Hansel and Gretel, Peter and the Wolf, The Sorcerer's Apprentice, Excerpts from Bastien and Bastienne.*

Adrian Pecknold's Canadian Mime Theatre — *Shapes and Shadows.*

Members of the Company: Tom Alway, Malcolm Armstrong, Christine Bennett, Colin Bernhardt, Mervyn Blake, Pamela Brook, Trudy Cameron, J. Kenneth Campbell, Joyce Campion, Carol Carrington, Jane Casson, Susan Chapple, Dinah Christie, Patrick Christopher, Stanley Coles, Giuseppe Condello, Jack Creley, Richard Curnock, Neil Dainard, Peter Donat, Eric Donkin, Peter Elliott, Bernerd Engel, Donald Ewer, Eillean Ferguson, Gary Files, Patricia Gage, Pat Galloway, Robin Gammell, Marilyn Gardner, Lewis Gordon, Mari Gorman, Patricia Grant, Suzanne Grossman, Sheila Haney, Edward Henry, Martha Henry, Roland Hewgill, Ian Hogg, Ruby

Holbrook, Elva Mai Hoover, William Hutt, Marc Jacobs, Jeff Jones, Joel Kenyon, Michael Liscinsky, Karen Ludwig, Barry MacGregor, Iris MacGregor, Stephen Markle, Robin Marshall, Howard Mawson, Robert McKennitt, Elizabeth Milne, William Needles, Bette Oliver, Blaine Parker, Gerard Parkes, Wyman Pendleton, Leon Pownall, Douglas Rain, Jack Roberts, Hamish Robertson, Stewart Robertson, Paul Roland, Joseph Rutten, Mary Savidge, Elsie Sawchuk, David Schurmann, Joseph Shaw, Donna Sherman, Brian Sinclair, Charles Sitler, Edwin Stephenson, Don Sutherland, Powys Thomas, Joseph Totaro, Tony van Bridge, Kenneth Welsh, Tim Whelan, Carolyn Younger.

Music

Festival Concerts with Alfred Brendel, pianist; Lorin Hollander, pianist; Patricia Kern, mezzo-soprano; B. B. King; Alexandre Lagoya, guitarist; Melanie; Jean-Pierre Rampal, flautist, Janos Starker, cellist; Jon Vickers, tenor; Gyorgy Sebok, pianist; Charles Reiner, pianist.

Eight Saturday Morning Chamber Music concerts with Pierre Bernac Master Class Singing Recital; Classical Quartet of Montreal, Charles Reiner, pianist; Hungarian Quartet; Lagoya Master Class Guitar Recital; Orford Quartet, Katrina Vournasos, pianist; Rideau String Quartet of Ottawa; Stephen Staryk, violinist and Joseph Schwartz, pianist; Vaghy Quartet.

Eight Music at Midnight after-theatre concerts were presented at the Rothmans Art Gallery in cooperation with the Stratford Art Association featuring guest artists.

Three Master Classes of one week each were conducted by Alexandre Lagoya, guitarist; Pierre Bernac, baritone; and Jean-Pierre Rampal, flautist.

Other Activities

International Film Festival — Stratford's Seventh International Film Festival opened Sept. 10 at the Avon Theatre, with the North American première of the National Theatre of Great Britain's production of Strindberg's *Dance of Death*, starring Sir Laurence Olivier. The next ten days brought an exciting assortment of films from around the world, including important new Canadian works such as Claude Jutra's *Mon Oncle Antoine*, which went on to sweep the 1971 Canadian Film Awards. There were 2 p.m. and 9 p.m. showings daily, Sept. 11 through Sept. 19, with double bills most afternoons and two special midnight presentations. A Mary Pickford retrospective was held each evening at 7 p.m. and programmes of children's films were shown on Saturday mornings. Visiting filmmakers attended informal discussions at a daily morning coffee hour and at the Cinema Club each night after the show.

Workshops — Under the direction of Michael Bawtree, the Drama Workshop held classes in voice, movement, singing, fencing and makeup which were taken voluntarily by members of the company and staff. Several original dramas, written and directed by members of the company, were given public performances. Workshop presentations also included recitals, readings and a Brecht-Weill revue.

Art and Theatre Exhibits — *The Stratford Festival Exhibit* — The Festival and the Rothmans Art Gallery jointly produced a display of costumes, properties, costumes designs and photographs shown at the Gallery. Rothmans Art Gallery also presented three other exhibitions throughout the season: *Vasarely in Retrospect, Body Art* (Carl Bucher) and Outdoor Sculpture.

Two Shakespeare Seminars of one week each were conducted by McMaster University, Hamilton.

1972

As You Like It — directed by William Hutt, designed by Alan Barlow, music by Harry Freedman, lighting by Gil Wechsler.

Lorenzaccio — by Alfred de Musset, translated by John Lewin, directed by Jean Gascon, designed by Michael Annals, music by Gabriel Charpentier, lighting by Gil Wechsler.

King Lear — directed by David William, designed by Annena Stubbs, music by Louis Applebaum, lighting by Gil Wechsler.

She Stoops To Conquer — by Oliver

Goldsmith, directed by Michael Bawtree, designed by Desmond Heeley, music by Raymond Pannell, lighting by Gil Wechsler.

The Threepenny Opera — by Bertolt Brecht and Kurt Weill, English adaptation by Marc Blitzstein, directed by Jean Gascon, designed by Robert Prévost, music direction by Alan Laing, lighting by Gil Wechsler.

La Guerre, Yes Sir! — by Roch Carrier, translated by Suzanne Grossman, with Le Théâtre du Nouveau Monde company, directed by Albert Millaire, designed by Mark Negin, lighting by Gil Wechsler, music by Gabriel Charpentier.

Mark — by Betty Jane Wylie, directed by William Hutt, designed by Art Penson, lighting by Ian Johnson.

Pinocchio — by Carlo Collodi, adapted and directed by John Wood, music by Alan Laing, designed by John Ferguson, lighting by F. Mitchell Dana.

Members of the Company: Edward Atienza, Mary Barton, Christine Bennett, Colin Bernhardt, Mervyn Blake, Theodore Britton, Pamela Brooke, Michael Burgess, Leo Burns, Trudy Cameron, J. Kenneth Campbell, Stanley Coles, Vincent Cole, Giuseppe Condello, Dan Conley, Jack Creley, Daniel Davis, Eric Donkin, Bernerd Engel, Denise Fergusson, Michael Fletcher, Christine Foster, Roy Frady, Carl Gall, Pat Galloway, Marilyn Gardner, Lewis Gordon, Edward Henry, Roland Hewgill, Eric Hutt, William Hutt, John Innes, Jeff Jones, Lila Kedrova, Joel Kenyon, Jean Leclerc, Maureen Lee, Monique Leyrac, Anne Linden, Michael Liscinsky, Barry MacGregor, Iris MacGregor, Robin Marshall, Doug McGrath, William Needles, Stephen Nesrallah, Blaine Parker, Antony Parr, Nicole Pelletier, Nicholas Pennell, Henry Ramer, Krysia Read, Jack Roberts, Anton Rodgers, Pam Rogers, Joseph Rutten, Mary Savidge, Elsie Sawchuk, Alan Scarfe, David Schurmann, Errol Slue, Carole Shelley, Elizabeth Shepherd, Sylvia Shore, Thomas Stebing, Sean Sullivan, Don Sutherland, Anni Lee Taylor, Powys Thomas, Joseph Totaro, Tony van Bridge, William Webster, David Wells, Jonathan Welsh, Kenneth Welsh, Jack Wetherall, Tim Whelan, Kenneth Wickes.

Music

Orpheus — by Gabriel Charpentier, translated and adapted by Michael Bawtree, directed by André Brassard, music direction by Ursula Clutterbuck, choreographed by Richard and Shirley Cohen, designed by Art Penson, lighting by F. Mitchell Dana.

Patria II: Requiems for the Party Girl — by R. Murray Schafer, directed by Michael Bawtree, music direction by Serge Garant, designed by Eoin Sprott, lighting by F. Mitchell Dana.

Members of the Company: Christine Bennett, Michael Burgess, Richard Cohen, Giuseppe Condello, Suzette Couture, Lewis Gordon, Jean Leclerc, Veronique LeFlaguais, Phyllis Mailing, Stephen Markle, Robin Marshall, Monique Mercure, Allan K. Migicovsky, Nicole Pelletier, Roland Richard, Pam Rogers, David Schurmann, Jonathan Welsh.

Festival Concerts with Alexandre Lagoya, guitarist; Rudolf Firkusny, pianist; Itzhak Perlman, violinist; Roberta Peters, soprano; Antonio Janigro, cellist; Van Cliburn, pianist.

Eight Saturday Morning Chamber Music concerts with the New Chamber Winds, Hungarian Quartet, Alberta Trio, Orford Quartet, Vaghy Quartet, Classical Quartet and Lorand Fenyves, violinist, and Menahem Pressler, pianist.

Music for a Summer Day—a special day of music featuring the New York Philharmonic with Eric Leinsdorf conducting, and concerts by The Beaux Arts Trio; Jean-Pierre Rampal, flautist; the Dorian Woodwind Quintet; and the Canadian Brass.

Eight Music at Midnight after-theatre concerts were presented at the Rothmans Art Gallery.

Three Master Classes of one week each were conducted by Alexandre Lagoya, guitarist; Antonio Janigro, cellist; and Jean-Pierre Rampal, flautist..

Other Activities

International Film Festival — Stratford launched its Eighth International Film Festival September 16 with the North American première of *Antony and Cleopatra* attended by Charlton

Heston, the film's director and star. The over thirty films screened during the Festival included short-subject and feature-length films by Canadian and international filmmakers and a retrospective showing of films from the great days of Hollywood musicals. The double-bill musical matinees featured the 1930's hits of Fred Astaire and Ginger Rogers and such Busby Berkeley extravaganzas as *Gold Diggers of 1935*. Evening showings at 7 p.m. and 9 p.m. offered a selection of exciting films from all parts of the world. Two special Saturday morning children's programs and informal daily coffee hour discussions with visiting filmmakers rounded out the eight-day Festival.

Workshops—The Workshop held classes and instruction in make-up, movement, dance, yoga, voice, fencing, singing and mask improvisation which were voluntarily attended by members of the company and staff. Other activities included drama presentations directed by members of the company and chamber music concerts featuring members of the drama orchestra. The Workshop was under the direction of Michael Bawtree, and co-ordinated by Robert Handforth.

Exhibits — Stratford's City Hall was the site of the Festival City Exhibition comprising the Stratford Festival Exhibit and an exhibit by the City of Stratford tracing the development of the City from the 19th century through the birth of the Festival to the present. The Festival Exhibit was a twenty-year panorama of the theatre's history as seen through costumes, props, pictures, film and documents. Rothmans Art Gallery presented *Appel's Appels*, a major exhibition of paintings and sculpture by the contemporary Dutch artist Karel Appel.

Two Shakespeare Seminars of one week each were conducted by McMaster University, Hamilton.

Tony van Bridge in *G.K.C.*, a one-man show based on the writings of Gilbert Keith Chesterton.

1973

The Taming of the Shrew — directed by Jean Gascon, designed by Desmond Heeley, music by Gabriel Charpentier, lighting by Gil Wechsler.

She Stoops to Conquer — by Oliver Goldsmith, directed by Michael Bawtree, designed by Desmond Heeley, music by Raymond Pannell, lighting by Gil Wechsler.

Othello — directed by David William, designed by Annena Stubbs, music by Louis Applebaum, lighting by Gil Wechsler.

Pericles — directed by Jean Gascon, designed by Leslie Hurry, music by Gabriel Charpentier, lighting by Gil Wechsler.

A Month in the Country — by Ivan Turgenev, translated by Andrew MacAndrew, directed by William Hutt, designed by Brian Jackson, lighting by Gil Wechsler.

The Marriage Brokers — by Nikolai Gogol, translated by Alexander Berkman, directed by William Hutt, designed by Murray Laufer, lighting by Gil Wechsler.

The Collected Works of Billy the Kid — by Michael Ondaatje, directed by John Wood, designed by John Ferguson, music by Alan Laing, lighting by Gil Wechsler assisted by Mark Hylbak.

Inook and the Sun — by Henry Beissel, directed by Jean Herbiet and Felix Mirbt, designed by Michel Catudal, puppets created by Felix Mirbt assisted by Ian Osgood, special movements by Jill Courtney, lighting by Mark Hylbak.

Members of the Company: Roger Allan, Edward Atienza, Nancy Beatty, Pat Bentley-Fisher, Colin Bernhardt, Ronald Bishop, Mervyn Blake, Sara Botsford, Theodore Britton, Pamela Brook, Daniel Buccos, Nachum Buchman, Trudy Cameron, Joyce Campion, Stanley Coles, Patricia Collins, Jack Creley, Richard Curnock, Cherry Davis, Diane D'Aquila, Scot Denton, Bob Dermer, Michael Donaghue, Eric Donkin, Ted Follows, Christine Foster, Leonard Frey, Carole Galloway, Pat Galloway, John Gardiner, Joan Gaskell, Lewis Gordon, Dawn Greenhalgh, Harding Greenwood, Brian Gromoff, Amelia Hall, Sheila Haney, Edward Henry, Martha Henry, Art Hindle, Andrew Henderson, Roland Hewgill, P. M. Howard, Eric

Hutt, Lila Kaye, Joel Kenyon, Marilyn Lightstone, Michael Liscinsky, Ian Macdonald, Barry MacGregor, Roberta Maxwell, Sylvia Maynard, Richard Monette, Neil Munro, William Needles, Raymond O'Neill, Nicholas Pennell, Kenneth Pogue, Douglas Rain, John Reymont, Jack Roberts, Anne Rushbrooke, Alan Scarfe, Joseph Shaw, Brian Sinclair, Christopher Spence, Don Sutherland, Anni Lee Taylor, Powys Thomas, Gordon Thomson, Joseph Totaro, Tony van Bridge, Jack Wetherall, Angela Wood.

Music

Exiles — by Raymond and Beverly Pannell, directed by Michael Bawtree, set design by Eoin Sprott, costume design by John Ferguson, photography by Beverly Pannell, lighting by Robert Scales. *Members of the Company*: Jason Czajkowski, Bob Bermer, Candy Kane, Phyllis Mailing, Janette Moody, Edward Pierson, Gary Reineke, Gary Relyea, David Schurmann, Gene Watts.

Eight Saturday Morning Festival Concerts with the Orford String Quartet; Tsuyoshi Tsutsumi, cellist; Toronto Winds; Ararat Trio; Canadian Brass; Bouchard et Morisset, duo pianists; Czech String Quartet, Oscar Ghiglia, guitarist.

Music for a Summer Day Opus 2 No.1 — A special day of music featuring the New York Philharmonic with Michael Tilson Thomas conducting, and concerts by the Vermeer Quartet and Ronald Turini; Lilit Gampel, violinist; Air Transport Command Band; Alexandre Lagoya, guitarist.

Music for a Summer Day Opus 2 No.2 — A special day of music featuring the Chicago Symphony Orchestra with Lawrence Foster conducting, and the following concerts: Sacred Music with Jacob Barkin, cantor, Douglas Haas, organist and The Gentlemen and Boys of St. Simon's Church Choir; Beaux Arts Trio; Philippe d'Entremont, pianist, and the New York Brass.

Nine Music at Midnight after-theatre concerts were presented at the Rothmans Art Gallery.

Two Master Classes of one week each were conducted by Alexandre Lagoya, guitarist and Jean-Pierre Rampal, flautist.

Other Activities

International Film Festival — Stratford launched its Ninth International Film Festival September 15 with the North American première of Joseph Losey's *A Doll's House*. Over thirty films were screened during the festival including short-subject and feature-length films by Canadian and international filmmakers and a matinee retrospective showing of films featuring Douglas Fairbanks from 1920 to 1927. Evening showings at 7 p.m. and 9:30 p.m. offered a selection of exciting films from all over the world. A special Saturday morning children's program and informal daily coffee hour discussions with visiting filmmakers rounded out the eight-day Festival.

Workshops — Under the supervision of coordinator Constance Brissenden, classes were held in make-up, text interpretation, mask, tap dancing, fencing, voice, movement, historical dance and special lectures on Shakespearean Theatre and theatre training which were voluntarily attended by members of the company and staff. Thirty music Workshops were given by the Festival chamber music group, musicians from the Festival drama orchestra and musicians from the Third Stage. Most of these concerts occurred after a performance and were attended by the general public. Nine acting workshops were presented by Company members and attended by members of the company and staff. For three and one-half weeks in September an Advanced Properties Workshop was given by members of the Festival Properties department for professional craftsmen and advanced students in the field of theatrical property making. This workshop was attended by 11 participants who came from all parts of Canada.

Exhibits — Stratford's City Hall was the site of the Stratford Festival Exhibit. The exhibition commemorated the Festival's 1973 Euporean tour with pictures, posters and other material documenting the Company's highly acclaimed productions of *King Lear* and

The Taming of the Shrew. The Rothmans Art Gallery presented *The Art of Mexico Today*, a major exhibition of paintings by three of Mexico's leading artists.

Two Shakespeare Seminars of one week each were conducted by McMaster University, Hamilton.

1974

The Imaginary Invalid — by Molière, translated by Donald M. Frame, directed by Jean Gascon, designed by Tanya Moiseiwitsch, music by Gabriel Charpentier, lighting by Gil Wechsler.

Love's Labour's Lost — directed by Michael Bawtree, designed by Sam Kirkpatrick, music by Alan Laing, lighting by Gil Wechsler.

Pericles — directed by Jean Gascon, designed by Leslie Hurry, music by Gabriel Charpentier, lighting by Gil Wechsler.

King John — directed by Peter Dews, designed by Brian Jackson, music by Louis Applebaum, lighting by Gil Wechsler.

La Vie Parisienne — by Jacques Offenbach, translated by Jeremy Gibson, directed by Jean Gascon, set design by Robert Prévost, costume design by François Barbeau, music direction by Raffi Armenian, lighting by Gil Wechsler.

Walsh — by Sharon Pollock, directed by John Wood, designed by John Ferguson, music and sound by Alan Laing, lighting by Michael J. Whitfield.

Ready Steady Go — by Sandra Jones, directed by Arif Hasnain, designed by Grant Guy, music by Berthold Carriere, lyrics by Sandra Jones, lighting by Michael J. Whitfield.

Members of the Company: Don Allison, Edward Atienza, Ken Atkinson, Michael Ball, Diana Barrington, John Bayliss, Rod Beattie, Nancy Bell-Fuller, Pat Bentley-Fisher, Jean Begmann, Mervyn Blake, Sara Botsford, Jean François Boucher, Bonnie Britton, Pamela Brook, Daniel Buccos, Michael Burgess, Douglas Campbell, Graeme Campbell, J. Kenneth Campbell, Barbara Carter, Patricia Collins, Jack Creley, Richard Curnock, Diane D'Aquila, John J. Dee, Diane Dewey, Rosemary Dunsmore, Mary Lou Fallis, Donna Farron, Denise Fergusson, Edwina Follows, Neil Freeman, Pat Galloway, Marilyn Gardner, Gabriel Gascon, Robert Godin, John Goodlin, Lewis Gordon, Luba Goy, Dawn Greenhalgh, Patricia Griffin, Amelia Hall, David Hemblen, Edward Henry, Martha Henry, José Hernandez, Susan Hogan, Howard Hughes, Donald Hunkin, William Hutt, Tim Jones, Terry Judd, John Keane, Joel Kenyon, Sheena Larkin, Lise LaSalle, Anne Linden, Hardee T. Lineham, Michael Liscinsky, Ian Macdonald, Barry MacGregor, Marti Maraden, Serge Maquis, Susan Mitchell, Tony Moffat-Lynch, Sam Moses, Jan Juszynski, William Needles, Wolfgang Oeste, Nicholas Pennell, Briain Petchey, Kenneth Pogue, Douglas Rain, Derek Ralston, Duncan Regehr, Jack Roberts, Pam Rogers, Stephen Russell, Penny Speedie, John Stewart, Powys Thomas, Gordon Thomson, Robert Thomson, Robert Vigod, Jonathan Welsh, Jack Wetherall, Christina Williams, Elias Zarou, Gene Zerna.

Music

The Summoning of Everyman — composed by Charles Wilson, libretto by Eugene Benson, directed by Michael Bawtree, designed by Susan Benson, musical direction by Raffi Armenian, lighting by Michael J. Whitfield.

The Medium — by Gian-Carlo Menotti, directed by Michael Bawtree, designed by Susan Benson, musical direction by Raffi Armenian, lighting by Michael J. Whitfield.

Members of the Company: Keith Batten, Darryl Beschell, Garnet Brooks, Eleanor Calbes, Maureen Forrester, Barbara Ianni, Dan Lichti, Phyllis Mailing, Philip May, Lynda Neufeld, Janis Orenstein, George Reinke, Alvin Reimer, Phil Stark, Larry Zacharko.

Eight Saturday Morning Concerts with the Festival Singers; the Canadian Brass; One Third Ninth; Anna Chornodolska and John Newmark; Stratford Festival Ensemble; Purcell String Quartet; Camerata; Lorand Fenyves and Elyakim Taussig.

Five Sunday Concerts with Maureen Forrester accompanied by Raffi Armenian; Stratford Festival Ensemble with Phyllis Mailing; Barry Tuckwell and

John Newmark; Trio di Trieste; and John Lill.

Six Music at Midnight after-theatre concerts were presented at the Rothmans Art Gallery.

Three Master Classes were conducted by Maureen Forrester in Mahler Lied Interpretation; Ray Still in Oboe; and Stuart Knussen in Double Bass.

Other Activities

International Film Festival — major international films, experimental works from young Canadians, and a retrospective series made up Stratford's Tenth International Film Festival. Among over thirty screenings were the International Series of films by such directors as Renoir, Fellini, and Louis Malle; Robin Spry's controversial NFB feature, *Action: The October Crisis (1970)* world-premièred as part of A Day with the Canadian Filmmakers; Great Stars from The Mary Pickford Company were seen in a retrospective of The Big Films of Yesterday. For ten September days the Avon Theatre was the source of exciting cinema, Stratford's important contribution to Canadian film awareness.

Workshops — Under the supervision of Don Shipley, classes were held in make-up, historical and tap dance, yoga, fencing, French, acrobatics and text interpretation, which were voluntarily attended by members of the company and staff. Other activities included numerous drama presentations, directed by members of the company, and concerts of folk and chamber music featuring members of the Festival orchestra.

Exhibits — Stratford's City Hall was the site of the Stratford Festival Exhibit. Costumes, properties, designs and photos were gathered to create a tribute to Tanya Moiseiwitsch. Elements of her productions at Stratford, for the major theatres of Great Britain and in the United States provided a vivid introduction to the work of this remarkable designer.

Two Shakespeare Seminars of one week each were conducted by McMaster University, Hamilton.

1975

Saint Joan — by Bernard Shaw, directed by William Hutt, designed by Maxine Graham, music by Berthold Carriere, lighting by Gil Wechsler.

Twelfth Night — directed by David Jones, designed by Susan Benson, music by Harry Freedman, lighting by Gil Wechsler.

Measure for Measure — directed by Robin Phillips, designed by Daphne Dare, music by Louis Applebaum, lighting by Gil Wechsler.

Trumpets and Drums — by Bertolt Brecht, translated by Kyra Dietz and Alan Brown, directed by Robin Phillips, designed by Daphne Dare, music by Alan Laing, lighting by Gil Wechsler.

The Comedy of Errors — directed by Robin Phillips and David Toguri, designed by Jeffery Sisco, lighting by Gil Wechsler; music by Alan Laing, arranged and directed by Berthold Carriere.

The Two Gentlemen of Verona — directed by Robin Phillips and David Toguri, designed by Molly Harris Campbell, lighting by Gil Wechsler, music by Martin Best.

The Crucible — by Arthur Miller, directed by John Wood, designed by Susan Benson, lighting by Gil Wechsler.

Fellowship — by Michael Tait, directed by Bernard Hopkins, designed by John Ferguson, lighting by Michael J. Whitfield.

Oscar Remembered — compiled and performed by Maxim Mazumdar, directed by William Hutt, designed by Gayle Tribick, lighting by Michael J. Whitfield.

Kennedy's Children — by Robert Patrick, directed by Bill Glassco, designed by John Ferguson, lighting by Michael J. Whitfield.

The Importance of Being Earnest — by Oscar Wilde, directed by Robin Phillips, designed by Molly Harris Campbell, lighting by Robert Scales.

Basic set for the Avon Theatre and the Third Stage designed by Daphne Dare. *Members of the Company:* Mia Anderson, Andrew V. Arway, Denise Baillargeon, Bob Baker, Guy Bannerman, Keith Batten, Gary Bayer, Rod Beattie, Brian Bedford, Robert Benson, Pat Bentley-Fisher, Mervyn Blake, Geoffrey Bowes, Daniel Buccos, Barbara Budd,

Jackie Burroughs, Graeme Campbell, J. Kenneth Campbell, J. Winston Carroll, Douglas Chamberlain, Marc Connors, Richard Curnock, Eric Donkin, Brenda Donahue, Martin Donlevy, Denise Fergusson, Michael Fletcher, Pat Galloway, Gale Garnett, John C. Goodlin, Lewis Gordon, Diane Grant, Lynne Griffin, Patricia Hamilton, Max Helpmann, Sheila Haney, Martha Henry, Meg Hogarth, Elva Mai Hoover, Bernard Hopkins, Linda Huffman, Don Hunkin, Peter Hutt, William Hutt, John Innes, Terence Kelly, Tom Kneebone, Jan Kudelka, Larry Lamb, Sheena Larkin, Michael Liscinsky, Barry MacGregor, Stephen Macht, Frank Maraden, Marti Maraden, Maxim Mazumdar, Richard Monette, Robert More, William Needles, Robin Nunn, Odetta, Blaine Parker, Richard Partington, Nicholas Pennell, Doris Petrie, Douglas Rain, Jack Roberts, Stephen Russell, Melody Ryane, Dena Saxer, Nan Stewart, John Sweeney, Robert Vigod, Neil Vipond, Ian Wallace, Jack Wetherall, Richard Whelan, Kathleen Widdoes, Leslie Yeo.

Music

The Fool — by Harry Somers, libretto by Michael Fram, directed by Jan Rubes, musical direction by Raffi Armenian, designed by John Ferguson, lighting by Michael J. Whitfield.

Le Magicien — music and libretto by Jean Vallerand, directed by Pat Galloway, musical direction by Raffi Armenian, designed by John Ferguson, lighting by Michael J. Whitfield.

Ariadne Auf Naxos — by Richard Strauss, libretto by Hugo von Hofmannsthal, directed by Jan Rubes, musical direction by Raffi Armenian, designed by John Ferguson, lighting by Michael J. Whitfield.

Members of the Company: Robert Calvert, Barbara Carter, D. Glyn Evans, Mary Lou Fallis, Giulio Kukurugya, Gary Relyea, Brian Roberts, Roxolana Roslak, Janice Taylor, Jeannette Zarou.

Six Sunday Concerts with the Stratford Festival Ensemble; Gisela Depkat and Raffi Armenian; Cleo Laine and John Dankworth; the Stratford Festival Ensemble with Janice Taylor, Glyn Evans, Victor Martens, Philip May, and Giulio Kukurugya; and with Janice Taylor, Otto Armin, and William Aide; Bruce Cockburn.

Three Music at Midnight after-theatre concerts were presented at the Gallery/Stratford.

Master classes were conducted by Steven Staryk on violin; Barry Tuckwell on French Horn; and Ray Still on Oboe.

Other Activities

International Film Festival — Over fifty films were screened at the Avon Theatre during the eight days of the Festival. Among them were some of the best of Harold Lloyd, the great American comic; films from the catalogue of Rock Demers' Faroun Films, in a tenth-anniversary tribute; new works from the Netherlands, Hungary, and Japan; from Britain, *Royal Flash*, directed by Richard Lester; from France, John Frankenheimer's *The Impossible Object*. The award-winning *Eliza's Horoscope* and Claude Jutra's latest film, *Pour le Meilleur et pour le Pire* were included in Stratford's second Day with the Canadian Filmmakers.

Workshops — This year in a wide-ranging program, activities were focussed on a single theme, the Greeks. Early in September a two-week "mini-festival" was held. Lecturers, composers, dancers and playwrights were invited to Stratford to work with the company on a dozen projects. These visitors included such internationally known experts as Peter Arnott, Kas Piesowoski and Jan Kott.

As well, under the sponsorship of the Canada Council, Yoshi and Company conducted a five-day workshop drawn from Japanese theatre and religions. Emphasis was on the physical aspect of Oriental acting technique.

Workshop organizers were Don Shipley, Blaine Parker and John Plank.

Two Shakespeare Seminars of one week each were conducted by McMaster University, Hamilton.

1976

Hamlet — directed by Robin Phillips and William Hutt, designed by John Pennoyer, lighting by Gil Wechsler, music by Berthold Carriere, basic set designed by Daphne Dare.

The Tempest — directed by Robin Phillips and William Hutt, designed by John Ferguson, lighting by Gil Wechsler, music by Berthold Carriere, basic set designed by Daphne Dare.

The Way of The World — by William Congreve, directed by Robin Phillips, designed by Daphne Dare, music by Louis Applebaum, lighting by Gil Wechsler, choreography by Earl Kraul.

The Merchant of Venice — directed by Bill Glassco, designed by Susan Benson, music by Morris Surdin, lighting by Gil Wechsler.

Antony and Cleopatra — directed by Robin Phillips, designed by Daphne Dare, music by Louis Applebaum, lighting by Gill Wechsler.

Measure for Measure — directed by Robin Phillips, designed by Daphne Dare, music by Louis Applebaum, lighting by Gil Wechsler.

A Midsummer Night's Dream — directed by Robin Phillips, designed by Susan Benson, music by Alan Laing, lighting by Michael J. Whitfield.

The Importance of Being Earnest — by Oscar Wilde, directed by Robin Phillips, set design by Daphne Dare, costume design by Molly Harris Campbell, lighting by Gil Wechsler.

Eve — by Larry Fineberg, based on the novel *The Book of Eve* by Constance Beresford-Howe, directed by Vivian Matalon, designed by John Ferguson, lighting by Gil Wechsler.

Three Sisters — by Anton Chekhov, directed by John Hirsch, designed by Daphne Dare, lighting by Gil Wechsler. *Members of the Company:* Mia Anderson, Bob Baker, William Ballantyne, Keith Batten, Paul Batten, Keith Baxter, Rod Beattie, Robert Benson, Patricia Bentley-Fisher, Mervyn Blake, Domini Blythe, Walt Bondarenko, Paul Bowman, Jeremy Brett, Daniel Buccos, Barbara Budd, Jackie Burroughs, Graeme Campbell, Les Carlson, Dorian (Joe) Clark, Hume Cronyn, Richard Curnock, Eric Donkin, Martin Donlevy, James Edmond, Frances Fagan, Denise Ferguson, David Fox-Brenton, Pat Galloway, John Goodlin, Don Goodspeed, Lewis Gordon, Amelia Hall, Max Helpmann, Martha Henry, Bernard Hopkins, Don Hunkin, James Hurdle, Stuart Hutchison, Peter Hutt, William Hutt, Patricia Idlette, Gerald Isaac, Joel Kenyon, Tom Kneebone, Jan Kudelka, Larry Lamb, Michael Liscinsky, Barry MacGregor, William Merton Malmo, Nick Mancuso, Frank Maraden, Marti Maraden, Richard Monette, Robert More, William Needles, Robin Nunn, Richard Partington, Nicholas Pennell, Douglas Rain, Jack Roberts, Stephen Russell, Melody Ryane, Alan Scarfe, Nathan Scott, Maggie Smith, Barbara Stephen, Jessica Tandy, Tony van Bridge, Cathy Wallace, Gregory Wanless, Jack Wetherall, Richard Whelan, Victor A. Young, Louis Zorich.

Music

Six Sunday concerts with The Stratford Festival Ensemble. Master Classes, intensive sessions with visiting musicians in collaboration with members of the Stratford Festival Ensemble with: Steven Staryk (violin); John Fletcher (tuba); and William Bennett (flute). Seven Pop, Jazz and Folk Concerts on the Festival Stage: Oscar Peterson, Cleo Laine and John Dankworth, The Chuck Mangione Quartet, the Preservation Hall Jazz Band, Murray McLauchlan, Odetta and Anne Murray. The popular Music at Midnight Concerts were presented once again at the Gallery/Stratford.

Other Activities

Workshops — The Stratford Festival Workshops explored a new script, *Breakthrough* by Bryon Wade. Workshop sessions were held by guest directors, John Van Burek and Eric Steiner, with actors drawn from the Festival and the playwright himself in residence for the sessions.

As well, Robin Phillips conducted intensive practical classics with students from the senior year of the National Theatre School. They worked on scenes from Albee's *Tiny Alice* and Strindberg's *Miss Julie*. The students had access to all the facilities of the Stratford Festival and frequently received instruction from such members of the company as Martha Henry and Maggie Smith. The presence of the NTS students at Stratford was stimulating and exhilarating both for the visitors and for the company here.

Two Shakespeare Seminars of one week each were conducted by McMaster University, Hamilton.

1977

A Midsummer Night's Dream — directed by Robin Phillips, designed by Susan Benson, music by Alan Laing, additional music by Berthold Carriere, lighting by Gil Wechsler.

All's Well That Ends Well — directed by David Jones, designed by Tanya Moiseiwitsch, music by Louis Applebaum, lighting by Gil Wechsler.

Richard III — directed by Robin Phillips, designed by Daphne Dare, music by Louis Applebaum, lighting by Gil Wechsler.

Much Ado About Nothing — directed by Marigold Charlesworth, designed by Brian Jackson with Jack King, music and sound montage by Allan Rae, lighting by Gil Wechsler.

As You Like It — directed by Robin Phillips, designed by Robin Fraser Paye, music by Berthold Carriere, lighting by Gil Wechsler.

Romeo and Juliet — directed by David William, designed by John Ferguson, lighting by Gil Wechsler, music by Berthold Carriere.

Ghosts — by Henrik Ibsen, directed by Arif Hasnain, designed by John Pennoyer, lighting by Gil Wechsler.

Miss Julie — by August Strindberg, directed by Eric Steiner, set design by Daphne Dare, costume design by Janice Lindsay, lighting by Gil Wechsler, music by Berthold Carriere.

The Guardsman — by Ferenc Molnar, directed by Robin Phillips, designed by Daphne Dare, lighting by Gil Wechsler.

Hay Fever — by Noël Coward, directed by Robin Phillips, set design by Lawrence Schafer, costume design by Daphne Dare with John Pennoyer, lighting by Michael J. Whitfield.

Members of the Company: Stewart Arnott, Karen Austin, Bob Baker, Rodger Barton, Christopher Ball, Keith Batten, Paul Batten, Rod Beattie, Brian Bedford, Robert Benson, Christopher Blake, Mervyn Blake, Domini Blythe, Walt Bondarenko, Paul Bowman, Peter Brikmanis, Christopher Britton, Barbara Budd, Graeme Campbell, Dorian (Joe) Clark, Richard Curnock, Jennifer Dale, Vincent Dale, Margot Dionne, Peter Donaldson, Eric Donkin, Martin Donlevy, Frances Fagan, John Goodlin, Don Goodspeed, Lewis Gordon, Richard Hardacre, Max Helpmann, Martha Henry, Bernard Hopkins, Stephen Hunter, Peter Hutt, William Hutt, Pamela Hyatt, Patricia Idlette, Gerald Isaac, Alicia Jeffery, Joel Kenyon, François-Regis Klanfer, Barry Kozak, John Lambert, Leo Leyden, Barry MacGregor, C. R. MacPherson, Barbara Maczka, Francesca Mallin, William Merton Malmo, Frank Maraden, Marti Maraden, F. Braun McAsh, Dion McHugh, Richard McMillan, Richard Monette, Robert More, Marylu Moyer, William Needles, Robin Nunn, Richard Partington, Florence C. Paterson, Nicholas Pennell, John Pollard, Douglas Rain, Stephen Russell, Robert Ruttan, Melody Ryane, Mary Savidge, Alan Scarfe, Robert Selkirk, Maggie Smith, Barbara Stephen, Barbara Stewart, Winston Sutton, Frank C. Sweezey, Margaret Tyzack, Colleen Wagner, Gregory Wanless, Jack Wetherall, Richard Whelan, Ian White, Elaine Wood, Tom Wood, Leslie Yeo, Elias Zarou.

Music

Six Monday evening Popular, Jazz, and Folk Concerts included: Gordon Lightfoot, Ella Fitzgerald, Sylvia Tyson, The Preservation Hall Jazz Band, Anna Russell, and Keith Jarrett.

Other Activities

Workshops — The Workshops were organized around the theme of chorus, loosely defined as actors moving, speaking or thinking together. There were four two-week sessions: Frau Til Thiele conducted movement and mime classes; Wally Siebert, from the University of Alberta, taught the basic vocabulary of tap-dancing; director and translator John Van Burek prepared choric scenes from Michel Tremblay's *Saint Carmen of the Main,* in the first work on the play done in English Canada; director Alec Stockwell and composer Richard Bronskill worked on choric possibilities, in sound and music, of R. D. Laing's *Knots.* The program was under the supervision of Literary Manager Urjo Kareda.

Two Shakespeare Seminars of one week each were conducted by McMaster University, Hamilton.

Exhibition: Made Glorious: Stage Design at Stratford: 25 years. An exhibition of costumes and designs celebrating the silver anniversary of the Stratford Festival, mounted by the Gallery Stratford with the assistance of the Stratford Festival.

1978

A Gala Shakespeare Revel

The Merry Wives of Windsor — directed by Peter Moss, design and lighting by Phillip Silver, music by Raymond Pannell.

Macbeth — directed by Robin Phillips and Eric Steiner, designed by Daphne Dare, music by Louis Applebaum.

The Winter's Tale — directed by Robin Phillips and Peter Moss, designed by Daphne Dare, music by Louis Applebaum, lighting by Gil Wechsler.

As You Like It — directed by Robin Phillips, designed by Robin Fraser Paye, music by Berthold Carriere, lighting by Gil Wechsler.

Julius Caesar — directed by John Wood, designed by Susan Benson, sound by Alan Laing, lighting by Michael J. Whitfield.

Titus Andronicus — directed by Brian Bedford, designed by Desmond Heeley, music by Gabriel Charpentier, lighting by Michael J. Whitfield.

The Devils — by John Whiting, directed by Robin Phillips, costume design by John Pennoyer, set design by Daphne Dare, music by Berthold Carriere, lighting by Michael J. Whitfield.

Uncle Vanya — by Anton Chekhov in a new English translation by John Murrell, directed by Robin Phillips and Urjo Kareda, designed by Daphne Dare, music by Berthold Carriere, lighting by Michael J. Whitfield.

Judgement — by Barry Collins, directed by Robin Phillips, designed by Michael Maher, lighting by Michael J. Whitfield.

Heloise and Abelard: Love Letters from the Middle Ages — from poems by Ronald Duncan with additional material by Ann Hutchinson, directed by Keith Batten, designed by Michael Maher, music by Berthold Carriere, lighting by Michael J. Whitfield.

Private Lives — by Noël Coward, directed by Robin Phillips and Keith Batten, designed by Festival Design Team, music by Noël Coward, arranged by Berthold Carriere, lighting by Michael J. Whitfield.

Candide — book adapted from Voltaire by Hugh Wheeler, music by Leonard Bernstein, lyrics by Richard Wilbur with additional lyrics by Stephen Sondheim and John Latouche, directed by Lotfi Mansouri, choreography by Brian Macdonald, musical direction by Berthold Carriere, designed by Mary Kerr, lighting by Michael J. Whitfield.

Ned and Jack — by Sheldon Rosen, directed by Peter Moss, designed by Shawn Kerwin, lighting by Harry Frehner.

Medea — by Larry Fineberg, directed by John Palmer, designed by Shawn Kerwin, lighting by Harry Frehner.

Four Plays by Samuel Beckett — *Not I,* directed by Alan Scarfe; *Footfalls,* directed by Ted Follows; *From An Abandoned Work,* directed by Peter Moss; *Come and Go,* directed by Richard Monette, designed by Shawn Kerwin, lighting by Harry Frehner.

Stargazing — by Tom Cone, directed by Pamela Hawthorn, designed by Shawn Kerwin, lighting by Harry Frehner.

Members of the Company: Stewart Arnott, Karen Austin, Theodore Baerg, Bob Baker, Rodger Barton, Keith Batten, Paul Batten, Stephen Beamish, Rod Beattie, Brian Bedford, Robert Benson, Christopher Blake, Mervyn Blake, Domini Blythe, Paul Bowman, Christopher Britton, Barbara Budd, Graeme Campbell, Helen Carscallen, Richard Curnock, Jennifer Dale, Margot Dionne, Peter Donaldson, Eric Donkin, Wilfrid Dubé, David Dunbar, Mary Durkan, Edward Evanko, Michael Fletcher, Ted Follows, Edda Gaborek, Maurice Good, Lewis Gordon, Dawn Greenhalgh, Susan Gudgeon, Jeffrey Guyton, Richard Hardacre, Dean Hawes, Max Helpmann, Martha Henry, Bernard Hopkins, Donald Hunkin, Stephen Hunter, Peter Hutt, William Hutt, Patricia Idlette, Gerald Isaac, Alicia Jeffery, Richardo

Keens-Douglas, Lorne Kennedy, Joel Kenyon, François-Regis Klanfer, Barry Kozak, John Lambert, Anne Linden, Pamela Macdonald, Barry MacGregor, Anna MacKay-Smith, C. R. MacPherson, Barbara Maczka, Frank Maraden, Marti Maraden, Andrea Martin, Roberta Maxwell, F. Braun McAsh, James McGee, Dion McHugh, Richard McMillan, Jim McQueen, Richard Monette, Marylu Moyer, William Needles, Nicholas Pennell, Jennifer Phipps, John Pollard, Douglas Rain, Maida Rogerson, Stephen Russell, Robert Ruttan, Mary Savidge, Alan Scarfe, Robert Selkirk, Maggie Smith, Rex Southgate, Barbara Stephen, Barbara Stewart, Winston Sutton; Caralyn Tomlin, Michael Totzke, Robert Vigod, Colleen Wagner, Cathy Wallace, Gregory Wanless, Peggy Watson, Jack Wetherall, Richard Whelan, Ian White, John Wojda, Barrie Wood, Tom Wood, Elias Zarou, Carol Zorro.

Music

There were five Popular, Jazz, Folk, and Operatic Concerts on the Festival Stage: Bruce Cockburn, Oscar Peterson, Dan Hill, Liona Boyd, Louis Quilico and Gino Quilico.

Other Activities

Workshops — The main Workshop activity in the 1978 season was an extended, six-week program devoted to the development of Larry Fineberg's script *Devotion*. The play itself had been scheduled for production during the 1978 season, but the illness of its director, Robin Phillips, forced its cancellation. Nevertheless, the leading actors cast in the production — Martha Henry, Tom Wood, Jennifer Phipps, Marti Maraden and Helen Carscallen — all participated in the Workshop, working in collaboration with the playwright. Kathryn Shaw, from the New Play Centre in Vancouver, supervised the Workshop.

In addition, there were two further ensemble workshops for the Stratford Festival company. Hazaros Surmejan, of the National Ballet, conducted a workshop in ballet mime, in order that the company might become aware of the kind of mental preparation and concentration required for this technique. Gabriel Charpentier led a workshop on rhythm and sound, working through experimental rhythm techniques toward the presentation of a scene from *The Eumenides*.

Finally, there was a workshop presentation, by members of the *Candide* company, of songs from the musical *The Golden Apple,* a satiric version of the Judgement of Paris legend, with lyrics by John Latouche, who was a lyricist for *Candide.*

Two Shakespeare Seminars of one week each were conducted by McMaster University, Hamilton.

1979

Gala Performance

Love's Labour's Lost — directed by Robin Phillips and Urjo Kareda, designed by Daphne Dare, music by Berthold Carriere, lighting by Michael J. Whitfield.

The First Part of Henry IV — directed by Peter Moss, designed by Daphne Dare and John Pennoyer, music by Gabriel Charpentier, lighting by Michael J. Whitfield.

The Second Part of Henry IV — directed by Peter Moss, designed by Daphne Dare and John Pennoyer, music by Gabriel Charpentier, lighting by Michael J. Whitfield.

Othello — directed by Frances Hyland, designed by Robin Fraser Paye, music by Norman Symonds, lighting by Michael J. Whitfield.

Ned and Jack — by Sheldon Rosen, directed by Peter Moss, designed by Michael Maher, lighting by Harry Frehner.

Richard II — directed by Zoe Caldwell, designed by Daphne Dare, music by Berthold Carriere, lighting by Michael J. Whitfield.

The Importance of Being Earnest — by Oscar Wilde, directed by Robin Phillips, designed by Daphne Dare, lighting by Michael J. Whitfield.

Happy New Year — based on the play *Holiday* by Philip Barry, music and lyrics by Cole Porter, adapted and directed by Burt Shevelove, musical director: Buster Davis, choreography by Donald Saddler, costumes designed by Robin Fraser Paye, set and properties by Michael Eagan, lighting by Michael J. Whitfield.

The Woman — by Edward Bond, directed by Peter Moss and Urjo Kareda, designed by Susan Benson, music by Berthold Carriere, lighting by Michael J. Whitfield.

King Lear — directed by Robin Phillips, designed by Daphne Dare, music by Berthold Carriere, lighting by Michael J. Whitfield.

The Taming of the Shrew — directed by Pamela Hawthorn, designed by John Pennoyer, lighting by Harry Frehner, music by Richard Bronskill.

Victoria — by Steve Petch, directed by Kathryn Shaw, designed by Sue LePage, lighting by Harry Frehner.

Barren/Yerma — an improvisation inspired by Lorca's *Yerma,* directed by Pam Brighton, designed by Michael Eagan, lyrics and music by Cedric Smith assisted by Terry Jones, lighting by Harry Frehner.

Members of the Company: Stewart Arnott, Karen Austin, Rodger Barton, Paul Batten, Rod Beattie, Leigh Beery, Christopher Blake, Mervyn Blake, Ingrid Blekys, John Bluethner, Domini Blythe, Jessica Booker, Barbara Budd, Graeme Campbell, Patrick Christopher, William Copeland, Clare Coulter, Philip J. Craig, Stephen Cross, Richard Curnock, John Cutts, Diane D'Aquila, Margot Dionne, Peter Donaldson, Eric Donkin, Wilfrid Dubé, Craig Dudley, David Dunbar, Kirsten Ebsen, Edward Evanko, Ted Follows, Carol Forte, Edda Gaborek, Sophie Gascon, Richard Gira, Maurice Good, Donna Goodhand, Lewis Gordon, Jeffrey Guyton, Amelia Hall, Richard Hardacre, Dean Hawes, Max Helpmann, Martha Henry, David Holmes, William Hutt, Gerald Isaac, Alicia Jeffery, Geordie Johnson, Lorne Kennedy, Joel Kenyon, François-Regis Klanfer, John Lambert, Barry MacGregor, Barabara Maczka, William Merton Malmo, Frank Maraden, Marti Maraden, F. Braun McAsh, Robert McClure, Dion McHugh, Anne McKay, Richard McMillan, Jim McQueen, Wally Michaels, Richard Monette, Marylu Moyer, William Needles, Bob Ouellette, Stephen Ouimette, Angelo Pedari, Nicholas Pennell, Jennifer Phipps, John Pollard, Douglas Rain, Paul Rapsey, Pamela Redfern, Maida Rogerson, Stephen Russell, Alan Scarfe, LeRoy Schulz, Cedric Smith, Victoria Snow, Rex Southgate, David Stein, Barbara Stewart, Hank Stinson, Heather Summerhayes, Winston Sutton, Michael Totzke, Peter Ustinov, Barry Van Elen, Gregory Wanless, William Webster, Ian White, John Wojda, Barrie Wood, Tom Wood.

Music

There were four jazz concerts and two pop music concerts on the Festival Stage: Dizzy Gillespie, Sarah Vaughan, The Preservation Hall Jazz Band, Gary Burton Quartet, Valdy, Kate and Anna McGarrigle.

Other Activities

Workshops — The 1979 Workshops included scene classes conducted by assistant director Gregory Peterson, which were available to the whole company. Among the works developed with Mr. Peterson was a new show, *A Flash in the Pan*, written and performed by Hank Stinson.

Company and individual movement and voice classes were given by Jeffrey Guyton and Lloy Coutts, respectively.

Mary Matthews Brion conducted Workshops in the Alexander Technique.

A guest specialist, Eric Fredrickson, conducted a fencing Workshop co-ordinated by Patrick Crean.

Two Shakespeare Seminars of one week each were conducted by McMaster University, Hamilton.

Exhibitions: Costumes and designs from Susan Benson's *A Midsummer Night's Dream* (1976-7) and *Julius Caesar* (1978) were selected by the Associated Designers of Canada for inclusion in Theatre Design Explorations, an exhibition mounted for the Prague Quadrennial. This exhibit won a special award for excellence.

1980

Twelfth Night — directed by Robin Phillips, set and properties by Daphne Dare, costumes by Ann Curtis, music by Berthold Carriere, lighting by Michael J. Whitfield.

Henry V — directed by Peter Moss, set by Daphne Dare, costumes by John Pennoyer with Daphne Dare, music by Gabriel Charpentier, lighting by

Michael J. Whitfield.

Titus Andronicus — directed by Brian Bedford, designed by Desmond Heeley, music by Gabriel Charpentier, lighting by Michael J. Whitfield.

Much Ado About Nothing—
directed by Robin Phillips, set by Daphne Dare, costumes and properties by Robin Fraser Paye, music by Louis Applebaum, lighting by Michael J. Whitfield.

The Seagull — by Anton Chekhov, in a new version by John Murrell, directed by Robin Phillips and Urjo Kareda, designed by Daphne Dare, music by Berthold Carriere, lighting by Gil Wechsler.

The Beggar's Opera — by John Gay, directed by Robin Phillips and Gregory Peterson, set by Daphne Dare, costumes by Sue LePage, musical direction, choral arrangements and orchestration by Berthold Carriere, lighting by Michael J. Whitfield, choreography by Jeff Hyslop, additional lyrics by Ned Sherrin and Caryl Brahms.

Virginia — by Edna O'Brien, directed by Robin Phillips, set by Phillip Silver, costumes by Ann Curtis, music by Berthold Carriere, lighting by Michael J. Whitfield, sound montage assembled by Roger Gaskell/Gie Roberts.

The Servant of Two Masters — by Carlo Goldoni, in a new version by Tom Cone, directed by Peter Moss, set by Michael Eagan, costumes by Janice Lindsay, music by Norman Symonds, lighting by Michael J. Whitfield, choreography by Jeff Hyslop.

The Gin Game — by D. L. Coburn, directed by Mel Shapiro, designed by Michael Eagan, lighting by Michael J. Whitfield.

Bosoms and Neglect — by John Guare, directed by Mel Shapiro, designed by Phillip Silver, lighting by Michael J. Whitfield.

Foxfire — by Susan Cooper and Hume Cronyn, directed by Robin Phillips and Peter Moss, designed by Daphne Dare, music by Jonathan Holtzman, lighting by Michael J. Whitfield, song lyrics by Susan Cooper, Hume Cronyn and Jonathan Holtzman.

King Lear — directed by Robin Phillips, designed by Daphne Dare, music by Berthold Carriere, lighting by Michael J. Whitfield.

Long Day's Journey into Night — by Eugene O'Neill, directed by Robin Phillips, designed by Susan Benson, music by Berthold Carriere, lighting by Michael J. Whitfield.

Brief Lives — adapted by Patrick Garland from the writings of John Aubrey, directed by Martha Henry, set by Daphne Dare assisted by Design Team, costumes by Sue LePage, additional music by Berthold Carriere, lighting by Harry Frehner.

Henry VI — adapted and directed by Pam Brighton, designed by Michael Eagan, music by Berthold Carriere, lighting by Harry Frehner.

Members of the Company: Scott Baker, Rodger Barton, Rod Beattie, Stephen Beamish, Brian Bedford, Robert Benson, Christopher Blake, Mervyn Blake, Dwayne Brenna, Norman Browning, Barbara Budd, Graeme Campbell, Brent Carver, Patrick Christopher, David Clark, Patricia Collins, Patricia Conolly, William Copeland, Lloy Coutts, Hume Cronyn, Richard Curnock, John Cutts, Katia de Pena, David Dunbar, Maurice E. Evans, Janet Feindel, Carol Forte, Edda Gaborek, Pat Galloway, Sophie Gascon, Maurice Good, Donna Goodhand, Lewis Gordon, Janice Greene, Luce Guilbeault, Jeffrey Guyton, Amelia Hall, David Harris, Max Helpmann, Martha Henry, Sten Hornborg, William Hutt, Keith James, Alicia Jeffery, Ray Jewers, Geordie Johnson, Lorne Kennedy, Joel Kenyon, Robert LaChance, Diana Leblanc, William Merton Malmo, Barry MacGregor, Roberta Maxwell, F. Braun McAsh, Robert McClure, Richard McMillan, Jim McQueen, Richard Monette, Marylu Moyer, Elizabeth Murphy, Sean T. O'Hara, Stephen Ouimette, Irene Pauzer, Nicholas Pennell, Jennifer Phipps, Douglas Rain, Kate Reid, Astrid Roch, Michael Ross, Stephen Russell, Booth Savage, Mary Savidge, Goldie Semple, Errol Slue, Maggie Smith, Wesley Stevens, Jessica Tandy, Michael Totzke, Reg Tupper, Davena Turvey, Peter Ustinov, Barry Van Elen, Bruce Vavrina, Paul Wagar, Cathy Wallace, Gregory Wanless, Peggy Watson, William Webster, Jack Wetherall, John Wojda, Elias Zarou.

Music

Three concerts by the Stratford Youth Choir, under the direction of Robert Cooper, with notable guest stars: The Stratford Youth Choir and their guest William Hutt; The Stratford Youth Choir and their guest Peter Ustinov; The Stratford Youth Choir and their guests Jessica Tandy and Hume Cronyn.

Other Activities

Two Shakespeare seminars of one week each were conducted by McMaster University, Hamilton; three Shakespeare seminars of one week each were conducted by the University of Toronto, Scarborough College.

Exhibition: The Trappings of Kings. An exhibition of properties and costumes from recent historical plays at Stratford, including the sculptured steel horses from *Richard II* (1979) as well as helmets, weapons and armour, banners, thrones and regalia.

1981

The Misanthrope — by Molière, translated into English verse by Richard Wilbur, directed by Jean Gascon, designed by Desmond Heeley, music by Alan Laing, lighting designed by David F. Segal.

Coriolanus — directed by Brian Bedford, designed by Desmond Heeley, music by Gabriel Charpentier, lighting by Michael J. Whitfield.

The Taming of the Shrew — directed by Peter Dews, designed by Susan Benson, music by Stanley Silverman, lighting by Harry Frehner.

The Comedy of Errors — directed by Peter Dews, designed by Susan Benson, music by Stanley Silverman, lighting designed by Michael J. Whitfield.

H.M.S. Pinafore — book by W. S. Gilbert, music by Arthur Sullivan, musical direction by Berthold Carriere, directed by Leon Major, set design by Murray Laufer, costumes designed by Astrid Janson, choreography by Judith Marcuse, lighting by Michael J. Whitfield.

The Rivals — by Richard Brinsley Sheridan, directed by Brian Bedford, designed by David Walker, music by

Berthold Carriere, lighting designed by David F. Segal.

The Visit — by Friedrich Dürrenmatt, adapted by Maurice Valency, directed by Jean Gascon, set design by John Ferguson, costumes designed by Molly Harris Campbell, music by Alan Laing, lighting by David F. Segal.

Wild Oats — by John O'Keeffe, directed by Derek Goldby, set design by Phillip Silver, costumes designed by John Pennoyer, music by Berthold Carriere, lighting by David F. Segal.

Members of the Company: Jan Austin, Shaun Austin-Olsen, Kenneth Baker, Scott Baker, Barrie Baldaro, Diana Barrington, Rodger Barton, Stephen Beamish, Rod Beattie, Brian Bedford, Anthony Bekenn, Mervyn Blake, Peter Boretski, Arthur Brand, Michael Burgess, George Buza, Len Cariou, Barbara Chilcott, Patrick Christopher, David Clark, Janet Coates, Wendy Creed, Stephen Cross, Richard Curnock, Keene Curtis, Ian Deakin, Daniel Delabbio, Elise Dewsberry, Keith Dinicol, Margot Dionne, Eric Donkin, Terence Durrant, Desmond Ellis, Colm Feore, Sharry Flett, Colin Fox, Pat Galloway, Paul Gatchell, Dennis Goodwin, Lewis Gordon, Lynne Griffin, Jeffrey Guyton, Mary Haney, Ron Hastings, Max Helpmann, Jeremy Henson, Peter Hutt, William Hutt, Scott Hylands, Deborah Jarvis, John Jarvis, Debora Joy, Eric Keenleyside, Patricia Kern, Avo Kittask, David Langton, Leo Leyden, Arthur Lightbourn, Anne Linden, Richard March, Ted Marshall, Paul Massel, Loreena McKennitt, James McLean, Peter Messaline, Dale Mieske, Richard Monette, Elizabeth Murphy, Barney O'Sullivan, Kenneth Pearl, Nicholas Pennell, Kenneth Pogue, Miles Potter, Paul Punyi, Pamela Redfern, Fiona Reid, Mary Rutherford, Ronn Sarosiak, Alexis Smith, Scott Smith, Gerald Smuin, Reid Spencer, Heather Suttie, Katherine Terrell, Marcia Tratt, Walter Villa, Peggy Watson, Dale Wendel, Lynn West, Tim Whelan, Jim White, Sandy Winsby, Karen Wood, Susan Wright.

Music

The Stratford Festival presented six pop and jazz concerts in the Festival Theatre: Judy Collins, Cleo Laine and John

Dankworth, The Preservation Hall Jazz Band, Mel Tormé, John Abercrombie, Ralph Towner, Solos and Duets, Sonny Rollins, Rob McConnell and The Boss Brass.

Other Activities

Workshops — Numerous workshop productions, open to the public, were presented by members of the 1981 Festival company.

Two Shakespeare Seminars of one week each were conducted by McMaster University, Hamilton; two Shakespeare seminars of one week each and one weekend Shakespeare seminar were conducted by the University of Toronto, Scarborough College.

Exhibition: A Most Rare Fashion. Originally mounted by the McCord Museum, Montréal, as Costume Design at Stratford in 1980, this exhibition consisted of twelve of the most exquisitely designed costumes from recent Festival productions along with their original designs.

1982

Julius Caesar — directed by Derek Goldby, designed by John Pennoyer, music by Berthold Carriere, lighting by Michael J. Whitfield.

The Merry Wives of Windsor — directed by Robert Beard, designed by Susan Benson, music by Berthold Carriere, lighting by Harry Frehner.

The Tempest — directed by John Hirsch, designed by Desmond Heeley, music by Stanley Silverman, lighting by Michael J. Whitfield.

Arms and the Man — by George Bernard Shaw, directed by Michael Langham, designed by Desmond Heeley, music by Stanley Silverman, lighting by Michael J. Whitfield.

The Mikado — book by W. S. Gilbert, music by Arthur Sullivan, direction and choreography by Brian Macdonald, musical direction by Berthold Carriere, set design by Susan Benson and Douglas McLean, costumes designed by Susan Benson, lighting by Michael J. Whitfield.

Translations — by Brian Friel, directed by Guy Sprung, set design by Phillip Silver, costumes designed by Debra Hanson, lighting by Harry Frehner.

Mary Stuart — by Friedrich Schiller, translated and adapted by Joe McClinton, Stratford version by Joe McClinton, and Michal Schonberg, directed by John Hirsch, set design by Ming Cho Lee, costumes designed by Tanya Moiseiwitsch, music by Stanley Silverman, lighting by Beverly Emmons.

Blithe Spirit — by Noël Coward, directed by Brian Bedford, associate director Robert Beard, designed by David Walker, music arranged by Berthold Carriere, lighting by Michael J. Whitfield.

A Midsummer Night's Dream — The Shakespeare 3 Company directed by Peter Froehlich, designed by Patrick Clark, lighting by Steven Hawkins.

All's Well That Ends Well — the Shakespeare 3 Company directed by Richard Cottrell, designed by Christina Poddubiuk, lighting by Steven Hawkins.

Letters of Love and Affection — with Irene Worth.

Damien — by Aldyth Morris, with Lewis Gordon, directed by Guy Sprung, designed by Barbra Matis, lighting by Steven Hawkins.

A Variable Passion — compiled by Nicholas Pennell, additional material by Elliott Hayes, produced by Michal Schonberg, designed by Douglas McLean, lighting by Steven Hawkins.

Members of the Company: David Agro, Shaun Austin-Olsen, Marie Baron, Richard Binsley, Mervyn Blake, Simon Bradbury, James Bradford, Douglas Campbell, Graeme Campbell, Helen Carey, Len Cariou, Aggie Cekuta, Nicolas Colicos, Timothy Cruickshank, Richard Curnock, Ian Deakin, Katia de Pena, Elise Dewsberry, Keith Dinicol, Margot Dionne, Curzon Dobell, John Dolan, Peter Donaldson, Eric Donkin, Maurice E. Evans, Colm Feore, Sharry Flett, Colin Fox, Glori Gage, Pat Galloway, Chris Gibson, Lewis Gordon, Allison Grant, Tammy Grimes, Amelia Hall, Mary Haney, Deryck E. Hazel, Max Helpmann, Raymond Hunt, Henry Ingram, Christina James, John Jarvis, Debora Joy, Avo Kittask, Beverly Kreller, Robert LaChance, Elizabeth Leigh-Milne, Richard March, Ted Marshall, Biff McGuire, Loreena

McKennitt, Richard McMillan, Jack Medley, Jim Mezon, Dale Mieske, Richard Monette, Tony Nardi, Irene Neufeld, Anita Noel-Antscherl, Nicholas Pennell, Miles Potter, Karl Pruner, Paul Punyi, Kelly Robinson, Astrid Roch, Robert Rooney, Stephen Russell, Gidon Saks, Carole Shelley, Michael Shepherd, Michael Simpson, Karen Skidmore, Scott Smith, Gerald Smuin, Martin Spencer, Reid Spencer, Allen Stewart-Coates, Jean Stilwell, Heather Suttie, R. H. Thomson, Marcia Tratt, Kate Trotter, Craig Walker, Joan Warren, Tim Whelan, Ian White, Karen Wood, Susan Wright, Peter Zednik.

Shakespeare 3 Company: Lee J. Campbell, Nicky Guadagni, Thomas Hauff, David Huband, Kieron Jecchinis, Eric Keenleyside, Charmion King, Paul Massie, Diego Matamoros, Seana McKenna, John Novak, Fiona Reid, Joseph Shaw, Nicholas Simons, Cheryl Swarts, William Vickers.

Music

The Stratford Festival presented eight pop and jazz concerts in the Festival Theatre: Len Cariou, Oscar Peterson, The Preservation Hall Jazz Band, Kris Kristofferson, Chick Corea/Gary Burton, Benny Goodman, Primavera Quartet, Bruce Cockburn and Roberta Flack.

Other Activities

A series of seven Celebrity Lectures in the Festival Theatre: Northrop Frye; Hugh MacLennan; Samuel Schoenbaum; Arthur Miller; Panel: Jean Gascon, Edward Gilbert, John Hirsch, John Wood with moderator Don Harron; and Robertson Davies.

Workshops — Numerous workshop productions including Blake, Cahoot's Macbeth, Dock Brief, Elephant Man, Generals Die In Bed, Gimme Shelter, Krapp's Last Tape, Lovers, When I Am, Readings of Macbeth and Troilus and Cressida. Music workshop concerts included works by Poulenc, Britten, Schoenberg, Sanquet, traditional Irish music and an excerpt from Don Carlos. Other workshops included Sonnets with Kristen Linklater, text with Nicholas Pennell, scene studies with William Needles, stage fighting with R. H. Thomson, and Douglas Campbell conducted an extended series of workshops on his production of St. Joan.

Exhibitions: In celebration of the Festival's 30th anniversary season, a retrospective exhibit consisting of properties, designs and photographs was installed in the Festival Theatre's lower promenade. In the upper promenade, busts by Pauline Redsell-Fediow and portraits by Grant MacDonald were displayed in a tribute to the stars of the Festival's early acting companies. Visitors to the theatre also saw the première exhibition of eighteen tapestries designed by leading contemporary Canadian artists.

Leslie Hurry: A Painter For The Stage: This exhibition at the Gallery Stratford was mounted in memory of designer Leslie Hurry (1909-78). Paintings, designs, costumes and properties were drawn from theatre collections in Canada, England and the United States. A series of Talks on Design were held in conjunction with this exhibit. Participants included Desmond Heeley, Phillip Silver, David Walker, Susan Benson and Nicholas Pennell.

After opening at the Gallery Stratford for its 1982 summer season, the Hurry exhibition toured to the Library and Museum of Performing Arts at Lincoln Center in New York, the Dallas Public Library, the McNay Art Institute in San Antonio, Texas, The Art Gallery of Northumberland in Cobourg, Ontario, The Agnes Etherington Art Centre at Queen's University in Kingston, Ontario, and the McCord Museum in Montreal.

In addition, costumes from the Festival were displayed in conjunction with chairs from the Montreal Museum of Fine Arts in a new exhibition entitled *Chairs and Their Costumes*, mounted at the London Regional Art Gallery during the summer months.

Out-of-Season Activities

1956

In January the Festival Company, headed by Anthony Quayle and Coral Browne, appeared in Toronto and on Broadway in Tyrone Guthrie's production of *Tamburlaine the Great* by Christopher Marlowe. In April the company was engaged by Leonid Kipnis Film Productions Ltd. to produce a film version of *Oedipus Rex*. Tyrone Guthrie directed with Douglas Campbell in the title role. In September the company appeared at the Edinburgh Festival in *Henry V* and *Oedipus Rex* directed by Michael Langham. The film version of *Oedipus Rex* was also shown at the Edinburgh Film Festival. In December the Festival Company appeared for the first time on TV with Bruno Gerussi in the title role of *Peer Gynt* by Henrik Ibsen, sponsored by the International Nickel Company.

1958

In February two plays were produced for a six-week international tour. Directed by Michael Langham, designed by Tanya Moiseiwitsch, Shake-speare's *Two Gentlemen of Verona* and *The Broken Jug* by Donald Harron, (adapted from Heinrich von Kleist), were presented in London, Ont., Toronto, Montreal, and the Phoenix Theatre, New York. The cast included Helen Burns, Douglas Campbell, Bruno Gerussi, Amelia Hall, Eric House and Douglas Rain. On September 20, Sir John Gielgud opened his North American tour of *The Seven Ages of Man* in the Festival Theatre.

1960

In September the *H.M.S. Pinafore* company appeared at the Phoenix Theatre, N.Y., for a six-week presentation under the auspices of Contemporary Productions. Tyrone Guthrie directed the Gilbert and Sullivan operetta with the Stratford principals in the leading roles. This production was also seen on the CBC-TV network.

1961

For a second time a Festival Gilbert and Sullivan production played for six weeks at the Phoenix Theatre after being televised by the CBC. The presentation was *The Pirates of Penzance* directed by Tyrone Guthrie. Leading roles were taken by the Stratford principals and the operetta later toured major cities of the United States for eight weeks.

1962

During February and March ten leading actors of the Festival Company toured universities in a special production entitled *Two Programmes of Shakespearean Comedy*, devised and directed by Michael Langham. Production costs were shared by the Canada Council and the universities themselves.

On February 8 the Stratford Festival's production of *H.M.S. Pinafore*, directed by Tyrone Guthrie, opened at Her Majesty's Theatre in London to be followed a week later by the Stratford production of *The Pirates of Penzance*, both under the auspices of Contemporary Productions. The two operettas played a six-week season with many of the original casts and were later presented in Los Angeles, San Francisco and Vancouver.

1963

In April, Michael Langham staged *The Affliction of Love* for the Festival of Performing Arts television series in the United States. Mr. Langham devised the script using excerpts from several Shakespearean plays.

The cast included John Colicos, Kate Reid, William Hutt, Douglas Rain, Peter Donat, Eric Christmas and Martha Henry. Shown in seven U.S. cities, the series was produced by David Susskind and James Fleming and sponsored by Standard Oil of New Jersey.

1964

The Stratford Festival accepted an invitation from the Chichester Festival Theatre, Chichester, England, to celebrate the 400th anniversary of William Shakespeare's birth with the presentation of *Timon of Athens, Love's Labour's Lost* and Molière's *Le Bourgeois Gentilhomme*, during a three-week engagement, April 6 to April 25, in Chichester.

1967

The Michael Langham-directed production of *Henry V*, presented during the 1966 Stratford Festival, was taped in colour for a CTV network television presentation on January 29.

Sponsored by the Centennial Commission, the Festival Company toured Canada under the Festival Canada banner, with productions of *Twelfth Night* and *The Government Inspector*.

The Company accepted an invitation to present *Antony and Cleopatra* and *The Government Inspector* at Expo 67 in October.

1968

The John Hirsch-directed production of Peter Raby's adaptation of the Dumas novel *The Three Musketeers* was taped in colour for television and shown in March, 1969, over the CBC.

A Midsummer Night's Dream, staged by John Hirsch, toured Montreal, Ottawa and Ann Arbor, Michigan, in March/April.

1969

On the six-week spring tour to Chicago, Ann Arbor and Montreal, the company presented the Jean Gascon-directed production of Ben Jonson's *The Alchemist* and the John Hirsch-directed production of *Hamlet*.

Following a month-long engagement in Stratford, *Hadrian VII*, directed by Jean Gascon set off on a 38-week tour of the United States.

At the close of the 1969 Festival season, the Festival presented a seven-month season, November 20, 1969-May 9, 1970, at the National Arts Centre in Ottawa. Productions presented were: John Hirsch's production of *Hamlet*, re-staged by Keith Turnbull, and Jean Gascon's production of *The Alchemist* performed in repertory, October 20-November 15 in the Theatre.

First school tour, *Bust Out* by Philip Spensley, directed by Peter Scupham, played to Grade 9 & 10 students in the Ottawa area, November 17-December 5.

Four Plays by Jean-Claude van Itallie ("It's Almost Like Being", "I'm Really Here", "Interview" and "Motel"), directed by Keith Turnbull, designed by Tina Lipp with music by Georgi L. M. Nachoff and Karol Rattray, was presented November 20-December 6 in the Studio.

Sauerkringle by John Hirsch, directed by Robert Sherrin, designed by Don Lewis, with music by Alan Laing, played from December 26 to January 4 in the Theatre.

1970

In the Theatre of the NAC, Stratford's season continued with Brendan Behan's *The Hostage* directed by Colin George, designed by Mark Negin, and Boris Vian's *The Empire Builders*, directed by Carl M. Weber, designed by Mark Negin, playing in repertory February 2-March 7.

Second Ottawa school tour, *As You Like It* by Peter Hay, directed by Timothy Bond, was presented to Grade 13 and University students March 2-20.

Three Plays by Mrozek ("Out at Sea", "Charlie", and "Striptease"), directed by Robert Sherrin, designed by Joseph Cselenyi, were performed March 5-21 in the Studio.

Shakespeare's *The Merchant of Venice*, directed by Jean Gascon, and Sheridan's *The School for Scandal*, directed by Michael Langham, were presented in repertory March 30-April 25 in the NAC Theatre, as part of the eleven-week 1970 spring tour which included one week in Urbana, four weeks in Chicago and two weeks in Montreal, prior to the Ottawa engagement.

James Reaney's *The Easter Egg*, directed by Timothy Bond, designed by Jack King, with music by Georgi L. M. Nachoff and Karol Rattray, was the final Ottawa Studio production, April 23-May 9.

Two productions were staged at the NAC by Stratford in the fall: *Tartuffe* by Molière, and Shakespeare's *Cymbeline*. Both were directed by Jean Gascon with music by Gabriel Charpentier. Designs for *Cymbeline* were by Tanya Moiseiwitsch and for *Tartuffe* by Robert Prévost.

1971

On the ten-week spring tour, the company presented Shakespeare's *Much Ado About Nothing* directed by William Hutt, designed by Alan Barlow, music by Harry Freedman and lighting by Gil Wechsler, and John Webster's *The Duchess of Malfi* directed by Jean Gascon, designed by Desmond Heeley, music by Gabriel Charpentier and lighting by Gil Wechsler in repertory at the Tyrone Guthrie Theatre in Minneapolis from February 24 to March 13, and at the Theatre of the National Arts Centre in Ottawa from March 22 to April 17.

1972

The 1971 Stratford production of Feydeau's *There's One in Every Marriage* directed by Jean Gascon, designed by Alan Barlow and lighting by Gil Wechsler, opened at the Royale Theatre in New York on January 3. The show was produced for Broadway by David Merrick.

The Company embarked on a nine-week spring tour presenting Shakespeare's *As You Like It* directed by William Hutt, designed by Alan Barlow, with music by Harry Freedman and lighting by Gil Wechsler, and Alfred de Musset's *Lorenzaccio* directed by Jean Gascon, designed by Michael Annals, with music by Gabriel Charpentier and lighting by Gil Wechsler at the Tyrone Guthrie Theatre in Minneapolis from February 21 to March 11 and at Ottawa's National Arts Centre from March 20 to April 15.

1973

On January 24, the Company opened its unprecedented seven-week sold-out European tour with a command performance of *The Taming of the Shrew* for Queen Margrethe of Denmark at the New Royal Theatre in Copenhagen. This European tour was made possible through the support of the Dept. of External Affairs. Prior to departing for Europe, the touring productions of *The Taming of the Shrew*, directed by Jean Gascon, designed by Desmond Heeley, with music by Gabriel Charpentier and lighting by Gil Wechsler, and *King Lear*, directed by David William, designed by Annena Stubbs, with music by Louis Applebaum and lighting by Gil Wechsler, played to near capacity houses at Montreal's Maisonneuve Theatre January 11-20. Following a four-day run in Copenhagen (January 24-27), the Company continued on to the Schouwberg Theatre in Utrecht (January 30-31), the Royal Theatre in The Hague (February 3), the National Theatre in Warsaw (February 7-10), the Slowackiego Theatre in Krakow (February 13-14), the Mxat Theatre in Moscow (February 20-25) and the Soviet Lenin Theatre in Leningrad (March 1-5).

1974

On February 15 the Company opened its seven-week tour of Australia with Molière's *The Imaginary Invalid* at the National Theatre in Perth. Following the Perth engagement (February 15-February 23) the Company performed at the Princess Theatre in Melbourne (February 26-March 7), Her Majesty's Theatre in Adelaide during the Adelaide Festival (March 9-March 23) and ended the tour performing at the new Opera Theatre in Sydney (March 26-April 6). *The Imaginary Invalid* was directed by Jean Gascon, designed by Tanya Moiseiwitsch, with music by Gabriel Charpentier and lighting by Robert Scales.

1975

The Company's first national tour since 1967 opened February 10 at the Playhouse Theatre in Winnipeg with *The Two Gentlemen of Verona* and the following night with *The Comedy of Errors*. After Winnipeg (February 10-15) the Company travelled to Saskatoon's Centennial Auditorium (February 18-19); on to Regina and the Saskatchewan Center of the Arts (February 22-23); Edmonton's Northern Alberta Jubilee Auditorium (February 25-26); and Calgary's Southern Alberta Jubilee Auditorium (February 28-March 1). After engagements at the Queen Elizabeth Theatre in Vancouver (March 5-9) and the Royal Theatre in Victoria

(March 12-13) the Company travelled to Ottawa where *The Comedy of Errors* played a three-week engagement as part of the National Arts Centre's subscription series (March 17-April 5). The final engagement of the eleven-week tour was at the Place des Arts in Montreal (April 8-20) where both plays were performed. Both plays were co-directed by Robin Phillips and David Toguri, basic set by Daphne Dare, with lighting by Gil Wechsler. Designs for *The Comedy of Errors* were by Jeffrey Sisco, for *The Two Gentlemen of Verona*, by Molly Harris Campbell.

1976

The Festival's first Kingston, Ontario, engagement began when the curtain rose for *The Tempest* on March 4 at the Grand Theatre. Richard Monette's *Hamlet* opened the following night and the production of *Hamlet* featuring Nicholas Pennell opened March 6. Upon completion of the Kingston run March 13, the production transferred to Montreal's Place des Arts (March 16-27). The final stop on the tour was Ottawa, where *Hamlet* was presented March 29 to April 17 as part of the National Arts Centre's subscription series. Both plays were co-directed by Robin Phillips and William Hutt, basic set by Daphne Dare, with lighting by Gil Wechsler and music by Berthold Carriere. Designs for *Hamlet* were by John Pennoyer, for *The Tempest*, by John Ferguson.

1977

Robin Phillips directed a production of Ferenc Molnar's *The Guardsman* with Maggie Smith. Brian Bedford and several members of the Festival Acting Company at the Ahmanson Theatre in Los Angeles. This production opened in December, 1976, for a limited engagement.

In February, Mr. Phillips directed a production of Eugene O'Neill's *Long Day's Journey into Night*, with William Hutt, Jessica Tandy and several members of the Festival Acting Company in London, Ontario, for Theatre London.

1979

Robin Phillips' production of *The Lady of the Camellias*, a new version of the Dumas classic by Suzanne Grossman, had its World Première at Theatre London, November 28, 1979. The production featured Martha Henry as Marguerite Gauthier, with a cast comprised largely of members of the Stratford acting company.

1980

The Festival production of *Virginia* began a 12-week engagement at London's Haymarket Theatre in January, 1981. Written by Edna O'Brien, the production was directed by Robin Phillips, set design by Phillip Silver, costumes by Ann Curtis, music by Berthold Carriere, lighting by Michael J. Whitfield; Maggie Smith, Patricia Conolly and Nicholas Pennell appeared in the cast.

1981

The Festival production of *Wild Oats* toured to the National Arts Centre in Ottawa November 3-21. Written by John O'Keeffe, directed by Derek Goldby, set design by Phillip Silver, costumes designed by John Pennoyer, music by Berthold Carriere and lighting by David F. Segal. Performances of *The Taming of the Shrew* and *H.M.S. Pinafore* were taped and broadcast by CBC-TV.

1982

The Festival production of *The Mikado* toured to the National Arts Centre in Ottawa (November 10-14). Directed and choreographed by Brian Macdonald, musical direction by Berthold Carriere, set design by Susan Benson and Douglas McLean, costume design by Susan Benson, lighting design by Michael J. Whitfield.

Translations by Brian Friel toured to the National Arts Centre in Ottawa (September 28-October 16). Directed by Guy Sprung, set design by Phillip Silver, costume design by Debra Hanson, lighting design by Harry Frehner, *Translations* was then remounted at Toronto Free Theatre in January, 1983.

Blithe Spirit by Noël Coward transferred to the Royal Alexandra Theatre in Toronto. Directed by Brian Bedford, associate director Robert Beard, designed by David Walker, music arrangement by Berthold Carriere, lighting design by Michael J. Whitfield.

Blake by Elliott Hayes, directed by Richard Monette, starring Douglas Campbell, played at the London Regional Art Gallery (November 6-7) following its workshop production during the season.

Performances of *The Tempest* and *The Mikado* were televised by the CBC.

·S·T·R·A·T·F·O·R·D·

Selected Bibliography

Davies, Robertson, et al. *Thrice the Brindled Cat Hath Mewed.* Toronto: Clarke Irwin, 1955.

Forsythe, James. *Tyrone Guthrie: A Biography.* London: Hamish Hamilton, 1976.

Good, Maurice. *Every Inch a Lear.* Intro. by Peter Ustinov. Vancouver: Sono Nis, 1982.

Guthrie, Tyrone. *In Various Directions.* New York: Macmillan, 1965.

———. *My Life in the Theatre.* New York: McGraw-Hill, 1959.

———, and Davies, Robertson. *Renown at Stratford.* Toronto: Clarke, Irwin, 1953.

———, et al. *Twice Have the Trumpets Sounded.* Toronto: Clarke, Irwin, 1954.

Knelman, Martin. *A Stratford Tempest.* Toronto: McClelland and Stewart, 1982.

Monsarrat, Nicholas. *To Stratford With Love.* Toronto: McClelland and Stewart, 1963.

Raby, Peter, comp. and ed. *The Stratford Scene, 1958– 1968.* Intro. by Michael Langham. Toronto: Clarke, Irwin, 1968.

The Stratford Papers on Shakespeare. Documents prepared for the Stratford Seminars, and published by McMaster University Press. Stratford Festival Archives.

Index